THE CAMBRIDGE COMPANION TO
FRIEDRICH SCHLEIERMACHER

Known as the 'Father of modern theology' Friedrich Schleiermacher is
without a doubt one of the most important theologians in the history of
Christianity. Not only relevant to theology, he also made significant contributions in areas of philosophy such as hermeneutics, ethics, philosophy
of religion, and the study of Plato, and he was ahead of his time in
espousing a kind of proto-feminism. Divided into three parts, this
Companion deals first with elements of Schleiermacher's philosophy, such
as metaphysics, epistemology of religious knowledge, ethics, hermeneutics,
and contributions to Plato scholarship. Second it discusses theological topics
such as sin and redemption and Christology, and the final section is
devoted to Schleiermacher's understanding of culture. This is the first
book in English introducing readers to all the important aspects of
Schleiermacher's thought in a systematic way, containing essays by the
some of the best Schleiermacher scholars in Germany and in the English-
speaking world.

JACQUELINE MARIÑA is Associate Professor of Philosophy at Purdue
University. She specializes in Kant, Schleiermacher, and philosophy of
religion. She has published a number of book chapters and scholarly
articles that have appeared in the following journals: *Journal of the
History of Philosophy, Kant-Studien, Faith and Philosophy, Journal of
Religion, and Religious Studies.* She is currently at work on a book entitled
Transformation of the Self in the Thought of Friedrich Schleiermacher.

CAMBRIDGE COMPANIONS TO RELIGION

A series of companions to major topics and key figures in theology and religious studies. Each volume contains specially commissioned chapters by international scholars which provide an accessible and stimulating introduction to the subject for new readers and non-specialists.

Other titles in the series

THE CAMBRIDGE COMPANION TO CHRISTIAN DOCTRINE
edited by Colin Gunton (1997)
ISBN 0 521 47118 4 hardback   ISBN 0 521 47695 8 paperback

THE CAMBRIDGE COMPANION TO BIBLICAL INTERPRETATION
edited by John Barton (1998)
ISBN 0 521 48144 9 hardback   ISBN 0 521 48593 2 paperback

THE CAMBRIDGE COMPANION TO DIETRICH BONHOEFFER
edited by John de Gruchy (1999)
ISBN 0 521 58258 x hardback   ISBN 0 521 58751 6 paperback

THE CAMBRIDGE COMPANION TO LIBERATION THEOLOGY
edited by Chris Rowland (1999)
ISBN 0 521 46144 8 hardback   ISBN 0 521 46707 1 paperback

THE CAMBRIDGE COMPANION TO KARL BARTH
edited by John Webster (2000)
ISBN 0 521 58476 0 hardback   ISBN 0 521 58560 0 paperback

THE CAMBRIDGE COMPANION TO CHRISTIAN ETHICS
edited by Robin Gill (2001)
ISBN 0 521 77070 x hardback   ISBN 0 521 77918 9 paperback

THE CAMBRIDGE COMPANION TO JESUS
edited by Markus Bockmuehl (2001)
ISBN 0 521 79261 4 hardback   ISBN 0 521 79678 4 paperback

THE CAMBRIDGE COMPANION TO FEMINIST THEOLOGY
edited by Susan Frank Parsons (2002)
ISBN 0 521 66327 x hardback   ISBN 0 521 66380 6 paperback

THE CAMBRIDGE COMPANION TO MARTIN LUTHER
edited by Donald K. McKim (2003)
ISBN 0 521 81648 3 hardback   ISBN 0 521 01673 8 paperback

THE CAMBRIDGE COMPANION TO ST. PAUL
edited by James D. G. Dunn (2003)
ISBN 0 521 78155 8 hardback   ISBN 0 521 78694 0 paperback

THE CAMBRIDGE COMPANION TO POST-MODERN THEOLOGY
edited by Kevin J. Vanhoozer (2003)
ISBN 0 521 79062 x hardback   ISBN 0 521 79395 5 paperback

THE CAMBRIDGE COMPANION TO MEDIEVAL JEWISH PHILOSOPHY
edited by Daniel H. Frank and Oliver Leaman (2003)
ISBN 0 521 65207 3 hardback   ISBN 0 521 65574 9 paperback

THE CAMBRIDGE COMPANION TO JOHN CALVIN
edited by Donald K. McKim (2004)
ISBN 0 521 81647 5 hardback   ISBN 0 521 01672 x paperback

THE CAMBRIDGE COMPANION TO URS VON BALTHASAR
edited by Edward T. Oakes, SJ and David Moss (2004)
ISBN 0 521 81467 7 hardback   ISBN 0 521 89147 7 paperback

THE CAMBRIDGE COMPANION TO REFORMATION THEOLOGY
edited by David Bagchi and David Steinmetz (2004)
ISBN 0 521 77224 9 hardback   ISBN 0 521 77662 7 paperback

THE CAMBRIDGE COMPANION TO AMERICAN JUDAISM
edited by Dana Evan Kaplan (2005)
ISBN 0 521 82204 1 hardback   ISBN 0 521 52951 4 paperback

THE CAMBRIDGE COMPANION TO KARL RAHNER
edited by Declair Marmior and Mary E. Hines (2005)
ISBN 0 521 83288 8 hardback   ISBN 0 521 54045 3 paperback

Forthcoming

THE CAMBRIDGE COMPANION TO THE GOSPELS
edited by Stephen C. Barton

THE CAMBRIDGE COMPANION TO ISLAMIC THEOLOGY
edited by Tim Winter

THE CAMBRIDGE COMPANION TO EVANGELICAL THEOLOGY
edited by Timothy Larsen and Daniel J. Treier

THE CAMBRIDGE COMPANION TO THE QUR'AN
edited by Jare Dummen McAulisse

THE CAMBRIDGE COMPANION TO

FRIEDRICH SCHLEIERMACHER

Edited by Jacqueline Mariña

CAMBRIDGE
UNIVERSITY PRESS

CAMBRIDGE UNIVERSITY PRESS
Cambridge, New York, Melbourne, Madrid, Cape Town, Singapore, São Paulo

CAMBRIDGE UNIVERSITY PRESS
The Edinburgh Building, Cambridge CB2 2RU, UK

Published in the United States of America by Cambridge University Press, New York

www.cambridge.org
Information on this title: www.cambridge.org/9780521891370

© Cambridge University Press 2005

This book is in copyright. Subject to statutory exception
and to the provisions of relevant collective licensing agreements,
no reproduction of any part may take place without
the written permission of Cambridge University Press.

First published 2005

Printed in the United Kingdom at the University Press, Cambridge

A catalogue record for this book is available from the British Library

ISBN-13 978-0-521-81448-5 hardback
ISBN-10 0-521-81448-0 hardback
ISBN-13 978-0-521-89137-0 paperback
ISBN-10 0-521-89137-x paperback

Cambridge University Press has no responsibility for
the persistence or accuracy of URLs for external or
third-party internet websites referred to in this book,
and does not guarantee that any content on such
websites is, or will remain, accurate or appropriate.

Contents

Notes on contributors   *page* ix
Acknowledgments   xiii
Abbreviations   xiv
Introduction   1

Part I *Schleiermacher as Philosopher*   13

  1 Metaphysical foundations: a look at Schleiermacher's
     Dialectic   15
     MANFRED FRANK

  2 Faith and religious knowledge   35
     ROBERT MERRIHEW ADAMS

  3 Schleiermacher's ethics   53
     FREDERICK C. BEISER

  4 The philosophical significance of Schleiermacher's
     hermeneutics   73
     ANDREW BOWIE

  5 The art of interpreting Plato   91
     JULIA A. LAMM

Part II *Schleiermacher as Theologian*   109

  6 Shaping an academic discipline: the *Brief Outline*
     on the Study of Theology   111
     RICHARD CROUTER

  7 Sin and redemption   129
     WALTER E. WYMAN, JR.

  8 Christology and anthropology in Friedrich Schleiermacher   151
     JACQUELINE MARIÑA

  9 Schleiermacher's understanding of God as triune   171
     FRANCIS SCHÜSSLER FIORENZA

 10 Providence and grace: Schleiermacher on justification
     and election   189
     DAWN DeVRIES AND B. A. GERRISH

11 Schleiermacher's *Christian Ethics* 209
EILERT HERMS

12 Schleiermacher's exegetical theology and the
New Testament 229
CHRISTINE HELMER

Part III *Culture, Society, and Religion* 249

13 Culture, arts, and religion 251
DAVID E. KLEMM

14 Schleiermacher and the state 269
THEODORE VIAL

15 Schleiermacher, feminism, and liberation
theologies: a key 287
THANDEKA

16 Schleiermacher yesterday, today, and tomorrow 307
TERRENCE N. TICE

Schleiermacher bibliography 319
References 325
Index 337

Notes on contributors

Robert Merrihew Adams taught philosophy for many years at UCLA, and retired recently from the Clark Professorship of Moral Philosophy and Metaphysics at Yale University. He is currently a Visiting Professor of Philosophy at the University of Oxford, where he is also a Senior Research Fellow of Mansfield College. His publications include *The Virtue of Faith and Other Essays in Philosophical Theology* (1987), *Leibniz: Determinist, Theist, Idealist* (1994), and *Finite and Infinite Goods: A Framework for Ethics* (1999).

Frederick C. Beiser is Professor of Philosophy at Syracuse University. He has been a major contributor to work on the history of modern philosophy, especially the history of German philosophy (Kant and German idealism) and the English Enlightenment. His book *The Fate of Reason: German Philosophy from Kant to Fichte* won the 1987 Thomas J. Wilson Prize for the best first book. He is the editor of *The Cambridge Companion to Hegel*. He has won Thyssen and Humboldt research fellowships to study at the Free University of Berlin and was a 1994 Guggenheim Fellow. He received a 1999–2000 NEH Faculty Fellowship (at Indiana University), and he has won awards for his outstanding undergraduate teaching.

Andrew Bowie is Professor of Philosophy and German at Royal Holloway College, University of London. His books include: *Schelling and Modern European Philosophy* (1993), *From Romanticism to Critical Theory* (1997), *Aesthetics and Subjectivity: From Kant to Nietzsche* (2003), and *Introduction to German Philosophy from Kant to Habermas* (2003), and he has translated editions of Schelling's *On the History of Modern Philosophy* and Schleiermacher's *Hermeneutics and Criticism*. He is currently writing a book, *Music, Philosophy, and Modernity*.

Richard Crouter is John M. and Elizabeth W. Musser Professor of Religious Studies Emeritus at Carleton College in Northfield, Minnesota. His publications include: *Friedrich Schleiermacher, Between Enlightenment and Romanticism* (2005), editor and trans. with Julie Klassen, *A Debate on Jewish Emancipation and Christian Theology in Old Berlin* (2004), editor and trans., *Friedrich Schleiermacher, On Religion: Speeches to its Cultured Despisers* [1799] (1996), and he is co-editor of *Zeitschrift für Neuere Theologiegeschichte / Journal for the History of Modern Theology*, 1994–.

Dawn DeVries is the John Newton Thomas Professor of Systematic Theology at Union Theological Seminary and Presbyterian School of Christian Education in Richmond, Virginia. She is the editor and translator of *Servant of the Word: Selected Sermons of Friedrich Schleiermacher* and the author of *Jesus Christ in the Preaching of Calvin and Schleiermacher.*

Francis Schüssler Fiorenza is the Stillman Professor of Roman Catholic Theological Studies at Harvard Divinity School. He is the author of *Foundational Theology: Jesus and the Church*, has co-edited a two-volume work, *Systematic Theology: Roman Catholic Perspectives*, has co-authored with James Livingston, *Modern Christian Thought*, vol. II: *The Twentieth Century*, has co-edited and translated with James Duke: *Schleiermacher: Open Letters to Dr. Lucke*, and has published more than 150 essays on theology and the history of modern theology.

Manfred Frank is Professor of Philosophy at Tübingen University. He is the author of numerous books and articles dealing with themes such as Kant's philosophy, early idealism and early romanticism, hermeneutics, neo-structuralism and self-consciousness from the point of view of both analytic and continental traditions. His work on self-consciousness has laid the groundwork for dialogue among analytic and continental traditions. His books, too numerous to list, have been translated into several languages and include *Das individuelle Allgemeine. Textstrukturierung und -interpretation nach Schleiermacher* (1977), *Was ist Neostrukturalismus?* (1983) *Das Sagbare und das Unsagbare* (1989), *Der kommende Gott* (1982, expanded edition 2003), *Unendliche Annäherung* (1997), and *Selbstgefühl* (2002).

B. A. Gerrish is John Nuveen Professor Emeritus at the University of Chicago Divinity School and a Fellow of the American Academy of Arts and Sciences. Among his books pertinent to the present volume are *Tradition and the Modern World: Reformed Theology in the Nineteenth Century* and *Continuing the Reformation: Essays on Modern Religious Thought.*

Christine Helmer is Associate Professor of Theology at Claremont School of Theology in Claremont, California. She is the author of *The Trinity and Martin Luther: A Study on the Relationship Between Genre, Language and the Trinity in Luther's Works (1523–1546)* (1999), as well as co-editor of a number of edited volumes including *Schleiermachers Dialektik: Die Liebe zum Wissen in Philosophie und Theologie* (2003) with Christiane Kranich and Birgit Rehme-Iffert, and *Schleiermacher and Whitehead: Open Systems in Dialogue* (2004) in co-operation with Marjorie Suchocki, John Quiring, and Katie Goetz.

Eilert Herms is Professor and Dean of the Evangelical Theological Faculty at Tübingen. From 1996 to 2002 he served as chair of the *Wissenschaftlichen Gesellschaft für Theologie* and is currently the director of the Institut für Ethik at Tübingen. He is the author of numerous scholarly articles and books including *Herkunft, Entfaltung und erste Gestalt des Systems der Wissenschaften bei Schleiermacher* (1974), *Menschsein im Werden: Studien zu Schleiermacher* (2003) and *Von Glaubenseinheit zur Kirchengemeinschaft* (2003). With Günter Meckenstock, he is co-editor of *KGA* 1.4 (2002).

David E. Klemm is Professor of Philosophical Theology in the Department of Religious Studies in the College of Liberal Arts and Sciences at the University of Iowa. His research interests include a new project on "theological humanism" as a constructive proposal for current theology of culture, as well as ongoing contributions to studies of Paul Ricoeur and Friedrich Schleiermacher within their respective cultural contexts.

Julia A. Lamm is Associate Professor of Theology at Georgetown University. She is author of *The Living God: Schleiermacher's Theological Appropriation of Spinoza* (1996), as well as several articles on Schleiermacher's theology, philosophy, and ethics. She is currently writing *Schleiermacher's Plato: The Construction of a New Platonism*, the research for which she began while an Alexander von Humboldt Fellow in Berlin.

Jacqueline Mariña is Associate Professor of Philosophy at Purdue University. She specializes in Kant, Schleiermacher, and philosophy of religion. She has published a number of book chapters and scholarly articles that have appeared in journals such as *Journal of the History of Philosophy, Kant-Studien, Faith and Philosophy, Journal of Religion*, and *Religious Studies*. She is currently at work on a book entitled *Transformation of the Self in the Thought of Friedrich Schleiermacher*.

Thandeka is Associate Professor of Theology and Culture at Meadville/Lombard Theological School in Chicago, co-president of the Center for Community Values and an affiliated minister at the Unitarian Universalist Church in Rockford, Illinois. She is the author of *The Embodied Self: Friedrich Schleiermacher's Solution to Kant's Problem of the Empirical Self* (1995) and *Learning to be White: Money, Race and God in America* (1999). Thandeka is currently working on volume one (doctrine of human nature) of her systematic theology, which will be published in 2006. An ordained Unitarian Universalist minister and theologian, she was given the !Xhosa name Thandeka, which means "beloved," by Archbishop Bishop Desmond Tutu in 1984.

Terrence N. Tice is Emeritus Professor of Philosophy at the University of Michigan. He was the initial chair of the American Academy of Religion's Schleiermacher Group, and he is the longtime chair of the Schleiermacher Society. He is an interdisciplinary scholar who has authored or edited numerous books, translations, bibliographies, and articles in Schleiermacher studies.

Theodore Vial is Batten Associate Professor of Religious Studies at Virginia Wesleyan College. He is author of *Liturgy Wars: Ritual Theory and Protestant Reform in Nineteenth-Century Zurich* (2004) and has published articles on historical theology and theory in *Numen*, the *Harvard Theological Review, Zeitschrift für neuere Theologiegeschichte/Journal for the History of Modern Theology*, and *Method and Theory in the Study of Religions*.

Walter E. Wyman, Jr. is Professor of Religion and Weyerhaeuser Professor of Biblical Literatures at Whitman College (Walla Walla, Washington). He is the author of *The Concept of Glaubenslehre: Ernst Troeltsch and the Theological Heritage of Schleiermacher* and co-editor of *Revisioning the Past: Prospects of Historical Theology*. He has published a number of essays on Schleiermacher, Harnack, and Troeltsch.

Acknowledgments

First, I would like to thank my family, Franklin Mason, my husband, and Curtis, Katie, and Gabriel, my children, who put up with the long hours that I devoted to this volume. Terrence Tice provided advice in the initial stages of the conception of the book, and Richard Crouter proved an invaluable guide throughout. Not only was he a resource in offering sound advice from beginning to end of the project, he also checked the translation of the chapter by Eilert Herms. Karl Ameriks was kind enough to check the translation for Manfred Frank's chapter. Both my student, Andrea White, and my husband worked on the index. Christine Helmer was helpful in getting Manfred Frank and Eilert Herms on board for the project, making this a truly international effort. Finally, the editors at Cambridge University Press for this series, Kevin Taylor and Kate Brett, have been enormously helpful. Kevin Taylor worked closely with me at the beginning stages of the process, and Kate Brett has overseen the rest of the process of production. Their input has been invaluable, and the volume is much better for it.

The final stages of this volume were completed at the Center for Humanistic Studies at Purdue University, which provided a semester off from my teaching duties during the fall of 2004. I am grateful to Purdue for this time to devote to research.

Jacqueline Mariña

Abbreviations

AO	*Ästhetik* (Odebrecht edition)
AF	*Athenaeums Fragmente*
BO	*Brief Outline* (*Kurze Darstellung*)
CF	*Christian Faith* (*Glaubenslehre*)
CE	*Christian Ethics* (*Die christliche Sitte*)
ChrEve	*Christmas Eve* (*Weihnachtsfeier*)
Dial O	Odebrecht edition of the *Dialectic* (*Dialektik*)
Dial J	Jonas edition of the *Dialectic* (*Dialektik*)
KGA	*Schleiermacher Kritische Gesamtausgabe*
LJ	*The Life of Jesus* (*Das Leben Jesu*)
OR	*On Religion. OR* will be followed by the name of the translator to indicate translation cited (*Über die Religion*).
PS	*Pädagogische Schriften*
PT	*Praktische Theologie*
SW	*Sämtliche Werke*
ThEnz	*Theologische Enzyklopädie (1831/32)*
UK	*Über den Umfang des Begriffs der Kunst*

Note on sources

Full references to the editions and translations of Schleiermacher's work will be found in the list of the primary sources. Works most commonly cited are referred to by the abbreviations, and the reference will be internal to the text. Other references to Schleiermacher's work will be cited by short title in the end notes. All secondary works will be cited by author and date in the notes, and full citations will be found in the bibliography.

Introduction

Friedrich Daniel Ernst Schleiermacher (1768–1834) was an eminent classicist, philosopher, and theologian. He is most famous for his contributions to theology, for which he is known as "the father of modern theology." He is without doubt one of the greatest Christian theologians of all time, standing in the same rank as Augustine, Aquinas, and Calvin.[1] His theological work had, and continues to have, an enormous influence, even when this influence has not always been recognized as his. It is well known that he introduced many of the ideas at the forefront of nineteenth-century German liberal Protestant theology. His influence has not been limited to liberal theology, however. Many of his insights decisively changed the understanding of the way in which the areas of theology are related to one another. For instance, the basic thrust of his argument regarding the "four natural heresies of Christianity," has been widely accepted, as has his claim that the doctrine of the Trinity is the *result* of reflection on the fundamental experience of redemption in Christ and the common Spirit of the church that flows from it. Moreover, Schleiermacher's discussion of the relation of Christology to soteriology, that is, his argument that the doctrines of the person and work of Christ are inherently related (so that the "activity" of Christ cannot be separated from his "dignity") has had an enormous impact. Whereas before Schleiermacher dogmatic textbooks tended to discuss the two topics in isolation, after him the topics were generally discussed together.

While Schleiermacher is best known for his contributions to theology, his contributions to philosophy have been notably significant as well, in particular in the areas of philosophy of religion, hermeneutics, and classical philosophy; his contributions to ethics are now just beginning to achieve the recognition they deserve in the English-speaking world.[2] It is well known that Schleiermacher's *On Religion* is a foundational text in the theory of religion, providing a theoretical basis for the comparative study of religion and for religious pluralism.[3] Not only has Schleiermacher been recognized as a pioneer of philosophical hermeneutics, but the work of Manfred Frank in Germany and Andrew Bowie in England has shown the continued relevance of his contributions to the field today. As Julia Lamm notes in her chapter in this volume, Schleiermacher's translations of Plato were a momentous event in the philosophical, philological, and literary world of his day, so much so that his translations are still in use today and continue to carry significant authority; his interpretation of Plato changed the entire course of Plato studies.

Schleiermacher was born the son of a Prussian army chaplain in Breslau in lower Silesia in 1768. His early education was provided by the Moravian Brethren (Herrnhuter), a strict pietist community that strove to be true to the reformist aims of P. J. Spener's *Pia Desideria* (1675). At Niesky (1783) Schleiermacher was exposed to an enlightened humanistic curriculum. His talents were recognized, and he was advanced to the seminary at Barby (1785). There he formed a secret club in which he and his classmates read Kant, Goethe, and other contemporary German writers. As a result of this exposure, as well as of the narrow theological pedagogy of that school, he began to have doubts about certain Christian doctrines. In 1787 he transferred to the more liberal University of Halle, where he continued in theology, with philosophy and classical philology as minor fields. Nevertheless, Schleiermacher never renounced his early religious training. In a letter to George Reimer in 1802 he wrote, "I have become a Herrnhuter again, only of a higher order."[4]

An extremely brief outline of Schleiermacher's appointments follows. In 1790 he passed his academic theological examinations at Berlin. From 1790 to 1793 he served as a private tutor for the aristocratic Dohna family at Schlobitten in East Prussia, and then was pastor in Landsberg from 1794 to 1796. In 1796 he became chaplain to a hospital in Berlin. He spent 1802–4 in Stolpe because of scandal and unhappiness in Berlin, but by 1804 he was teaching at Halle. As a result of the French occupation he left Halle in 1806–7 and moved to Berlin. By 1810 he was appointed professor of theology at the University of Berlin and in 1811 became a member of the Berlin Academy of Sciences. He remained at the University of Berlin, where he was professor and four-time dean of the theological faculty, lecturing on various topics until his death in 1834.

Throughout his life Schleiermacher was extraordinarily prolific, writing in such areas as theology, New Testament studies, philosophy of religion, ethics, psychology, and hermeneutics. Given the extent of his influence in so many areas, this volume will be divided into three parts. The first part of the volume is devoted to Schleiermacher's philosophy and philosophy of religion; the second to his theology, and the third to issues in culture, society, and religion.

Since Schleiermacher's metaphysical views are foundational for his philosophy of religion, the first chapter is devoted to Schleiermacher's metaphysics. In that chapter, "Metaphysical foundations: a look at Schleiermacher's *Dialectic*," Manfred Frank provides an insightful analysis of Schleiermacher's understanding of the highest transcendent ground that is the basis for both ethics and metaphysics. This ground is discovered through dialectic, a science of knowledge transcending the opposition between knowing and doing. Instead of tracing Schleiermacher's thought to Kant, Professor Frank pursues a new line of thought that follows Schleiermacher's Spinozist and Leibnizian inheritance as mediated by Eberhard in order to interpret Schleiermacher's views on judgment and concept formation. In light of Schleiermacher's Leibnizian inheritance, he makes sense of Schleiermacher's famous theory of a continuous "transition" between sense and understanding in light of the "numerical identity" of the foundational power. Professor Frank then provides a careful analysis of Schleiermacher's identity theory of judgment and its implications. He then explores Schleiermacher's four formulas of the unconditioned, transcendent ground, and provides an in-depth analysis of how the transcendent ground is accessed in the immediate self-consciousness.

In his chapter, "Faith and religious knowledge," Robert Merrihew Adams provides a critical analysis of Schleiermacher's epistemology of religion and its theological implications. In showing how the feeling of absolute dependence has an implicit reference to a being much greater than ourselves, he deals with the question of how the *immediate* self-consciousness can have an intentional object. In answer to this he points to the fact that while the feeling of absolute dependence is a characteristic of ourselves, it is a *relational* characteristic, and as such has implications that move beyond the nature of the immediate self-consciousness taken by itself. This is because for Schleiermacher causal relations are part of the implicit content of forms of immediate self-consciousness, although what we are aware of is only our own pole of the causal relation. Hence the immediate self-consciousness contains an implicit reference to that upon which we are dependent. Given this analysis, Professor Adams then asks whether for Schleiermacher faith is conceptually structured or not, reflecting on the implications of Schleiermacher's claim that the same religious consciousness can express itself in quite different propositions. Finally he discusses the question of the theological interpretation of the religious consciousness in the light of two test cases, Schleiermacher's eschatology and Christology.

Frederick C. Beiser tackles Schleiermacher's philosophical ethics in chapter three, "Schleiermacher's ethics." He distinguishes five stages in the development of Schleiermacher's ethics. (1) From 1789 to 1796 Schleiermacher is preoccupied with Kant and questions regarding the compatibility of determinism and moral responsibility; he is also concerned with the question of the highest good, and begins to defend an ethic of self-realization. (2) From 1796 to 1802 Schleiermacher is influenced by the romantic circle in Berlin and becomes critical of the tradition of the *Aufklärung*, questioning its view of religion and morality. He develops the themes of individuality, sociality, and love, which will continue to play a role in his ethical thought. (3) From 1802 to 1804 he prepared for his later system with his criticisms of past ethical systems; and (4) in Halle and Berlin begins a period of system building (1806–16). (5) From 1819 to 1832 Schleiermacher partially consolidates his ethical views and relates them to his metaphysics. Ethics is one of the two fundamental sciences of the infinite or absolute, and as such it is intrinsically related to religion. Schleiermacher adopts a vitalistic metaphysics departing significantly from Spinoza, and this foundation has significant consequences for his ethical theory. The world is a living organism that develops through differentiation and externalization whereby the subjective becomes objective – and a movement of assimilation and internalization – whereby the objective becomes subjective.

In his chapter, "The philosophical significance of Schleiermacher's hermeneutics," Andrew Bowie discusses the continuing philosophical relevance of Schleiermacher's hermeneutics. He notes that there are two diametrically opposed positions regarding how it is possible to interpret a text or utterance. According to the structuralist position, the meaning of an utterance is determined by the publicly available meanings of the words that constitute it. On the other hand, the intentionalist position holds that the meaning of an utterance lies in the intention of the speaker. The history and inner life of the speaker is of decisive importance in determining its significance. Schleiermacher calls these the "grammatical" and "psychological" poles of language, respectively. Professor Bowie argues that if understood in the context of his *Dialectic*, Schleiermacher's hermeneutics can help us move beyond this impasse. Schleiermacher holds that we cannot strictly separate receptivity and spontaneity because both share a single underlying root. This plays a crucial role at several levels, the first being how we move from sense-data to the ordinary world of tables and chairs. How the sense-data is organized will depend on the interpretive work of language: there is no bedrock given in receptivity. Wittgenstein's famous "duck-rabbit" is a useful example of this. Similarly, just as sense-data provide no bedrock "given," neither do the publicly available meanings of words. While language users begin from there, their own mental activity is important in shaping and sometimes even recasting those publicly available meanings. The level of the subject's activity in shaping these meanings will vary from activity to activity, from quite high in aesthetic endeavors to low in scientific ones. For Schleiermacher, hermeneutics is "the art of understanding ... the ... discourse of another person correctly." Both grammatical and psychological elements are vital to this task.

In her chapter, "The art of interpreting Plato," Julia Lamm notes that Schleiermacher's hermeneutical theory was developed as he interpreted Plato. Schleiermacher's groundbreaking Plato translations and interpretations made extensive use of the historical-critical method; they required both an extensive understanding of the historical context in which a text was written as well as close attention to the text itself. Unlike interpreters like Tenneman, Schleiermacher insisted that we need to pay close attention to Plato's dialogues themselves instead of positing an esoteric Platonic teaching. In focusing on Plato's artistic genius, the unity of Plato's works could be discovered. Professor Lamm points out three principles that Schleiermacher used in understanding the artistry, and thereby the unity in Plato's works. First, a work must be understood as an organic whole with essential natural connections; second, the collection of what appears scattered must be collected and the work must be divided into its natural parts; and third, the importance of the dialogue form must be recognized. Armed with these interpretive principles, Schleiermacher hoped to find not only the unity lying behind the Platonic corpus, but also to provide a chronology of Plato's work. Both tasks were interdependent. Finally, Professor Lamm calls attention to the fact that for Schleiermacher understanding is an art; the interpreter must not only dissect a work, but he must be able to put the pieces back together again, that is, to understand a literary corpus as a living whole. Interpretation is therefore itself an artistic process.

Richard Crouter's essay, "Shaping an academic discipline: the *Brief Outline on the Study of Theology*," begins part two of the book on Schleiermacher's theology and sets the context for the following chapters. In his chapter Professor Crouter takes a look at Schleiermacher's theological method, noting that Schleiermacher balances the need for a rational perspective in theological method with a grasp of the significance of the contingent character of historical existence. Philosophical theology is the "root" of theology insofar as it identifies the essence of Christianity "in its givenness," relates it to other religions (apologetics), and picks out its own aberrations (polemics). Nevertheless, this original essence of Christianity must manifest itself in history. As such, historical theology, which reaches from the age of the apostles through contemporary dogmatics, is thereby assigned the task of confirming the results of philosophical theology by examining how the essence of Christianity has appeared in history. Moreover, historical theology lays the foundation for practical theology, which Schleiermacher considered the "crown" of theology. The three main subfields of historical theology, exegetical theology, church history, and dogmatics, have tight internal correlations. So too, the three main divisions of theology, philosophical theology, historical theology, and practical theology are inherently related, presupposing and informing each other dialectically. Professor Crouter discusses the merits of Schleiermacher's anchoring of dogmatics in history, and why such anchoring need not compromise doctrinal statements. Lastly, he explores Schleiermacher's understanding of practical theology as the crown of theology.

In his chapter, "Sin and redemption," Walter E. Wyman notes that sin and grace are at the heart of Schleiermacher's understanding of Christianity; the principle problem Schleiermacher confronts is how to give an account of these concepts after the Enlightenment. Schleiermacher thus sets out to rethink these ideas and to show how his revisionist understanding was consistent with the earlier credal statements. As Professor Wyman notes, Schleiermacher's methodological innovation is a theology of consciousness. Both sin and redemption are located in consciousness, and this means that an exploration of both involves an exploration of the nature of consciousness. At the same time, Schleiermacher remains in dialogue with the tradition, in particular the confessions of the sixteenth century. After exploring Schleiermacher's developmental account of sin, his account of it in terms of intellect and will, and his social account, Professor Wyman turns his attention to Schleiermacher's account of redemption. He provides an analysis of Schleiermacher's understanding of the means of redemption and reconciliation, as well as of Schleiermacher's understanding of the phenomenology of grace, namely regeneration and sanctification. Finally Professor Wyman discusses the resources that Schleiermacher's theology has for theology today and identifies possible limitations in Schleiermacher's theology.

In my chapter, "Christology and anthropology in Friedrich Schleiermacher," I discuss Schleiermacher's understanding of both the person and work of Christ. Schleiermacher's dialogue with the orthodox Christological tradition preceding him, as well as his understanding of the work of Christ, is founded on a critical analysis of the fundamental person-forming experience of being in relation to Christ and the community founded by him. I provide an analysis of Schleiermacher's discussion of the difficulties surrounding the use of the word "nature" in relation to Jesus' humanity and divinity, and then move to discuss how Schleiermacher understands both the humanity and divinity of Jesus, as well as how the two stand in relation to one another. In the original divine decree Jesus Christ is ordained as the person through which the whole human race is to be completed and perfected, and the essence of perfect human nature is to express the divine. This is the essence of Schleiermacher's solution to the Christological problem, that is, of how the divine and the human can converge in one person. I then move to discuss Schleiermacher's understanding of the work of Christ as involving two interrelated moments. The first is the awakening of the God-consciousness. The second involves the self-expression of this God-consciousness in the form of Christian love in the community of believers. As such, the principle work of Christ is the founding of the kingdom of God.

Francis Schüssler Fiorenza provides a penetrating analysis of Schleiermacher's doctrine of the Trinity in his chapter, "Schleiermacher's understanding of God as triune." He replies to numerous objections to Schleiermacher's exposition of the Trinity, from the charge that Schleiemarcher marginalizes the doctrine to the more extreme charge by Robert Jenson (echoing that of Johann Adam Möhler) that Schleiermacher is an Arian who has simply dropped the inherited Trinitarian position. On this interpretation, for Schleiermacher God is one eternally unknown monad behind diverse manifestations. Against these misunderstandings, Professor Fiorenza points out that for Schleiermacher the love and wisdom of God are not mere attributes but also expressions of the very essence of God, and as such are not the revealed manifestations of a hidden unknown monad. God is known as love and wisdom through the Christian experience of redemption in Christ and the common Spirit in the church that flows from it; the doctrine of the Trinity is a result of reflection on this fundamental experience. As Professor Fiorenza notes, this theological move proved to be extremely influential, but what remained in question was whether this biblical affirmation of the divinity of the Father, Son, and Holy Spirit necessitated a speculative doctrine about inner differentiation within God. While Schleiermacher stressed that knowledge of the divine essence was possible, he denied that the Christian experience of redemption implied the original and eternal existence of distinctions within the divine essence. Schleiermacher's understanding of the divine causality as well as his epistemological modesty led him to shy away from speculations about the interior relations of the Trinitarian persons. Given this analysis, Professor Fiorenza concludes that

Schleiermacher's conception of the Trinity should not be equated with an Arian or a Sabellian view.

In their chapter, "Providence and grace: Schleiermacher on justification and election," Dawn DeVries and B. A. Gerrish discuss the interrelations of the concepts of providence, justification, and election, paying particular attention to the theological location in which these doctrines are placed. They argue that what Schleiermacher thought about both justification and election was partly formed by his discussion of God's providence in part one of the *Christian Faith*; the doctrine of providence, in particular Schleiermacher's thoughts on the relation of divine to natural causality, regulates what can be said about the divine operations of grace in justifying the sinner and election. God's relations to the world are all functions of a single divine decree, which is oriented towards a single goal, that of the establishment of the kingdom of God. As such, statements about providence, justification, and election must be understood from the perspective of this single divine decree, which is directed to the realization of the final *telos* of the world as a whole.

In his chapter, "Schleiermacher's *Christian Ethics*," Eilert Herms situates Schleiermacher's Christian ethics in the larger context of his thought as a whole. After discussing the relation between ethics and faith, the relation of historical theology to philosophical theology, and theology's place in the theory of human knowledge as a whole, he provides a painstaking analysis of the content of the *Christian Ethics*. Christian piety is characterized by a double motive, grounding both a desire for knowledge and the desire to act. While the content of the *Christian Faith* is concerned with the former, Christian ethics is concerned with the latter. Christian ethics answers the question, how must the religious self-consciousness develop itself, and what must come of it? In answering this question, Schleiermacher provides an analysis of the conditions under which the immediate self-consciousness, as determined by Christ's redemptive activity, becomes an incentive to action. Since all action presupposes a lack and serves to overcome it, these are incentives that take place in the *emerging* blessedness of the Christian. Professor Herms explores the character of the three kinds of incentives to Christian action identified by Schleiermacher: the incentive to actions that *re-establish* the flesh as the organ of the spirit, the incentive to *expansive* actions extending the dominion of spirit over those areas not yet grasped by it; and *representing* or *expressive* actions that express what it is to be in the community of the redeemed. Finally, the nature of these actions in both the family and the civil state is discussed.

Christine Helmer examines Schleiermacher's exegetical works in the larger context of Schleiermacher's theological and philosophical thought in her chapter, "Schleiermacher's exegetical theology and the New Testament." First, she shows that in affirming the priority of the experience of Christ over Scripture, Schleiermacher was able to engage in a scientific investigation of the New Testament canon that did not pose a threat to the ecclesial use of the Bible. Second, she provides an analysis of Schleiermacher's understanding of the goal of exegetical theology as the fixing of the canon, namely the determination of the original apprehensions of Christ. Third, she examines how Schleiermacher's exegetical methodology was informed by the critical disciplines of hermeneutics and dialectic, and lastly, she explores the relationship between dogmatic and exegetical theology in Schleiermacher's thought.

The last part of the book begins with David Klemm's chapter, "Culture, arts, and religion," in which he provides an analysis of Schleiermacher's understanding of how religion should relate to culture. The cultured despisers of religion are aware of the conditioned character of positive religions, while the true believers in positive religion often ascribe absolute truth to their beliefs and are unaware of their culturally conditioned character. While all religions are positive and as such are historically and culturally conditioned, Schleiermacher attempts to identify elements common to all religions. The strength of positive religion is that it proceeds from a living intuition of the universe. Professor Klemm reads Schleiermacher as advocating an appreciation of this moment of living vitality in positive religion while at the same time recognizing the limited and conditioned character of all human apprehensions of the infinite. This is the task of philosophical theology, which is a self-conscious and reflexive way of thinking about and experiencing religion in its truth. Professor Klemm next discusses the extent to which Schleiermacher's understanding of Christian revelation played a role in his contribution to comparative religion, and concludes that there is no necessary connection between Christianity and Schleiermacher's philosophical theology. Finally, Professor Klemm discusses the role of the arts in fostering spirituality as Schleiermacher understands it.

In his chapter, "Schleiermacher and the state," Theodore Vial shows that, contra the Enlightenment view of the state as an artificial machine designed only to protect the individual in his or her personal activities against external threats, Schleiermacher viewed the state as a vital organism necessary for human progress to occur. Through the state individuals can bring their energies together, harmonize them, and through their common efforts achieve great things. Moreover, in its institutions the state expresses the spirit of people. As such, the state represents the completion of human life. In light of his discussion of Schleiermacher's theoretical commitments regarding the nature of the state, Vial examines Schleiermacher's activity as citizen, including his participation in intrigues against Napoleon, the preaching of sermons with political content, his editorship of a political newspaper, and his efforts for the reunification of the Lutheran and Reformed churches in Prussia.

In her essay, "Schleiermacher, feminism, and liberation theologies: a key," Thandeka notes the contradictory conclusions that scholars have reached concerning Schleiermacher and feminism. While some find him sympathetic to contemporary feminist issues, others find him hostile, pointing to his stance against the political, educational, and social liberation of women. Thandeka proposes to move beyond this impasse through an exploration of Schleiermacher's "doctrine of the soul," containing an analysis of how human feeling is organized and the effect of this organization on human consciousness. In his "doctrine of human affections" Schleiermacher used a set of gender images that transcended the restrictive gender biases of his own time. According to Schleiermacher there is a proto-gender, an original state of the self that precedes gender. Schleiermacher named this gender "artist." It is the original state of the soul before it is split into male and female genders. Thandeka provides an analysis of the roots of this idea in Schleiermacher's theorizing upon the experience of music and how music evokes different affective states in the listener. Her analysis reveals both the resources Schleiermacher's theory has to offer for contemporary feminism, as well as its limitations.

Finally, in his chapter, "Scheiermacher yesterday, today, and tomorrow," Terrence N. Tice provides a summary of Schleiermacher's identity and achievement, discusses the history of his reception in the English-speaking world as well as the recent growth of Schleiermacher scholarship, and makes note of areas in Schleiermacher scholarship that still need to be explored.

Schleiermacher was such a polymath, and his thought so rich that no single volume can do justice to his work. Yet the seventeen authors contributing to this volume are among the top Schleiermacher scholars in the world, and their chapters provide thought-provoking introductions and analyses of the thought of this great thinker. It is my hope, and theirs as well, that this volume will stimulate many others to continue to investigate his work and the relevance of his insightful legacy to the world today.

Jacqueline Mariña

Purdue University, Fall 2004

Notes

1 Johannas von Kuhn of the Catholic Tübingen school noted in 1839 that "among all the theologians of later and contemporary times, only Schleiermacher can be compared to [Thomas Aquinas] so far as scientific force and power are concerned." This judgment is no less true today. Cited in Sockness 2003, 317n.

2 See Sockness 2003, Sockness 2004, and Mariña 1999, as well as Beiser's chapter in this volume.

3 See Mariña 2004b, as well as David Klemm's chapter in this volume.

4 Rowan 1860, 283–4.

Part I

Schleiermacher as Philosopher

1 Metaphysical foundations: a look at Schleiermacher's *Dialectic*[1]

dedicated to Willem van Reijen on his sixty-fifth birthday

MANFRED FRANK

(translated by JACQUELINE MARINA and CHRISTINE HELMER)

THE NATURE OF THE WORK

Strictly speaking, Schleiermacher does not have a metaphysics, if by this is meant a foundational philosophical doctrine. He was not convinced that metaphysics could grasp the highest object of the human mind, or that it could exhaustively deal with the essential interests of the human spirit. He reserved the expression "metaphysics" for the systematic exposition of descriptive truths.[2] Alongside such a system he placed ethics, or morals, as a system of action (not only right action). The "highest" lies beyond the knowledge claims of both, and as such, must be named their transcendent ground. It cannot be represented adequately through the means of either discipline. This ground is called "transcendent" because it "lies beyond every possible experience and every possible determined thought" (Zusatz to §85 of the 1831 lectures). Schleiermacher wished to "dispense entirely" with the distinction, introduced by Kant, between the "transcendental" (grounding the knowability of objects of experience) and the "transcendent" (extending beyond the limits of experience) (*Dial* J, 38).

Instead of "metaphysics," Schleiermacher called his first philosophy, in the Platonic tradition, "Dialectic." The word choice is inspired by the Platonic practice of διαλέγεσθαι and it characterizes "dialectic" as "the art of conversation in pure thinking" (F 2001 II, 5ff.). "Pure" refers to a kind of thinking not distracted by artistic/aesthetic or practical considerations, but motivated solely by the cooperative search for truth. In light of the epistemic transcendence of its object, for Schleiermacher one criterion of truth is consensus; another is the coherence of our beliefs. However, the *definition* of truth is, as for Kant, the correspondence (or agreement) of thought with its object (*Dial* O, 135 ff.; § 95). Disagreement in the formation of our beliefs can be "maximal" if the communal fixing or individuation of the object is in question. However, Schleiermacher does not consider this a real possibility. This is because a typical dialectical conflict begins when different thinkers/ speakers think not simply differently, but in contradictory ways about an object. And they can do this only given the quasi transcendental conditions of the identity of an object, to which not only different (yet logically equally possible), but contradictory determinations (predicates) are assigned. Hence dialectical praxis presupposes the identity of the thing referred to, and therefore a realistic theory of truth. This differentiates Schleiermacher's project sharply from that of Hegel.

The *Dialectic* would have been Schleiermacher's principal philosophical work had he not succumbed to pneumonia in February of 1834, as he was preparing the introduction for publication. He had first begun his lectures on the foundations of philosophy with his appointment in 1810 to the theological professorship of the newly founded Friedrich-Wilhelms University of Berlin. In the summer semester of 1811 he offered a systematic presentation of his foundational philosophical beliefs. Through these lectures Schleiermacher sought to combat Fichte's philosophical predominance and to reject the dialogical forgetfulness of Fichte's "philosophizing from a highest principle."[3]

Schleiermacher was strongly interested in ethical issues from a philosophical perspective. However, he noted the one-sided and foundationalist way in which Fichte resolved them. On the other hand, in Schelling's philosophy of nature he recognized a physicalistic antidote to this praxis-oriented trajectory that did not suit him either. As he already makes clear in his *Grundlinien* (1803), dialectic should be a science of knowledge transcending the opposition between knowing and doing, theory and praxis. Schleiermacher also hoped to counter Hegel's logical idealization of reality through his own lectures on dialectic. Admittedly, dialectic was a basic concept of Hegel's own method. But unlike Schleiermacher's view of dialectic, Hegel's aimed at a final grounding of a system of all theoretical and practical knowledge (absolute knowledge). Schleiermacher's *Dialectic*, in contrast, resonates with early romantic, anti-foundationalist, and partially realist themes. Schleiermacher stands in the psychologizing, empiricism-friendly tradition of thinkers, some of whom took up Kant, such as Schmid, Novalis, and Fries. On the other hand, this psychologizing tendency was also lively in followers of Leibniz, such as Platner, Tetens, or Schleiermacher's teacher in Halle, Eberhard. The tendency to psychologize basic transcendental concepts is especially marked when Schleiermacher speaks of the "organic function" instead of sensation. However, fundamentally Schleiermacher no longer took strict *a priori* concepts for empirical items.[4] The driving intuition behind his *Dialectic* is a realist one since it presupposes, with Schmid and Novalis, a "being" prior to and outside of consciousness from which the "organic" data originates. It is anti-foundationalist since it does not ground knowledge in a logical principle, but rather, situates the beginning of knowledge "in the middle" (*Dial O*, 195, 390, § 291 of the manuscript from 1814). This oscillation between speech and response points to a Kantian regulative Idea, rather than to a preestablished principle, since each understanding attained is revisable. Along with Plato, Schleiermacher calls this movement between thesis and antithesis, or the overcoming of a contradiction in individual thought, διαλέγεσθαι, henceforth, dialectic. As a romantic thinker Schleiermacher is not a German idealist, if by such a thinker is meant someone who believes s/he has grasped the absolute through infallibly valid concepts or as a ground in consciousness.

KANTIAN AND LEIBNIZIAN PRESUPPOSITIONS

The *Dialectic* is the most unmanageable of Schleiermacher's works, but is, nonetheless, his foundational philosophical œuvre. After 150 years, the text remains a riddle. The way in which it has been transmitted complicates matters: Schleiermacher based all his lectures on dialectic (1818, 1822, 1828, as well as the final lectures of 1831) on the handwritten manuscript of 1814. He therefore never had an edited version of the *Dialectic* prepared for publication. When he finally got around to preparing it, he never moved beyond the important "Introduction" of 1833. As a result, scholars must make do with student notes. The first of these were compiled by the first editor of the *Dialectic*, Ludwig Jonas, who reproduced the underlying text of 1814–15 and supplemented it with excerpts from his notes. A critical edition of this version has appeared recently in the *Kritische Gesamtausgabe*, edited by Andreas Arndt (Arndt 2002).

Another problem lies in situating the *Dialectic* in relation to Schleiermacher's philosophical contemporaries. For too long, scholars were fixated by Schleiermacher's relation to Kant and German idealism, assuming that the *Dialectic* belonged to this tradition. Since no interpretative progress was made given this assumption, a new line of thought was pursued following Schleiermacher's Spinozist (through Jacobi and Heydenreich) inheritance as mediated by Eberhard, among others. This line of thought was more fruitful than that of the Kantian trajectory for interpreting Schleiermacher's remarkable views on concept and judgment formation. Moreover, from this perspective new light was cast on Schleiermacher's self-professed (but never thoroughly investigated) connection to Schelling. It brings together the idea of a maximum/minimum, as well as that of the upper and lower limits of the real and ideal series. According to Schelling, these ideas were far more influenced by Leibniz than Kant. In his review April 1804 review of Schelling, Schleiermacher viewed them as radiating from Schelling's famous "point of indifference."[5]

Schleiermacher shared Schelling's opinion that Leibniz's philosophy was, in its essential points, the same as Spinoza's. This opinion was first formulated by Heydenreich in his *God and Nature According to Spinoza* (1789). There Heydenreich compared Leibniz's criterion of identity for monads (the identity of indiscernables) with Spinoza's proof in the fifth proposition in the first part of the *Ethics*. He concluded that once this criterion of identity is posited, there can be only one substance.[6] Properties of monads reflecting those of the central monad are, as such, represented identically in all. The "fulgarations," as Leibniz noted, are the informational seeds of *one* substance. All substances are exhaustively characterized through the same determinations, and hence, are all one, according to Leibniz's principle of the identity of indiscernables. In this way, the identity of distinct realms (the real and the ideal; in Schleiermacher, being and thought) became a predominant theme in philosophy.

Kant had correctly assessed the danger of a re-Leibnizianization of his philosophy. The real danger was not the further development of his idea of the suitability of the "I" and its consciousness of its own unity as a principle of deduction for validity claims. It was, rather, the metaphysical monism stemming from Leibniz, powerfully bubbling up in Schelling. According to the Leibnizian view, the monads misinterpret those activities that they cannot immediately attribute to themselves as mediated by sensation, and as such, interpret them as confused perceptions of the causal activity of objects. Schleiermacher follows Leibniz (as does Schelling) in assuming that "*agere* and *pati* differ only by degrees," so that "the antithesis between I and not-I is overcome."[7] Schleiermacher notes that "in the expression 'passibility' we posit the ground of a subject's change outside of itself"(*Dial* O, 365). Eberhard considered such a case as a "deception" due to a limiting condition: "when the soul is hindered in its activities, it hinders *itself*."[8] Schelling stands completely in this tradition when he refers to Leibniz's position in the following way: "Matter is nothing in itself; it is only the appearance of the imperfect representations of the monads."[9]

I will limit myself to discussing two other ideas Schleiermacher borrowed from Leibniz by way of Schelling (and possibly under Eberhard's influence). Schelling did not take his concept of absolute spirit by further developing Kant's idea of the "I". Rather, Schelling took over Kant's understanding of the organism as a self-regulating principle. Schelling reformulated the idea of "being simultaneously cause and effect of oneself" into the idea that the absolute is *by means of itself* simultaneously both that which affirms and that which is affirmed.[10] Moreover, this "doubled" self-relation is the real essence of spirit. In this way, the Kantian restriction of the "as if" is boldly eliminated.[11]

Schelling's idea has two immediate consequences, both formative for Schleiermacher. First, if the absolute "by means of itself" is simultaneously that which does the affirming and that which is affirmed, then the subject and object of the infinite self-affirmation are also, each in themselves, the entire and single absolute. Their differences from each other can only be understood as the predominance or retreat of one moment in relation to the other. Schelling frequently speaks of changing "exponents" under which the identity relation is at any one time posited. These are the affirming and the affirmed, and each is in itself an infinite unity. I call this idea the "preponderant synthesis." The second consequence is implied by the first. The operation of the preponderant synthesis rests on an identity theory of judgment. In light of this Schelling spoke, not of a "simple" identity, but rather of a "doubled" one, an "identity of identity," or a "redoubled life" of all particular essences in themselves and in the absolute.[12] Since Schelling, like Schleiermacher, takes the copula of a proposition to be a sign of identity, he explains the structure of a simple subject–predicate judgment in the following way: properly understood, a proposition about the identity of the affirming with the affirmed has to do with the conjunction of two judgments. The first is "X is A" and the second is "X is B."[13] The ideal and the real are identified not *as* A or *as* B, that is, not as predicates, but rather insofar as they both have been brought into being (gewesen werden) through X. They are thereby held in being transitively, or in other words, they instantiate or express the same subject,[14] a subject that Schleiermacher also claims may be called absolute. In the strong sense of identity, X (the subject of both partial judgments) is only identical with itself, since the predicates may differ among themselves.[15] Hence, the absolute's power to bind together is only, so to speak, delegated to the copula. In the first sketches of his "Absolute system of identity,"[16] Schelling already distinguishes between the so-called "essence" (or "*An-sich*") and the "form" of the absolute. By "form" he meant the form of the proposition in which the one brings itself (as subject) to understanding through a predicate.[17]

Schleiermacher takes over the ideas of the preponderant synthesis and the identity theory of judgment in the following ways. First, he speaks of a predominance or retreat of the organic vis-à-vis the intellectual, or willing vis-à-vis thinking (F 2001 I, § 239.2, 300). He notes that there is a fundamental "identity of both functions" (*Dial* O, 360), and posits "a knowledge that takes the predominant form of a concept ... and a knowledge that takes the predominant form of a judgment" (F 2001 I, § 197, 254–5). This idea he takes directly from Eberhard and indirectly from Schelling. Eberhard also had as his starting point the "identity of reason and sensation."[18] This assumption is common to the entire Leibnizian school. One begins with the simple "foundational power" (*Grundkraft*) of the soul "of which the powers of knowledge and sensation (*Empfindung*) are merely modifications."[19] Otherwise we cannot explain how the manifold "transitions" between actions or states of the soul's life are events of one and the same being.

This doctrine lies at the basis of Schleiermacher's famous theory of "transition." The assumption of a continuous transition between sense (*Sinn*) and understanding (*Verstand*) makes sense in light of the "numerical identity" of the foundational power. This assumption of unity implies that a minimum of sensibility dwells in the understanding and vice versa. Either "unity" can be brought about only by the "predominance" of one function over the other (*Dial* O, 142–4, 157). Eberhard's insight about sensation and thinking as "restrictions" of one "primal power" (*Urkraft*) clearly prefigures Schleiermacher's own view that "the naming of thought and sensation is determined solely by which characteristics have the upper hand in each state."[20] Hence the difference between sense and understanding is reduced to the predominance of, or retreat by, one function over against the other. Schleiermacher notes, "we can only think of the antithesis between receptivity and spontaneity as a relative, not as an absolute antithesis. A minimum of power must also be posited in receptivity" (*Dial* O, 255ff.).

The assumption of innate ideas is incompatible with the denial of a complete antithesis between spontaneity and receptivity. This assumption directly excludes organic functions from playing a role in concept production. Hence, for Schleiermacher, "innate" means "preceding thinking," and by it "nothing other is meant than that in all items there is the same orientation to the same system of concepts" (*Dial* O, 151). This capacity, however, cannot be explained by organic functions and is difficult to reconcile with the claim that there are "differing degrees of the intellectual and the sensible," with no pure form of either (F 2001 I, 1818 lecture to § 195.2, 253, n. 93). Schleiermacher notes that "the concepts whose formation is predetermined by reason develop in everyone when they are occasioned by the organic function." This sounds as if only the *disposition* for concept formation (which includes individual concepts) is innate in all persons (§ 176.4). However, Schleiermacher continues, its "content" is given through reason alone (*Dial* O, 233) "insofar as we deny the development of the concept from the organic affections" (F 2001 I, § 175; lectures of 1818 to notes to § 186.4 = *Dial* J, 119). As such, the organic function disturbs the pure rational unfolding of the communication developing among interconnected intelligences. "Additionally, differences in concept formation producing the subjective must first be sought in the organic function" (marginal notes to § 177, *Dial* J, 107). Schleiermacher's point is inconsistent with the thesis of a continuous transition between both functions and their varying degrees. It seems to imply that the "individual factor," that is, the "individual coefficient," can never be eliminated entirely (F 2001 II, C 249; cf. F 2001 I, § 191, 249–50 and § 256.2, 312–13). While agreement in conversation is the goal, its achievement can never be guaranteed.

The idea that the preponderant synthesis includes a conception of judgment as a form of identity is also taken from Schelling and indirectly from Leibniz. Recall that Schelling claims that sense and understanding (in relation to their objects, nature, and spirit) are essentially one, and only distinguish themselves according to the predominance or retreat of one side vis-à-vis the other. If the proposition is considered the original "form" of this identity, then subject and predicate cannot be distinguished specifically, but only in relation to their logical function. The result is a monistic ontology in accordance with which those entities for which the subject term stands can be coordinated with no other specific entities than those for which the predicate term stands. Moreover, the copula stands precisely for the essential identity between two realms of reality. This means that Schleiermacher does not think that singular expressions stand for natural objects and that predicate expressions stand for properties progressively characterizing them. Rather, he thinks that both are concepts. Moreover, concepts are essentially nothing but bundles of properties whose elements are called "predicates." They are related as "higher" to "lower concepts." By "higher," Schleiermacher means concepts whose extension is greater, so that concepts with lesser extension "fall under them." A concept is analyzed when the predicates contained in it are enumerated; this results in an intensional characterization of the concept (*Dial* O, 195).

This means, further, that Schleiermacher must refer the differences between objects, for which concepts stand, back to the difference between combinations of predicates in a concept. Objects cannot be distinguished from one another simply in virtue of their place in the spatial and temporal continuum. Such a proposal was put forward by Kant against Leibniz.[21] Together with Leibniz and Eberhard, Schleiermacher believes that there are individual concepts: "The individual is the lowest level of the concept" (*Dial* O, 225).

THE IDENTITY THEORY OF JUDGMENT AND ITS IMPLICATIONS

This view is thoroughly un-Kantian. Kant understood concepts as classificatory terms or sets *under* which objects are subsumed. Even a concept with the smallest extension subsumes objects under itself. Hence the language of individual concepts is misleading. For Kant, the fixing of an object occurs intuitively through pointing, and not through the work of the concept. The standpoint of Leibniz and his students, from which Kant critically set himself apart, is, on the contrary, intensional. The Wolffian school held subject concepts to be bundles of predicates that could be analyzed through predication, and as such, could be partially identified. Predicates do not fall *under*, but are contained *in*, a concept. They are elements in the concept and do not instantiate it. This type of relation is that of inherence. As such, Schleiermacher's talk of a successive enrichment of the subject concept through the process of judgment needs to be corrected in the following way: partners vying for the validity of their truth claims are mistaken if they consider the growth of their knowledge to be synthetic.

The description of these relations between concepts affects a key element of Schleiermacher's convictions. Along with Leibniz and Schelling, he assumes a "ground of the terms of a proposition."[22] Indicated by the copula, the ground connecting the terms is their identity. As such, the predicate inheres in the subject[23] and stands intensionally for a part in a bundle of predicates that Schleiermacher calls the "complete concept" (in opposition to individual judgment). The relation of *inesse* implies ontological homogeneity between the two Kantian sources of knowledge, in accordance with the law of the preponderant synthesis (*Dial* J, 56, 1818 lectures). Predicates are incomplete parts of concepts. A is contained in B or is implied by B when it is impossible that an object falls under A but not under B. Furthermore, the concept A is contained in B if all simple constitutive parts of A are also constitutive parts of B. The concept "animal" is contained in the concept "human." It follows from this that true judgments are analytic statements. This is true not only for tautologies, but also for so-called synthetic statements (such as "A = B"). These can be converted into analytic judgments through a further specification of what is actually contained in the subject concept (such as "AB = B"). Schleiermacher was praised by Lotze and Sigwart for his belief that there are actually no synthetic statements (§ 308; *Dial* J, 563.5).

In light of the "great principle of identity," Leibniz, Schelling, and Schleiermacher similarly blur the border between metaphysics and logic (in relation to ontology and epistemology). While the principle of distinction names the individuating conditions for *objects*, and is thereby ontological, the second identity condition holds between propositions, and is therefore logical. In regard to the second, Leibniz argued that two expressions are identical when one can be substituted for the other in statements without loss in their truth value (*salva veritate*). The first, known as the "principle of the identity of indiscernables," is ontological and has to do with inner-worldly substances. In regard to it Leibniz argued that "it is not true that two substances can resemble each other completely, meaning according to all their intrinsic determinations, yet differ only according to number [*solo numero*]."[24] These two applications of the principle of identity – the logical and the ontological – need to be carefully sorted out. It is doubtful that they have to do with one and the same law.

Schleiermacher, however, was aware of this. The correspondence theory of truth to which he was committed obliged him to refer concepts and predicates to entities existing in a mind-independent reality. Classes of objects are specified by concepts that correspond to them. "Being" corresponds to the highest extension, "chaos" to the smallest. This is similarly the case with upper and lower limits of judgments (or predications). At the upper limit is what Schleiermacher misleadingly calls the "absolute subject," that is, the subject term that has completely saturated its predicates (F 2001 I, § 200, 258). At the lower limit is the chaotic mass of predicates that have not yet been assigned to a subject (§ 203, 260–1). Since Schleiermacher conceives of the dialectical process as a path from emptiness to fullness, the maximal extensional indetermination ("being") must be maximally intensionally filled up at the process' end. At this point, "being" coincides with the "absolute subject." This makes sense given the Leibnizian presupposition that (logical) subjects are bundles of concepts (predicates) (F 2001 II, 413, 1822 lectures to § 310).

THE FOUR FORMULAS FOR THE TRANSCENDENT GROUND

The four formulas for the transcendent ground result from the positing of that which in reality (ontically) corresponds to both upper and lower limits of concept and judgment. God or the highest power corresponds to the highest level of the concept; material chaos, or the lowest appearance corresponds to the lowest limit of the concept.[25] The latter is called the lowest appearance since it cannot be considered as the power of a yet lower appearance. Just as each concept stands in relation to a higher (*genus proximum*) or lower (*differentia specifica*) one, so, too, is the system of powers and appearances similarly ordered (§ 181–2). Each power can be understood as the appearance of a yet higher one, and each appearance as the power of a yet lower one. Schleiermacher assigns the highest limit of a judgment – the absolute subject – to providence (or absolute necessity). The lower limit of the judgment (as the mere unconscious totality of all causal relations) he assigns to fate (§ 200, § 202; cf. *Dial* O, 261ff.). All four formulas represent the transcendent ground, although they do so inadequately.

The question arises as to why the identification of God with a (Leibnizian) highest power is not "transcendent enough" to represent the highest unity adequately. Already in § 149, Schleiermacher stressed that insofar as the antithesis between thought and object is overcome in it, the idea of the absolute unity of being is no longer a concept. This unity is specified first as the unity between the ideal and the real, then as the highest power. In § 136, the ideal and the real are understood as modes of the "idea of being" (cf. § 153). As such, it approximates Spinoza's substance, at least given Schelling's reading, according to which Leibniz and Spinoza agree on the most important points.[26] Both Leibniz and Spinoza assumed that the set of all predicates ascribable to the same subject without contradiction (the maximum of compossibles)[27] are one set and as such are to be ascribed to one and only one absolute subject. If there were two subjects to which the set of predicates were ascribed, then they could not be distinguished through any predicate. According to the principle of the identity of indiscernables, they would be identical. In his fragment on Leibniz (No. 44 from 1797–8), Schleiermacher makes the same point. "Everything is only one, and every individual is nevertheless a whole."[28] Hence, herein lies the tension between two candidates for the post of the highest unity.

This is a difficult point in Schleiermacher's lectures. Ludwig Jonas is of help here, providing helpful citations and commentary. Jonas first stresses the inconsistency in Schleiermacher's notes. Schleiermacher's criticism of a pantheistic formula for the highest Being (the unconditioned, primal ground, or absolute) is generally that the absolute cannot be thought of "as one in the same series as all entities contained under it" (*Dial* J, 115). A similar formulation is "The Godhead cannot be in the same series, and therefore is never something known" (marginal notes to § 186, 1818 lectures, 121). Against Schelling he notes that his absolute remains "wholly posited under the form of the highest concept, and therefore does not correspond to that which transcends it." It thereby still remains in "the realm of powers as appearances" (§ 183.3). A variant of this formulation stresses the dissimilarity between the absolute and that which is comprehended under (or in) it (§ 186, marginal notes to § 188.1). On the other hand, genus and species are on a level where transitions can be made to the genus/species above or the genus/species below, according to the laws of specification or generalization (*Dial* O, 242). In such a way "our knowledge of God would be homogeneous with our knowledge of physics and ethics, and such a construction ... cannot be the highest" (§ 188).

Schleiermacher attempts a third formulation to distinguish the transcendent ground from the pantheist natural–philosophical concept of the highest substance. The unity of this pantheistic idea remains "in an antithesis" or is "marked by traces of duality." It "is conditioned by something else," which for Schleiermacher means that it is included in the antithesis unfolded from it, and which falls under it (*Dial* O, 241^2, 243^3, C 244, $245^{2/3}$, 247^1, 247, 248^1; these formulations are missing in the notes to 1814–15 and the 1818 lectures).

In view of this third attempt, Jonas remarks that Schleiermacher, in §§ 128–37, had indeed "found the antithesis between ideal and real as the highest, and the idea of being as the unity comprehending and unfolding the antithesis" (*Dial* J, 115). What is still missing from this idea in order that it may adequately represent the unconditioned? It cannot be that it does not lie beyond the reach of our concepts. This is true of the limits of concepts and judgment as well. Jonas notes that for Schleiermacher the "limit of the concept was one that fell into the antithesis .... The unity of being *is no longer a concept because there is nothing above it*" (§ 200). The "highest subject" occurs along with the "highest living power, which cannot be subsumed under anything higher," and itself does not appear. Jonas writes that Schleiermacher does not have simply this highest concept limit (not subsumable by anything higher) in mind. Although this limit is the identity of the real and ideal, nevertheless, it

> lies in the same series with everything else. Furthermore, that unity, which absolutely lies above the concept, even the highest concept, is the one that cannot be approached no matter how far one climbs up [the system of concepts]. This unity is also not identical with the totality of knowledge and being, but is their absolute foundation. It is truly the unconditioned which conditions all else, while the absolute

subject (the highest power, the highest genus) conditions all else in such a way that it itself remains conditioned by everything else.

(*Dial* J, 115)

Schleiermacher also rejects other formulas for God or the origin of the world for similar reasons, most clearly in the 1818 lectures to § 186 (*Dial* J, 118–19). As the lowest limit of the concept, matter cannot explain consciousness. (While this may be true, Schleiermacher only makes the claim dogmatically.) In combination with a God giving it form, we do not escape from a duality. If we posit God as its creator, matter becomes a nothing, a *nihil privativum*, and hence nothing having independent being (cf. 246, *C* 244). Schleiermacher has generally little to say of the idea of the creation from nothing; it "has no speculative worth," and leads to atheism (298, 300). A reason for this is that the idea of the activity of creation can remove the idea of time in words but not in reality. This is the old paradox of the temporal creation of time (268).

THE DOCTRINE OF THE TRANSCENDENT GROUND

No author has stressed the objectlessness and the non-reflexive character of the immediate self-consciousness as much as Schleiermacher. He is unique in relating immediate self-consciousness to the insight that self-consciousness does not arise in virtue of its own being, but is absolutely dependent on Being. For Schleiermacher, feeling is the original mode of dependent self-consciousness. His theory of feeling and faith crowns a tradition and gives it a clear focus.

In the years 1793–4, Schleiermacher excerpted and commented upon Jacobi's *Spinozabüchlein*. His most important notes on Spinoza and Leibniz stem from this study (*Spinozismus* and *Kurze Darstellung des Spinozisteschen Systems*).[29] These notes can be used to interpret his later and richly developed thoughts on Being as transcending reflection, as well as the indirect grasp of "Being" in feeling. In the *Dialectic* (particularly that of 1822) and in the Introduction to the *Christian Faith* (1821 and 1830), Schleiermacher assumes that the unity of self-consciousness cannot be explained by its reflexive character (the subject–object relation in which each bit of consciousness consists). It must consequently be understood as the representation of a higher and seamless unity, which Schleiermacher, along with Jacobi, called "Being." Insofar as it is beyond reflexivity, the one Being *ipso facto* transcends consciousness. Like most of his contemporaries, for example, Fichte, Schleiermacher understood consciousness to be a solely objective or intensional kind of representing; "consciousness" does not stand for pre-reflexive interiority. Being is grasped solely through feeling. In *Spinozismus*, Schleiermacher notes:

> The actual, true and real in the soul is the feeling of Being, the immediate concept, as Spinoza calls it. This, however, cannot be perceived. Only individual concepts and expressions of the will can be perceived, and apart from these, there exists nothing else in the soul at any moment of time. Can one for this reason say that individual concepts have their distinct, individual being? Nothing actually exists except the feeling of Being: the immediate concept. Individual concepts are only its revelations. Can one say that the immediate concept exists only as thinking in another? By no means. The immediate concept is the actual, essential ground of the soul. All those individual concepts inhere in its modes (understanding and will). Nevertheless, one must not go on from this to say that the immediate concept is the sum of the individual concepts.[30]

Schleiermacher understands the feeling of Being as the "ground of the soul." This expression comes from Baumgarten,[31] but Schleiermacher changes its function. In the second speech of *On Religion*, he speaks of a "ground-feeling (*Grundgefühl*) of infinite and living nature."[32] As in his later writings, "immediate self-consciousness" has two dimensions: an inner-temporal psychic phenomenon and a supra-temporal (the manifestation of the transcendent unity). In the early writings, feeling already has the character of a unity that exists before, or better, founds the synthetic "grasping-together" of individuals. It is furthermore not "thinking in another." This means it is not grounded in a conscious turning to a second object, in the manner of a reflection. Rather, it rests in itself. The remaining "concepts" and "modes," such as willing and thinking (as Schleiermacher notes in terms that resemble those of Spinoza) "inhere" in it. If the opposite were true, how the different concepts and modes make the transition from one to the next would be unintelligible. This transition presupposes a qualitative identity between the *terminus a quibus* and the *terminus ad quos*. Like Eberhard, Schleiermacher thought of the river of the soul's life and the arising transitions between types of representation as continuous.[33] Consequently, thinking and sensing are fundamentally one and the same, although each accords with the changing predominance of one determination over the other. As such, Schleiermacher brusquely contradicts Kant's dualism, which drives an unbridgeable wedge between not only sense and thought, but also thinking and willing. Feeling contains an immediate reference to existence; it is the "feeling of Being."

In the years between 1820 and 1822 Schleiermacher fills out this outline with feeling as the site of an experience of transcendent Being. A significant benchmark along the way is the second speech in *On Religion* (1799). In this speech, Schleiermacher distinguishes between "intuition" (*Anschauung*), oriented towards the grasp of external objects, and "feeling" (*Gefühl*). The same distinction between perception and sensation is drawn later in the *Dialectic*. Intuitions represent the world, while sensations are states in the subject.[34] Feelings shape the qualitative or phenomenal character of sense impressions. Schleiermacher can thereby say "that each intuition, in accordance with its nature, is connected to a feeling," while the converse does not hold.[35] Schleiermacher does not always meticulously observe this distinction, and hence he sometimes speaks of intuition, and sometimes of the feeling of either the "infinite" or the "universe." The essential point, however, is that intuitions are immediate and individual representations of the world.[36] In contrast to concepts, which according to Schleiermacher's minimum/maximum continuum have a higher degree of spontaneity, intuitions are maximally "passive."[37] This must be the case if they are to represent the self's absolute (meaning not diminished by any self-activity) dependence on the absolute. Only as a sensuous being is the individual passively affected by objects in the world; only in religious feeling does the subject experience itself as absolutely dependent on the universe. Since realism is the theory that defines reality as the cause of knowledge, Schleiermacher calls his standpoint one of a "higher realism."[38] In both the *Kurze Darstellung* and in the second speech, Schleiermacher brings his understanding of the universe close to Spinoza's substance.[39] And like Spinoza, Schleiermacher describes the object which causes the feeling of absolute dependence as located above the system of descriptive truths ("metaphysics") and the system of action ("morals").[40] This train of thought is reiterated in the second speech. Pious self-feeling is identified as the point at which activity and thinking are brought together. It is the site of transition from one to the other.

The *Dialectic*, too, refers to the distinction between thinking and willing, most clearly in the 1822 lectures. The possibility of transition between the two distinct modes of the understanding and the will lies at the point of the unity of feeling. In the fifth chapter, Schleiermacher specifically determines the transcendent ground as the qualitative identity between knowing and willing. This identity is the final and highest identity, which is "represented" in and from feeling. Preceding it are all types of unities of a lower kind, which mediate the relations within thinking, such as the organic and intellectual functions, concept, and judgment. As the identity of thinking and willing, this new determination of the transcendent ground results from the end-point of Schleiermacher's method, which corrects, step by step, the one-sided formulas that he previously proposed for the transcendent ground. For a more complete determination of spirit, the one-sidedness of thinking must finally be supplemented by willing. The transition from thinking to willing and from willing to thinking belongs to the phenomenal apparatus of our conscious life (F 2001 II, 20, 23, 278ff.).

There must be an instance to which the operation of the transition can be attributed. It must never be zero, as Schleiermacher says (F 2001 II, 286²). The soul's states are constantly changing. The point at which one state changes into another does not appear. In order to justify this phenomenon, a unity must be found which itself does not appear, and which is therefore transcendent. As such, it mediates the transitions from one state to the next. Schleiermacher speaks of a "transcendent ground of both," which "must be the same in both" (F 2001 II, 280). It makes its appearance in the immediate self-consciousness, and is thereby called "feeling" when the aspect of dependence on the transcendent ground, rather than the transitional one, is held in view. Self-consciousness is a mental state like others. Its extension is, like others, temporal. But unlike other mental states, self-consciousness is retained through all phases of the temporal stream. Sometimes it emerges more strongly, sometimes it is more withdrawn, but it "never disappears entirely" (280). The transition has a temporal extension, which is "negated" in the identity of its ground (286). As such, immediate self-consciousness still bears the traces of a rift without which it could not unite the two poles. Moreover, without it there could be no temporal continuity between moments. Schleiermacher writes that the identity between thinking and willing in immediate self-consciousness is only a "relative" one (F 2001 I, 271ff. [215 and 215.1]; cf. 274). The identity is a fleeting transition in time, so that there is always a thought between two acts of the will and an act of the will between two thoughts (F 2001 II, 286, 292). In time and as time, the pure identity obviously cannot show itself. Nevertheless, a continuous transition cannot be explained by the distinctiveness of the phases. The transition manifests an identity which, as such, cannot be represented (268). Consequently, the moment of identity cannot appear by itself in self-consciousness. In every temporal transition, the functions of thinking and willing are "posited together"(292). Sometimes more, sometimes less, the predominance of one is corrected by its retreat and the predominance of the other in what follows. Thus, it can be said of the immediate self-consciousness that the transcendent ground is "represented" in it. The unity, which is actually not accessible to self-consciousness, grounds the temporally extended self-consciousness. The transcendent ground mediates the transition between numerically distinct, but also qualitatively different, states of self-consciousness. In regard to this mediating function, Schleiermacher can say, "We are now outside the realm of the antithesis" (288²). We are not really, but only insofar as the mediation brings the method to completion.

In his understanding of the transcendent ground, Schleiermacher brings together two important ideas. One is the idea that the basal phenomenon of our conscious life is not a knowledge *of* something, but is, rather, feeling. The second is that we are not the source of our own existence. This fact is signalled by our elementary self-feeling, which connotes not activity, but passivity. This idea stands in opposition to the absolutism of the "I" proposed by Fichte, which misunderstands itself as the *omnitudo realitas*, as the "Being" absorbing everything into itself.

While Schleiermacher seems to identify feeling and immediate self-consciousness, the two terms describe the same kind of mental state, but pick out two different aspects of it. In immediate self-consciousness, the state and its content are known pre-reflexively. This is not an intentional act focusing on something represented *as* an object. As such, Schleiermacher notes that the immediate self-consciousness is not a "knowledge about something," it is not "reflective" or an "objective consciousness" (*CF*, §§ 4 and 5). Formulations in the 1822 *Dialectic* are similar. The "subject–object antithesis remains completely excluded and is not applicable." "Immediate self-consciousness does not have knowledge of an "I"; this only arises through the reflective self-consciousness" (F 2001 II, 287ff.). On the other hand, as feeling, the same phenomenon is not bound to the pre-reflexive mediation of the transition between the soul's states. It is not bound to its capacity to have itself (*"Sich-selbst-habens"*), but to its lack of Being (288).

Schleiermacher is unclear as to the meaning of "Being."⁴¹ At one moment he represents "being" as the result of a progressive abstraction, that is, as the extensionally richest and intensionally poorest of all concepts. But he then shifts his understanding of transcendence: the highest concept transcends concepts since it can no longer be thought of as the specification of a higher genus. This is the sense of transcendence that we find in § 4 of the *Christian Faith*. Self-consciousness must be absolutely dependent in regard to its existence, since it is not responsible for its own existence (and this radical dependence includes its freedom, which is just as "thrown" as the capacity to think). On top of this we find yet a third sense of "Being," standing for the ground of unity of subject and object; immediate self-consciousness is the only place where it can make its appearance. (According to Schleiermacher, it is "represented.") Only here do the results of an analysis of self-consciousness coincide with the experience of Being. In self-consciousness we thereby have evidence for the truth of the identity theory that treats the transcendent ground as the One and All.

Schleiermacher's understanding of the transcendence of this ground fluctuates between "transcendent" (in the Kantian sense) and "transcendental" (in the pre-Kantian sense) (F 2001 I, 178). For Schleiermacher the transcendent ground represents the transcendent ground of objects of both outer and inner experience, that is, it is the ground of both subject and object (F 2001 II, C 289). If all "real thinking" fills time, how can the transcendent ground be represented in the immediate self-consciousness if its representation fills time but it does not? Only if feeling, as a mode of real consciousness, is directly oriented not to the transcendent ground, but only to its own incapacity to adequately represent it. In other words, for Schleiermacher, it is not possible to reflect on the absolute ground; it is only possible to reflect on the self's absolute lack of grounding in itself. Consciousness feels itself to be *absolutely* dependent on Being, and this dependence is indirectly represented as the dependence on the Absolute. When immediate self-consciousness (or feeling) flickers from one to the other pole of the reflexive rift, this does not shed light on the positive fullness of a supra-reflexive identity, but rather on its lack. Schleiermacher notes that in the moment of "transition" (286) from object to subject of reflection, self-consciousness always traverses the space of a "missing unity" (C 290, § LI). Since the self cannot attribute this lack to its own activity, it must recognize this lack as the effect of a "determining power transcending it, that is, one that lies outside its own power" (C 290). The self can only ascribe to itself the ground of *knowledge* of this dependence. Schleiermacher can thereby say that the cause of this feeling of dependence is not "effected by the subject, but only arises *in* the subject" (CF, § 3.3). However, in feeling, the activity of the self is "never zero," for "without any feeling of freedom a feeling of absolute dependence would not be possible" (CF, § 4.3).

QUESTIONS REGARDING SCHLEIERMACHER'S THOUGHT

I have shown that Schleiermacher's thesis of Being's transcendence to consciousness is indebted to Leibniz. However, for Leibniz, God's transcendence was merely a contingent matter, stemming from a lack of information of the individual monads. It was not a fundamental feature of his philosophy. Indecisiveness regarding why Being is transcendent to consciousness is one of the principal weaknesses of Schleiermacher's thought. How was it possible that Schleiermacher left this question unanswered? The answer lies in the correspondence theory of truth he adopted, which demands the integration of a realistic theory of being, à la Kant. As the later Schelling had demonstrated, such a realist theory is not consistent with Absolute Idealism. I have already stressed the realistic aspirations of the *Dialectic*. Schleiermacher had shown that conflicting claims of knowledge presuppose a common reference to an *identical* object transcending thought. "All thinkers have *the same object* as the object of their thought" (*Dial* O, 140²). A "maximum of strife" (*Dial* O, 21ff.; cf. §§ 86ff.; *Dial* O, 135ff.) between conflicting claims to knowledge, which occurs when there is disagreement as to which object is being talked about, can only be avoided through the causal intervention of reality. This, however, contradicts the Leibnizian idea of the complete concept determining the individual completely. Here individuals are *species infimae*.

This reconstruction, which interprets Schleiermacher as adopting the Leibnizian idea of individuals as *species infimae*, contradicts Schleiermacher's causal theory of reference. What makes us believe that a representation refers to an outer object is that the object causes the representation. Even the content of feeling is interpreted as a representation or "mirroring" of an entity lying outside of consciousness, that is, the transcendent ground. Such formulations leave the discourse of Leibniz and Wolff behind and decisively hook up with that of Kant. Kant had described causality as a dynamic fundamental principle that brought reality into play. Concepts do not anticipate reality in the way that they do mathematical entities. Rather, reality is given through perception.[42] And in problematic but nevertheless clear formulations, Kant notes that the content of reality depends upon things in themselves.

Unlike the relation to concrete objects, the relation to Being is not mediated by sensation. Hence, Schleiermacher spoke of feeling. The conscious relation to Being is not presented as a causal one only because the dependence of consciousness on Being is absolute (unlike the relative dependence of things on one another) (*CF*, § 4). This relation negates the homogeneity of all moments implied by the idealistic fundamental principles of Bishop Berkeley. Hence, Schleiermacher discovered a fourth dimension of "identity" transcending all our concepts. That it transcends our concepts is fundamental for his philosophy. When the "power of the subject" is broken by it (as Schleiermacher notes in a marginal note to § 4.3 of the *Christian Faith*), this is not because of complicated reasons regarding the fact that the limits of the concept cannot be thought. Rather, a new insight into the meaning of "Being" comes into play, one that cannot be reconciled with the basis of Leibniz's philosophy, or that of Schelling's philosophy of identity. This is the turning point at which a theory of the conditions of knowledge turns into a doctrine of faith.

Notes

1 Citations to the *Dialectic* will be placed in the body of the text. The following abbreviations will be used: F 2001 refers to my edition of the *Dialectic* (see *Dialektik*, ed. M. Frank), which contains the foundational text of 1814–15. "F 2001 I" refers to the first volume; "F 2001 II" to the second, followed by the paragraph and/or page number. All citations making use of §, followed by a number, are to this text. *Dial* O refers to the Odebrecht edition of the *Dialectic*, containing a collection of notes to the lectures from 1822; it is reprinted in the second volume of F 2001. *Dial* J refers to Jonas edition of the *Dialektik*; it is reprinted in the first volume of F 2001. *C* refers to what Jonas believed to be the handwritten notes to the lectures of 1822, which appear under the main text of the Odebrecht edition; it is also reproduced in F 2001 II.

2 For instance, in the second speech in *On Religion* [*OR*], Schleiermacher notes that metaphysics "classifies the universe and divides it into this being and that, seeks out reasons for what exists, and deduces the necessity of what is real while spinning the reality of the world and its laws out of itself." *OR*, Crouter, 98.

3 On this point, see Frank 1997.

4 Such an understanding of strict *a priori* concepts as empirical ones results from this psychologizing tendency, which understands the way the mind processes data as a fact of human nature, and hence as empirical.

5 Schleiermacher, *Schriften*, ed. Arndt, 280ff.

6 Schelling 1856, vol. I.6, 104.

7 *KGA* I.2, 85, no. 36.

8 Eberhard 1776, 68.

9 Schelling 1856, vol. I.6, 106.

10 Schelling 1856, vol. I.6, 161, 164, 173.

11 Schelling 1856, vol. I.6, 386.

12 Schelling 1856, vol. I.4, 134 n.; I.6, 165; cf. 173, 187.

13 Schelling 1946, 26ff.

14 Schelling 1946, vol. I.7, 205 n. 1; cf. II.3, 227^2.

15 Schelling 1946, 27^2.

16 Cf. Schelling 1856, vol, I.4, 113 and II.1, 371.

17 Schelling 1856, vol. I.4, 116ff.; §§ 4 and 5.

18 Cf. F 2001 I, 201 (§ 122) and 421–3; also *Dial* O, 360, regarding the identity of both functions.

19 Eberhard 1776, 17ff., and 31.

20 Eberhard 1776, 58.

21 Kant 1998, A 263 = B 319; A 271ff. = B 327.

22 Leibniz to Arnauld (July 14, 1686). There he notes, "This is my great principle."

23 Mates 1986, 84ff.

24 Leibniz, *Discourse on Metaphysics*, 1686, § 9; cf. *Monadology*, § 9, in Leibniz 1989, 41–2; 214.

25 F 2001 I, 241–2, 243–4, §§ 183, 185.

26 Frank 1986, 103–12.

27 Mates 1986, 44.

28 Fragment No. 44 on Leibniz from 1797–8, *KGA* I.2, 288.

29 *KGA* I.I, 511ff., 559ff., 583ff.

30 *KGA* I.I, 535.

31 "FUNDUS ANIMAE," § 511 of Baumgarten 1757.

32 Schleiermacher, *Shriften*, 102; cf. *OR*, Crouter, 112ff.

33 Eberhard 1776, 17ff.

34 Schleiermacher, *Shriften*, 109ff.; F 2001 I, 249 (§ 190); *Dial* O, 127, 135, 250; cf.
    Eberhard 1776, 45ff.

35 Schleiermacher, *Shriften*, 109.

36 Ibid. 104.

37 Ibid. 103.

38 Ibid. 102.

39 Ibid. 102ff.

40 Ibid. 95.

41 Translator's note: In this translation, if "being" is used in the sense of the "being
    of beings," or "common being," it is rendered with a lower case " b;" if its sense
    corresponds to the idea of "the ground of Being," it is rendered with a capital "B."

42 Kant 1998, A 225 = B 272ff.

2 Faith and religious knowledge

ROBERT MERRIHEW ADAMS

Schleiermacher, famously, regards religious faith and theology as grounded in religious consciousness, and thus as broadly empirical. This is the source of much of the fascination of his religious thought, and also of many of the objections that have been raised against it. The aim of this chapter is to provide a critical analysis of Schleiermacher's epistemology of religion and its theological implications. In the limited space available we will concentrate on his masterpiece, the *Christian Faith*, looking from time to time for relevant background in other works.

RELIGIOUS CONSCIOUSNESS AND ITS OBJECT

Schleiermacher has been accused of replacing God with human consciousness as the object of theology and religious thought. The charge is not exactly groundless. He himself said (in a text from the period of the *Christian Faith*) that "it can rightly be said that in religion everything is immediately true, since nothing at all is expressed in its individual moments except the religious person's own state of mind" (*KGA*, I.12, 136; *OR*, Oman, 108).[1] An important motive for this claim is explicit in the statement: to the extent that religion does not go beyond the religious person's own state of mind, it can hope to have the certain truth commonly ascribed to direct ("immediate") experience of one's own consciousness. The accusation of anthropocentrism or subjectivism thus has some relation to Schleiermacher's focus on experience.

To conclude, however, that religious faith and theology, in Schleiermacher's view, are not about God, but only about human states of mind, is to adopt a badly one-sided reading. There is plenty of evidence in his writings about religion, early and late, that he regarded religious consciousness as having at least an implicit intentionality or reference to a being much greater than ourselves. How he conceives of this reference is one of the difficult things to understand in Schleiermacher; it will be our next concern.

In an important recent criticism, Wayne Proudfoot has written that "Schleiermacher is trying to have it both ways. The religious consciousness [according to him] ... is both intentional ... and immediate," where "a mental state is intentional if it can be specified only by reference to an object," and immediate insofar as "it is not dependent on concepts or beliefs." Proudfoot objects that what is intentional "cannot be independent of [conceptual] thought" because of its object reference.[2]

It is certain that Schleiermacher (at least in his mature writings) held that religious consciousness, in its most essential form, is preconceptual or independent of concepts, in the sense of not being structured by concepts. Both in the *Speeches* and in the *Christian Faith* he distinguishes the fundamental religious consciousness from speculation or thinking on the one hand, and from ethics or doing on the other hand. Religion does not need the grounding in more or less "speculative" metaphysics that so many philosophical theologians have tried to give it, nor the grounding in morality that Kant proposed as its sole proper basis. Religion "has its own province in the mind in which it reigns sovereign" (*KGA*, I.2, 204; *OR*, Crouter, 17). Its province is constituted by a faculty or faculties different from those of conceptual thought and voluntary action. I believe this is consistent with Schleiermacher's treating religious consciousness as having at least an implicit intentionality, but the intentionality of a nonconceptual religious consciousness may be importantly different from that of conceptual thought or language.

The intentionality of religious consciousness is most obvious, and its nonconceptual character perhaps least clear, in the first edition of the *Speeches*, in 1799. There the central religious consciousness is characterized as intuition (*Anschauung*) and feeling, and the senior partner is clearly intuition (a sort of mental seeing, distinct from any systematic theory). "Intuition of the universe ... is the highest and most universal formula of religion" (*KGA*, I.2, 213; *OR*, Crouter, 24). The formula wears its implication of intentionality on its face: intuition *of* the universe. Schleiermacher holds explicitly that "the universe and the relationship of the human being to it" is the object (*Gegenstand*) of religion, as also of metaphysics and morality (*KGA*, I.2, 207; *OR*, Crouter, 19). Not only does religious intuition have an object; it relates to the object as having a certain character. "Thus to accept everything individual as a part of the whole and everything limited as a presentation (*Darstellung*) of the infinite is religion" (*KGA*, I.2, 214; *OR*, Crouter, 25).

In the second edition of the *Speeches*, in 1806, feeling becomes the senior partner; indeed, it displaces intuition entirely, not everywhere, but in many of the key passages of the second Speech, on the essence of religion.[3] This change has been much discussed in the secondary literature. Two things are clear and worth noting here. One is that by 1806 intuition has acquired a more theoretical cast in Schleiermacher's thought, and is associated at least as much with science as with religion.[4] The other is that already in the first edition intuition is seen as looking outward to the object, feeling as turned inward toward the center of the self (*KGA*, 1.2, 220–2; *OR*, Crouter, 31–?). Defining the essence of religion as a matter of feeling rather than intuition is thus in line with the view that the primary religious consciousness is a sort of *self*-consciousness.

Even as feeling, however, religious consciousness still seems to have intentionality in the second edition of the *Speeches*. It is "the one and all of religion to feel everything that moves us in feeling, in its highest unity, as one and the same" (*KGA*, 1.12, 68; *OR*, Oman, 49–50). Here what moves us in feeling is *felt as* having a characteristic that is obviously seen as religiously significant.

In the *Christian Faith* Schleiermacher's formula for the "essence" of religion – or more precisely, of "piety" or personal religiousness[5] – is that it is a "feeling of absolute dependence" (*CF* [1830], § 4.3). It consists in the fact "that we are conscious of ourselves as absolutely dependent, or, equivalently, as in relation with God" (§ 4). These formulations again bear obvious implications of intentionality. The fundamental religious consciousness is a feeling *of* absolute dependence, a consciousness *of* ourselves *as* absolutely dependent. It is consciousness of a characteristic of *ourselves*, to be sure, but it is a *relational* characteristic. We can hardly be absolutely dependent unless there is something, other than ourselves, on which we are absolutely dependent. This something, "the *whence* that is implied [*mitgesetzt*] in this self-consciousness ... is to be designated by the expression 'God'," and Schleiermacher adds that he takes this to be "the truly original meaning" of the word "God," which gets its content, in this context, from reflection on the feeling, and not from any knowledge of God that is prior to the feeling (§ 4.4).

Can we say then that according to the *Christian Faith* the essential religious consciousness, the feeling of absolute dependence, has God as an intended object? Not without qualification. Despite the tight connection of this feeling with consciousness of "something distinct from us" on which we are dependent, "still the self-consciousness does not therefore become consciousness of an object, but it remains self-consciousness" (*CF*, 1821–2, § 9.1). According to the 1822 lectures on *Dialectic*, indeed, there is no contrast of subject and object at all in the feeling that is pure immediate self-consciousness

(*Dial* O, 287). The whence of absolute dependence is not given in the feeling itself of absolute dependence, as part of the conscious content of that feeling. How then do we get the idea of God as such a whence? It is *inferred* from the description or interpretation of the essential religious consciousness *as* a feeling *of* absolute dependence.

It is important at this point that we are concerned with an idea or representation (*Vorstellung*) that is expressed linguistically, by a word ("God"). This is part of the professedly philosophical introductory sections of the *Christian Faith*; but like Christian theology's doctrines or faith-propositions (*Glaubenssätze*), the description here of a feeling as one of absolute dependence is an interpretation (*Auffasssung*) of a religious state of mind, presented in speech (cf. *CF*, 1830, § 15). And philosophy's interpretation, as far as it goes, agrees perfectly with theology's: the feeling is a consciousness of absolute dependence, and hence of relation with God. The inference that a whence of the absolute dependence is implied is based no doubt on a *concept* of absolute dependence, and issues in a representation or concept of God which has God as an intentional object in a way that Proudfoot could accept because it is not "independent of thought."

Can we say then that according to the *Christian Faith* God is not an intentional object of the essential religious consciousness, the feeling of absolute dependence, but only of thoughts that reflect on that feeling? Not without qualification. For Schleiermacher is plainly committed to the *correctness* of his interpretative description of piety as a feeling *of* absolute dependence. He gives us no reason to think that this feeling can be specified or identified except in terms of religious concepts expressing such intentionality, as Proudfoot rightly points out.[6] And Schleiermacher seems equally committed to the correctness of the inference from absolute dependence to a whence that can be called "God." If he is right on these points, then surely it is fair to say that God, as the "whence," is implied or co-posited (*mitgesetzt*) in the feeling of absolute dependence, and in that sense is implicitly an intentional object of the feeling.

Does this (as Proudfoot charges) compromise Schleiermacher's classification of the essential religious consciousness as nonconceptual, as in itself "neither a knowing nor a doing but a determination of feeling or of immediate self-consciousness" (*CF*, 1830, § 3)? That deserves, I think, to remain a controversial issue. The question is whether there can be, and indeed are, states of consciousness that are not conceptually structured but are best understood by us by analogy with the intentionality of conceptual thought. More than one influential philosophical movement is committed to a negative answer to this question, but it is not obvious that the negative answer is correct. What Schleiermacher seems to be affirming is a sort of self-consciousness, a feeling of how it is with us, that is not conceptually structured but which we can express by assimilating it to conceptually structured claims about how it is with us; and some may find that quite plausible.

This is connected with issues about "the given." Feeling, for Schleiermacher, is a given in the sense that it is a conscious state that is what it is independently of any conceptual interpretation that we give to it. However, this view does not carry with it two implications that many find objectionable. (1) Feeling, I believe, should be understood here as nonconceptual only in the sense that it is not *structured* by concepts. This does not imply that feeling is *causally independent* of conceptual thought. In fact it is evidently Schleiermacher's view that the feeling of absolute dependence will exist in a pure, clear, strong form only in contexts in which it is supported by appropriate conceptual thought. This appears, for instance, in the relation of the feeling of absolute dependence to the sequential development in each individual of self-consciousness, from infantile to mature, in *CF*, 1830, § 5.1–3. (2) Most important is the other point: the givenness of feeling does not guarantee the truth of anything we say about the feeling. A verbal characterization of a feeling is a conceptual interpretation of a nonconceptual state of consciousness, and as such it can be mistaken, or at any rate off target. Thus dogmatic propositions can have more or less "ecclesiastical value," depending on their "relation [of more or less adequate correspondence, I take it] to the religious emotions themselves" (§ 17.1).

Indeed, even granting that we have states of nonconceptual self-consciousness that are best understood by analogy with the intentionality of conceptual thoughts, we may still wonder whether Schleiermacher has rightly interpreted any such state in speaking of a feeling of absolute dependence. There are possible theoretical as well as introspective reasons for misgivings on this score. Schleiermacher holds that such a feeling is "an essential element of human nature" (*CF*, 1830, § 6.1), and hence presumably present, permanently, in typical human adults. Introspectively, then, you should be able to find it in yourself; look for a feeling of not having made yourself to be as you are [of *Sichselbstnichtsogesetzthaben*] with respect to your whole condition and particularly with respect to your consciousness of your own spontaneity, freedom, and action on other things (§ 4.1 and 3). My own experience, and that of my students, suggests that it is not easy to be sure, introspectively, whether we have it.

At the level of theory, some may be troubled by the *Christian Faith*'s clear implication that causal relations to other things (not only to God but also to the rest of the created universe [*CF*, 1830, § 4.1–2, § 8.2]) are part of the implicit content of forms of immediate self-consciousness. This is perhaps the most obvious point at which Schleiermacher's view of experience differs from views that have prevailed in anglophone empiricism, which have typically followed Hume (and Malebranche) in denying that any causal relationship can be part of the content of immediate experience. In German thought, on the other hand, the assumption that such implicitly causal facts about the self can be part of the content of self-consciousness was not unprecedented. Kant, for instance, states that the "I think," which we must always be able to have as part of our consciousness, "expresses the act of determining my existence."[7] The issue probably deserves to remain controversial.

One might wonder whether Schleiermacher himself is consistent on this point; for the first edition of the *Christian Faith* contains a note in which we may be tempted to see him as expressing a more Humean point of view. Commenting on the dependence of human ills (*Übel*) on sin, he says that "strictly speaking, no causal relation in itself can be perceived and grounded, without any presupposition, purely through experience" (*CF*, 1821–2, § 99). Although this note, like a number of others, is dropped from the second edition, I think it is probably consistent with the claim of a feeling of absolute dependence. What Schleiermacher is denying in the context of the note is the possibility of immediate experience of a causal relation between two types of experienced particulars. What he affirms in his account of God-consciousness is the possibility of immediate consciousness of oneself as active or affected, and thus of one's own pole of what is implicitly a causal relation, but not of the other, divine pole, which must be inferred and is only an implicit object of the feeling.

FAITH IN GOD

Glaube (faith or belief) is much less prominent than self-consciousness and feeling as a topic of Schleiermacher's writings on religion; but he does develop a concept of faith, and it is particularly important in the *Christian Faith* (as the title would lead us to expect). In the first edition of the *Christian Faith* he defines faith as "nothing but the assenting certainty that accompanies the pious emotions" (*CF*, 1821–2, § 6). "Faith in God," likewise, in the second edition, is "nothing but certainty about the feeling of absolute dependence as such – that is, as conditioned by a being posited outside us, and as expressing our relationship to that being" (*CF*, 1830, § 14.1).

In these formulations faith is tightly linked to feeling. A theological proposition floating free of religious feeling cannot be the object of an authentic faith, in Schleiermacher's view. This is not to say that faith is itself a part or aspect of religious feeling. He describes it rather as something that *accompanies* the pious emotions. Is faith conceptually structured, or not? A note in Schleiermacher's hand on § 14.1 of the 1830 edition of the *Christian Faith* suggests that he did think of it as conceptually structured. Adopting formulations of his former student August Twesten, he identifies faith with "the determination of our representing and knowing which the religious feeling immediately brings with it. (In general, faith [is] a holding as true that rests on feeling.)"[8] I think "representing and knowing" here are most plausibly understood as conceptual (cf. *CF*, 1830, § 4.4).

Is the object of faith in God, then, a conceptually articulated doctrine about God? I think that is not Schleiermacher's view; rather, as he says, faith in God is *about* the feeling of absolute dependence. This does not mean that what faith is certain of is its *interpretation* of the feeling. What faith in God holds as true is principally the feeling itself. Can feelings, then, be true? Schleiermacher plainly implies that they can, and that his faith is committed to the truth of the feeling of absolute dependence (*CF*, 1830, § 40.3).

This is not to say that Schleiermacher thought that faith in God is independent of conceptually formed assent to propositions about God. He explicitly held that "the feeling of absolute dependence could not have any truth" if certain propositions about God and the creation were true (*CF*, 1830, § 40.3), and likewise that Christian piety is incompatible with some forms of speculation or philosophy, apparently including "genuinely atheistic systems of philosophy" as well as some versions of pantheism (*CF*, 1830, § 8 postscript 2 and § 28.3; *BO*, § 214). Perhaps his best formulation of the theoretical commitments of faith in God is suggested by his statement that a Christian theologian is free "to attach himself to any form of speculation so long as it allows an object to which the feeling of absolute dependence can relate itself" (*CF*, 1830, § 50.2). That there is such an object is what must be believed about God in faith in God.

It is significant that in this formulation the divine object is specified in terms of its relation to the feeling of absolute dependence. In these statements the topic is what propositions are *compatible* with Christian piety, and each of the statements occurs in a context in which Schleiermacher emphasizes the diversity of theoretical positions that are compatible with piety. The truth-commitment of his faith in God seems to be roughly of the form: "I am certain of the truth of the feeling of absolute dependence, and if it is true, then there must be an object of which *something like this* is true."

The "assenting certainty" that he defines as faith is a certainty about the truth of religious feeling, and not about the truth of any conceptualized doctrinal formulation. It is only the religious feeling that is related directly or immediately to God; the conceptual articulation is related to God only indirectly, by its relation to the feeling. Schleiermacher seems to see this as significantly softening any theoretical commitment involved in assenting to a doctrinal proposition, when he says about "theological concepts" (according to notes from his 1818 lectures on *Dialectic*) that "if one says ... they are to be nothing but presentations of the way in which the consciousness of God is in our self-consciousness, then one can consent to them, because then they do not purport to be immediate presentations but only indirect ones" (*Dial* J, 159).

Two ideas that further loosen the connection between the truth of religious feeling and the truth of doctrines based on it play an important part in Schleiermacher's thought. They are expressed with particular vividness in the second and third editions of the *Speeches*. (1) He held that a religious consciousness essentially the same may be expressed in quite different propositions, which may even be theoretically inconsistent with each other. "Thousands could be moved religiously in the same way, and very likely each would make different signs to characterize his feeling, led not by his sensitivity [*Gemüth*] but by external relationships." Even of the difference between personal and impersonal ideas of deity it is claimed that which of them a person with a given "sense for the deity ... will adopt depends merely on what he needs it for, and to which side his imagination principally inclines, to that of being and nature or to that of consciousness and thinking" (*KGA*, I.12, 72, 124; *OR*, Oman, 52f., 97f.).[9]

(2) For philosophers of religion one of the most interesting ideas in Schleiermacher's work is that of a superiority of religious feeling or religious consciousness in comparison with religious concepts and doctrines in regard to the truth or adequacy of their relation to the religious object. A person's "piety, the divine in his feeling, must be better than his concept." Both personal and impersonal conceptions of God "are faulty, and as neither of them corresponds to its object," neither of them has religious value, "except insofar as it rests on something in the mind, of which it has fallen far short." The value of each depends on the fact that it "presents at least one element of the feeling" (*KGA*, I.12, 121; *OR*, Oman, 95). (The lines about concepts of God failing to correspond with their object and falling far short of religious feeling were added in the 1821 edition of the *Speeches*, and thus in the period of the *Christian Faith*.) If the suggestion is intended that religious feeling does "correspond to [the divine] object," has "truth" as

correspondence in that way, and that is why it is superior, it is not explicit here; and I have not found these ideas explicitly presented in the *Christian Faith* itself.

In Schleiermacher's *Dialectic* the comparative adequacy of thinking and feeling in relation to the divine object is handled explicitly, and more even-handedly than in the *Speeches*. In the 1814–15 lectures "perfection and imperfection are equally apportioned to both [thought and feeling], only on different sides." Compared with respect to completeness, "The religious feeling ... is something really complete," whereas "the intuition of God [here placed in the theoretical faculty] is never really complete," because it is "only an indirect schematism," a sketch that thought is unable to finish. With respect to purity, on the other hand, the thought or intuition of God "is entirely free [*rein*] of everything heterogeneous," whereas the religious feeling "is never pure [*rein*], for the consciousness of God in it is always in relation to something else." The sides of the comparison are intimately related. As a parallel passage from the lectures of 1818 indicates, the purity of the thought is a matter of seeking as its intended object the divine "in and for itself," whereas religious feeling is consciousness of God only insofar as it is consciousness of something else (the self and the world) as absolutely dependent (*Dial* J, 152f.). And the reason why feeling is more complete than speculative thought here is presumably not that feeling can complete what speculation cannot, but rather that knowing the divine as it is in itself is a task that we cannot complete at all, whereas our absolute dependence is completely present in religious self-consciousness.[10]

Reticence about the divine as it is in itself is one of the most marked and most persistent features of Schleiermacher's religious thought. Far from claiming more access than thought can have to a divine thing in itself, religious feeling and a theology properly based on it do not address the subject of the inherent nature of such a thing even to the incomplete extent that philosophical speculation may address it. From the first edition of the *Speeches* in 1799 to the definitive edition of the *Christian Faith* in 1830, he insists that religious consciousness is consciousness of something other than ourselves only insofar as it is consciousness of our being causally affected by something. Saying in the second edition of the *Speeches*, that what you "feel and perceive in [religion's] stirrings is not the nature of things, but their action on you" (*KGA*, I.12, 67; *OR*, Oman, 48), he restates in terms of feeling a claim already made in terms of intuition in the first edition (*KGA*, I.2, 213f.; *OR*, Crouter, 24f.).

In the *Christian Faith* this point carries over into the thesis that "all the divine attributes to be dealt with in Christian faith-doctrine [*Glaubenslehre*] must go back in some way to the divine causality, since they are only to elucidate the feeling of absolute dependence" (*CF*, 1830, § 50.3). Although what Schleiermacher says about the attributes of God – for instance, that God is omniscient and that God is love (§§ 55, 167) – may sometimes seem to ascribe some intrinsic character to God, nevertheless it is all to be understood, strictly speaking, as being about the divine causality, as that causality is felt from our side in the feeling of absolute dependence. We may see a skeptical strand in Schleiermacher's thought about God at this point, but it remains a pious skepticism, and may also be seen as a way of honoring the otherness of God.

In this it is connected with a long tradition of theologians (such as Maimonides and Aquinas) who have been reluctant to claim positive knowledge of the divine nature as it is in itself. Schleiermacher places his own view explicitly in that context, commenting that it is "praiseworthy that Albertus Magnus, and several after him, have chosen to derive all divine attributes from the concept of the eternal causality" (*CF*, 1821–2, § 64.3). Referring to three ways that have been accepted for arriving at divine attributes, the ways of eminence (or removal of limits), of negation, and of causality, Schleiermacher insists on the preeminence of the way of causality (*CF*, 1830, § 50.3). Indeed, it is hard to think of a theologian who has adhered more rigorously or more exclusively than he to the way of causality.

The most obvious reason for this adherence is explicitly stated by Schleiermacher himself: "the concept of causality stands in the closest connection with the feeling of absolute dependence itself" (*CF*, 1830, § 50.3). The formative influence of the (causal) idea of absolute dependence on his doctrine of God is rather similar, I think, to that of the idea of "first cause" on Aquinas' doctrine of God. Some of the divine attributes – eternity, omnipresence, omnipotence, and omniscience – are articulated and affirmed by Schleiermacher simply on the basis of reasoning about what must be true of anything on which we (and the world) are absolutely dependent. Other attributes of God – holiness, justice, love, and wisdom – he derives from specifically Christian consciousness, not just of absolute dependence, but also of sin and of redemption through Christ. These latter, however, still remain for him exclusively attributes of the divine causality as such.

Schleiermacher's commitment to absolute dependence as the content of the essential religious consciousness is momentous for the shape of his theology. A theology might have to be very different from his if its principal foundation were in experience interpreted as communication with a divine Person or as glimpses of a transcendent Good. In connection with the latter possibility, which was historically accessible to Schleiermacher in the interaction of philosophical theology with the Platonic tradition, it is note-worthy that, among his philosophical heroes, he follows Spinoza and not Plato in identifying good with what advances the development of human life, which for Schleiermacher means especially its domination by the religious consciousness (*CF*, 1830, § 70.2–3; cf. §§ 57.1 and 60).[11] He adheres rigorously to the way of causality in ascribing evaluative predicates to God only on the basis of God's causal relation to the developmental goods and evils in human life (see especially §§ 83–4, and 166).

FAITH IN CHRIST

If we stopped with what Schleiermacher says about "faith in God," we would have a very one-sided account of his conception of faith, ignoring the role faith plays in the largest (and, in his own opinion, the most important) part of his theology. He identifies "faith in Christ" with "the certainty that through the influence of Christ the state of needing redemption is taken away and that [of redemption] brought about." Unlike faith in God, which is a certainty, but one that concerns a feeling that expresses a relation to "a being posited outside us," faith in Christ is "a purely factual certainty, but the certainty of a fact that is entirely inward" (*CF*, 1830, § 14.1). The feeling of absolute dependence still plays a part in the self-knowledge that grounds this faith in Christ; for the inward fact about which faith in Christ is certain is a fact about the feeling of absolute dependence. It is not the fact of merely *having* the feeling of absolute dependence. That is not enough to constitute redemption, for it is quite consistent with the feeling of absolute depen-dence being severely hindered by sin – that is, by tendencies in the self that prevent it from developing and from dominating one's mental life as it should. The inward fact of which faith in Christ is certain is rather the fact that in one's own case such sin has been removed and displaced by a dramatically fuller development and dominance of the feeling of absolute dependence.

There is also, of course, the certainty of the less obviously inward fact that this has happened "through the influence of Christ"; but insofar as we focus on the inward fact, it can seem to be a pretty straightforwardly empirical fact. As Schleiermacher emphasizes, the certainty about it is not about anything external, but about the development of one's own feelings and mental life. Moreover, this aspect of his interpretation of religious experience seems less exposed to doubt than his account of the feeling of absolute dependence. The latter may well remain controversial, as noted above; but it is hardly to be doubted that many Christians have experienced a dramatic increase in the power and happiness, or "blessedness," of their religious consciousness in their contact with Christianity, as Schleiermacher claims.

The doctrinal propositions of Schleiermacher's *Christian Faith* do not all have the same epistemological basis. Some purport to express the implicit content of the feeling of absolute dependence. Others propose an empirical description of the history of that feeling and of related states of mind, as we see in the present context. Others offer explanations of aspects of that history. The argument that supports the proposition that "we are conscious of sin, partly as grounded in ourselves, and partly as having its ground outside our own existence" (*CF*, 1830, § 69), for example, seems to be empirically grounded phenomenological and causal reasoning of a sort that could be found in the work of many social theorists. More often, however, even in propositions that are directly or indirectly about the sin and redemption that Christians have experienced in themselves, there is also an element of what we could call theological interpretation, which for Schleiermacher is always an implication of relation to the divine causality; and much of what is most interesting in Schleiermacher's theology depends on this. Here there is room to develop this point only in relation to two areas of doctrine: eschatology and Christology.

Eschatology is of particular interest for the study of Schleiermacher's epistemology. He himself emphasizes that doctrines of the "last things" are on weaker ground epistemologically precisely because the experience now available to us does not include the future (*CF*, 1830, § 157.2; cf. § 159.2). This leads Schleiermacher to hedge round with qualifications his assent to traditional doctrines of the last things, but he does endorse in his theology some propositions of predictive force. A clear example is his repudiation of the doctrine of eternal damnation; if there is to be a life after death, he thinks it, emphatically, more reasonable to conceive of it as one in which everyone will eventually be redeemed (§ 163 appendix). And he thinks his Christianity commits him to a prediction about the future religious history of the world, which surely does not have a straightforwardly empirical basis (though it does not get all the way to the last things): "it is essential to our faith that every nation will sooner or later become Christian" (§ 120 postscript).

What is Schleiermacher's basis for such predictions? He is not as articulate as one might wish about his epistemology at this point. He says in this connection that "in our being conscious of our spiritual life as communicated perfection and blessedness of Christ," there is contained something that "is at the same time faith in the reality of the consummated church, though only as an efficacious motive force within us." He adds that there is not such a good basis for taking "this efficacious principle" to be manifested in time in the ways that eschatology suggests (*CF*, 1830, § 159.2). But he evidently sees such a moving force both as experienced in Christian consciousness and as having an inherent teleology. The teleology of Christian life, which can be experienced also as a challenge or demand (§ 83.1), seems to lie behind such eschatological predictions as he is willing, cautiously, to make.

This teleology is also a feature of the divine causality, and specifically of the divine love, the attribute with which God is most identified for Schleiermacher (*CF*, 1830, § 167). He defines the divine love as "the attribute by virtue of which the divine essence imparts itself," and says it is "known in the work of redemption" (§ 166). It is in effect God's property of causing redemption, or equivalently of causing the perfecting of human religious consciousness. This is a teleologically ordered causality. "When we trace to the divine causality our consciousness of fellowship with God, restored through the efficacy of redemption, we posit the planting and extension of the Christian church as object of the divine government of the world" (§ 164). Significantly, God's love figures explicitly in Schleiermacher's reasons for his (predictive) rejection of eternal damnation.[12]

This teleology of love is, I believe, the only teleology that Schleiermacher ascribes to the divine causality. And he denies that God's love can be known, apart from redemption, "in all arrangements of nature and orderings of human affairs that protect and further life" (*CF*, 1830, § 166.1). In this respect what Schleiermacher thinks can be seen about the divine causality through specifically Christian experience is importantly different from what he thinks can be seen through the more general feeling of absolute dependence alone.

This is not to say that two distinct divine causalities are seen here. How could an additional causality of anything in the world be added to the causality on which absolutely everything in the world is absolutely dependent? Yet Schleiermacher does think the *way* in which God causes redemption is different from the way in which God causes anything else. "The power of the God-consciousness in our souls ... because we are conscious of it not as our own doing," may be ascribed "to a special divine impartation," which is a causality distinct from "that general divine concurrence without which even sin could not be done" (*CF*, 1830, § 80.1).

In what sense can there be a special divine impartation here, given that the divine causality is one and indivisible? This question goes to the heart of Schleiermacher's Christology. He identified the special existence of God in Christ with a special relationship of the human life of Christ to the divine causality.[13] Specifically, "in the redeemer both are the same: his spiritual originality, torn free from every disadvantageous influence of natural heredity, and that being of God in him that likewise proves itself creative" (*CF*, 1830, § 94.3).

The "spiritual originality" mentioned here is also the primary form of the "special divine impartation" that constitutes grace. Schleiermacher is very reluctant to characterize anything in particular in the world as supernatural. He sees the perfect God-consciousness of Jesus and the redeemed God-consciousness of Christians as intrinsically natural; human nature is in principle capable of such religious consciousness (*CF*, 1830, § 13.1). And he sees the propagation of Christ's God-consciousness to his disciples, and then from person to person in the church, as "no miracle, but just the ethical becoming natural of the supernatural, for every outstanding force draws mass to itself and holds it fast" (§ 88.4; cf. § 108.5). The one thing that is supernatural is precisely the originality of the redeemer, the fact (as Schleiermacher claims) that Christ's perfect God-consciousness has no explanation in the historical particulars of its "natural heredity," or in "the state of the circle ... in which it emerges and goes on to operate" (§ 13.1). It is the fact that "in relation to the hitherto all-encompassing and, for [human] formation, all-dominant corporate life of sinfulness, the new is also something that has come into being supernaturally" (§ 88.4). And this relatively supernatural event (rather than any doctrine about it or any document recording it) is the one thing in Christianity that is most properly regarded as *revelation* (§ 13.1).

CONCLUSION: VULNERABILITY AND INVULNERABILITY

There is no doubt that Schleiermacher aspired to render Christian faith, and to some extent theology, invulnerable to rational criticism, especially to criticism emanating from other intellectual disciplines. That is part of the point of his appeal to immediate consciousness (e.g., *KGA*, 1.12, 136; *OR*, Oman, 108), and it is the point of his efforts to understand "every dogma that really represents an element of our Christian consciousness" in such a way that "it does not leave us entangled with science" (*KGA*, 1.10, 351).[14] There is also no doubt that he is at best partially successful in this aspiration.

His difficulties are nowhere more acute than in his Christology. As I noted above, the essential Christian certainty seems, on Schleiermacher's account, to extend to a fact not entirely inward: that the redemptive development of Christian religious consciousness has come about "through the influence of Christ." Schleiermacher's main argument for this extension is that by virtue of its experienced character as consciousness of an actual religious perfection and blessedness in which it participates without itself perfectly exemplifying it (e.g., *CF*, 1830, § 110.3), the Christian consciousness can only be explained as arising through the influence of a Christ in whom it arose in full perfection, Jesus being the one to whom Christian history points as that Christ (§ 93.1–4).

Even if one insists, as Schleiermacher surely would and should, that it is not the details but only the general character of these claims that must be regarded as sound if the certainty of Christian faith is not to be undermined or abandoned, his theology remains committed to rather extensive historical views about the psychology of Jesus – more extensively committed to views of that sort than he might need to be if his Christology focused as older Christologies had done on metaphysical claims about the incarnation. Whether these views about the consciousness of Jesus are correct is a historical question to which it seems that historical evidence must be relevant. Indeed it might be thought that such questions "can be answered only through a historical investigation," as was objected to Schleiermacher in his lifetime by his younger contemporary F. C. Baur (quoted in *KGA*, I.7/3, 267).

To be sure, historical evidence about Jesus is now widely thought to have proved inadequate to settle such questions. This has left many theologians thinking that Christian faith needs a primary basis in present Christian experience as Schleiermacher proposed, or at any rate in some sort of present contact with the power of the gospel. Still, historical questions seem inescapably involved in any attempt to connect present experience with Jesus of Nazareth, and the question whether Schleiermacher has provided adequate grounds for what seem in part to be historical beliefs is one on which his theology remains open to challenge. How convincing, for instance, is his explanatory argument for the perfection of Christ's God-consciousness? (cf. Baur in *KGA*, I.7/3, 250.)

With regard to less Christological issues related to faith in God, which are less historical and more philosophical, Schleiermacher seems to claim for theology a strong invulnerability to philosophical objections. Theology and philosophy are to be so separate, he says, that "so peculiar a question as whether the same proposition can be true in philosophy and false in Christian theology, and vice versa, will no longer be asked" (*CF*, 1830, § 16 postscript). Likewise he claims that a "contradiction" between "the speculative consciousness" and "the pious self-consciousness" (as respectively the highest objective and subjective functions of the human mind) must always be a "misunderstanding." But this invulnerability seems to vanish immediately after the second of these claims when Schleiermacher himself imagines "such a contradiction" nonetheless arising, and allows that "if ... someone rightly or wrongly finds the source of the misunderstanding on the religious side, then this can certainly lead to giving up piety altogether, or at least Christian piety" (§ 28.3). And I believe that vulnerability of this sort is indeed implied by Schleiermacher's account of faith in God, as I have interpreted it.

I don't think this greatly worried Schleiermacher. The one thing he thought theology really needed philosophy to admit is the existence of God, or more precisely "an object to which the feeling of absolute dependence can relate itself" (*CF*, 1830, § 50.2); and his *Dialectic* makes clear that he thought philosophy would amply justify positing the existence of a being to whom this role could be assigned. Not that he sees such a philosophical argument as part of the epistemological foundation of theology. Faith in God appears in his dogmatics as an element in Christian faith, and falls, I believe, within the scope of his statements that his dogmatics is written "only for Christians," and that in it "we entirely renounce every proof for the truth or necessity of Christianity, and presuppose instead that every Christian, before entering" the study of dogmatics, "already has in himself the certainty that his piety cannot assume any other form than this," which I think is supposed here to amount to certainty of the truth of Christian faith (*CF*, 1830, § 11.5), or perhaps even "the proof of faith" (*CF*, 1821–2, § 18.5).

This certainty is for Schleiermacher something "which the religious feeling immediately brings with it" (see the text cited in note 8). It is grounded not in reasoning about the self-consciousness, but in the self-consciousness itself, and thus is accessible only to those who have the relevant consciousness (cf. *CF*, 1830, § 13 postscript). In Christian dogmatics, at least, he proposes to proceed by taking for granted this certainty and its soundness, as (arguably) we must necessarily proceed with some beliefs or others in any rational inquiry. It may be thought a bold step to treat in this way beliefs as pervasively contested as religious beliefs are; but the legitimacy of doing just that remains in fact an object of lively discussion in contemporary philosophy of religion.[15]

Notes

1 A semi-colon separates references to the German original and an English translation of the same passage. While I have sometimes adopted the rendering of a cited translation, I commonly quote in my own translation.

2 Proudfoot 1985, ii, 237, n. 7.

3 See Richard Crouter's introduction to the first edition (1988) of his translation of *On Religion* [*OR*], 57–64.

4 *KGA*, I.12, 56; mistranslated in *OR*, Oman, 39. Cf. *KGA*, I.2, 212; *OR*, Crouter, 23.

5 Andrew Dole called my attention to the importance of this distinction in Schleiermacher.

6 Proudfoot 1985, 11, 18.

7 Kant 1998, B 157n.

8 Quoted in the apparatus to § 14.1 in *KGA*, I.13.1, 115. "Holding as true" (*Fürwahrhalten*) is the most general term for assent, covering all the types and grades of truth-ascription, in the Canon of Kant's *Critique of Pure Reason*, which Schleiermacher (and Twesten) may have in mind here.

9 For an affirmation of cultural (if not individual) variability of conceptualization of essentially the same religious content, from the period of the *Christian Faith*, see *KGA*, I.12, 135f.; *OR*, Oman, 107 (explanation 7).

10 I am not sure whether Schleiermacher has changed his views, and if so, in what ways, when he says, in notes for his *Dialectic* lectures of 1828, that "the way of having the transcendent in religious feeling is not a higher one." Metaphysics, ethics, and religious feeling seem there to be set on a par as all relating to God as a whence on which we are dependent (*Dial* J, 475).

11 This is discussed more fully in Adams 1996, 566–7.

12 Schleiermacher, *Über die Lehre von der Erwählung*, *KGA*, I.10, 217. On this point and on the teleology of divine causality, see Adams 1996, 570–6.

13 I am indebted to an unpublished paper by Edward Waggoner for illumination on this point.

14 From the second of Schleiermacher's two published letters to Lücke on the *Christian Faith*.

15 See, e.g., Plantinga and Wolterstorff 1983.

3 Schleiermacher's ethics

FREDERICK C. BEISER

THE ROLE OF ETHICS

Of all areas of philosophy, ethics was perhaps the most important for Schleiermacher. Throughout his career he remained devoted to the subject. One of his first endeavors was a translation of Books 8 and 9 of Aristotle's *Nicomachean Ethics*. It was his main interest in the early Halle and Schlobitten years, when he wrote essays on such topics as the meaning of responsibility, the highest good, and the purpose of life. The romantic writings of his early Berlin period (1796–1802) – the *Monologen*, *Athenäumsfragmente*, and *Vertraute Briefe* – were manifestos for "a moral revolution." Schleiermacher's first published treatise in philosophy, his 1803 *Grundlinien einer Kritik der bisherigen Sittenlehre*, was a thoroughgoing critique of past ethics. Once his academic career began, ethics remained at the center of his agenda. In Halle and Berlin he would lecture on philosophical ethics eight times.[1]

Any student of Schleiermacher's ethics immediately confronts a formidable obstacle. For all the importance he gave to the subject, Schleiermacher never published his own system of ethics. He had long nurtured plans for a system, but they never came to fruition. The *Grundlinien* was only a critical preparation for his system. All that remains of the system are two sets of manuscripts, the *Brouillon zur Ethik* (1805–6) and the *Ethik* (1812–13). The *Brouillon* consists entirely of notes for Schleiermacher's Halle lectures; the *Ethik* consists of lecture notes for the Berlin lectures, but it is also a draft for a published compendium. While the *Brouillon* is very sketchy and rough, the *Ethik* contains carefully formulated numbered theses with a commentary. Schleiermacher wrote a complete draft of the *Ethik* in (1812–13), and then rewrote substantial parts of it in 1814, 1816, and 1817.[2] There are significant differences between these drafts.

Starting in 1819 Schleiermacher gave a series of addresses on ethical and political topics to the Berlin Academy of Sciences, which are the most mature expression of his ethical views.[3] Unfortunately, though, these were on sundry topics and it is difficult to discern the general vision behind them. Schleiermacher himself once said that anyone who read these addresses and knew his *Grundlinien* would be able to make out his ethical views. But this was to overrate his readers and to underrate his own lectures, which provide a systematic overview absent in the other writings.

The very concept, "Schleiermacher's ethics," is misleading because it suggests he had a final and complete system, or at least a consistent and characteristic doctrine. But he never finished his system, and in the course of his long career his thinking about ethics underwent several transformations. To be sure, there were fundamental continuities in Schleiermacher's ethical thought, themes that can be traced back to his first essays, but there are also discontinuities, even reversals and ruptures. In his later years his views were more stable and consolidated, but even then there are striking differences between versions of his system. Like all good philosophers, Schleiermacher never ceased to rethink and revise his views in the light of later reflection.

Very crudely, we can distinguish five stages in the development of Schleiermacher's ethical thought. First, an early stage of exploration in his Halle, Schlobitten, and Drossen years (1789–96). Second, a stage of discovery within the romantic circle in Berlin (1796–1802). Third, a period of transition, when he prepared for his later system with his criticisms of past ethics (1802–4). Fourth, the period of system-building in Halle and Berlin, beginning with the *Brouillon zur Ethik* and ending with the last manuscript of his *Ethik* (1806–16). Finally, a period of partial consolidation, marked by the lectures to the Academy of the Sciences (1819–32). Inevitably, any periodization is somewhat artificial and arbitrary, and this is especially so in the case of such a complex figure as Schleiermacher.

THE PROBLEM OF FREEDOM

The central concern of Schleiermacher's early ethical writings was the problem of freedom. More specifically, Schleiermacher was troubled by the issue of moral responsibility in a deterministic universe. Is moral responsibility illusory if a person's actions are determined according to causal laws? If not, what does moral responsibility mean? Schleiermacher reflected on these questions for years, first at Halle, when he wrote one of his first philosophical essays on the topic, his *Gespräche über die Freiheit* (1789), and then at Schlobitten, when he devoted his most substantive early work to it, his *Über die Freiheit* (1790–2). His reflections on this issue were decisive for his later ethical thought.

The main stimulus for Schleiermacher's early reflections on freedom was Kant's first and second *Critiques* and the *Groundwork of the Metaphysics of Morals*, which Schleiermacher had carefully studied in Halle.[4] It is important to keep in mind, however, that Kant's *Religion* (1792) and *Metaphysik der Sitten* (1796–8) had still not appeared. These works revise Kant's earlier account of freedom, so that Schleiermacher's critique does not affect them. Schleiermacher's concern was Kant's controversial claim that freedom is possible only if the moral agent belongs to a noumenal or intelligible world distinct from the phenomenal or empirical world of nature. In the first *Critique* Kant held that moral responsibility implies transcendental freedom or spontaneity, a power to begin a series of events without determination by any prior cause (*B* 561). Such a requirement could be secured, Kant argued, only if the agent were not within the natural order, where every event has a prior cause that determines it into action. Moral freedom and determinism are compatible only if moral actions have two causes: the noumenal will or moral intention of the agent and the phenomenal causes of nature.

The main topic of the *Freiheitsgespräch*, only parts of which survive (*KGA*, I.I, 135–64), is Kant's transcendental concept of freedom. This manuscript is a dialogue between two characters, Sophron and Kleon, who discuss the merits and implications of Kant's concept. Kleon represents a skeptical and naturalistic standpoint, and Sophron attempts to defend a qualified form of Kant's theory. Kleon objects to Kant's concept that even inner freedom must have its causes and that its actions must fit into the general course of nature (*KGA*, I.I, 149). Sophron defends Kant's claim for the independence of the will on the basis of the Leibnizian–Wolffian theory of the soul as a faculty of representation. According to this theory, the representations of reason arise from the soul itself and not from sense experience, where the mind is strictly passive (150–3). Sophron explains moral virtue from the soul's striving for harmony and perfection, which is the source of all pleasure for it (157–8). This does not reduce moral action to the striving for pleasure, he explains, because there is a distinction between the pleasures of sense and those of reason. Although he usually defends Kant, Sophron thinks Kant has gone too far in his claims for the powers of practical reason. He agrees with Kant that reason has the power to create *laws* by itself, independent of all motives of pleasure; but he disagrees with Kant that it has the power to produce *actions* by itself. We act morally, Sophron claims, only if the moral law is an object of pleasure, where we are motivated to act according to it from love (161).

The *Freiheitsgespräch* has been understood as the first statement of Schleiermacher's early determinism.[5] The main evidence cited for this claim is Schleiermacher's statement to Brinkmann that he wanted to treat "the power of the will like every other."[6] But this reading is problematic because the dialogue does attempt to defend Kant's claim for the independence of the will, and it makes a distinction between two orders of events, noumenal and phenomenal. Although Schleiermacher argues that pleasure must serve as an incentive for moral action, he is careful to explain that it is a moral pleasure distinct from the physical pleasures of the natural world. When Schleiermacher states that he wants to treat the will like any other power all he means is that he will consider it part of the general power of representation in the usual manner of the Leibnizian–Wolffian psychology.

Über die Freiheit is the longest and most substantial of Schleiermacher's early writings on ethics. This manuscript is essentially a defense of determinism or compatibilism against the incompatibilism of Kant and Jacobi. Although Schleiermacher chiefly addresses Kant, he probably also has in mind Jacobi, and more specifically Jacobi's famous charge that all naturalism ultimately ends in fatalism. It is unclear whether Schleiermacher's aim was to defend Spinoza against both Kant and Fichte. Although he had no firsthand knowledge of Spinoza's writings until the 1800s, he knew about Spinoza's philosophy from Jacobi's *Briefe über die Lehre von Spinoza* as early as 1787.[7] There are unmistakable allusions to Spinoza's doctrine in crucial places in the manuscript.[8] It is striking, however, that Schleiermacher declares that his only aim is to investigate the concept of freedom and that he has no metaphysical or theoretical proof for determinism (*KGA*, I.I, 228–9, 245). So, if Schleiermacher already had Spinozist sympathies, he was still not ready openly to argue for them.

Schleiermacher's express aim in *Über die Freiheit* is to reconcile the concepts of responsibility and obligation with determinism (*KGA*, I.I, 244–5). He wants to defend determinism against the common objection that it undermines the imputation of responsibility. According to this objection, determinism means that all actions are necessary and cannot be otherwise; but responsibility implies that an action could be otherwise. It was indeed for just this reason that Kant placed freedom and determinism in different ontological realms.

The basis of Schleiermacher's argument for the compatibility of responsibility and determinism is his analysis of the concept of responsibility. Schleiermacher makes two fundamental points about judgments of responsibility. First, these judgments are primarily about the character or the worth of the agent (*KGA*, I.I, 247). When we judge the worth of an action we also implicitly judge the character of the person who performs it; we consider how the person would act in similar cases (247–8). Second, judgments of responsibility do not concern the causes for an action but simply whether they conform to principles or ideals (250, 265). We judge whether the person is fit to achieve certain ends, but we do not consider *how* that person achieves them (250). In this respect Schleiermacher likens judgments of responsibility to aesthetic judgments: just as an aesthetic judgment concerns the merits of the work, regardless of how it arose, so a moral judgment concerns the merits of the action, regardless of the mechanism behind it (258 9).

On the basis of this analysis Schleiermacher claims that responsibility is compatible with determinism. Both points mean that these judgments retain their point or value even if all the agents' actions are determined. According to the first point, the aim of these judgments is to change the general character of the agent, so that he or she acts differently in the future; so it does not matter whether specific past actions on specific occasions are necessary. We must distinguish, Schleiermacher argues, between "the grounds for the reality of each individual case" and the "grounds for the possibility of all cases in general" (*KGA*, I.I, 253). In other words, though a specific action in specific circumstances is determined, we still think that the person is in general obliged to fulfill his moral obligations (253). Even if the particular act on a particular occasion is necessary, judgments of responsibility are not abrogated because they concern what a person in general should do (253). According to the second point, a judgment of responsibility will not lose its value, no matter what the causal account of the action, because its sole purpose is to determine the value of the action from some moral point of view. It does not presuppose any specific account of the mechanism of the action (250, 265–6).

Schleiermacher's theory of responsibility implies, therefore, that a person is responsible under two conditions. First, the action comes from the character of the person, so that the person can claim that it is *his* or *her* action. Second, the person can change or alter their character in the future; they do not have to act in the same manner. Schleiermacher thinks that both points are perfectly compatible with the necessity of individual actions.

Like many compatibilists, Schleiermacher contends that responsibility is not only compatible with determinism but also requires it. He argues that the assessment of the morality of an action presupposes that it derives from the person's character, and that this assumes that there are causes for the action within the person's character that bring about certain results on certain occasions (*KGA*, I.I, 254–5). Although the concept of responsibility does not imply any *specific* causal account of the agent's actions, it does imply that the action is the effect of the agent; in other words, although it does not presuppose *how* the agent executes his power of action, it does presuppose *that* he has such a power, or that he can be the cause of his action (260). The whole practice of punishment, Schleiermacher argues, is justifiable only on the assumption that actions have necessary causes (269). Punishment works only because it assumes that bringing to bear certain sanctions will have certain consequences with people; if the cause of their actions was some unknowable X, we would have no reason to believe that the sanctions would have any effect on the agent (269). Schleiermacher's main objection to incompatibilism is that it makes the causes of moral actions completely mysterious (245). After banishing metaphysics from the theoretical realm, he complains, Kant had reintroduced it through the back door into the practical realm.

Schleiermacher never abandoned the position he developed in *Über die Freiheit*, which established the foundation for much of his later ethical thought. This was the basis for his later critique of moral imperatives, his insistence on the self's dependence on the universe, and his emphasis on the interconnection between ethics and natural science.

THE ENDS OF LIFE

Freedom was not the only concern of Schleiermacher's early writings. Another issue that came close to it in importance was the classical question of the highest good. This was the main subject of his *Über das höchste Gut*, which was written in 1789, and his *Über den Wert des Lebens*, which was written in late 1793 (*KGA*, I.1). Both these writings laid important ground for Schleiermacher's mature views. The concept of the highest good eventually became the central concept of the 1812–13 *Ethik*.

Über das höchste Gut is essentially a polemic against Kant's concept of the highest good in the second *Kritik*. According to Kant, the highest good consists neither in happiness nor virtue alone but in the direct proportion of happiness to virtue. Schleiermacher interpreted Kant as affirming that although our moral obligations depend for their validity on reason alone, we are still sensible beings who need the stimulus of happiness to act according to the moral law. Belief in the reality of the highest good is therefore a command of practical reason. Schleiermacher made several objections to his understanding of Kant's concept. First, the addition of happiness to the highest good compromises the concept of virtue with motives of sensibility (*KGA*, I.1, 95). We should love virtue for its own sake, and not admit any sensible incentives for it. Second, the concept of the highest good should be a regulative ideal, and so a goal for action, not an object of belief (100). Third, Kant cannot combine the concepts of happiness and virtue because they belong to heterogeneous realms: happiness has its source in sensibility and virtue its basis in reason; to diminish the difficulty of uniting them, Kant simply projects the highest good into an unknowable beyond (102–3). We cannot examine here the merits of Schleiermacher's critique; but it interests us for its importance for his later ethical views. *Über das höchste Gut* was important for Schleiermacher's rejection of dualism and the traditional Christian doctrine of supernatural rewards and punishments.

Über den Wert des Lebens is an investigation of the great question whether life is worth living. Schleiermacher laments that so few reflect on this question, and resolves to know the answer even if it is the hard truth that life is pointless. He raises the general question about how we should measure the value of life, and finds this standard in humanity itself (*KGA*, I.I, 407). He rejects the attempt to measure the value of life by some standard outside it; those who appeal to the idea of God are caught in a circle, he argues, because their concept of God ultimately depends on their idea of what man should be (407). The final goal of our life should be the promotion of our humanity (*Humanität*), which consists in the realization of our characteristic powers of desiring and willing. We should develop these powers so that they are in harmony, that is, we know how to satisfy our desires and limit them to what we can know (410). Schleiermacher rejects hedonism because, on balance, life leads to more pain than pleasure; the hedonist could value life, he argues, only by having a very selective memory that allows him to repress its many trials and tribulations (397–8). Yet, contrary to his earlier critique of Kant, Schleiermacher now thinks there is an important place for pleasure in the account of the highest good. Although it should not be an end in itself, it should be "the sign of the harmony of my powers" (411), the enjoyment that comes from exercising my will and power of knowing (412–15).

The tension in Schleiermacher's earlier and later views about the highest good point to a deeper conflict in his early ethics. Schleiermacher was still undecided about the fundamental source and criterion of morality itself. In the two essays on freedom and in *Über das höchste Gut* Schleiermacher had adopted an essentially Kantian criterion of morality, which saw its source and criterion in practical reason. Yet in *Über den Wert des Lebens* Schleiermacher explicitly defends an ethic of self-realization, according to which the standard of value is what preserves and promotes the development of our humanity.[9] While he at first wanted to purge reason of any connection with sensibility, he is now adamant on connecting them.

There was a conflict, then, between Kant's rationalist ethic and the classical humanist ethic of excellence.[10] The tension will later be resolved to the advantage of humanism, though, as we shall soon see, a humanism with a religious foundation.

ROMANTIC FRENZIES

Schleiermacher's Berlin years (1796–1802), the years of his association with the romantic circle, were some of the most formative for this ethical thought. It was during these years that he first conceived some of the central themes of his mature ethics. There was also an important shift in Schleiermacher's thinking. While the earlier writings were very much in the tradition of the *Aufklärung*, Schleiermacher now becomes critical of that tradition. He questions its anthropology, its political theory, and, most importantly, its conception of the relationship between religion and morality.

In the Berlin years Schleiermacher gave no systematic exposition to his new ethical views. Most of his thinking takes place in fragments, notebooks, and in scattered passages of the *Reden, Monologen,* and *Vertraute Briefe.* He suggests his ideas rather than argues for them; they are proposed and never elaborated. This was only in keeping with "the thetic style" of the romantics, which stressed the limitations of discursive thought and the value of proposing new ideas without scholastic accompaniment. The task of systematic elaboration and consolidation fell to the mature ethical works.

In any case, it would be absurd to measure the contribution of Schleiermacher's romantic period in academic terms alone. These were the years when Schleiermacher, Novalis, and the Schlegel brothers declared – and to some extent enacted – their "moral revolution," their own revaluation of all values, which had an enormous influence on the moral and social climate of their age. The main manifesto of this revolution was the *Athenaeumsfragmente*, which contained a critique of the immorality of past morality, and which proposed the moral and social ideals for a new age.

Schleiermacher's ethical thinking in the Berlin years reflects the new gospel of the romantic circle. Its central themes are individuality, sociability, and love. Each theme deserves separate comment.

Individuality

In the *Monologen* Schleiermacher suggests that one of the main shortcomings of Kantian ethics had been its failure to account for the intrinsic worth of individuality. Kant had laid such great emphasis upon the value of acting according to universal rules that he had neglected the value of individual differences (*KGA*, 1.3, 17–18). Each person develops humanity in their own unique and distinctive way, Schleiermacher contended, and one of the aims of ethics should be to encourage the development of this individuality (*Eigenthümlichkeit*). In one respect this ethic of individuality was simply an extension of the ethics of excellence or self-realization already present in Schleiermacher's earlier writings. There he held that the end of life should be self-realization, the unification of all one's characteristic powers into a single living whole; but he now adds to this that each person should develop and unify his powers in a manner characteristic of himself or herself alone. Hence, after writing in the *Reden* that perfection consists in uniting the drives toward activity and passivity, he noted that every individual has a unique way of uniting them so that they are "an individual portrait of humanity" (*KGA*, 1.2, 192).

While Schleiermacher was not the first to protest against the uniformity of Kant's ethics, it would be wrong to conclude that there is nothing new or distinctive about Schleiermacher's ethics of individuality. For, unlike Schiller, Schlegel and Humboldt, the ultimate source of his doctrine appears to have been Spinoza. It is striking that in many passages of the *Spinoza Studien* Schleiermacher focuses upon the "*principium individuationis*," the principle by which each thing is distinguished from others.[11] Schleiermacher held that individual differences do not disappear in Spinoza's single universal substance but that each finite thing has a distinctive value as an appearance of the infinite. It was this religious dimension that lay behind Schleiermacher's individualism. Hence, in the *Reden*, he argued that since each individual is a manifestation of the divine, and since the divine appears equally in all its manifestations, every person has an infinite value as this unique person (*KGA*, 1.2, 215, 229–30).

Sociability

Sociability (*Geselligkeit*) means that a person develops his or her humanity and individuality only through interaction with others. Individuality never meant for Schleiermacher, as it meant for Hobbes, going my own path and competing with others for power, prestige, and property. Like Novalis and Hegel, he questioned the individualist anthropology of the social contract tradition, according to which each individual has a fixed nature prior to his entrance into society and the state. He too went back to the classical tradition of Plato and Aristotle, which stressed how each individual is a social and political animal. We become who we are, Schleiermacher held, only through interaction with others. We have a desire to express ourselves to others, and a need to be recognized by them (*KGA*, 1.2, 268).

One of the most important expressions of Schleiermacher's ideal of sociability is his 1799 essay "Versuch einer Theorie des geselligen Betragens."[12] Here Schleiermacher argues the case for having a sphere of social life, independent of political control and the necessities of the economic world, where individuals could interact as equals and engage in free conversation. The purpose of such social gatherings was nothing more than social interaction itself, the free exchange of feelings and ideas. This essay was partly a rationalization of the literary salons of the romantic circle in Berlin, but it was also a protest against the rigid social distinctions of late eighteenth-century society, which inhibited the development of individuality and concealed the humanity within everyone alike.

Schleiermacher understood sociability on both a social and political level. If on the social level it meant the demand for spheres of social life independent of political control, on the political level it signified the fact that each individual could develop his powers only through his participation in political life. In the *Monologen* he laments the loss of the virtue of the ancient republics, where each individual was ready to sacrifice himself for the sake of the public good (*KGA*, 1.3, 33). Everything goes astray, he wrote in one of his notebooks,[13] when society becomes a means to satisfy egoism. Social and political relations are not simply means toward individual ends, instruments for the increase of happiness: rather, they are ends in themselves, the medium of self-realization.

Love

In the Berlin years Schleiermacher attempted to restore love to its supreme place in ethics. In the *Reden* he declared that one intuits the universe only through others, and that one intuits others only through love (*KGA*, 1.2, 228). In the *Monologen* he stated that love should be the center of everyone's life, their "first and last" (*KGA*, 1.3, 22). It was indeed love that weds together the apparently conflicting themes of individuality and sociability. What proves the need to develop a person's individuality in and through others is nothing less than the primal need to love and be loved. In stressing the importance of love Schleiermacher was again reacting against Kant, who had given love a much diminished role in ethics.[14] Kant had distinguished between a practical and pathological love: while practical love has a moral value, it amounts to little more than benevolence; pathological love, which expresses itself in feeling and desire, has no moral value at all.[15] Schleiermacher questioned Kant's distinction; he resisted any reduction of practical love to benevolence, and maintained that even pathological love has moral value. Love was the great mediator between the realms of reason and sensibility, and it was indeed the key to joining together what Kant had so disasterously divided.

One of the most important aspects of Schleiermacher's ethic of love was its emphasis upon sexual equality, more specifically the right of women to realize their own individuality as well as men. The most important expression of this *credo* is Schleiermacher's catechism for women in *Athenaeumsfragmente* No. 364. Since the romantic call for sexual equality was primarily moral rather than political – the romantics were not advocating women's suffrage or right to work – it would be anachronistic to see them as pioneers of contemporary feminism. Still, it would be unjust to underrate the romantic contribution to sexual equality and emancipation.

One of the most important problems in Schleiermacher's ethical thought – the precise relationship between morality and religion – first emerges in the Berlin years. In his early writings Schleiermacher, true to the tradition of the *Aufklärung*, maintained that moral principles should have their validity independent of religion. Hence in his early *An Cecilie* (1790) he saw religion as a primitive form of morality, a step on the road to the development of freedom and reason (*KGA*, I.1, 194–9); and in his *Über das höchste Gut* he had criticized Kant for compromising the moral law through religious incentives. The reappraisal and defense of religion in the Berlin years, however, changed Schleiermacher's thinking about the relationship between morality and religion. In important respects religion now becomes the foundation of morality, and not only as a stimulus to perform duties that have an independent rational basis. While Schleiermacher still seems intent on preserving some autonomy for morality, the morality that is independent of religion shrinks down to nothing more than a doctrine of duties. The higher ethical standpoint, which recognizes the value of love and individuality, has its foundation in religion.

Schleiermacher was far from having resolved this issue during his Berlin years. His failure to resolve it is apparent from a tension in the *Reden*. Schleiermacher both sharply separates, yet intimately joins, religion and morality; he argues for both their interdependence and independence. He had two motivations to separate religion and morality. One was to preserve the autonomy of religion, to prevent it from being a mere instrument to aid morality and the state. Hence Schleiermacher stresses that the chief purpose of religion is solely the intuition of the universe; its aim is not action, and still less does it attempt to determine our duties (*KGA*, I.2, 208). He makes several sharp contrasts between religion and morality. While religion cultivates our passive and sensitive side, morality develops our active and rational side (211). Whereas morality assumes that our actions are free, having their source in the will alone, religion supposes that they are necessary, the product of the universe acting through us (212). If morality is *idealistic*, making man the center of the universe so that the world conforms to him, religion is *realistic*, making the universe its center so that he conforms to it (212). Another motivation for separating religion and morality was to maintain the autonomy of morality. Schleiermacher was still enough of a Kantian to realize that we should do duty for the sake of duty alone. Hence he insists that, though we should do everything *with* religion, we should do nothing *because* of religion (219). Although religion should accompany all our actions like a "holy music," moral actions should be done for the sake of morality alone.

Yet, for all his contrasts between religion and morality, Schleiermacher was also determined to join them. Hence Schleiermacher writes that it is only through religion that a person becomes a complete human being (212–13). With its emphasis on universal rules morality degenerates into "uniformity and homogeneity;" and it is only religion that introduces "multiplicity and individuality" (213). Religion is the foundation for the recognition of individuality because it reveals that the infinite is within everyone alike, and that the living whole cannot be without each of its distinctive embodiments (192, 229–30). Indeed, it is only through the power of intuition, which is cultivated by religion, that it is possible to grasp every person in their innerness and individuality (*AF*, No. 336). The inferior position of morality, and its dependence upon religion, was best put in one of the *Gedanken und Einfälle* of the Berlin years, where Schleiermacher baldly declares that one cannot have morality without religion, and that morality without religion is nothing more than correctness (*KGA*, I.2, 25: *AF*, No. 89).

THE DREARINESS OF STOLP

In early summer 1802 Schleiermacher was transferred by the Berlin consistory to serve as *Hofprediger* in the small village of Stolp in the Pommerian hinterland. Schleiermacher referred to his time in Stolp as his "exile," for he was banished there for his liberal views and lifestyle.[16] He felt cut off from all his friends and the rich cultural life of Berlin. He was also anxious, awaiting Eleonore Grunow's decision to stay with her husband or make a new life with him. When the decision went against him he fell into despair.

It was in these desolate circumstances that Schleiermacher wrote his *Grundlinien einer Kritik der bisherigen Sittenlehre*, the only formal philosophical treatise he published in his lifetime. He began the book in late summer 1802, and finished it virtually a year later in August 1803. The dreary circumstances made for a dreary book.[17] The *Grundlinien* is written in the driest and densest prose, lacking all the wit, fervour and immediacy of his Berlin writings. Schleiermacher himself admitted the obscurity and difficulty of the work. True to its title, the *Grundlinien* is essentially a critical work, an attempt to provide an internal critique of the chief ethical systems of the past from Plato to Fichte. Schleiermacher's chief targets are Kant and Fichte, who are almost always unfavourably compared to Plato and Spinoza. Schleiermacher saw the critical exercises of the *Grundlinien* as preparation for the construction of his own ethical system. It is indeed a transitional work, consolidating many of his earlier ideas while laying the foundation for his later systematic sketches. The central thesis of the book reveals its preliminary role: that ethics is still very far from the status of a science. Schleiermacher's ideal of a science is perfectly foundationalist: a system organized and derived from a single leading idea (121/119).[18] In the *Grundlinien* there is no trace of the anti-foundationalism of the romantic circle in Jena. Schleiermacher thinks that there can be only one complete and consistent system of ethics (10/8); and he explicitly defends the view that all ethical concepts form an organic whole (245–53/243–51). He will later become less sanguine about the possibility of achieving his systematic ideals.

Although the *Grundlinien* claims to be an immanent critique, examining each system by its own standards so that exposition and criticism are one (10, 11/8, 9), it cannot be said that this is Schleiermacher's real procedure. There is no exposition: he presupposes on the part of his reader a complete and thorough knowledge of each system; and his standard of criticism is his paradigm of science rather than the ideals of the author. Schleiermacher faults past systems not because they are inconsistent, but because they are incomplete according to his ideal of science (255–6/253–4), and because they leave out whole dimensions of ethical experience (247–53/245–51). Sometimes his criticisms are patently unfair; for example, he criticizes Kant's ethics for its formalism on the grounds that it cannot derive the content of specific maxims (57, 100/55, 98).

Nevertheless, for all its shortcomings, the *Grundlinien* makes some justified complaints against the systems of the past: that they have failed to examine in depth the concepts of love and friendship (277/275); that they limit the spiritual side of man to his reason (271–2/269–70); that they stress *what* we should do and neglect *how* we should do it (259/257); that they are so concerned with the foundation of the state that they ignore all forms of free human association (276/274). All these criticisms were implicit in the

Berlin writings; now they come forward in a single powerful phalanx in Book 3.

The *Grundlinien* also anticipates some of the fundamental themes of the later systematic sketches. For the first time Schleiermacher states his comprehensive conception of ethics: "nothing that concerns real human action lies beyond the realm of ethics" (263/261). Schleiermacher insists on expanding the realm of ethics beyond its narrow limitation to duties, insisting that every aspect of human conduct where the will is involved is the concern of ethics (154/152). He explicitly states in his later thesis that there are no morally indifferent actions – actions that are simply permissible – because all human actions are done according to the will (135/133). He also argues that the concepts of virtue, duty, and the good are all primitive and fundamental to the development of an ethical system (130/128), one of the central themes of all his later writings.

THE LATER CONCEPT OF ETHICS

Although Schleiermacher felt his exile in Stolp would end only with death, it lasted but two years. In 1804 he was called by the Prussian monarch himself to be a professor of theology and philosophy at the University of Halle. One of his first lecture courses, held in the winter semester 1804–5, was on ethics. Unfortunately, the drafts for these first lectures have been lost.[19] But the drafts for the 1805/06 lectures survive under the title *Brouillon zur Ethik*. These notes are essentially exploratory; they collect materials for a system, though they are hardly rigorously organized and developed. They are divided into ninety-four short *Lehrstunden*, each of which consists of schematic sentences that were the basis for Schleiermacher's oral delivery. The drafts for his mature system first arose in connection with his 1812–13 lectures in Berlin, and Schleiermacher added to them in the following years. These drafts were first published after Schleiermacher's death under the title *Entwurf eines Systems der Sittenlehre*; but they are now known simply by the short title Schleiermacher gave to some of them: "*Ethik.*"

In a short introductory survey it is impossible to do justice to the depth and details of Schleiermacher's mature system. I will limit myself, therefore, to investigating one fundamental concept central to the system, his concept of ethics itself. There is no shorter and easier way to have some understanding of his system as a whole and his thinking about ethics in general.

Schleiermacher's mature conception of ethics is ultimately based upon his metaphysics. In both the 1812 and 1816–17 introductions to his *Ethik* he conceives of ethics as one of the two fundamental sciences of the absolute or infinite. He understands the infinite as pure indivisible unity, the complete identity of subject and object, and the finite as the multitude of individual things. Although the infinite is pure unity or identity, it appears in different forms or manifestations. It has two fundamental manifestations: one is objective and appears as nature; the other is subjective and appears as reason. While it is the job of physics to expound nature, it is the task of ethics to expound reason. Though they have separate domains, ethics and physics are interdependent since each describes how its specific manifestation interpenetrates its opposite, and so how they are joined in the absolute. Physics explains how the objective becomes subjective, how the various stages of nature reach their highest degree of organization and development in reason, and ethics explains how the subjective becomes objective, how reason acts upon and transforms nature.

Schleiermacher's insistence that ethics be understood as one part of metaphysics ultimately goes back to his early determinism and Spinozism. These made him see the individual as only one part of the universe, and his actions as an appearance or manifestation of the laws of nature as whole. Ethics has to assume that the individual is free, Schleiermacher wrote in his *Brouillon*, but it also has to recognize that free action is a manifestation of the laws of nature as a whole (7/83).[20] Schleiermacher's earlier equivocation about the relation between morality and religion is now resolved in favor of religion, or better a metaphysics that expresses the fundamental intuition behind religion. To some extent that tension still troubled Schleiermacher in Stolp, because the *Grundlinien* reaffirms the autonomy of ethics but also praises Plato and Spinoza for deriving ethics from the higher principle of the infinite (10, 36–8/8, 34–6). Yet in the final 1816–17 exposition of the *Ethik*, Schleiermacher states explictly that he will not treat ethics as an independent science and that he will not begin its exposition from a moral principle (192/524).[21]

It would be a serious mistake, however, to think that Schleiermacher's conception of ethics goes back to his determinism and Spinozism alone. For in his mature ethical writings Schleiermacher's metaphysics is not strictly Spinozist but involves an important transformation of Spinozism. Schleiermacher's conception of the infinite is fundamentally organic. He sees the world as a living organism, which undergoes a process of development like all living things. This development consists in a movement of differentiation and externalization – whereby the subjective becomes objective – and a movement of assimilation and internalization – whereby the objective becomes subjective. In the *Brouillon* Schleiermacher describes the basic intuition (*Grundanschauung*) behind his ethics as the idea that the universe is "ein Lebendes und Beseeltes," an idea that he refers back to the ancients (8/84).[22] This vitalistic metaphysics marks a fundamental departure from Spinoza, who had defended a mechanical explanation of events, and who had eschewed all final causes.

Once we place Schleiermacher's ethics within this metaphysical context, it is easy to understand some of his otherwise apparently puzzling statements about ethics. One of these statements is his constant insistence – beginning in the 1805–6 *Brouillon* – that ethics should not be understood as a normative science, where these norms consist in either counsels of prudence or categorical imperatives. Schleiermacher questions the distinction between "is" and "ought" that lay behind the ethics of Hume, Kant, and Fichte.[23] The distinction is bogus, he argues, because we can understand what a thing is only by a norm, and we can understand what we ought to do only by knowing what we can do or be. Behind Schleiermacher's arguments there stood his organic conception of the world, according to which what a thing is has to be understood by function. For such a worldview the normative/declarative distinction makes no sense.

Another of these statements is Schleiermacher's claim – in both the 1805–6 *Brouillon* and 1812–13 *Ethik* – that ethics is history. He is perfectly explicit that ethics is nothing more than "a description of the laws of human action." *Prima facie* the equation is puzzling, but it too follows immediately from his metaphysics. If ethics deals with how the subjective becomes objective, with how reason acts upon nature, then it is history, because history is essentially the realm in which human beings act in the world. In the new 1816–17 introduction to his *Ethik* Schleiermacher somewhat retreated from this equation of ethics with history. He explained that there is both a contemplative and reflective form for the study of nature and reason. The contemplative study of nature is physics, and its contemplative study is natural history. The contemplative study of reason is ethics, and only its reflective form is history (204/536). Though Schleiermacher somewhat demoted the role of history, he still saw ethics as the study of human action in general, whose closest exemplar was history.

Covering the entire realm of human action, Schleiermacher's historical conception of ethics is intentionally and explicitly broad. There is no aspect of human activity that does not fall under the domain of ethics, Schleiermacher argues, because ethics deals primarily with the will, and the will is behind all our activity. As soon as the will operates the question arises of *how* it should do so, and so the further question arises which option it should choose. But as soon as we consider choices we are, willy-nilly, doing ethics. Armed with this broad conception of ethics, Schleiermacher then questioned the concept of the permissible, the idea that there are some actions that are morally indifferent and not subject to ethical precepts.[24] Since ethics deals with all human actions, and since all human actions should lead to the creation of the highest good, no actions are completely indifferent. Although some actions are permissible with respect to some determinate rules or indeterminate principles, there are no actions that are permissible as such because they do not fall under any rules or principles whatsoever.

Given such a broad conception of ethics, it is not surprising when Schleiermacher refuses to classify his ethics in terms of the usual categories. His is not an ethics of duty, of virtue, or of the good; rather, it is all at once. He insists that the concepts of duty, virtue, and the good are all fundamental to ethics, and that none is reducible to the others. Each concept is necessary because it focuses on one aspect of human action: the good upon the end of action, duty upon the norms that govern it, and virtue about the power to produce the good and to act on duty. He maintains that each concept could provide a complete account of human action, and so all of them can be regarded as alternative explanations of one and the same subject matter. Hence Schleiermacher's exposition in the 1812–13 *Ethik* is divided into a doctrine of virtue (*Tugendlehre*), a doctrine of duty (*Pflichtlehre*) and a doctrine of the good (*Güterlehre*).

It is striking, however, that of all these concepts Schleiermacher gives primacy to the good, and more specifically to the concept of the highest good. It is one of the most noteworthy features of Schleiermacher's ethics that he gave this concept such supreme importance. In the 1812–13 *Ethik* he maintains that it is the basis of duty and virtue: these concepts presuppose it though it does not presuppose them (16/256). This concept had been the subject of some of his earliest essays; and it was the main subject of two of his final addresses to the Berlin Academy.[25] In these addresses Schleiermacher argues the case for restoring this classical concept to its central place in ethics. One of the main reasons modern ethics is in such a deplorable state, he contends, is because it has failed to address questions of fundamental importance to human life. The question of the highest good is the central question of ethics, and it is has the most immediate bearing on the conduct of life.

In one of the few English treatments of Schleiermacher's philosophy, Richard Brandt limited Schleiermacher's contributions to the realms of epistemology and theology, and excluded his ethics, which he regarded as no longer "tenable."[26] Brandt's assessment was essentially based upon his critical view of the metaphysics that supported Schleiermacher's ethics. We do not, however, have to accept the details of that metaphysics to recognize the importance and relevance of Schleiermacher's ethics. If it is not recognized as one of the fundamental areas of his philosophical achievement, the problem lies with the public rather than the author.[27] Schleiermacher's comprehensive conception of ethics; his insistence that ethics broaden its horizons, that it investigate such important phenomena as love, free sociability, and friendship; his demand for the restoration of the highest good; his critique of the fact–norm distinction; and his insistence that our ethics ultimately depend upon our general metaphysical view of the world – all these remain a challenge to ethics today. If the subject is as dreary in 2002 as it was in 1802 it is because we have failed to listen to powerful voices like his own.

Notes

1 In Halle Wintersemester 1804–5 and 1805–6; in Berlin in 1808, in Wintersemester 1812–13, and in the Sommer Semester of 1816, 1824, 1827, and 1832. From 1806 to 1831 Schleiermacher also lectured twelve times on theological ethics, *Christliche Sittenlehre*. In this chapter my main concern is his philosophical ethics. On the theological ethics see Birkner 1964 as well as Herms' essay in this *Companion* (ch. 11).

2 For a complete list of the manuscript remains, see Hans-Joachim Birkner's introduction to *Ethik (1812–13)*.

3 The most important of these addresses on ethics proper are "Über die wissenschaftliche Behandlung des Pflichtbegriffs" (1826); "Über die wissenschaftliche Behandlung des Tugendbegriffs" (1820); "Über den Unterschied zwischen Naturgesetz und Sittengesetz" (1828); "Über den Begriff des Erlaubten" (1829); "Über den Begriff des höchsten Gutes. I." (1832); and "Über den Begriff des höchsten Gutes. II." (1832).

4 For an in-depth discussion of Schleiermacher's attempt to think through issues in Kant's ethics, see Mariña 1999; cf. Lamm 1994.

5 See Dilthey 1972, 138, and Blackwell 1982, 10, 37, 39.

6 Schleiermacher to Brinkmann, July 22, 1789, *KGA*, V.1, 140.

7 See Schleiermacher to his father, May 17, 1787: *KGA*, V.1, 79. Dilthey denied that Schleiermacher had any knowledge of Spinoza when he wrote this manuscript. See Dilthey 1972, 140, 141–2. He is corrected by Blackwell 1982, 125–6. Since Jacobi's *Briefe* was still the main source of his knowledge of Spinoza in his 1794 studies, Schleiermacher was probably as well informed about Spinoza in 1787 as he was in 1794.

8 See Blackwell 1982, 72.

9 This conflict was already implicit in an earlier essay, the 1790 *An Cecilie*, where Schleiermacher argues that the standard of morality should be unity of sensibility and intellect. See *KGA*, I.1, 202, 204.

10 Dilthey's claim (in Dilthey 1972, 96), that Schleiermacher was a Kantian all his life in making reason the basis for moral obligation is simply false.

11 See "Spinozismus," *KGA*, I.1, 547–54; and "Kurze Darstellung des Spinozistischen Systems," *KGA*, I.1, 573–4.

12 *KGA*, I.2, 163–84.

13 *Vermischte Gedanken und Einfälle (Gedanken I)*, KGA, I.2, 28, #102.

14 This becomes fully clear only in the later *Grundlinien*. See *Schleiermachers Werke*, I, 280–1.

15 Kant 1997, 399.

16 On the circumstances surrounding the composition of the *Grundlinien*, see Nowak 2001, 122–31; see also Braun's introduction to *Schleiermachers Werke*, lxiv–lxvii.

17 I concur with the judgments of Nowak 2001, 127 and Braun, "Einleitung," lxvi.

18 The first number refers to volume I of the edition of Otto Braun, the second refers to III.1 of the *Sämtliche Werke* [henceforth *SW*].

19 See Hans-Joachim Birkner's "Einleitung" to *Brouillon zur Ethik*, xviii.

20 All references to the *Brouillon* cite first the page numbers of Birkner's edition and then those of the Braun edition.

21 All references to the *Ethik* are first to the edition of Hans-Joachim Birkner, *Ethik (1812–13)*, and then to the Braun edition.

22 See too Schleiermacher's statement in the 1816–17 version of the new introduction to the *Ethik*: "The complete unity of finite being as the interpenetration (*Ineinander*) of nature and reason in one all inclusive organism is the world" (202/534).

23 Schleiermacher's critique of that distinction appears in his academy address "Über den Unterschied zwischen Naturgesetz und Sittengesetz," *Werke*, I.396–416 (*SW*, III.2, 397–417).

24 See *Grundlinien*, 135–7/133–5, and "Über den Begriff des Erlaubten," KGA, III.2, 417–444.

25 See "Über den Begriff des höchsten Gutes," *Werke*, I.445–67 (*SW*, III.2, 446–68); and "Über den Begriff des höchsten Gutes. II," *Werke*, I.468–94 (*SW*, III.2, 467–95).

26 Brandt 1941, I, 167.

27 For an excellent account of the reception of Schleiermacher's ethics in both Germany and the English-speaking world, see Sockness 2003.

4 The philosophical significance of Schleiermacher's hermeneutics

ANDREW BOWIE

MODELS OF INTERPRETATION

Many of the most controversial theoretical debates of recent years in the humanities have been concerned with the relationships between text, author, and reader. What underlies the differences between those who announced the "death of the author," on the basis of the claim that the language an author employs does not gain its meaning from the author's mental acts, and those who continued to write literary interpretation based on research into the life of the author as a means of establishing authorial intentions, is the wider question of the relationships between language, the people who employ it, and the world in which it is employed. Given the lack of any widespread consensus about how these relationships are to be conceived, it is not surprising that a great deal of controversy was generated. The controversy was deepened by the fact that decisions about the relationships also take one into fundamental philosophical questions concerning freedom and self-determination, and language and truth, in modernity.

Two characteristic extremes in the debates about language and its users suggest a model that will recur in a variety of ways in what follows. In some versions of structuralism the subject is "subjected" to the constraints of a language over which he/she has no fundamental power. The subject's relationship to language is consequently "receptive": language is received from the external world and the subject has no significant effect on the meanings it conveys. In strong intentionalist conceptions the author is the source of the authority over the meanings of the text he/she produces. The subject therefore has a "spontaneous" relationship to language: meaning relies on the mental acts of the producer of the text. In the first of these conceptions the task of interpretation is to gain access to significances that transcend what the producer of an utterance knew when producing that utterance. One problem here is that what these significances are understood to be can be dictated in advance by the theoretical assumptions of the interpreter, being based, for example, on class ideology in certain kinds of Marxist interpretation, or on repressed desire in psychoanalytical interpretations. In the second conception, the assumption is that what matters is the extent to which an author produces something individual, which therefore has to be understood via the particular inner life which gives rise to it. This assumption has the advantage of adverting to a vital aspect of writing in modernity, namely the dimensions of texts that simply cannot be accounted for by identifying general historical, linguistic, and other factors that may have played a role in their genesis. The problem is that the spontaneous inner life of the author manifests itself via what the author has received from the external world, namely the language and forms of expression of a particular society and era. Schleiermacher's hermeneutics is based precisely on the attempt to get round the dilemmas involved in both structural and intentionalist approaches.

Extreme versions of structuralism and intentionalism have increasingly come to be seen as inadequate to the phenomena they explore. The reasons why were already evident in Hamann's critique of Kant in 1784, which influenced some of the most important subsequent thinking about language in Germany, including that of Schleiermacher. Hamann argues that "words are both pure and empirical *intuitions* as well as pure and empirical *concepts*: *empirical* because the sensation of sight or sound is affected by them, *pure* in so far as their meaning is not determined by anything which belongs to those sensations."[1] Words would not have meanings if they were merely objects in the world, so they require the spontaneous cognitive activity associated with concepts, but meanings would not be possible without the objective existence of the signifier. As Schleiermacher realized, in the wake of Hamann, aspects of both structuralism and intentionalism are inescapable in any serious engagement with a text. In the terms suggested above, an account which somehow caters for both the "receptive" and the "spontaneous" aspects is required to escape the implausible consequences of both positions.

In what follows I want to show that Schleiermacher's search for ways of avoiding a complete separation of the passive and the active in his accounts of textual understanding has a greater philosophical significance than has generally been appreciated. His avoidance of a complete polarization of passive and active links ideas from the hermeneutics to many other issues in his philosophy. In the hermeneutics the receptive aspect in the subject's relationship to language involves what Schleiermacher terms the "grammatical." The vocabulary, syntax, grammar, morphology and phonetics of a language are received by the subject from the object-world, and they can be "mechanized." This is confirmed by the fact that rules of language can, as we now know, be programmed into a computer. The spontaneous aspect involves what Schleiermacher refers to as the "psychological" or the "technical," which has to do with the ways in which the subject employs language for its own individual purposes. We will see how these aspects relate later.

If one is to believe most accounts of his work on hermeneutics, Schleiermacher belongs solidly in the intentionalist camp, regarding interpretation as the empathetic attempt to "feel one's way" into the mind of an author in order to understand their text. Moreover, if one follows Gadamer's influential account in *Truth and Method*, Schleiermacher is part of a questionable tradition in modernity that spans the human and the natural sciences. The source of this tradition is Descartes' founding of philosophical certainty in self-consciousness, which turns what is to be understood into the object of a "method," rather than, as Gadamer does, regarding understanding as a non-objectifying "fusion of horizons" between interpreter and interpreted. The hermeneutic task that emerges in this tradition is supposedly a *reconstruction* of the "original determination of the work" as an object from the past.[2] Establishing this "determination" depends on the idea of subjective "*feeling*, thus an immediate sympathetic and congenial understanding" of the author's spontaneity.[3] The problem is therefore the problem for intentionalism that we just encountered: sympathetic or empathetic understanding relies on the objective resources of a language not created by the author.

This kind of objection to Schleiermacher's work relates to a widespread move at the end of the nineteenth century against "psychologism." The objection to psychologism in interpretation is that the aim of any philosophical account of language must be to establish how words possess a meaning that is independent of what any particular speaker may happen contingently to intend at any moment. Gadamer's objection to Schleiermacher's supposed attachment to empathetic understanding connects Gadamer to aspects of the analytical philosophy of language, from Bolzano and Frege to the present, which "drives thoughts out of consciousness" and into language.

Were Schleiermacher to have meant what Gadamer and many others say he did, his hermeneutics could happily be consigned to an – admittedly significant – role in the history of ideas. However, it is clear that these accounts in fact involve a considerable distortion of Schleiermacher's thinking. The full reasons for the distortion are too complex to go into here, but one key factor is the failure to read Schleiermacher's texts on hermeneutics – which can, not least because they are also concerned with precepts for textual criticism, appear as rather dry methodological manuals for interpretation – in the context of his other philosophical work, particularly his *Dialectic*. If one does read the texts on hermeneutics in this context, a very different image of Schleiermacher's work emerges, which offers much for contemporary debate. New approaches to Schleiermacher's work were already initiated by the work of Manfred Frank in the late 1970s.[4] Frank saw Schleiermacher's work in relation to new versions of textual theory in the structuralist and post-structuralist traditions, such as those of Barthes and Derrida. However, perhaps the best way now to approach Schleiermacher's major insights is via an idea that is central both to his philosophy and to some contemporary philosophical positions.

THE ROLE OF THE *DIALECTIC*

One of the main targets of contemporary pragmatism is the attempt to describe how the "content" provided by the world is organized into reliable cognitions by a "scheme" furnished by the mind or language. This content is the sense-data of the empiricists, or what Kant saw as the intuitions provided by receptivity which were ordered by the spontaneously functioning schemata of the categories. In this kind of model, as Donald Davidson puts it, "there should be an ultimate source of evidence the character of which can be wholly specified without reference to what it is evidence for."[5] The problem is how to get from a founding source, such as "sense-data," which nobody has ever seen, to the everyday world of tables, people, etc. that we do see. The underlying point is that the attempt to specify what lies on the different sides of the divide between mind and world always involves the problem of how the two sides connect. Contemporary philosophers trained in the analytical tradition, like Robert Brandom and John McDowell, have, in the wake of the work of Wilfrid Sellars, recently turned their attention to Hegel precisely because he rejects a model that depends upon fixing separate subject and object sides.[6]

Schleiermacher rejects the Hegelian conception of the completion of philosophical knowledge, at the same time as still arguing that any separation of receptivity and spontaneity is only ever relative, because they share a single, underlying source. Whereas Kant makes receptivity and spontaneity topically separate, Schleiermacher sees their relationship as a shifting one, in which the more active side has preponderance in, for example, aesthetic production, and the more passive side has preponderance in knowledge of objects. Neither side is ever in play without some degree of the other side also being in play. In everyday perception we may just habitually identify an object as something, where there will be a relative minimum of activity, but we can also actively decide to redescribe an object in new terms. This is not merely a subjective matter, as the terms can become accepted as a new objective description. What, though, does this conception do to Schleiermacher's account of how to arrive at true descriptions of an objective world in the *Dialectic*, a text of which, it is important to remember, he never wrote a definitive version? Here things get difficult, and there is no clear overall answer to this question, not least because Schleiermacher himself is not consistent in his arguments.

There are two contrasting ways of looking at these inconsistencies. One is to look at the sources of his key ideas and to interpret these ideas as versions of those sources.[7] Whilst enlightening us about the contexts of the work, this approach does, though, tend to leave us with a pretty implausible set of conflicting conceptions that are of historical, but not necessarily of deeper philosophical interest. The other approach sees Schleiermacher's difficulties as pointing towards ideas of a kind that have only recently been more fully articulated. Many of the points at which Schleiermacher is inconsistent tend to be the points where he is trying to get beyond his influences to new ways of seeing the issues. I shall adopt the second approach. This approach is a kind of rational reconstruction – with the attendant neglect of some significant aspects of the texts – but it still has solid support in other aspects of the texts and in certain aspects of the historical context.

An obvious place where Schleiermacher's inconsistencies are apparent is in relation to the issue of "realism." Even though it is frequently claimed that Schleiermacher belongs to German idealism, commentators have argued that he actually adheres to a version of realism. This is because he talks about a being which exists outside consciousness: "In all thought something is posited which is outside thought. One thinks *something* does not only mean thought is determined but also that it relates to something posited outside itself" (*Dial* J, 48); or in another formulation: "Disagreement *per se* presupposes the acknowledgement of the sameness of an object, as well as there being the relationship of thinking to being at all."[8] However, for these claims necessarily to entail a realist position the assumption would have to be that true thoughts or assertions "correspond" to this being. Here things are not so simple. The fact that we share the *normative* presupposition that there is something to be right about when we exchange speech acts about matters of truth and objectivity, does not, as Richard Rorty has recently argued, entail a realist *ontology*, with all the attendant commitments. Agreeing about the whiteness of snow is *not* agreeing about "reality."

As Rorty puts it: "Why cannot we get Reality (aka How the World Really Is In Itself) right? Because [unlike the norms for snow] there are no norms for talking about it."[9] The norm that would be required would involve agreement on the correspondence theory. Like Kant, Schleiermacher does in fact often invoke correspondence as the criterion of truth. Also like Kant, though, he is frequently overtly suspicious of the idea of truth as correspondence, for reasons relating to what Rorty contends.

The problem is that the theory of correspondence seems to do no real philosophical work, and it is not actually clear that one can make sense of it. In the first *Critique* Kant admits:

> For what does one understand if one speaks of an object which corresponds to knowledge, which is consequently also different from that knowledge? It is easy to see that this object should only be thought of as something at all = X, because outside our knowledge we have nothing which we can set over against this knowledge as corresponding to it.[10]

Correspondence is, Schleiermacher insists, only "the postulate of completed knowledge," because "our thought never completely corresponds to the object" (*Dial* O, 137–8). More strikingly: "But as far as the expression knowledge corresponds to being is concerned: one could replace it with many others, all with the same value; but what it means does not get any clearer thereby, for because it is what is prior [*das Ursprüngliche*] in the orientation towards knowledge, from which everything else develops, it cannot be explained" (*Dial* J, 49). He also prefigures Frege's objection that: "It would only be possible to compare an idea with a thing if the thing were an idea too,"[11] when he says "One could say that correspondence of thought with being is an empty thought, because of the absolute different nature and incommensurability of each."[12] At best, therefore, correspondence looks like a regulative idea, and Schleiermacher sometimes suggests that he cannot rely on it to establish an account of truth.

This question is central to understanding what is at issue in the links of Schleiermacher's hermeneutics to his *Dialectic*. The problem with a theory of truth such as correspondence was suggested by Frege in 1897. If one defines an idea as true "if it corresponds to reality" one has to try to see if any particular idea corresponds, to see "in other words whether it is true that the idea corresponds to reality," and this means that one always has to presuppose truth in trying to define it. Consequently "truth is obviously something so original and simple that a reduction to something even more simple is impossible."[13] Echoing Kant's line on correspondence, Frege ends up with what seems to many people to be the only consistent position with regard to the correspondence theory, namely the position that all true sentences correspond to the same thing, "the True." Donald Davidson, who also thinks defining truth is impossible, has given the best explanation of why Frege ends up in this position. Finding what a true sentence corresponds to is the basic problem: "One can locate individual objects, if the sentence happens to name or describe them, but even such location makes sense relative only to a frame of reference, and so presumably the frame of reference must be included in whatever it is to which a true sentence corresponds ... if true sentences correspond to anything at all it must be the universe as a whole." There is therefore "no interest in the *relation* of correspondence if there is only one thing to correspond to since, as in any such case, the relation may as well be collapsed into a one-place predicate: '*x* corresponds to the universe.'" In that case it makes more sense just to say "*x* is true."[14] Realism requires a correspondence theory, but truth does not. Davidson therefore thinks that trying to use realism to explain truth gets things the wrong way round, and leads to insoluble dilemmas. The simple point is that the number of ways the furniture of the world can be divided up in language is indeterminably large. It is therefore unconvincing or uninformative to assume that every new articulation of the truth about things is already somehow "present in the things out there," waiting to be "corresponded to," unless one makes Frege's assumption. Otherwise one has to invoke a norm – correspondence – that seems to have no specifiable content, rather than just relying on truth, which is presupposed in the very use of language.

The notion of the universe to which all true statements correspond is one way of construing the notion of the "absolute," and one of the problems with the notion is precisely that it can turn out to be either completely empty, or, by the same token, indeterminately full. It is this consequence that Hegel seeks to escape with his absolute idealist philosophy of immanence. It is generally agreed that, unlike Hegel, Schleiermacher does not regard the absolute as being articulable in philosophy. The absolute identity of Being and knowledge is, he claims, "nowhere given to us," so we are faced with an endless "approximation" to it, which means we are always located between two inaccessible extremes.[15] He consequently argues that "before the completion of real knowledge absolute knowledge is given only in a divided way and ... it only really exists in the inexpressible thought of the unity of divided knowledge" (*Dial* J, 144). In consequence: "The idea of absolute Being as the identity of concept and object is therefore not knowledge" (87). Schleiermacher gets into difficulties because he justifiably wants to hold on to the idea of truth as an absolute notion, but often seeks to do so by making traditional metaphysical assumptions about fixed differences inherent in being to which true concepts will correspond. In a formulation which seems to prefigure Frege he argues that, "behind the difference of separate knowledge we must necessarily presuppose a universal identity, and by this we hold firm to the idea of the purity of knowledge, even if we cannot show an object in which it manifests itself" (69).

This presupposition of universal identity leads him, though, to the following dilemma: "Only the absolute as it never appears for itself in consciousness and the contentless idea of mere matter are free of all relativity. The subtractive procedure of excluding everything from the domain of knowledge that is tinged with relativity would permit no real knowledge at all" (*Dial* J, 230). How, then, is it possible to have "real knowledge?" Schleiermacher rejects skepticism on the pragmatic grounds that "external being is receptive to our reason and also takes on the ideal imprint of our will" (150). This still does not, however, provide *epistemological* certainty that would be free of relativity. Two routes suggest themselves in relation to this dilemma. One is simply to return to the epistemological problems concerning the absolute involved in the moves from Leibniz, to Kant, and to German idealism. The other is a move in the direction of pragmatism. Schleiermacher makes both moves, and this is, it seems to me, why the *Dialectic* remains such a problematic text. The pragmatic side of Schleiermacher's thought is, though, more congruent with his conception of the art of hermeneutics.

The pragmatic dimension is evident in Schleiermacher's characterization, against Fichte and Hegel, of the task of the *Dialectic*: "instead of setting up a science of knowledge in the hope that one can thereby put an end to disagreement it is now a question of setting up a doctrine of the art [*Kunstlehre*] of disagreement in the hope that one can thereby arrive at common bases for knowledge" (*Dial* O, 43). For Schleiermacher "art" is "that for which there admittedly are rules, but the combinatory application of these rules cannot in turn be rule-bound," on pain of a regress of rules for rules, which would render the activity impossible.[16] He also refers to hermeneutics as a "Kunstlehre," and the tasks of the *Dialectic* and of the hermeneutics both depend upon ideas about interpretation. Knowledge is here not seen in terms of representation, but as based in communication: "the art of finding principles of knowledge can be none other than our art of carrying on conversation" (*Dial* O, 77). Like Jürgen Habermas, he is led by this assumption towards a consensus theory: "knowledge in its temporal development is the agreement of all in thinking" (*Dial* J, 487), but, also like Habermas, he realizes this does not give an account of truth: "there is error and truth in language as well, even incorrect thought can become common to all" (*Dial* O, 374).[17] The basic consequence is, though, that one has to accept the impossibility of cognitive foundations: "Beginning in the middle is unavoidable."[18] He does hang on to the notion of correspondence by positing both a state when concept and object were not separate, and a future, regulative idea of knowledge where they are re-joined. This move, however, repeats the idea of the empty or indeterminately full absolute: "Just as certainly as we cannot give up the [regulative] idea of knowledge, we must presuppose this primal being in which the opposition between concept and object is removed," but this presupposition is made "without being able to carry out any real thinking in relation to it" (*Dial* J, 145).

Real thinking, therefore, simply cannot rely on the kind of foundations sought in the attempt to conceptualize the absolute. Schleiermacher's pragmatic moves relate to his doubts about the usefulness of notions involving completed knowledge. Actual knowledge claims, he argues, involve a version of what are now seen as Quine's arguments about the analytic/synthetic distinction, arguments which Davidson sees as having got rid of the search for specifiable "meanings" in the philosophy of language, in favor of looking at the holistic relations between words. Schleiermacher does not reject the analytic/synthetic distinction, but sees it just as a pragmatic aspect of understanding the use of concepts:

> The difference between analytical and synthetic judgments is a fluid one, of which we take no account. The same judgment (ice melts) can be an analytical one if the coming into being and disappearance via certain conditions of temperature are already taken up into the concept of ice, and a synthetic one, if they are not yet taken up ... This difference therefore just expresses a different state of the formation of concepts. (*Dial* J, 563)

In actual language use the analytic/synthetic distinction cannot therefore be regarded as a logical distinction, and this precludes any attempt to establish knowledge on the basis of logical rules and sense-data of the kind characteristic of the founders of analytical philosophy. The crucial factor is therefore the way in which we interpret how a term is used, and this depends upon the contexts of life in which it is employed, thus on a holism where no concept can be determined in isolation from other concepts.

Schleiermacher gets into considerable difficulty in attempting to explain how ever-different empirical input results in reliable concepts, because he ultimately wishes concepts to reflect a fixed order of being – and this even leads him as far as the idea of innate concepts. Once again, though, his problems give rise to prescient ideas. Central among these is his doctrine of the "schema," which he characterizes as an "intuition that can be shifted within certain limits."[19] The schema is intended to solve the empiricist problem of how to get from sense-data to a world of identical, intersubjectively communicable, knowledge:

> at different times the same organic affection [this is Schleiermacher's term for the content of receptivity] leads to completely different concepts. The perception of an emerald will at one time be for me a schema of a certain green, then of a certain crystallization, finally of a certain stone ... For anything which is perceived is never completely resolved into its concept, and determining this relativity, without which the concept would not be able to result at all, depends upon intellectual activity, without which even perception could not be limited.   (*Dial* J, 103)

Consequently: "The absolute identity of schematism in knowledge only exists as the demand/claim [*Anspruch*] of individuals, but nothing that completely corresponds to it can be shown."[20] There cannot be one essential concept of a thing which could "grasp the whole content of the organic affection" (*Dial* J, 103). At the same time, there is nothing to say that such differing schemata cannot all result in appropriate statements of the facts.

The situation is, though, further complicated by the fact that the input that individuals schematize into communicable form has a different history for each person, and this is what leads to the need for interpretation, even when the same locutions are employed in the same situation by different speakers. Schleiermacher gives the example of trying to teach a child what "green" means by holding up a green object: "But how is the child to know whether it is to connect "green" with the form or the weight or with something else in the object?" (*Dial* J, 103). Davidson refers to the need for revisable interpretative "passing theories" which cannot be generalized to all cases of the use of an expression because interpretation relies on context and specific background knowledge. (This, as we shall see a bit later, is part of what Schleiermacher means by "divination.") Schleiermacher talks of a

> further element whereby the area of knowledge is limited, by virtue of which in thought everyone is different from everyone else. This is the individual [*das Individuelle*]. To the extent that there is some of this everywhere no act will completely correspond to the Idea of knowledge [in the sense of the "complete concept"] until after this element has been eliminated. And this can be only indirectly solved if the totality of the Individual as such, i.e. with its foundations, is known, and with this we have a completely endless task.   (*Dial* O, 131)

The question of individuality leads from Schleiermacher's conception of language in the *Dialectic* to the most productive way to understand his hermeneutics.

It should already be clear that the more narrow focus of the hermeneutics on textual interpretation needs to be seen in relation to the *Dialectic*, which connects the issues to general questions of truth and communication. The combination of the two, upon which Schleiermacher himself insists, brings him close in certain respects to the kind of broader conception of interpretation as a fundamental way of being in the world that is developed by Heidegger and Gadamer, as well as to key ideas in contemporary pragmatism.

HERMENEUTICS

Schleiermacher first gave lectures on hermeneutics in 1805, and he worked on the topic virtually until the end of his life. His most well-known work on hermeneutics, a compendium of texts from different periods published posthumously in 1838 as *Hermeneutics and Criticism*, is mainly concerned with the interpretation of the New Testament, but he always insists that there is no difference between interpreting religious texts and interpreting secular texts. The sometimes confused history of his texts on hermeneutics has been a further obstacle to an adequate assessment of their content. Much critical effort has been expended, for example, on tracing the supposed development of his account of the relationship between the individual/psychological/technical, and the grammatical/structural aspects of interpretation. Recent research has, however, shown that he used material from 1805 for his last lectures in 1832–3, and it now seems clear that his approach actually remained much the same throughout this period.[21] His basic claim regarding this version of the spontaneous/receptive, technical/grammatical divide is simple: "These are not two kinds of interpretation, instead every explication must completely achieve both."[22] This is not in fact possible, so the aims of the technical and grammatical are regulative ideas. The difference of Schleiermacher's account of hermeneutics from that of Gadamer derives from this assumption. Gadamer claims "it is enough to say that one understands *differently, if one understands at all*,"[23] rather than assuming that there is true and false understanding based on a regulative idea of complete understanding. Understanding is therefore something that happens in any fusion of horizons between text and interpreter. For Schleiermacher, in contrast, it involves a truth claim that can never be definitive, because the necessary evidence is never all present.

Schleiermacher asserts that hermeneutics is "the art of understanding ... the ... discourse of another person correctly."[24] However, he also
insists that it must be considered in relation to dialectic. Hermeneutics seeks
the specific intentions of the individual in the contexts of their utterances.
These intentions are obviously not exhausted by the possible general validity of those utterances. The relationship between intentions and validity is
therefore decisive in the relationship between hermeneutics and dialectic.
Schleiermacher rejects what is now termed "social externalism" – "understanding and interpreting an agent's speech in terms of what others mean
by the same words"[25] – for the same reasons as Davidson. Interpreting what
someone says without any reference to what they intend is fundamentally at
odds with how we come to understand anyone else's utterances at all. An
ineliminable aspect of how we come to understand is the comparison of
others' reactions to things with our own reactions in a shared objective
world, and many reactions make no sense unless we try to understand them
as the expression of an intention.

Davidson talks of a "triangulation," between the subject, other subjects, and the world, in which "knowledge of other minds and knowledge
of the world are mutually dependent; neither is possible without the
other."[26] Schleiermacher is often regarded as advocating an implausible
subjectivism, but he actually already makes much the same point as
Davidson:

> Even the most subjective utterance of all has an object. If it is just a
> question of representing a mood, an object must still be formed via
> which it can be represented ... There is nothing purely objective in
> discourse; there is always the view of the utterer, thus something
> subjective, in it. There is nothing purely subjective, for it must after all
> be the influence of the object which highlights precisely this aspect.[27]

The crucial issue is the intention of an utterance, which can, for example, be
to express an otherwise private affective inner state, or to assert a claim to
objective knowledge. Dialectic is concerned with general validity, in the
name of universal agreement, and the inherent generality of language
demands this, but agreement also relies on being able to interpret what a
particular individual means in a specific context:

> Looked at from the side of language the technical discipline of
> hermeneutics arises from the fact that every utterance can only be
> counted as an objective representation [*Darstellung*] to the extent to
> which it is taken from language and is to be grasped via language, but

that on the other side the utterance can only arise as the action of an individual ... The reconciliation [*Ausgleichung*] of both moments makes understanding and explication into an art.[28]

It is, therefore, "clear that both [hermeneutics and dialectic] can only develop together with each other" (*Dial* J, 261), so the relationship between apprehension of the individual and of the universal cannot be established in advance, and depends on the context of an utterance. In everyday understanding we rely on our command of the resources of a common language, on knowledge of the world in which things are said, and on particular knowledge of the beliefs, desires, etc. of the individual whose utterances we seek to grasp. Even if we become aware that what someone says is driven by structural factors of which they are not aware, our awareness can only develop in relation to all three sides of this triangle. Schleiermacher's insistence on the regulative idea of complete interpretation derives from the fact that the possibilities for engagement with each side of the triangle will always vary, depending on the circumstances of interpretation, from interpreting a directly spoken utterance, to interpreting a written text from the distant past.

The ability to communicate intrinsically relies on receptivity for objectively existing linguistic resources – which can function as ideology – and subjective spontaneity in employing them for our own particular purposes: "If language appears to come to [the child] first as receptivity, this only refers to the particular language which surrounds it; spontaneity with regard to being able to speak at all is simultaneous with that language."[29] Schleiermacher's version of the hermeneutic circle therefore results both from the fact that "each person is ... a location in which a given language forms itself in an individual [*eigentümlich*] way," and from the fact that "their discourse is only to be understood via the totality of language."[30] These two quantities, the individual and the totality, are not reducible to each other: if the latter is reduced to the former we have a completely implausible solipsistic intentionalism; if the former is reduced to the latter we have social externalism. Because language results from concrete "speech acts" the speech *act* is necessarily individual: it is your or my act at a particular time in a specific situation.[31]

The "stricter practice" of the "art" of hermeneutics therefore presumes that "misunderstanding results as a matter of course and that understanding has to be desired and sought at every point," because we can never be sure that we have grasped the content both of the psychological and of the grammatical.[32] Schleiermacher distinguishes between the psychological, which depends on as thorough a knowledge of the life of the individual as possible, and the technical, which relates to a person's deciding to engage in a particular form of utterance, such as writing a poem or a novel: "If we now assume that the utterance is a moment of a life, then I must seek out the whole context and ask how the individual is moved to make the utterance (occasion) and to what following moment the utterance was directed (purpose)."[33] This might again appear to push him towards a psychologistic, intentionalist conception, but he also maintains that the interpretation of first-person utterances is not to be governed by the authority of the writer/speaker.

The notion of "empathy" often associated with Schleiermacher – even though it is a word he does not employ – is therefore wholly out of place in his method:

> The task can also be put like this: "to understand the utterance at first just as well as and then better than its author." For because we have no immediate knowledge of what is in him, we must seek to bring much to consciousness which can remain unconscious to him, except to the extent to which he reflexively becomes his own reader. On the objective side he as well has no other data here than we do.[34]

The accusation of reliance on empathy is generally linked to Schleiermacher's claim that "divination" is a necessary part of understanding. His reason for saying this is, though, a logical one. He takes the case of primary language acquisition by children, which relies on divination and on comparison of the uses of a word in various contexts. The logical problem concerns how the process can begin at all:

> They do not yet have language, rather they are looking for it, but they also do not yet know the activity of thinking because there is no thinking without words: on what side do they begin [i.e. by comparison or divination]? They have not yet got any points of comparison but they only gradually acquire them as the basis of an unexpectedly quickly developing comparative procedure; but how do they fix the first thing?[35]

They fix it by divination, the ability to make ungrounded and revisable judgments about the relationships between words, which are inherently general, and particular things. He also applies this idea to playing a musical score: "in performance there is always something which cannot be represented either by signs or words and which has to be found by divination. The composite marks which are supposed to represent the idea [of the whole piece] are largely laughable."[36] Divination is Schleiermacher's term for what Davidson characterizes in terms of passing theories that cannot be reduced to a general methodology. The comparative process can only get underway after some elements are – at least temporarily – fixed, but this cannot itself be achieved by learning a linguistic rule. There are no linguistic "rules ... that would carry the certainty of their application within them," and there can be no rule for learning to apply the first rule.[37]

Importantly, this claim can be linked to the failure of attempts to define truth we considered above, though the issues need a lot more investigation than is possible here. In the case both of truth and of the understanding of rule-following one always has to presuppose an immediate grasp of what is at issue. The attempt to explain the learning of how to acquire rules leads to something that cannot itself be explained in terms of rules. What is in question here seems to be so fundamentally part of what we are that we cannot objectify it in terms of something else. This necessity for some kind of intuitive immediacy offers a way of trying to understand the significance of Schleiermacher's problematic concept of "immediate self-consciousness," or "feeling." Manfred Frank has shown that Schleiermacher belongs to a tradition that contends that "feeling, as the epistemic organ for a non-objective familiarity with oneself, is also the epistemic organ for the comprehension of Being in its radical pre-conceptuality, including, of course, one's own being."[38] Schleiermacher regards the existential continuity of immediate self-consciousness as playing an ineliminable role in judgment, and therefore in the articulation of truth. Without the immediate continuity of the subject as the principle of intelligibility that accompanies the different mediated moments of a judgment, the moments would, he claims, have no basis upon which to be related at all. Consequently, all judgment is "grounded in feeling."[39]

This might seem to lead back into questionable foundational epistemological territory, but Schleiermacher is clear that the aspect of self-consciousness designated by "feeling" cannot function as a philosophical foundation. Indeed, it is the *dependence* of the "I" on a ground that transcends it and that is not in its power that leads him to the notion. What he is concerned with is the fact that whereas the conscious, reflexive subject relies upon inferences that link different experiences for the ways it judges both its own identity and conceptualizes objects in the world, the immediate "I" must be the existential *basis* of any act of inference. There are many problems and complexities associated with Schleiermacher's claims in this respect, but they do suggest a dimension of intersubjective understanding that is perhaps still too little attended to, even by philosophers who have broken with representationalist assumptions.

In the *Ethics* and the *Aesthetics* Schleiermacher links feeling, in a sense which refers both to immediate self-consciousness and to the immediacy of private feelings in the everyday sense, to gesture, and to music: "just as the infinity of combination of articulated sounds belongs to human thought being able to appear in language, so the manifold of measured [*gemessen*] sounds represents the whole manifold of movements of self-consciousness, to the extent that they are not ideas, but real states of life."[40] Verbal language can convey the thoughts of one subject to another, depending, of course, on their being correctly interpreted. Understanding feeling requires the ability to grasp the significance of wordless gestures or music – like Adorno, he stresses the connection of the two – that cannot be determinate in the way words can. In the hermeneutics he also suggests that lyric poetry often expresses the movements of immediate self-consciousness, rather than propositionally articulable thoughts.[41] Echoing aspects of Schleiermacher, Dieter Henrich has claimed that "language can only be understood as a medium, but not as the instrument of agreement. Subjects cannot agree on the use of language, because the agreement would itself already presuppose its use. From this it follows that taking up communication presupposes a real common ground between subjects who mutually relate to each other" as self-conscious beings.[42] In this sense it could be argued that the social practice of music manifests a dimension of the relationships between subjects without which understanding even at a verbal level would be impossible. Arguments like this take one well beyond what can be adequately argued here, but they do suggest the resources that may still lie in Schleiermacher's work.

The main aim of this essay has been to suggest the continuing philosophical significance of Schleiermacher's hermeneutics. What, though, of the contemporary social significance of philosophy of this kind? The rejection in pragmatism of the assumptions of the kind of analytical philosophy that privileges the representational aspect of language over its communicative aspect is a result both of the increasing implausibility of empiricist arguments about the move from the primary "given" to its expression in language, and of the suspicion that philosophy oriented primarily towards the natural sciences runs the danger of "scientism." Bjørn Ramberg argues that "Scientism is not bad because it gets the world wrong ... but because it renders us subject to certain forms of oppression,"[43] namely forms which seek to exclude ways of looking at things that are not amenable to the methods of the natural sciences. Rorty thinks Ramberg's remarks are valuable for reinforcing the pragmatist desire to "break down the distinction between the knowing, theorizing, spectatorial mind and the responsible participant in social practices."[44] In the *Dialectic* Schleiermacher sometimes unsuccessfully tries to sustain this distinction, but the combination of the *Dialectic* with the hermeneutics promotes a view in which the normative aspects of all language use are necessarily prior: "Language never begins to form itself through science, but via general communication/exchange [*Verkehr*]; science comes to this only later, and only brings an expansion, not a new creation, in language" (*Dial* O, 511). The idea of a grounding scientific language that can somehow go back behind "general communication" and explain it in scientific terms was part of the mythology that drove – and still drives – some of the analytical tradition. The recent developments in American philosophy that oppose this idea are congruent with Schleiermacher's hermeneutic perspective and reveal the roots of a growing tradition that is concerned to sustain intersubjective rationality – including scientific rationality – without surrendering truth solely to the natural sciences.[45]

Notes

1 J. G. Hamann, in *SW*, III.286.
2 Gadamer 1975b, 158.
3 Gadamer 1975b, 179.
4 See Frank 1977.
5 Davidson 2001, 42.
6 McDowell thinks Kant can also be read as avoiding a complete separation of spontaneity and receptivity.
7 See Manfred Frank's outstanding introduction in his edition (2001) of Schleiermacher's *Dialektik*.
8 Schleiermacher, *Dialektik (1814–15), Einleitung zur Dialektik (1833)*, 132.
9 In Brandom 2000, 375.
10 Kant 1998, A 104.
11 Frege 1977, 3.
12 Schleiermacher, *Dialektik (1814–15)*, 18.
13 Frege 1990, 39.
14 Davidson 2001, 183–4.
15 Schleiermacher, *Dialektik (1811)*, 73.
16 From the secular "Allgemeine Hermeneutik" ("General Hermeneutics" of 1809–10), in Schleiermacher, *Hermeneutics and Criticism*, 229. This is the best condensed account of Schleiermacher's ideas on hermeneutics. The German can be found in Virmond 1985, 1271–1310.
17 See Bowie 2003.
18 Schleiermacher, *Dialektik (1814–15)*, 105.
19 Cited in Frank 1989, 28.
20 Schleiermacher, *Ethik (1812–13)*, 107.
21 For details see my Introduction to Schleiermacher's *Hermeneutics and Criticism*.
22 Ibid. 229.

23 Gadamer 1975b, 280.

24 Schleiermacher, *Hermeneutik und Kritik*, 75. This easily available edition is based on the edition of 1838, but misses out significant parts of the text. More of the text is available in English in Schleiermacher, *Hermeneutics and Criticism*.

25 Davidson 2001, 199.

26 Davidson 2001, 213.

27 Schleiermacher, *Hermeneutics and Criticism*, 257.

28 Schleiermacher, *Ethik*, 116. By art he means, as usual, an activity involving rules where there can be no rules for the application of the rules.

29 Schleiermacher, *Ethik (1812–13)*, 66.

30 Schleiermacher, *Hermeneutik und Kritik*, 78.

31 Schleiermacher, *Hermeneutik und Kritik*, 80.

32 Schleiermacher, *Hermeneutik und Kritik*, 92.

33 Schleiermacher, *Hermeneutik und Kritik*, 89.

34 Schleiermacher, *Hermeneutik und Kritik*, 94.

35 Schleiermacher, *Hermeneutik und Kritik*, 326.

36 Schleiermacher, *Ästhetik (1819–25) über den Begriff der Kunst*, 75.

37 Schleiermacher, *Hermeneutik und Kritik*, 81.

38 Frank 2002, 10.

39 Schleiermacher, *Ethik (1812–13)*, 73.

40 Schleiermacher, *Vorlesungen über die Aesthetik*, 394.

41 Schleiermacher, *Hermeneutik und Kritik*, 138.

42 Henrich 1999, 71.

43 Brandom 2000, 367

44 Brandom 2000, 371.

45 This chapter was completed with help from the Research Leave Scheme of the British Arts and Humanities Research Board.

5 The art of interpreting Plato

JULIA A. LAMM

INTRODUCTION

The art of interpreting Plato, according to F. D. E. Schleiermacher, consists in two things: that Plato be viewed as an artist, and that the interpreter be an artist as well as a scholar. This twofold guiding principle is easily recognizable as "romantic," and indeed many commentators have referred to Schleiermacher's view of Plato as "romantic." Yet the term "romantic," however accurate, is not in itself adequate in describing Schleiermacher's interpretation of Plato. The problem, of course, is that "romantic interpretation" carries many different meanings. Often it is taken to refer to a divinatory method of interpretation that imposes an ideal type irrespective of historical evidence; yet Schleiermacher was quite critical of such an approach. Moreover, a simple appeal to the term "romantic" overlooks the fact that there are many different "romantic" interpretations of Plato, among which Schleiermacher's was one, albeit arguably the most distinctive and influential. Finally, the modifier "romantic" eclipses the very important fact that Schleiermacher's interpretation of Plato is thoroughly "modern" – if not exactly the first modern interpretation, surely the most authoritative. It is its modern quality, inseparable from its romantic elements, that marked it as a watershed in the history of Plato interpretation. In short, nomenclature can never be an adequate substitute for a more substantive explanation, especially when we are speaking of two thinkers of the magnitude of Plato and Schleiermacher. I propose, therefore, that we examine what effect Schleiermacher's view of Plato as artist (and of himself as artist) actually had on his translation and interpretation of Plato. One important thing to keep in mind is that, for Schleiermacher, art and scholarship are inseparable.

A prior question must be addressed: Why is Schleiermacher's interpretation of Plato so important? Why not devote the same attention to his interpretation of other philosophers – such as Kant, or Spinoza, or even

Aristotle – who had influenced him? The answer is simple, really. Schleiermacher's translation of Plato's dialogues, along with his accompanying "Introductions," was a momentous event in the philosophical, philological, and literary world. His translation of Plato's dialogues, which itself has been hailed as "artistic," was so effective that it is still in use today and continues to carry significant authority. His interpretation of Plato's dialogues, as explicated in his "Introductions," changed the entire course of Plato studies and continues to reverberate even now, two centuries later.[1] Finally, an indication of the significance of his interpretation of Plato is that its influence extended beyond the field of Plato scholarship inasmuch as it led Schleiermacher to develop a theory of interpretation. It would not be too far afield to say that Schleiermacher's famous *Hermeneutics* emerged in part from his philological work of translating and interpreting Plato according to the demands set by the new criticism.

Plato's Works (*Platons Werke*)[2] appeared in six volumes, with the first five appearing between 1804 and 1809 – an amazing scholarly accomplishment. Originally, the project of translating all of Plato's works together, in conjunction with writing a "study" of Plato, had been a collaborative one between Friedrich Schlegel and Schleiermacher, who had been house-mates for a time. Schlegel, a renowned literary theorist and philologist, had first mentioned the project to Schleiermacher in 1799, shortly after Schleiermacher had finished writing his *Speeches on Religion*. Not long after they had begun their collaborative project, Schlegel raised the question in a letter to his collaborator, "How can two translate Plato together?" (*KGA*, v.3, 455 [ca. April 4, 1800]). As it turned out, two could not do it together – or, at least, not those two – and in 1803 the entire project became Schleiermacher's alone. Although it was Schlegel's name and reputation that had initially carried the project, Schleiermacher quickly honed the talents and confidence necessary to carry the project through.[3] The first volume was hailed as a work of genius. The philologist August Böckh wrote in a published review that "no one has so fully understood Plato and has taught others to understand Plato as this man."[4] Schleiermacher, he proclaimed, was that one "rare talent" who could present Plato as *philosophical artist*.

THE NEW CRITICISM AND THE PLATO RENAISSANCE

Late eighteenth-century Germany witnessed a renaissance in which classics – modern as well as ancient – were being translated into German. The German language, it was believed, had developed to just that point where it, and it best of all, could unlock the deepest meanings of classical texts. This sense of the development of the German language was itself fueled by the new historicism. Philology and (many areas of) philosophy came to be seen as inseparable from history, and scholars embraced and developed the new historical, critical method. By the very end of the century, the traditional definition of what constituted a "classic" was being challenged by the early romantics, who dissolved conventional categorization of literary forms and called for the establishment of an entirely new canon, one determined not by epoch or genre but by what F. Schlegel referred to as the "element of poetry." In the romantic canon, Plato, an ancient philosopher who had attacked the poets, is a "romantic" poet and artist; Shakespeare, a modern poet, is a "romantic" philosopher; and Spinoza, a modern rationalistic philosopher, is a "romantic" poet. This romantic re-classification was deeply committed to the new criticism.

All of this had powerful implications for Plato studies. There was a growing consensus that the historical critical method had to be applied to Plato's work, which had been largely neglected in Germany, especially in comparison to England and France. Consequently, there was a fundamental shift in orientation regarding Plato's philosophy, a shift that mirrored work being done in the interpretation of the New Testament. This meant, first of all, that claims about Plato's philosophy had to be grounded in the writings themselves – undefiled by dogmatic commitments, theological agendas, or other philosophical systems. Second, the writings had to be set in historical context. This required, third, that the chronological sequence and dates of the dialogues needed to be discovered. This newly stated ideal had yet to be achieved by 1800, when Schleiermacher entered the scene of Plato studies.

Unquestionably indebted to this "new situation,"[5] as E. N. Tigerstedt has termed it, Schleiermacher was the one who carried it forward by relentlessly pursuing its ideals and commitments. What was it that set his study of Plato apart from that of the other "modern" and "romantic" critics? On this point it may be instructive to attend to Schleiermacher's acknowledgment of debt to, and pointed criticism of, two of the most important Plato interpreters of his day: the Kantian philosopher, Wilhelm Gottlieb Tennemann; and the romantic theorist, Friedrich Schlegel, Schleiermacher's friend and collaborator in the Plato project. Both Tennemann and Schlegel were committed to approaching Plato via the new historicism. Yet each represented one side within the new situation: Tennemann the more historical (and philosophical); Schlegel the more literary (and philological). The failures of both demonstrated to Schleiermacher the weakness of a one-sided approach.

The strength and weakness of Tennemann's *System of Platonic Philosophy* (*System der platonischen Philosophie*, 1792) was his historical method, what Schleiermacher referred to as an "external" method – external, because it relied exclusively on historical evidence, or external markers. What defined Tennemann's scholarship as being truly "modern" is that he had sifted through all previous scholarship and had sorted out the historical from the conjectural. As a result, he was able to isolate certain dates and facts about Plato's life and works. Indeed, Schleiermacher began his own great study of Plato by referring his readers to the first, biographical part of Tennemann's study, "The Life of Plato." Schleiermacher had considered it so authoritative that he did not see the need to revisit it. Yet the great weakness of Tennemann's external method was that it could neither accomplish its own goals of dating and ordering the dialogues nor tell us much that is substantive about Plato or his philosophy. There were simply not enough external markers. This created a problem for Tennemann, who, unable or unwilling to relinquish the notion of a Platonic system, wound up betraying his own methodological commitments. He averred that Plato must have had a "double philosophy" – an "external" one found in the extant writings (what Schleiermacher referred to as the "exoteric" tradition), and a "secret" one (the "esoteric" tradition). Since his presentation of Plato's so-called system was therefore not based exclusively on the close examination of texts, he strayed from the new criticism. He did not forsake dogmatic tendencies after all, despite his intentions: having found no system in the written dialogues, he wound up imposing his own philosophical (Kantian) system. Schleiermacher proposed that, given the paucity of historical evidence, the external method needed to be supplemented by an "internal," by which he meant literary, method.

Schlegel, too, was convinced that an "internal" method was necessary. An artistic translation of Plato, he announced, was waiting to be discovered.[6] Schleiermacher agreed. Increasingly, however, they diverged on what this internal method involved. Schlegel focused more and more on irony as the *leitmotiv* that would help determine authenticity and order. Schleiermacher, in response, warned that such an approach would produce only fragments and inconsistencies, not argument. Although Schlegel had begun the Plato project committed to the very historicism he himself had advanced, Schleiermacher was concerned that Schlegel had come to occupy himself too much with the more theoretical questions. Schleiermacher emphasized that precise, painstaking work of "the higher grammar," which he, like Schlegel, understood to require both scholarship and art, was the more fundamental and necessary task. In Schleiermacher's understanding, the new (text) criticism involved close grammatical and comparative work within the text, whereby each part is worked through with precision and thoroughness. Such attention to the particulars would begin to yield the rest – the relation among the particulars, as well as the relation between particulars and the whole. They needed to have the trans-lations before them, Schleiermacher urged, before they could begin to determine the order and connection of the dialogues. "Philosophy and the higher grammar," he wrote to Schlegel, "should therein revise each other" (*KGA*, v.5, 47 [letter of February 7, 1801]).

Ironically, although Tennemann and Schlegel represented two different sides of the new modern approach to Plato, their respective forms of one-sidedness arrived at the same problematic result: the imposition of their own philosophies onto Plato. Both resulted, that is, in a form of idealism. Tennemann reached beyond the authentic texts to an unwritten or esoteric tradition (which he had originally rejected) in order to find the Platonic system. Schlegel, although anti-system, also departed from text criticism in order to follow his literary theory, a theory that yielded false conclusions regarding the authenticity of certain texts (e.g., that the *Apology* is inauthen-tic). To Tennemann, Schleiermacher said that the historical must be balanced by the internal or literary; to Schlegel, that the literary needed to be balanced by historical investigations and philological details. In both cases, the new (text) criticism restrained philosophical and idealistic urges. For Schleiermacher it was the text, the written text, the authentic written text.

In summary, Schleiermacher, like Tennemann and Schlegel, began the art of interpreting Plato committed to the new criticism; unlike them, however, he continued to adhere to the rules of criticism, using them as a touchstone. As the *sine qua non* of Schleiermacher's interpretation of Plato, criticism restrained different tendencies and temptations to stray from the authentic texts and consequently to import foreign meanings. Criticism, however, while an art, is not itself the art of interpreting. Later, in his lectures on hermeneutics, Schleiermacher explained the relation between criticism and interpretation:

> Hermeneutics and criticism, both philological disciplines, both
> theories belong together, because the practice of one presupposes the
> other. The former is generally the art of understanding particularly the
> written discourse of another person correctly, the latter the art of
> judging correctly and establishing the authenticity of texts and parts
> of texts from adequate evidence and data. Because criticism can only

recognize the weight to be attached to evidence in its relationship to the piece of writing or the part of the text in question after an appropriate correct understanding of the latter, the practice of criticism presupposes hermeneutics. On the other hand, given that explication can only be sure of its establishing of meaning if the authenticity of the text or part of the text can be presupposed, then the practice of hermeneutics presupposes criticism.

Hermeneutics is rightly put first because it is also necessary when criticism hardly takes place at all, essentially because criticism should come to an end, but hermeneutics should not.[7] How, then, do you move from criticism to hermeneutics?

In his "General Introduction" to *Plato's Works*, Schleiermacher explained that the translator-interpreter must have so thorough a knowledge of the history of Greek language and thought as to be able "to adduce something about the scientific state of the Hellenes at the time when Plato began his career, about the progress of the language in relation to philosophical ideas, about texts of the same genre that were available at the time and the probable extent of their circulation."[8] This expert knowledge of the whole – of the language shared by the author and his original audience, of the historical and intellectual context – is what in his *Hermeneutics* Schleiermacher would come to call the "grammatical" part of the explication: "Everything in a given utterance which requires a more precise determination may only be determined from the language area which is common to the author and his original audience."[9] Only with such thorough knowledge and expertise can the interpreter then move to assess the uniqueness of an individual's expression of the language. With regard to the Platonic dialogues, this means that the interpreter must be able to "feel where and how Plato is restricted by [the state of the language], and where he himself laboriously expands it."[10] In the *Hermeneutics*, Schleiermacher would come to call this the "technical" or "psychological" part of the explication. He always insisted, from this early articulation of it in his "General Introduction" through his later lectures on hermeneutics, that these two must co-exist and be interdependent; that each presupposes and requires the other. This is also why interpretation and explication are an art: "The successful practice of the art depends on the talent for language and the talent for knowledge of individual people."[11] Much more than learning a foreign language, therefore, the interpreter must have a "living awareness of language, the sense of analogy and difference."[12] Hence the art of understanding Plato begins in scholarship – in particular, in philology – but such scholarship always requires art. It can be extended to non-specialists if the translator-interpreter is an artist. Schleiermacher's goal was not to expound Plato's philosophy so much as it was to "make it possible for each reader, by means of an immediate and more exact knowledge of Plato's works, to come to his own view of Plato's *Geist* and teachings, whether that view be entirely new or just more complete." The key to such a view is to come to know Plato as "philosophical artist."[13]

HERMENEUTICS AND SOCRATIC CLUES

Schleiermacher clearly felt the weight of the long history of Plato interpretation. He decided to begin his own interpretation with misunderstanding – that is to say, with the question of why Plato had previously been so misunderstood. Early in his "General Introduction" Schleiermacher tried to account for why Plato, perhaps more than any other writer, had been so misunderstood. He identified two "incorrect judgments" about Plato and, in light of them, developed his own method for surmounting them. Understanding, in other words, sometimes begins in misunderstanding. First, there is the complete "failure to understand" (*Nichtverstehen*, 24) that stems from viewing Plato as a "dialectician" more intent upon tearing down arguments than on constructing his own. Second, there are the "misunderstandings" (*Mißverständnisse*, 34) that result from the appeal to some supposed esoteric Platonic tradition. The former line of interpretation failed because of its arbitrary division of Plato's works; the latter, because of its equally arbitrary, uncritical appeal to some esoteric system. Schleiermacher avoided both mistakes by making a distinction between "system" and "unity." Whether or not there is a Platonic system, there is clearly a *unity* in Plato's thought and works. Yet, if at the beginning of his quest to understand Plato he has only, on the one side, the particulars and details established by his "higher grammar" and, on the other, the woeful misunderstandings of previous interpreters, and if the new criticism eschews prior philosophical and dogmatic commitments, then on what basis can Schleiermacher affirm any unity? Schleiermacher located that unity not so much in Plato's philosophy as in his person, in his artistic genius.

Preliminarily, the view of Plato as artist accomplished two things. It conveyed an initial, albeit cursory, sense of some whole: "Even within a single text the particular can only be understood from out of the whole, and a cursory reading to get an overview of the whole must therefore precede the more precise explication."[14] Yet, because it is only cursory, it needs to be tested in relation to the texts. The view of Plato as artist also permitted Schleiermacher to turn to Plato himself for hints by seeking interpretive clues in the Platonic texts. Most especially, he turned to the *Phaedrus*, a notoriously difficult dialogue to interpret, and yet a dialogue the importance of which was beyond dispute.

In his ordering of the Platonic dialogues, Schleiermacher (erroneously, as it turned out) identified the *Phaedrus* as the first: it must have been chronologically the earliest because it is logically prior; it contained the "seeds" of his entire philosophy. Schleiermacher explained that his "Introduction to the *Phaedrus*," which immediately follows the "General Introduction" in the first volume of *Plato's Works*, is the longest of all the individual introductions because it is in the *Phaedrus* that Plato sets forth his basic method, a method that is inseparable from content (70). It is hardly accidental that, in discovering and explicating Plato's philosophical method, Schleiermacher articulated and developed his own method of interpretation. In other words, Schleiermacher's interpretative theory – his hermeneutics – emerged out of the praxis of translating and interpreting Plato. It thus makes sense to begin with the "Introduction to the *Phaedrus*." Although his "General Introduction" is nothing less than his methodological prolegomenon for the art of interpreting Plato, it was in working on the *Phaedrus* that Schleiermacher had arrived at many of those very principles and guidelines that he then developed in the "General Introduction."

Three of the most notorious problems of Plato interpretation arise in the *Phaedrus*: What is the main topic of the *Phaedrus*? How are the two parts of the dialogue related? And how seriously are we to take Socrates' stated preference for oral communication over writing? Schleiermacher answered each of these questions in an interesting and novel way and, in the process, discovered three Socratic clues which he then applied to the entire Platonic canon. He began his "Introduction to the *Phaedrus*" by addressing the felt need on the part of countless interpreters to assign various subtitles, and he warned that we must set aside all prejudice and look anew at the issue. In doing so, he found a Socratic clue. Paraphrasing Socrates (at *Phaedrus*, 264c) he noted that a speech must be formed like a living creature, with a body suitable to a mind and with well-proportioned parts (71). This principle of the organic body (or, the somatic metaphor) became for Schleiermacher a guiding principle of interpretation: a speech, a text, or a body of texts must be seen as an organic body with essential, natural connections and proportions. If this principle does not apply, the speech (or text) is not really worthy of our attention. Yet we know – as even his detractors admit – that Plato's dialogues are worthy of attention and that the *Phaedrus*, in particular, commands our attention. Therefore we are compelled to look further, beyond the appearance of unrelated parts, for essential relations. When anything stands in relation to a whole, Plato informs us, it behooves us to discover just what the necessary relation is.

Schleiermacher therefore decided that he should search for the real subject matter of the *Phaedrus* in the second part, rather than in the famous third speech of the first part. The second part, however, presents another obstacle to understanding. Socrates' criticism of rhetoric as a false art is not unexpected, but his redefinition of it in terms of dialectics is. In carefully considering what Plato means by making dialectics the true foundation of rhetoric, Schleiermacher came across a second Socratic clue: dialectics is an art, "a systematic art" (see *Phaedrus*, 276e, 265d). Dialectics is "true science" and "true art" because it proceeds by a twofold process of *collecting* together what appears scattered and *dissecting* a body along its natural joints (265d–e). Schleiermacher's translation of *technē* as *Kunst* communicates a double meaning of "art" as scientific method and aesthetic principle. The dialectical method is one that brings the many, the parts, together "in a systematic and completely exhaustive manner" (74). This is an aesthetic principle in that the "body" is an artistic unity, by which is meant everything is internally, harmoniously, complexly, and beautifully related. This second, aesthetic clue is really an extension of the first, but whereas the somatic metaphor tells us how to view a speech or text, this principle of dialectics as art tells us how to proceed. The Socratic method is to begin with well-known particulars and, by connecting similar concepts, to arrive at "higher" concepts; also, by means of dialectical movements between the inner and the outer, to propel ourselves "to the innermost soul of the whole work" (78). When these two basic movements are in turn connected with each other, this "scientific method" belongs to "art" (73).

These first two interpretative principles did not allow Schleiermacher to rest in his interpretation of the *Phaedrus* – otherwise he would have had to conclude that part one (with its three examples of rhetoric) is merely the playground for part two (with its redefinition of rhetoric in terms of dialectics); that would mean, however, that the relationship between the two parts is neither essential nor internal. Schleiermacher thus knew that he had not yet arrived at the "correct" view and that he had to push further "inward." This drove him back to the first part, to Socrates' famous speech. He then recognized *eros* as the "impulse" (*Trieb*), or the originating, inward force of the soul. Not accidentally, the innermost soul of the text is about the innermost spirit of the human. "Thereby all problems are solved," Schleiermacher concluded, "and this commends itself as the true unity of the work – bringing out, vivifying, and connecting everything" (79). The subject matter of the *Phaedrus* is therefore nothing less than philosophy itself. The *Phaedrus* is not about one philosophical theme or another – whether beauty, love, or rhetoric; it is, rather, the "breath of the whole" (87, cf. 67) The first part speaks to philosophy's impulse – love or *eros*; the second to its method – dialectics. These two, impulse and method, were always present in Socrates' exchanges and permeated his entire thought. Their separate presentation in the *Phaedrus* is one of the reasons why Schleiermacher determined the dialogue to be the first: Plato first presents separately what are really united so that we may understand them; through the remaining dialogues he will more and more reincorporate and reunite what, in reality, is not separate.

Yet, having found the unity, Schleiermacher still faced the further obstacle of Socrates' suspicion of writing, introduced toward the end of the *Phaedrus*. The perceived danger is that writing will introduce forgetfulness and make knowledge external rather than internal (*Phaedrus*, 275a). This was so problematic for Schleiermacher that he found the need to address it in his "General Introduction" rather than in the separate introduction to the *Phaedrus*. In addition to appearing to undermine Plato's very act of writing the dialogues, it also threatened to undermine Schleiermacher's own critical insistence that Plato is to be found in the extant documents alone. Those espousing the esoteric tradition appealed (and continue to appeal) to this passage as textual evidence that Plato's true philosophical teachings were handed down orally (and secretly) to his disciples and that the written dialogues were merely a decoy for the masses.

Schleiermacher, not surprisingly, interpreted Socrates' preference for *oral* communication as supporting evidence for his own claim regarding the importance of the dialogue form in Plato's *written* texts. This difficult passage provided him with another Socratic clue: it speaks to the purpose of philosophy, which is communication. Even though ideally the communication of ideas is done through dialogue, Schleiermacher suggested that Socrates nonetheless concedes that the risk of writing should be taken since the real purpose of dialogue is pedagogy: "Standing in the presence of and in lively interaction with the student, the teacher can know in each moment what the student grasps and so can assist the movement of the understanding whenever it falters" (39). Plato's method was a Socratic method insofar as his written dialogue, a "living composition" (75), perfectly imitated the "oral, living instruction" that Socrates had perfected (39). The imitation is necessary because the student, now the reader, although no longer in the presence of the teacher, must nevertheless be brought through the same processes of understanding. If the method of philosophy is dialectics, and its impulse *eros*, then its purpose is the kind of communication that brings the student-reader to knowledge. What is important, in other words, is the form of the dialogue, whether it be spoken or written.

Together, these three Socratic clues – the somatic metaphor, dialectics as art, and the importance of dialogue – all suggest that Plato is to be viewed as an artist. Whatever proclivities Schleiermacher-the-romantic may have had to interpret a genius like Plato as an artist, he found warrants for just such an interpretation in Plato's texts. The *Phaedrus* established the following for Schleiermacher: "That is the method of Plato and the triumph of his artistic [*künstlerisch*] mind, that in his great and varied forms nothing is without meaning and that he leaves nothing for chance or blind arbitrariness to determine; rather, for him, everything is appropriate and effective in accordance with everything else" (77).

PLATO AS ARTIST

We are now in a better position to judge what work Plato-as-artist actually did in Schleiermacher's interpretation of Plato. As we have seen, two convictions defined the new text criticism and its application to Plato: Plato is to be found only in those texts determined to be authentic; and discovering the original (chronological) ordering of the texts is crucial for understanding Plato's philosophy. The view of Plato as artist guided Schleiermacher in carrying out these two important philological tasks. I turn now to Schleiermacher's "General Introduction."

The artistic unity of the Platonic corpus

Included in the view of Plato as artist is the view of Plato's writings as works of art – indeed as *one* work of art. And, Schleiermacher pointed out, "We have no other telling evidence of his greatness and excellence than these writings" (33). One of the profound contradictions of the esoteric interpretation of Plato, as Schleiermacher saw it, was that, in either altogether denying the importance of the extant written dialogues or in assigning to them a secondary status, it undermined the very genius its adherents sought to extol and perpetuate. It is useless, Schleiermacher scolded, to lament over some lost treasure or to search in desperation for some hidden truth. Plato's extant writings are all we have and all we really need to have. Schleiermacher's argument regarding the exclusive authority of the authentic, written texts (hence his adamant rejection of the esoteric tradition) was so persuasive that it became the dominant scholarly assumption in Plato studies for the next century and a half. It followed simply from the central tenets of the new criticism, the main task of which is the determination of authenticity. This, then, was the "first" task of his Introductions: to determine and explain "which texts are really Plato's and which are not" (50).

The "second" task of his Introductions is that of "arranging" the authentic texts. To see the genius of Plato and to grasp the content of his thought, we must restore the original order of the dialogues. Just such a restoration is what Schleiermacher took to be his most important contribution to the field of Plato research. The problem with the external method is that, even had it been successful in dating and sequentially ordering the dialogues, it would have revealed very little about their meaning and relations. That is why Schleiermacher saw his internal method as a necessary complement and supplement to Tennemann's external method. Whereas Tennemann had been interested in trying to date the composition of various dialogues, Schleiermacher wanted to discern "the real and essential relation of the works of Plato to one another" (47). For him, restoring the original order of the dialogues was one and the same thing with explicating essential, necessary, and natural relations. Meaning and content are revealed through relations and interconnections. Indeed, that was why Schlegel and Schleiermacher had set out to translate *all* of Plato's works rather than just a few.

The task of arranging the dialogues was of such fundamental importance to Schleiermacher that he did not think the task of determining authenticity could be done apart from it. The two tasks, he maintained, "mutually support and confirm each other" (60). This relates back to the first Socratic clue. The dialogues judged to be authentic are not just some scattered, unrelated pieces. They rather "form a trunk [*Stamm*] from which the rest seem to be only offshoots, so that the relationship to them affords the best distinguishing feature for determining their origin. At the same time, regarding the second task of ordering, all essential moments of general connection must already be given in that trunk" (54). In other words, as he approached the twofold task he set out for himself in his Introductions, Schleiermacher kept in mind Socrates' saying that a speech should be seen as an organic body. This time Schleiermacher applied the somatic metaphor to not just one, but to all of the Platonic dialogues. They form a written *corpus*, in the stronger sense of that term.

Sticking closely to Socrates' elaboration of the process of collection and dissection (see *Phaedrus*, 265d–e), Schleiermacher argued that viewing Plato's works as a "living creature" or organic body means that no part is dispensable, that the various parts are organically (which is to say, essentially and vitally) connected, and that those connections can only be understood if "the whole nature of a body" (38) is recognized. Interpretation must therefore begin with an acquaintance with the whole – a body, a text, or set of texts – and must then proceed to dismember or dissect [*zerstückeln*] that body. Schleiermacher thus applied the first and second Socratic clues as he set about restoring the original order of the Platonic dialogues. The "vessels" and "bones" must be separated out and compared with each other. The end, however, of this process of dismemberment, dissection, or de-composition is not to leave a corpse behind. There is another part of the process of understanding that completes the dissection – namely a restoration of the original connections, a re-composition. It is this part of the interpretative process that distinguishes the artist from the mere analyst. Once each "limb" is understood (through the process of separation and dismemberment) as a whole in itself, its place in and contribution to the "body" can also be understood. Those "limbs" or parts must then be rejoined to the body, and only then can the body itself be understood. When applied to Plato's dialogues, this process of dis-membering and re-membering, de-composing and re-composing, allows us to restore the individual dialogues to the natural connection according to which "they, as continually more complete expositions, gradually developed Plato's ideas; the end being that, each dialogue is simultaneously seen as a whole in itself as well as in its connection with the rest, so Plato himself can finally be understood as philosopher and artist [*Philosoph und Künstler*]" (39).

Dialogue as "art form"

The view of Plato as artist also instructed Schleiermacher to pay attention to form. Along with his insistence that we adhere only to the extant written texts, Schleiermacher's attention to the dialogue form was perhaps his greatest contribution to Plato interpretation. It was inconceivable to Schleiermacher that a work of art would be considered apart from its form. The dialogue form is none other than Plato's "art form" (*Kunstform*). Yet most interpreters had considered the dialogue form to be either a nuisance or, worse, a deliberately placed obstacle intended to veil the real meaning and content of Plato's philosophical doctrines. In Schleiermacher's judgment, those who disparage the dialogue form as mere embellishment have no understanding of Plato whatsoever. Schleiermacher was only being consistent. His view of the unity of Plato's dialogues held as much for the unity – the indissolubility – of form and content as for the unity of the parts. In Plato's philosophy, he wrote, "form and content are inseparable, and each sentence is rightly understood only in its own place, and within the connections and restrictions, that Plato established for it" (38). More even than tolerating or appreciating the dialogue form, we are to relish and to praise it on account of its "mimetic and dramatic composition, by virtue of which persons and circumstances are individualized, and which, by general confession, radiate so much beauty and charm throughout the dialogues of Plato"(59).

That being said, the dialogue form was also an important tool for Schleiermacher insofar as it aided him in his two main philological tasks. As to the first and properly critical task, he distinguished between two stages: that of identifying those dialogues of the "first rank," which are those that form the main "trunk" or body; and that of identifying those dialogues of the "second rank," which although authentic are either occasional pieces (such as the *Apology*) or in some way peripheral. The second stage presents the most difficulties, since the characteristic marks of Plato are by definition not as clearly present as they are in dialogues of the first rank. Before Schleiermacher it had been common practice to employ two criteria in judging authenticity: the distinctiveness of the language, and the range of subject matter. To these two Schleiermacher added a third criterion – that of form and composition. The dialogue form, beautifully and exquisitely executed, was Plato's signature. Schleiermacher took this new criterion so seriously that he argued that the absence or even diminishment of the artful dialogue form should flag any text as dubious with regard to authenticity. In dialogues of the first rank, these three characteristics – language, subject matter, and form – are all present in a clear and mutually determining way. In dialogues of the second rank, such clarity and co-inherence fade. At this stage of interpretation, the criterion of form becomes the chief one because it is always present. Schleiermacher concluded "that this distinct form can never be wholly lacking, and that Plato, even in the most insignificant pieces (what he wrote as a study or on someone's order) will have applied some of this art" (17). Attention to the form of the dialogues thus "yields the surest canon for judging their authenticity" (59). As to how attention to form aided Schleiermacher in the second philological task of ordering the dialogues, it is necessary to consider his view of Plato as pedagogical artist.

The art of pedagogy

Schleiermacher's Plato was also an artist because he was the perfect teacher whose aim was "not only to explain his own thought to others in a lively way, but precisely thereby to excite and uplift theirs in a lively way" (38). Although the somatic and aesthetic principles – derived from the first and second Socratic clues – were indispensable for restoring some of the essential relations of the dialogues, they could not supply a full, chronologically sequential ordering of the dialogues, which was a central aim of the new criticism. Schleiermacher, as we have seen, was committed to restoring the original order of the dialogues, but he had, early on, grown skeptical about discovering a strict chronological ordering, complete with dates. There was simply not enough historical evidence to date, or even to arrange chronologically, a significant number of the dialogues. While he therefore maintained the external method as a "natural test" (i.e., external markers should be respected and be used to limit discoveries arrived at by the internal method), Schleiermacher sought another way of determining the original sequence of the dialogues, a sequence not necessarily fixed by dates. Plato's progressive pedagogy supplied that "progressive connection" (67). This line of interpretation is closely related to the third Socratic clue Schleiermacher had found in the *Phaedrus*: the essential character and purpose of the dialogue form is "to compel the soul of the reader to the spontaneous generation of ideas" (60).

According to Schleiermacher's interpretation of Plato as perfect, artistic pedagogue, the original ordering of the dialogues does not reflect some development of Plato's ideas; that is, his early dialogues do not contain immature and unformed views that were refined and corrected in the later dialogues. It reflects, instead, Plato's awareness of the process of learning, the needs of the reader-student in coming to knowledge, and the interconnection of the ideas being imparted. Plato, he explained,

> cannot progress further in another dialogue if he cannot assume as established the effect intended in an earlier dialogue, so that the same point amplified as the end of one dialogue must also be assumed as the beginning and ground of another. Now if Plato ended in separate presentations of the individual sciences, then one might assume that he had developed each gradually on its own and would have to discover two different sequences of dialogues, one pertaining to ethics and the other to physics. Since, however, he presents them as a connected whole, and it is characteristic of him to think of them everywhere as essentially connected and inseparable, so also are the preparations for them united and made through consideration of their common grounds and laws, and therefore there are not many, independent series of Platonic dialogues progressing next to one another but only one series comprehending everything within itself. (42–3)

The unity of the dialogues, therefore, is not only an organic whole or aesthetic unity, it is also a pedagogical, progressive unity.

The earlier dialogues are those which awaken and excite through the use of myth and especially vivacious dialogue form. The middle dialogues are those that develop and connect specific themes and doctrines and ideas. The later are those which present those same themes in a systematic, scientific way, connecting them under the two main categories of ethics and science. Yet even the most systematic and "scientific" of presentations – for instance, a university lecture – must contain some essential element of the living, reciprocal exchange between teacher and student through the dialogue form.

A TRILOGY OF TRILOGIES

With the aid of the *leitmotiv* of Plato-as-artist, and all that it included and entailed, Schleiermacher arrived at an ordering of the whole which was at once somatic, aesthetic, and sequential. The authentic dialogues of the first rank having been determined, and Plato's progressive pedagogy being kept in mind, the interpreter will begin to see the dialogues of the first rank fall naturally into groupings. The *Phaedrus, Protagoras*, and *Parmenides* fall in together as "the elementary part of the Platonic works" (67). Similarly, the *Republic, Timaeus*, and *Critias* fall in together on account of their "objective, scientific presentation" (63). These two groups form the bookends, so to speak, of the progressively ordered body of works. Each is an "inseparable whole" (64). With these two outer wholes in place, a middle grouping appears, although its order and relations are not as clear as in the other two groups. What is clear is the development of the philosophical method and the progression of certain ideas. In considering these three groups, it occurred to Schleiermacher that each comprises a trilogy of sorts. In short, Schleiermacher concluded that Plato's works together constitute a trilogy of trilogies.[15]

To invert this order, Schleiermacher claimed, especially the order of the two bookend trilogies, would offend the interpreter's philological "feeling"

Trilogies in the Dialogues

First Trilogy	Second Trilogy	Third (incomplete) Trilogy
1. *Phaedrus*	1. *Theaetetus*	1. *The Republic*
2. *Protagoras*	2. Sub-trilogy of *Sophist*, *Statesman*, and *Symposium* (a dialogue of the second rank)	2. (*Timaeus*)
3. *Parmenides*	3. *Phaedo* and *Philebus*	3. (*Critias*)

(65) – clearly an aesthetic principle in that the interpreter is one who must be an artist, who can sense perfect proportion, relations, and internal movements.

THE INTERPRETER AS ARTIST

It takes an artist to interpret an artist. The scholarship required for translating, interpreting, and explicating Plato's dialogues necessarily includes art – a keen sense of analogy and proportion, of the whole, of what is fitting; an ability to engage in an almost infinite process of connecting and relating, of applying rules, of testing and challenging, of creating and even destroying, of communicating and mediating. As we have seen, Schleiermacher saw his role as one of presenting a new view of Plato so that others might gain new access to his works. In other words, it is fair to say, Schleiermacher understood his own role, in part, as that of an author and mediator. In his study *Imagination and Authority: Theological Authorship in the Modern Tradition,* John E. Thiel has identified the romantic understanding of theological authorship as a major paradigm shift. With Schleiermacher in mind as the main Protestant representative of the romantic paradigm, Thiel explains, "The theologian's task was no longer seen as the mimetic representation of an objective revelation but as the imaginative construction of the historical experience of salvation."[16] The theologian's task as here described certainly has its parallels in Plato interpretation. Schleiermacher understood perhaps better than anyone in his day the historical nature of thought and communication, including his own. He endeavored not to provide a final, definitive account of Plato's philosophy so much as to recover the living and vital connections of the dialogues, to recapture their spirit, and to awaken something in the (early nineteenth-century German) reader. He anticipated that future generations of Plato scholars would come to different findings, as indeed they have done. Yet it says so much of his work on Plato that scholars have continued, throughout two centuries, to engage with Schleiermacher, either to refute his interpretation of Plato or to retrieve some of its insights.

Notes

1 An English translation of Schleiermacher's "Introductions" was made available early on by William Dobson (1836, reprint 1973) under the title *Introductions to the Dialogues of Plato.* His translation is useful but not really adequate for English-speaking scholars today. Schleiermacher's "Die Einleitungen zur Übersetzung des Platon" (1804–28) has recently been made available as an independent text in *Friedrich Daniel Ernst Schleiermacher, Über die*

Philosophie Platons, ed. Peter M. Steiner, 21–387. Translations given here are mine, based on this edition. All internal page references are to this edition. Cf. *Platon im Kontext: Sämtliche Werke auf CD-Rom, in den Übersetzungen und mit den Einleitungen in die Dialoge von Friedrich Schleiermacher*, Berlin: Karsten Worm, 1998.

2 *Platons Werke von F. Schleiermacher.* The ambitious aim of translating the entire *corpus* never came to fruition, since Schleiermacher never got around to finishing the seventh volume (which would have included the *Timaeus, Critias*, and *Laws*) before his death in 1834.

3 For a more detailed analysis of the conception of the Plato project, the central themes in Schleiermacher's "General Introduction" to the Platonic Dialogues, and the controversies surrounding it, see Lamm 2000, 206–39.

4 Böckh 1804, 83.

5 Tigerstedt 1974, 63.

6 Schlegel 1800.

7 Schleiermacher, *Hermeneutics and Criticisms*, 3–4.

8 Schleiermacher, "Einleitungen," 27.

9 Schleiermacher, *Hermeneutics and Criticism*, 30.

10 Schleiermacher, "Einleitungen," 28.

11 Schleiermacher, *Hermeneutics and Criticism*, 11.

12 Ibid. 11.

13 Schleiermacher, "Einleitungen," 28.

14 Ibid. 27.

15 For more on this ordering of a trilogy of trilogies and how it served Schleiermacher in interpreting Plato, see Lamm 2003, 1–25.

16 Thiel 1991, 21.

Part II

Schleiermacher as Theologian

6 Shaping an academic discipline: the *Brief Outline on the Study of Theology*

RICHARD CROUTER

> The fact that in such knowledge the knower's own being comes
> into play certainly shows the limits of method, but not of
> science.   (Gadamer, *Truth and Method*)

Few theologians in the history of the Christian church have been as rigorously self-reflective about the craft of theology as was Friedrich Schleiermacher. Always a master teacher, Schleiermacher developed a curriculum for Protestant theology that reflects a penchant for relating thought and practice. In his hands, theological methods must be engaged with actual history and the life of religious institutions. Of course, as an intellectual pursuit a secure starting point for theology must be given. Like Plato, arguably the favorite of his Greek predecessors, Schleiermacher's architectonic cast of mind insists on linking matters of intellectual principle and foundational insight to their specific, embodied details. Although less philosophical in some respects, his preferred Reformation theologian, John Calvin, exemplified an equally bold ambition and similarly systematic cast of mind.

Not surprisingly, the question of theological method runs deep in modern Christian thought. With the dawn of historical criticism and Newtonian physics few verities of the Christian faith could any longer be taken for granted. After the work of dramatist-critic Gotthold Ephraim Lessing (1729–81) the gulf between accidental truths of history and eternal truths of reason seemed permanent. At the end of the eighteenth century rival theological camps staked out positions, none of which Schleiermacher viewed with satisfaction. The Kantian view, in which Jesus exemplifies the moral ideal of practical philosophy, set no store by Christian doctrine, biblical theology, and the life of the church. That of a biblically based supernaturalism, in which the Bible's miracles prove the deity of Jesus, sought to shield this position from rational assaults. The speculative rationalism of Fichte and Hegel, Schleiermacher's successive philosophical colleagues in Berlin, subsumed the claims of theology beneath a dominant philosophical truth.

In contrast with these efforts Schleiermacher's lectures on theological encyclopedia address these issues in a novel way. In his day, not unlike our own, theology as an intellectual discipline was poorly defined, its tasks and methods anything but self-evident. In his words, "One cannot tell what theology means from the name alone, because it has served up many aberrant meanings ... Yet names cannot be changed arbitrarily; one can only precisely define how they are to be understood."[1] If the condition of theology has not improved today, and numerous intervening solutions have failed, we are nonetheless still challenged by his way of defining its component parts and illustrating their interrelationships. Schleiermacher's understanding of theology is philosophical while avoiding undue dependence on any specific school of philosophy, historical while not succumbing to historical relativism, and practical while placing its concern for lived religion squarely on the shoulders of a well-educated clergy. His theology has the avowed task of reconciling the substance of Biblical and creedal teachings with a distinctively modern account of Christian consciousness. Schleiermacher thus launched a systematic program of theological inquiry that stands apart from those of his contemporaries. Whatever we may think of his achievement, he was right to remind us that "one cannot tell what theology means from the name alone."

In what follows I first offer a context for understanding what makes Schleiermacher's *Brief Outline* distinctive in the history of theology. Its groundbreaking tripartite division of theology (philosophical, historical, and practical) is examined in the next three sections of this chapter. I then end by appraising certain issues within the work that continue to inform contemporary debates about Schleiermacher's theological method. Of course, the work provided a blueprint for the main principles of both editions (1821–2; 1830–1) of his magnum opus, the *Christian Faith*. This chapter does not explicitly address specific methodological issues that arise from within his dogmatics.[2] For the careful student of the *Christian Faith*, parallels with the *Brief Outline*'s recommendations are readily apparent and well worth analyzing. Yet it seems salutary to focus our present attention on the program of theology as it is laid out in the *Brief Outline*.

CONTEXT OF THE *BRIEF OUTLINE*

By the end of the eighteenth century the term "encyclopedia" had begun to be used for texts that introduced the premises and contents of a field of knowledge in ways that were not necessarily arranged alphabetically. Hegel's *Encyclopedia of the Philosophical Sciences* (1817) produced such a work for his system of philosophy. It was largely to counter the influence of the text we are analyzing that the Hegelian philosopher Karl Rosenkranz produced his own *Encyclopedia of Theological Sciences* (1831).[3] Such introductions often surveyed rival positions and provided literature in the field, while advancing their author's views. In contrast with much of this literature the *Brief Outline* makes scant reference to the thought of others. Although it was lean and skeletal even in its second edition, the text challenges its readers, as future pastor-theologians of the German Protestant churches, to appropriate a boldly personal, self-consistent vision of the theological task.

In presenting his ideas, we do well to acknowledge that Schleiermacher's tripartite division of theology (philosophical, historical, and practical) draws from a time-conditioned idiom regarding the academic disciplines.[4] Aspects of the *Brief Outline* are unthinkable apart from definitions given elsewhere in his system of the sciences. Following the ancient Greeks, Schleiermacher contrasts "ethics" (as the "speculative science of reason") with "physics" (as the "speculative science of nature"), a usage that reflects Aristotle's notion of rational human beings who live in a world (ethos) that is distinguishable from nature. Ethics seeks to attain a coherent and consistent view of the abiding forms of the human world; history ("the empirical science of reason") strives to understand the actual unfolding of it. Ethics and history operate on distinctive planes; the task of analyzing and clarifying concepts is distinguished from the task of grasping the world as it develops. It is relevant for the discussion that follows to observe that Schleiermacher further distinguishes between a *critical* theoretical discipline and a *technical* theoretical discipline or art, both of which relate contemplative to experiential knowing. Philosophical theology, as a *critical* discipline, connects what appears in history with the speculative task, while practical theology, as a *technical* discipline, consists of the art of relating what appears in history to practice.

These interrelated intellectual pursuits bear upon an analysis of the *Brief Outline* and inform its depiction of theological methodology. Yet caution is in order, since assumptions that inform Schleiermacher's disciplinary matrix do not neatly translate into the disciplinary debates of our own day. He maintains that the materials of dogmatic theology, like those of history, are empirical, and insists that humanly experienced religious reality, whether past or present, must be explicated intellectually. Unlike some exponents and defenders of religious thought, Schleiermacher thinks theology arises from the bedrock of a personal conviction that does not directly stem from proof or argument. Consistently with that approach, theology is construed as a "positive science," whose organizing center lies outside itself in the practical tasks for which the science exists.[5] Theology functions to prepare leaders for service in the Christian church, much as one goes about preparing well-educated barristers or physicians.[6] Readers with skeptical inclinations will not approach the *Brief Outline*'s teachings empathetically within the circle of Christian witness but will still be capable of grasping how theology as an academic discipline relates to its own ends.

Schleiermacher does not hold the view, sometimes attributed to Max Weber, that objectivity is best reached through value-free inquiry.[7] For it to become real, knowledge requires a subjective moment of judgment through which it is personally appropriated. *Brief Outline* (§ 101) acknowledges that historical studies "can never be wholly divested of the scholar's own particular viewpoints and opinions," even if we must try to keep our material free of these biases as much as possible. Like more recent students of historical epistemology, Schleiermacher holds that history seeks to make objective judgments about the past, even if "higher criticism carries out its task, for the most part, only by approximation" (§ 113).[8] Such approximations, however, are disciplined judgments, not just casual opinions. The commitment to grasping the human social world historically does not mean that Schleiermacher thinks we should, or even could, comprehend the human world as nothing but historical. By bringing reason to bear on the course of Christian history a student learns to "exercise his own discretion in matters of church leadership." "Nothing is more fruitless than a piling up of historical learning which neither serves any practical purpose nor offers anything for the use of others in its presentation" (§ 191). As the *Brief Outline* makes clear, dogmatics must be based upon a personal conviction of the Christian religion's truth. Like Nietzsche in *Use and Abuse of History for Life* (1874), the *Brief Outline* calls for a profound engagement, not just a scholarly encounter, with history. To study the Christian past chiefly for information or to establish a chronology remains useless. To analyze the meaning of theological teaching as it relates the essence of Christianity to the ongoing life of the church constitutes the agenda of the *Brief Outline*.

Intended to introduce new students to the discipline of theology, the *Brief Outline* is the central work in which to probe Schleiermacher's approach to theological method. It was his first major book to appear in English, some seventy-eight years before his dogmatics was translated.[9] Perhaps owing to its shape as an outline, the impact of the book in Germany and in the English-speaking world has been uneven. Only in recent years has more attention been given to this theological charter alongside the more famous dogmatics that refines its principles even further.[10]

Schleiermacher first lectured on "theological encyclopedia" at the University of Halle (1805–6). He published the first edition of the book in 1811 and a revised version in 1830. He lectured on this material twice in Halle and nine more times in Berlin, including 1831–2, when the lectures were transcribed by David Friedrich Strauß, whose astute theological mind was already evident.[11] Schleiermacher himself acknowledged that his definition of dogmatic theology in the 1811 edition "is too short and aphoristic."[12] Although the stark expression of the first edition seems more cohesive to some readers than its 1830 revision, the later formulations embody his most mature thought. Since the 1811 and 1830 editions were published as mere adumbrations of classroom lectures, neither version conveys everything that Schleiermacher wished to communicate. It is fortunate that the David Friedrich Strauß transcript of these lectures has been available since 1987.[13] Strauß likened the task of taking notes on Schleiermacher's lectures to "photographing a dancer in full motion."[14] His meticulously transcribed text provides Schleiermacher's own commentary on the book's theses and explanations.

LOCATING AND DEFINING THE ESSENCE OF CHRISTIANITY

In addition to using ethics to signal the study of what is human, Schleiermacher's first division of "philosophical theology" bears slight resemblance to the term's usage today. Far from seeking to demonstrate the truth of Christian teaching, "philosophical theology" for Schleiermacher might be paraphrased as "philosophical reflection on the form and content of a religion in its givenness." It undertakes the crucial task of locating and defining the "religious consciousness" and "church community" that are the bedrock of Christian existence. This task is accomplished through the complementary pursuits of apologetics (*BO*, §§ 43–53), which looks outward and locates the church with respect to its origins in history, and polemics (§§ 54–62), which looks inward and analyzes the community's aberrations and afflictions. Although he never wrote a work under the name philosophical theology, *On Religion* as well as most of the "borrowed propositions" in the "Introduction" of the *Christian Faith* fall into this category.[15]

When Schleiermacher published the first edition of his encyclopedia (1811) Hegel had not yet written his *Encyclopedia of Philosophical Sciences*, which seeks to ground the subfields of philosophy in a single principle.[16] But the speculative rationalism of his contemporary German idealists nonetheless influenced Schleiermacher's decision about how to use philosophy within theological inquiry. His dilemma was how to retain the dignity and power of a rational perspective, while allowing it to inform, and to be informed by, the contingencies of historical existence. Such a specific use of philosophical theology broke sharply with the indifference towards historic religion of Kant's rational theology and its sublation to philosophical reason of the German idealists.

Schleiermacher is committed to the idea that human beings are religious by nature and find religious meaning within communities. "Unless religious communities are to be regarded as mere aberrations, it must be possible to show that the existence of such associations is a necessary element for the development of the human spirit" (*BO*, § 22). Espousal of the view that religion is anthropologically necessary is today vigorously debated as a form of "religious essentialism."[17] Yet Schleiermacher appears to have been untroubled by such doubts; for him, "Christian consciousness" stands as a factual given. His unswerving insistence that the Christian instantiation of religion proceeds from the "concept of the pious community, not from the piety of the individual soul," seems to compete with his well-established individualism (*ThEnz*, 21 commenting on § 22). Personal conviction is never absent from the theological task. The primary spiritual datum is the reality of the church in empirical history, a claim that is both normative and demonstrable through the study of history. "If we look into the matter of how Christian theology arose in the beginning, the Christian church was always already earlier, and thus even now for each individual the Christian church is earlier than theology" (*ThEnz*, 32). A given primordial communal piety is chronologically as well as logically prior to the need of the church to develop theology and produce handbooks on church leadership. Such definitional and practical needs arise only with the passage of time in an effort to adjudicate the claims of rival religious communities.

Everything in Schleiermacher's approach to theology hinges on this awareness of the church's religious reality and the need to give it intellectual definition. If, as Schleiermacher maintains, practical theology is the crown toward which theology moves, philosophical theology is the root that identifies the reality of the church and thus gets the project off the ground.[18] This work of defining Christianity's essence philosophically, both in relation to other religions (apologetics), and with respect to its own aberrations (polemics) must be undertaken by every theologian. Schleiermacher directs our attention to "the two main points, the content of theology as the summation of all scientific elements, and the purpose of theology: the leadership of the Christian community," while adding that, "Christianity is a uniquely formed God-consciousness and a community that is founded upon it" (*ThEnz*, 20). The passage testifies to the reality of an original essence of Christianity manifest in history and of the pious community that mediates this content. Because of the need to clarify Christianity's content, inquiry into the essence of Christianity is required. Since the content of Christian consciousness is transmitted through a specific community, this historical resource must also be plumbed as a means of sustaining the original God-consciousness. If a degree of circularity appears in these claims, this is a price Schleiermacher appears willing to pay in order to avoid the pretension of deriving the content of theology from a single foundational starting point.

APPREHENDING THE CHURCH IN TIME AND PLACE

Schleiermacher's appeal to philosophical theology in the *Brief Outline* sets theology in motion by delineating the reality of the church, where Christian consciousness takes on geography and temporality. Historical theology, the work's second division, reaches from the age of the apostles through contemporary dogmatics. Although historical theology is analyzed more extensively (*BO*, §§ 69–256) than either philosophical (§§ 32–68) or practical theology (§§ 257–338), it is tightly interwoven with its corollary disciplines. Historical theology has the dual function of *confirming* philosophical theology, while *laying the foundation* of practical theology. "Since historical theology attempts to exhibit every point of time in its true relation to the idea of Christianity, it follows that it is at once not only the founding [*Begründung*] of practical theology but also the confirming [*Bewährung*] of philosophical theology" (§ 27).[19] Just how this works may be debated. But it seems reasonable to think that historical theology is assigned the task of confirming philosophical theology by examining how its definition of the essence of Christianity has stood up over time. Historical theology thus stands as a distinctive mode of inquiry that is intimately related to the other two divisions of theology.

Today it appears naïve to think that history can preserve meaning or somehow help to ground our moral choices. Historical study appears too much subject to revision to test our life choices effectively. But even in our day Schleiermacher's reasoning on the point has merit, provided that we share what we might call his realist approach to historical epistemology. This approach maintains that, despite the apparent vacillation of historical judgments, historical theology can reliably assay the reality of the Christian consciousness over time. This is so, because historical reasoning preserves not just facts, but repeatedly makes and defends claims about the meaning of those facts.[20] As an empirical inquiry, history feeds our reflection with data that includes highs and lows in the story of the church. Where such reflection encounters more pain than pleasure, say in the era of the Crusades, a negative judgment of those events is rendered only by comparison with the positive teaching of Christ on the love of one's neighbor. On Schleiermacher's view, not to acknowledge the vital significance of a Christian consciousness in history requires a supreme indifference to Christianity.

Like the three main divisions of theology, which stand in dialectical and reciprocal relationships, the subfields of historical theology (exegetical theology, church history, and dogmatics) have tight internal correlations. Outwardly these subfields are related by chronological narrative. Schleiermacher differentiates between the epochs of Christian history. Earliest Christianity should be studied first; it alone provides source material through which philosophical theology can identify the distinctive contours of the church. Dogmatics should be studied last; it frames the issues that inform the minds of pastors as they lead the church in the tasks of preaching and church governance. But the life of Christian faith past and present is grasped more as a living, quasi-organic, entity than as a timeline of events. Since *all of historical theology* reflects the constitutive principle of theology as built on a living tradition of faith (*BO*, § 81), biblical archaism and free contemporary spirituality both distort the truth of this tradition.

As Schleiermacher puts it, since the present "can only be understood as a result of the past ... the entire previous career of Christianity forms a second division of historical theology." Church history is not merely an auxiliary science for biblical exegesis but "rather, both are related to church leadership in the same way, and are not in a subordinated but are in a coordinate relation to each other" (*BO*, § 82). Historical theology draws upon the natural divisions of the modern study of history. Yet as a theological field historical theology is "the indispensable condition of all intelligent effort toward the cultivation of Christianity" and hence "all the other parts of historical study are subordinated to it" (§ 70). Schleiermacher goes to great lengths to rebut static views of the historical development of Christianity. He recognizes the period of the canon and the need for exegetical theology. But Christian meaning does not assume "definitive forms" just because of its *being in the earliest period*, and, however much there is need for exegesis, the term is somewhat arbitrary, since the *interpretation of texts* goes on in all three divisions of historical theology (§ 88).

For church history, the second division of historical theology, the twofold development of the church consists of the history of its common life (*BO*, §§ 166–76) and the history of its doctrines (§§ 177–83). Ethics and doctrine have not come into being merely for the sake of the present; they are bearers of the tradition in history. As historical theologians think about the course of Christian history they must decide how doctrine relates to "the utterances of primitive Christianity" and correlates with philosophical propositions that "are not engendered by the Christian faith as such." Church teaching develops from this oscillating movement between primitive Christianity and philosophical thought. Here the complexity of this interpretive process can only be adumbrated. The methods of inquiry within church history are endless and no one person can master the whole field (§ 184). This creative historical engagement with the church in history leads Schleiermacher to take up dogmatics as the contemporary systematic application of this inquiry (§§ 195–222), which in turn leads to material on Christian ethics as the practical counterpart of doctrine (§§ 223–31).

In turning to dogmatics Schleiermacher was well aware of the novelty of placing this field of inquiry within historical theology. His preference for the designations "dogmatics" or "dogmatic theology" over "systematic theology" is related to this choice. Even though systematic theology rightly stresses that "doctrine is not to be presented as a mere aggregate of propositions, whose coherent interrelation is not clearly known," it nonetheless "conceals, to the detriment of the subject, not only the historical character of the discipline but also its aim in relation to church leadership." As a result, "numerous misinterpretations are bound to arise" (*BO*, § 97). The 1831–2 lectures elaborate:

> One may thereby think that dogmatics is purely historical and the dogmaticians only express factual matters that have nothing to do with conviction. But if we return to the initial insight, this objection drops away, since no one would be a theologian except by virtue of his conviction about Christianity. (*ThEnz*, 99)

The term "dogmatics" puts emphasis on historic teachings that represent the common faith of the church. A church dogmatics is not a "truly scientific dogmatics or a rational theology" and it does not consist of the "private convictions" of the theologian, which might yield a "beautiful book, but not be dogmatics" (*ThEnz*, 99). The useful part of calling it systematic theology lies in showing that theology is not supposed to be just an aggregate of theological insights. But since "this is likewise the case with our designation and position" (*ThEnz*, 99–100), dogmatics remains the preferred name for his craft.

Far from compromising Christian truth, Schleiermacher's rationale for placing dogmatics within historical theology links expressions of doctrine to the actual life of the church. Every theologian must form a coherent picture of the present teachings of the church, "even though after this period runs its course, perhaps it will occur to no one to take a measure of the church exactly at this point" (*ThEnz*, 181). Not surprisingly, dogmatic theology must be undertaken by every generation for very practical reasons. The practical emphasis of these choices is underscored by the way *Brief Outline* follows the discussion of dogmatics and Christian ethics with "church statistics" (§§ 232–50), which inquires into the external conditions of the religious society.

His 1831–2 lectures show Schleiermacher contrasting his threefold arrangement of theology with the fourfold division that was standard in Germany, and subsequently in the English-speaking world.

> In the usual arrangement of theology the chief points are exegetical theology, historical theology, systematic theology, and practical theology. Only two of these, historical and practical, are acknowledged here and the exegetical and the dogmatic are both subordinated to the historical. Here dogmatics thus appears as a part of historical theology, while it usually appears as coordinated with historical theology. The same holds for exegetical theology, about which far fewer objections have been made. (*ThEnz*, 182–3)

It remains for us to clarify further the reasoning that stands behind this significant shift in understanding how dogmatic theology relates to history.

Examined closely, we can identify three features of dogmatics that contribute to his position. First, for Schleiermacher, anchoring dogmatics firmly in history does not compromise the doctrinal statements or put them at risk. As a science dogmatics requires the theologian to clarify and elucidate the ecclesial witness of the Christian consciousness. When Schleiermacher pursues dogmatics as historical theology, he does not abandon reason or personal conviction. Rather, the essence of Christianity (located by the apologetics and defended by the polemics of philosophical theology), lends underlying continuity to the church's historical, that is, developing, existence. Dogmatics differs from a mere account of church doctrine: "Whoever is not convinced of this doctrine, can of course provide a report about it, and about the manner in which its teachings cohere, but not preserve the value of this coherence by what he has established" (*BO*, § 196).[21] As we have seen, historical theology serves to *found* practical theology and to *confirm* philosophical theology. As an example of an empty and unproductive system of theology Schleiermacher cites the work of Julius August Ludwig Wegscheider (1771–1849), whose system of rationalist Protestant theology does not help a reader "locate the connection of individual ideas" (*ThEnz*, 187). To locate ideas, for Schleiermacher, is to encounter them in history (past and present). The necessary element, alongside speculative and empirical uses of reason, is faith (hence a *Glaubenslehre* or "doctrine of faith"), formed in response to the proclamation of the Christian community.

Second, dogmatic theologians do not work out of their own resources and imaginative powers. The dogmatic theologian does not risk willfulness by speaking individually, but incorporates in his work the symbolic confessions and controversial interpretations that have arisen within Christianity, especially historic Protestantism. The historic symbols, which first arose from Scripture, enable Schleiermacher to utilize the entire sweep of the Christian past as grist for his dogmatic mill. As a mature churchman Schleiermacher wrote an *Open Letter* (1831) to protest the theology of contemporary Breslauer theologians, Daniel von Cölln and David Schulz, who rejected the historic "symbolic confessions" and sought to impose their own confession on the church.[22] By contrast, a properly dogmatic Protestant theologian aims at a level of unity within Protestant teaching without insisting on uniformity. Whatever our judgments may be about the relative emphases and substantive choices offered by the details of Schleiermacher's dogmatics, his aim is to respect the historic expressions of the church's faith.

Third, being aligned within historical theology does not make dogmatic theology less argumentative. Theology must not smooth over controversy artificially. A merely external historical report ill serves dogmatics; the same is true of a wholly irenic theology. Such efforts leave out "the middle terms necessary to form a truly demonstrative argument" and will also weaken "the precision in defining concepts necessary for winning confidence in the presentation" (*BO*, § 197). Like philosophy, the discipline of a theology that draws from history must rigorously defend its claims. Even working historians pursue a similar goal, provided that their interpretations of the past are well-argued and reach beyond mere chronicle.

These three interrelated foci (the necessity of a theologian's personal conviction, the fact that conviction draws from historic biblical and church tradition, thus avoiding idiosyncracy, and the argumentative nature and defense of this inquiry) make it reasonable to view dogmatics as historical theology. For Schleiermacher there is no better way to make it clear that "the present moment is the result of the entire past, but especially of the most recent epoch" (*ThEnz*, 217). By positioning the work of dogmatics within (not beyond or above) historical consciousness Schleiermacher avoids the twin perils of a rank Biblicism and of an idiosyncratic individual philosophy of faith. The former truncates Christian consciousness by ending it with the apostolic age, while the latter acts as if Christian truth and meaning is oblivious to its past expressions. For Schleiermacher, "There is a great difference whether we have to preserve each phrase of the canon, or whether we say, the manner in which each phrase of the canon is expressed is the sheer expression of our conviction." He continues:

> This [the former of these views] is not at all possible, since our conviction results from the entire development that lies between us and the canon. If a theologian allows himself to move in a wholly natural manner, then he will not easily present his conviction in the field of dogmatics in biblical expressions, but in wholly other ones. The more scientific he wishes to be, the less the untreated expressions of the canon satisfy him; we have a history of the development of concepts before us, without reference to which we cannot adequately express our conviction.   (*ThEnz*, 242–3)

Like Hans Georg Gadamer, cited above (p. 111), Schleiermacher asserts that the claims of Christian theology are not less but more scientific, that is, conceptually coherent, for encompassing the theologian's own being and existence within history. In confronting biblical texts, their alien elements must be "referred back to the historical conditions under which language necessarily stands." But just as an adequate account of Christian theology's definitions of faith cannot merely be parroted from biblical phrases, it also cannot be reduced to the novel inventions of philosophy.

> Even though dogmatics calls for one's own conviction, it still should not be taken apart from the connection with historical theology and presented as systematic theology, for an ambiguity arises in this expression, namely that dogmatics has been placed under the diction of philosophy in a different manner than has been done here, where the organization, juxtaposition, and terminology have to be justified dialectically.   (*ThEnz*, 243)

For Schleiermacher a "correct use of philosophy runs through the treatment of all the theological disciplines." By contrast a wrong use of philosophy is "the death of exegesis and the death of history" (*ThEnz*, 244). All the reproaches against a "systematic dogmatics" – Schleiermacher uses the phrase one time in the Strauß lectures – rest upon a misunderstanding of these two uses of philosophy. "There is nothing of philosophical content in dogmatics, but what there is of philosophy in it is only the dialectical justification of the arrangement of the whole in its organization and further in its individual formulae" (*ThEnz*, 244). In the form of reflective and dialectical thinking philosophy provides an "intellectual location" and thus a warrant for religious meaning. In the end, for Schleiermacher, the potential misuse of an historical awareness is not nearly as great a potential enemy of dogmatics as the more popular alternatives of a biblical literalism or a rationalist system of theology.

LEADING AND GOVERNING THE CHURCH IN THE PRESENT

It remains for us to round out an understanding of Schleiermacher's theological program by exploring the idea of practical theology as its crown. His metaphor reminds us that practical theology is the place where the theologian's gifts yield fruit and exert leadership within the life of a congregation, the larger church body, and the world of human affairs.

Schleiermacher's commitment not just to the high and lofty status of practical theology but to its role in implementing theology leads him to reflect even more on the limits of methodology within his proposals. Compared to philosophical theology, which is a *critical* discipline, and historical theology, which is *empirical*, practical theology is *technical*, an art or skillful craft (*Kunstlehre*, or *technē*, in the Greek sense) that links thought to practice. Schleiermacher distinguishes between his proposed theological methods and the task of putting them to effective use in the church. For him, all aspects of theology point toward the care of souls, where the mind of a pastor/theologian meets those of individuals within a congregation. And in the care of souls line of work "no other means whatever are applicable ... than definite influences upon the hearts of people" (*BO*, § 263). Thus although constructs, definitions, and admonitions are indispensable for a proper understanding of theology, even where methods and correct teachings are assimilated perfectly by a theologian, it is not methods but the mind of the theologian implementing the methods that influences individuals within the religious community.

In the end, everything in this positive science depends upon the natural talents and cultivation of persons who are drawn into the service of the church (§ 336). Earlier in the *Brief Outline*, when discussing philosophical theology, Schleiermacher writes that "every theologian should produce the entirety of this part of his theology for himself" (§ 67; see also § 89), and that "apprehending things historically is a talent" that must be practiced in each person's life (§§ 155, 100). The most effective church leader not only "has most thoroughly and completely developed his philosophical theology," but also "the most appropriate methods will occur to the person whose historical basis for living in the present is the deepest and most diversified" (§ 336). True to his romanticist respect for individual ability and talent, Schleiermacher sees that implementing his theological method is hardly a matter of just having correct knowledge of theology. The highly articulated and coordinated theological methods and insight that he recommends require hermeneutical art for their enactment. Ministry is, in effect, the implementing side of theology, which rests on effectively communicating and mediating the meaning and truth of Christian faith. These themes, articulated when discussing practical theology, do not just arise in the book's final section. At its outset Schleiermacher expresses the need for passionate human engagement with theology. He writes: "No one person can perfectly possess the full compass of theological knowledge," and adds that "if one is to deal with any one of the theological disciplines in a truly theological sense and spirit, he must master the basic features of them all" (§§ 14, 16). This tension between desiring mastery and recognizing one's limits reflects Schleiermacher's characteristic realism about the human condition. Practical theology works from a unity between an "ecclesial interest" and a "scientific spirit" (§§ 257–8), while bestowing deliberative order upon Christian dispositions and feelings. At the same time, no handbook on theological method – even one as erudite and well considered as the *Brief Outline* – can ensure its own success.

With respect to its actual contents practical theology distinguishes between church service (*BO*, §§ 277–308) and church governance (§§ 309–34). Pastoral duties that function within a local congregation are contrasted with those in the wider church, in this instance, the German Protestant church as it relates to the larger culture. Church service, for Schleiermacher, consists of the tasks of preaching (an individual expression of the theologian) and liturgics (a more communal expression). Elements of edification, which consist of rousing the religious consciousness, co-exist with those of regulation, which consist of motivating Christian behavior (§ 293). At the level of practice, edification and regulation relate to the pursuits of dogmatics and Christian ethics within historical theology. Pedagogical tasks are central to this work, including catechetics as the task of educating children to be lively members of the ongoing body of the church. Missions reach out to those in the parish who have fallen away, become indifferent, or were never properly involved in the first place. The novelty of Schleiermacher's construal of "church service" lies not in his understanding of a pastor's duties but in his insistence that to enact these duties well one must draw from the insight and tasks of philosophical and historical theology.

Under church governance Schleiermacher places the necessary partici-pation of the pastor/theologian in the affairs of the wider church, including synodal meetings and decisions regarding German Protestantism as a whole. Such admonitions are not intended to apply to Roman Catholic Christianity, and probably not even to non-German Protestant churches. Yet his vision of church governance moves well beyond the quasi-political committee work of ecclesial bodies. Teaching and writing, the chief activ-ities by which Schleiermacher's legacy reaches us today, also contribute to church governance. Wolfgang Pleger doubtless overstates when he writes, "Schleiermacher's philosophy in all its parts is a philosophy of practice."[23] Praxis, for Schleiermacher, is thoroughly informed by theory. Along with other parts of Schleiermacher's theoretical work, the encyclopedia contri-butes to church governance by honing a curriculum for church leadership. Indeed, what are arguably Schleiermacher's most refined intellectual achievements, his published works on dogmatics and theological encyclo-pedia, have practical theology as their telos.

APPRAISING THE MODEL OF THEOLOGICAL STUDY

A review of these reflections on the *Brief Outline* might well begin with a warning and then issue a few reminders. First, the warning: It is a mistake to think that Schleiermacher's linear arrangement of his material should lead us to conclude that the methods and tasks of theology are sequentially valued. The carefully drawn correlations and cross-links within the encyclo-pedia are intended to serve the community of lived Christian faith that is presupposed as the raison d'être of such study. In this respect, *Brief Outline* resembles the *Christian Faith* in giving a highly intricate account of diverse yet interrelated teachings. Apart from the Strauß lecture transcript, the *Brief Outline* remains a mere sketch. Read sequentially, its 338 theses easily seem dull and rigid. Yet if the project is grasped dialectically, that is, in its multi-ply contending interrelationships, the life of the mind called theology is experienced as a reflective act that draws upon a vast array of materials. The challenge theology faces lies in its need to effect a balance between ecclesial and scientific interests. If we ask how Schleiermacher's encyclopedia differs from Hegel's, the answer is not that the former is less systematic or rigorous. The proper response is that Schleiermacher incorporates the lived religious community further into his discussion, while using that analysis to bestow order on the figurative and contingent dimensions of lived Christian existence.

We have seen that the realm of history looms large in his program. On this point his proposal remains controversial. For him, empirical historical work is not compromised when it is informed by certain normative claims about the tradition.

> No knowledge [*Wissen*] of Christianity is possible if one is satisfied only with an empirical approach and fails to grasp the essence [*Wesen*] of Christianity in contrast with other ways of faith and churches, and as the essence of piety and pious communities in relation to other activities of the human spirit.[24]

As Brian A. Gerrish has said of historical theology, "it would be an impoverishment of the discipline to hold it strictly to the positivistic historical ideal of just ascertaining the facts."[25] By 1800 the study of history in Germany was moving from the realm of personal narrative and rhetorical persuasion toward becoming a science (*Wissenschaft*), an aspiration that is already looming within the work we have examined.[26] For Schleiermacher, taking a scientific, that is, disciplined academic, approach to explicating the meaning of Christianity requires this approach to frame interpretations of religious history that are compelling to persons with a subjective stake not only in the project but also in its overarching aims.

Certainly the most controversial issue in Schleiermacher's program is his insistence that dogmatics belongs under historical theology. Writing in 1963, Hans-Joachim Birkner called attention to the relatively modest place of dogmatic theology within Schleiermacher's theological program:

> By arranging dogmatics within historical theology Schleiermacher, rather than having found successors, assured himself of many critics. The critics have conceived and rejected this arrangement mainly as a diminishment that seemed to prepare the way for, if not actually espouse, a consistent historicizing of dogmatics.[27]

Upon inspection, Schleiermacher appears to have legitimate reasons for his choices. He appears able to cast dogmatics under the umbrella of history because he holds the view that theological convictions of the community of faith are actually manifest in history. Today, such confidence that history and theology can flow so neatly together is widely thought to be lacking. Since "Schleiermacher's inclusive concept of historical theology signals the historicizing of theology,"[28] we may be assured that debate will continue. But it does not follow from this last observation that the turn to history in

Schleiermacher led to a relativizing sort of historicism. A profound confidence in the unity of reason prevents a slide into relativism. To be effective, a young vicar must combine a talent for dialectical thought with a sense of history and have sufficient powers of observation and empathy to interact effectively with the souls of his parishioners. For Schleiermacher, historical awareness is an indispensable part of being a theologian. Rightly delineated, it contributes mightily to the task of properly explicating the contents of the Christian consciousness.[29]

Notes

1 Friedrich Schleiermacher, *Theologische Enzyklopädie (1831–2): Nachschrift David Friedrich Strauß*, 2. Translations from this work, hereafter cited as *ThEnz*, are my own.
2 See B. A. Gerrish's masterful essay, "Friedrich Schleiermacher (1768–1834)," in Gerrish 1993, 147–77.
3 Rosenkranz 1831, 4.
4 For a lucid account of these disciplinary definitions in *BO*, see Wyman 1991, especially 104–8.
5 Birkner 1996, 104–5; B. A. Gerrish, "Ubi theologia, ibi ecclesia? Schleiermacher, Troeltsch, and the Prospect for an Academic Theology," in Gerrish 1993, 255–8.
6 For a critique of the view that Schleiermacher's theology is held together by this functional aim apart from the formal definition of an essence of Christianity, see Schröder 1996.
7 Georg G. Iggers argues against the view that Weber's social-scientific program rests upon value-free inquiry; see Iggers 1995, 129–52. Cf. Hardtwig 1998, 259.
8 Unless otherwise noted, citations of *Brief Outline* are from Friedrich Schleiermacher, *Brief Outline on the Study of Theology*, trans. Terrence N. Tice.
9 *Brief Outline of the Study of Theology*, trans. William Farrer.
10 Ziolkowski 2004, ch. 3, puts the *Brief Outline* at the center of Schleiermacher's project of historicizing theology.
11 Birkner 1996, 286.
12 *KGA*, I.6, LXVII.
13 See n. 1 above.
14 Sachs in *ThEnz*, XXXIX, citing Strauß (1876–8), v. 9
15 See Birkner 1996, 157–92; cf. Rössler 1994.
16 "What is reasonable is actual; and, what is actual is reasonable": Hegel 1892, 10.
17 Wilfrid Cantwell Smith in *The Meaning and End of Religion* offers an anti-essentialist critique of Schleiermacher that still clings to essentialism in the view of Talal Asad; see Asad 2001, 205–22.
18 For the crown and root metaphors see Schleiermacher, *Kurze Darstellung des theologischen Studiums zum Behuf Einleitender Vorlesungen*, ed. Scholtz, p. 10, § 26 [first edition], "Die philosophische Theologie ist die Wurzel der gesamten Theologie," and § 31, which reads, "Die praktische Theologie ist die Krone des theologischen Studiums."
19 Tice translation altered; Scholtz, 11.

20 For a contemporary non-metaphysical defense of historical truth, see Williams 2002. Whether Williams' approach would work in defending religious claims, however, remains to be argued.

21 Translated from Scholtz, 75.

22 *ThEnz*, 185 n. 42, citing Daniel von Cölln and David Schultz, *Über theologische Lehrfreiheit auf den evangelischen Universitäten und deren Beschränkung durch symbolische Bücher* (Breslau, 1830), and Schleiermacher's response, "An die Herren D. D. D. von Cölln und D. Schultz," [*Theologische Studien und Kritiken*, 1831, 3–29], printed in *KGA*, I.10, 297–426.

23 Pleger 1988, 3.

24 Translated from Scholtz, 8–9 (§ 21).

25 Gerrish, cited in Engel and Wyman 1992, 302–3.

26 Hardtwig 1998, 245–60.

27 Birkner 1996, 106. See also Fischer 2001, 74.

28 Engel and Wyman (1992) 3, drawing from Gerrish 1982, 208–9.

29 If Schleiermacher's theological method works for today, this can be the case only for those who share the key assumptions within his system of the sciences. To explore those assumptions further would require us to examine his unpublished lectures on ethics and dialectics, as well as the introduction to the dogmatics, a task that reaches well beyond this chapter.

7 Sin and redemption

WALTER E. WYMAN, JR.

Sin and redemption constitute the heart of Schleiermacher's understanding of Christianity. Christianity "is essentially distinguished from other such [monotheistic and teleological] faiths by the fact that in it everything is related to the redemption accomplished by Jesus of Nazareth" (*CF*, § 11);[1] "the distinctive feature of Christian piety lies in the fact that whatever alienation from God there is in the phases of our experience, we are conscious of it as an action originating in ourselves, which we call Sin; but whatever fellowship with God there is, we are conscious of it as resting upon a communication from the Redeemer, which we call Grace" (§ 63). The problem that Schleiermacher confronted was how to give an account of sin and grace after the Enlightenment, when fundamental questions about the credibility of Christian doctrines had been raised. Schleiermacher is committed to producing a dogmatics adequate to the modern world, that is, to meeting the challenge to the credibility of theology while remaining appropriate to the Christian tradition.[2] To carry out this project Schleiermacher boldly reinterpreted traditional doctrines to establish their credibility, while seeking to show how his revisionist formulas are consistent with both the New Testament and the Protestant confessions of the sixteenth century as the criteria of appropriateness. His discussion of sin and redemption exhibits his dual commitment to revision and fidelity to the Christian (specifically, Protestant) tradition.

As a glance at his open letters *On the Glaubenslehre* readily confirms, the specific historical context of Schleiermacher's revisionist enterprise was complex.[3] In a passage that helps to clarify the live options as he saw them, Schleiermacher argued that his position, which he perhaps misleadingly named "mystical," was the "true mean" between two extremes, the "magical" and the "empirical" (§ 100.3). The "magical," Schleiermacher's pejorative term for supernaturalism, held Christ's redeeming influence to be immediate, that is, not mediated by anything natural. The "empirical" position, Schleiermacher's term for Enlightenment rationalism, held Christ to be significant as teacher and example, thereby eliminating redemption in the strict sense (§§ 100.3, 101.3). Schleiermacher sought a third alternative to a supernaturalism that was no longer credible and a rationalism that failed to be appropriate to the essence of Christianity.

Schleiermacher reinterpreted both sin and redemption in terms of a conceptuality provided by a philosophical anthropology. In the "Introduction" to the *Christian Faith* he initially defined redemption as "a passage from a bad [*schlecht*] condition, which is represented as a state of captivity or constraint, into a better condition"(§ 11.2, translation altered). The bad condition he specified as "an obstruction or arrest of the vitality of the higher self-consciousness, so that there comes to be little or no union of it with various determinations of the sensible self-consciousness, and thus little or no religious life." In this initial definition Schleiermacher has utilized the philosophical conceptuality ("higher self-consciousness," "sensible self-consciousness") that he had developed earlier in the "Introduction." A grasp of Schleiermacher's thinking about sin and redemption presupposes, then, some acquaintance with that conceptual framework. In accordance with his methodological innovation, the theology of consciousness, he understands sin as an inhibition of the God-consciousness, and redemption as its quickening. He can, of course, put his point in much less technical terms: the condition from which humans are redeemed is "*Godlessness*, or, better, *God-forgetfulness*" (§ 11.2). In a major departure from the Augustinian tradition, sin is understood not as the result of a historical Fall that corrupted human nature, but as the "virtually inevitable" result of the way human beings develop in a natural and social context.[4] Nevertheless, in an argument that is as intricate as it is original, he affirms the doctrine of original sin. Redemption does not depend upon the atoning death of Jesus of Nazareth but on the perfection of his God-consciousness. Schleiermacher's major innovation is to show that sin and redemption can only be properly understood if the communal character of both is made central.

SCHLEIERMACHER'S PHILOSOPHICAL ANTHROPOLOGY

In his initial characterization of the "bad condition" from which redemption is necessary, what does Schleiermacher mean by "an obstruction or arrest of the vitality of the higher self-consciousness, so that there comes to be little or no union of it with the various determinations of the sensible self-consciousness" (§ 11.2)? To answer requires a brief exploration of Schleiermacher's philosophical analysis. By "the higher self-consciousness" Schleiermacher means "the feeling of absolute dependence." Analyzing human consciousness philosophically, Schleiermacher uncovers feelings of partial freedom and partial dependence in the self's relation to the world. That is, the self–world relation is a reciprocal relationship of activity and receptivity: the self can act to some extent upon the world, and the world influences the receptive self (§§ 4.1–2). He denies that there can be a feeling of absolute freedom: existence is given to human beings; it does not proceed from their "own spontaneous activity." By contrast, there is a feeling of absolute dependence: "the self-consciousness which accompanies all our activity, and therefore, since that is never zero, accompanies our whole existence, and negatives absolute freedom, is itself precisely a consciousness of absolute dependence; for it is the consciousness that the whole of our spontaneous activity comes from a source outside of us" (§ 4.3). Schleiermacher takes the crucial step of identifying the feeling of absolute dependence with "relation to God"; God is properly understood as "the Whence of our receptive and active existence" (§ 4.4). Thus Schleiermacher can speak simply of the "God-consciousness."

Indispensable for properly grasping Schleiermacher's philosophical anthropology is the realization that the feeling of absolute dependence is an *abstraction*: "a feeling of absolute dependence, strictly speaking, cannot exist in a single moment as such, because such a moment is always determined, as regards its content, by what is *given*, and thus by objects towards which we have a feeling of freedom" (§ 4.3). Thus the feeling of absolute dependence only occurs in a moment of consciousness always already constituted by the "lower" self-consciousness and in association with it (§ 5).

What is this "lower self-consciousness"? This is "the self-consciousness which, as expressing the connection with perceptible finite existence, splits up into a partial feeling of dependence and a partial feeling of freedom" (§ 5.1). Human "sensible life" in the widest sense of the term consists of perceptions (*Anschauungen*) and feelings (*Gefühle*). The former constitute the objective consciousness, which need not detain us further. It is the realm of feeling (or immediate self-consciousness) which arises from the self's relation to the world (including "social" and "moral" feelings) that Schleiermacher designates the "lower" or "sensible self-consciousness."

The relation of the sensible and the higher self-consciousness, then, is the crucial philosophical framework for Schleiermacher's reinterpretation of the Christian doctrines of sin and redemption. How does Schleiermacher understand that relationship philosophically? As an essential structure, the higher self-consciousness is "always self-identical" (§ 5.4). It can become concrete in consciousness only "on the supposition that the sensible self-consciousness is always conjoined with it." What is the nature of the conjoining? It is not a "fusion" (*Verschmelzung*) but rather a "co-existence

[*Zugleichsein*] in the same moment which "involves a relation [*Bezogensein*] of the two" (§ 5.3).[5] This means several things, First, it means that "the more the subject, in each moment of sensible self-consciousness ... takes at the same time the attitude of absolute dependence, the more religious he is" (§ 5.3). Second, it means that particular religious emotions arise in a concrete moment of consciousness when the always self-identical feeling of absolute dependence enters as a "constituent factor" into relation with the sensible self-consciousness, which "splits up ... into the antithesis of the pleasant and the unpleasant, or of pleasure [*Lust*] and pain [*Unlust*]" (§ 5.4). In the only concrete example he gives in the discussion, Schleiermacher states there can be "a sorrow of the lower and a joy of the higher self-consciousness, as for example whenever with a feeling of suffering there is combined a trust in God."

Schleiermacher's philosophical analysis establishes a conceptual framework and uncovers the condition of the possibility of sin: the higher self-consciousness must enter into a relationship with the sensible self-consciousness to form a moment of consciousness; the inhibition of the God-consciousness by the sensible self-consciousness constitutes the "bad condition." But this is not yet the Christian doctrine of sin – it is a philosophical anthropology. Schleiermacher's philosophy provides only the form, not the content, of Christian doctrines (§ 16 Postscript). How is sin understood and accounted for in the dogmatics proper?

REINTERPRETING SIN

The concrete Christian consciousness is, Schleiermacher maintains, always a consciousness of sin and grace: "it is the case that every Christian is conscious both of sin and grace as always combined with each other and never dissociated" (§ 64.1; see § 63.3). The consciousness of sin itself only arises "as the effect of the Redeemer's self-revelation, as indeed it certainly does come to full clarity only as we contemplate His sinless perfection" (§ 100.2; cf. §§ 88.2 and 14.2). The claims are methodologically important; not only is sin a distinctively Christian category, but any analysis of sin is an abstraction from concrete Christian experience.

The consciousness of sin

With § 66 we have Schleiermacher's theological definition of sin: "We have the consciousness of sin whenever the God-consciousness which forms part of an inner state, or is in some way added to it, determines our self-consciousness as pain [*Unlust*]; and therefore we conceive of sin as a positive antagonism of the flesh against the spirit." This definition contains three elements that need further analysis. First, as Schleiermacher makes explicit in the first paragraph (§ 66.1), sin and the consciousness of sin coincide. This follows strictly from the method of a theology of consciousness: there can be no "objective elucidation of sin." Sin is a disturbance of the religious consciousness. Second, it seems somewhat odd to describe the consciousness of sin as "pain." Why does Schleiermacher say that? Part of the problem of grasping Schleiermacher's meaning is terminological: *Unlust*, which is translated as "pain" here, is not a simple word.[6] According to Schleiermacher's analysis, the religious consciousness oscillates between a more and less; "if ... the determining power of the God-consciousness is felt to be limited, pain [*Unlust*] is bound up with it" (§ 62.1). But pain in what sense? Dissatisfaction? Actual mental suffering? Lack of joy? Granted that the God-consciousness is a structural element, why should its inhibition result in "pain," whatever is meant by that?

A passage from the sermon "The Power of Prayer in Relation to Outward Circumstances" may be of some help in ferreting out Schleiermacher's meaning:

> To be a religious man and to pray are really one and the same thing. To join the thought of God with every thought of any importance that occurs to us; in all our admiration of external nature, to regard it as the work of his wisdom; to take council with God about all our plans, that we may be able to carry them out in His name; and even in our most mirthful hours to remember His all-seeing eye: this is the prayer without ceasing to which we are called, and which is really the essence of true religion.[7]

Here Schleiermacher characterizes piety in more concrete terms than he employs in the *Glaubenslehre*. It is possible to work out from it what an inhibited God-consciousness would be, and why it might be characterized as unsatisfactory. Sinfulness would be an inability to "join the thought of God with every thought of any importance," an absence of a conscious relation to God in one's everyday existence. The problem of sin is a religious, not a moral problem; it is, as he says, "God-forgetfulness" (§ 11.2). By the experience of *Unlust* Schleiermacher apparently means a sense of incompleteness, mental discomfort, of things somehow out of joint, of the world lacking in religious meaning. It would make sense that this experience of "pain" would arise within the Christian community where the expectation of a pious consciousness is cultivated.

Third, Schleiermacher speaks of "a positive antagonism of the flesh against the spirit," thereby invoking Paul's vocabulary (there are several footnote references to Romans and Galatians in the paragraphs that follow). How does Schleiermacher understand the terms "spirit" and "flesh"? He is explicit that flesh means "the totality of the so-called lower powers of the soul" (§ 66.2); we may take it to mean, in Schleiermacher's philosophical vocabulary, the sensible self-consciousness. "Spirit" is a term referring to the human being's "inner side, as a self-active being in whom God-consciousness is possible" (§ 59.1). Spirit would refer, then, to the higher self-consciousness (or the capacity for it). This move accords well with his wider agenda to revise the tradition while maintaining continuity with it; Schleiermacher can claim that his distinctive conceptuality is continuous with the Pauline duality of flesh and spirit.

Original sin and actual sin

Schleiermacher's account of the universality of sin is dramatically revisionist. He recognizes the internal difficulties created by the traditional doctrine of the Fall of Adam and Eve and subjects it to some devastating criticisms. Not only does it fail to explain the origin of sin ("Adam must have been sundered from God before the first sin"), it is incoherent, for one can only act in accordance with one's nature, not upon it (§§ 72.2–3). Moreover, the doctrine of original sin assigns guilt to the individual for something "received from an external source," and so is "incredible" and "offensive" (§ 71.1). Therefore, Schleiermacher revises the doctrine to show how sin can be both universal and inevitable without being an inheritance from a particular act that changed human nature.

Schleiermacher's account of sin

In §§ 67–9 Schleiermacher presents a threefold account of the universality of sin without mentioning either the Fall or the term "original sin." In these propositions, Schleiermacher presents his analysis in his "own quite independent form of expression."[8] § 67 gives a developmental account; § 68 gives an account in terms of the intellect and will; § 69 gives a social account. Schleiermacher is not explicit about the relationship of the three accounts to each other; he must intend them to be differing aspects of a single comprehensive account.

The basic question here is: how does sin arise in human life? "We are conscious of sin as the power and work of a time when the disposition to the God-consciousness had not yet actively emerged in us" (§ 67). The basic point is that "flesh manifests itself as a reality before the spirit comes to be such, the result being that, as soon as the spirit enters the sphere of consciousness ... resistance takes place" (§ 67.2). It is a fact of human development, Schleiermacher is claiming, that the sensible self-consciousness appears before the higher self-consciousness; accordingly, it gets a head start, as it were: human beings become accustomed to experiencing the everyday world without consciously linking their experience to the thought of God; this condition hinders the emergence of pious awareness. In his second account, Schleiermacher states that sin is "a result of the unequal development of insight and will-power" (§ 68). Here Schleiermacher appeals to what he regards as a fundamental psychological fact already articulated by Paul in Romans 7: human beings can see what they want or ought to do before they can control their will.[9] Finally, "we are conscious of sin partly as having its source in ourselves, partly as having its source outside our own being" (§ 69). In this third account of the universality of sin, Schleiermacher develops an explicitly social account. People are social and historical beings. Later generations depend on earlier ones, and are shaped by them; fundamental dispositions, including "our evil nature [*Bösartigkeit*]," are received from others and are voluntarily perpetuated (§ 69.1). Schleiermacher picks up and develops this social dimension in the next stage in his argument.

Schleiermacher in dialogue with tradition

In § 70 Schleiermacher turns explicitly to the doctrine of original sin, prefacing his discussion with quotations from numerous confessional documents, both Lutheran and Reformed.[10] He asserts that the idea affirmed by the confessions of "a sinfulness present from the first in every human being is in perfect accord with what has been set forth above" (§ 70.1). Since "above" could only mean §§ 67–9, Schleiermacher here is boldly proclaiming the continuity of his revisionist account with the doctrine of original sin, despite his critical rejection of the Fall. Two ideas, both unintelligible and offensive to modern sensibilities, are at stake: that there is sinfulness "present in an individual prior to any action of his own" and that humans beings are completely incapable of good (§ 70).

Concerning the first point, the notion of a ground of sinfulness outside of the being of the individual reverts to the idea introduced in § 69, which Schleiermacher proceeds to develop further in § 71. If there is no Fall of the original pair, how is a sinfulness antecedent to the individual to be understood? In what sense is the individual responsible for it and thus guilty? This sinfulness that is prior to an individual's activity comes to him or her "through the sin and sinfulness of others" (§ 71.2). It is inherited, not in a biological or Augustinian sense, but socially and historically: individuals are raised by families and in cultures and nations where the common life is shaped by individuals and groups whose God-consciousness is always already deficient. To borrow a technical term from Schubert Ogden, human beings re-present sinfulness to each other.[11] Both "space" (the influence of one's contemporaries) and "time" (the influence of preceding generations) constitute the communal dimension of sin. This "inherited" predisposition to sinfulness is in turn owned or ratified by each individual in his or her voluntary actions; only by integrating original sin and actual sin can the former idea be made intellectually acceptable. In terms of the traditional distinctions, the sinfulness that is "originated" in the individual through social and historical influences becomes, through the voluntary action of the individual, "a growth in congenital sinfulness" within and a pernicious influence without (on contemporaries and successors), or "originating original sin." Sinfulness "must be something common to all … it is … in each the work of all, and in all the work of each; and only in this corporate character [*Gemeinsamkeit*] … can it be properly and fully understood" (§ 71.2).

Concerning the second point, the incapacity for the good, Schleiermacher states that "original sin is always issuing in actual sin" (§ 73). The "incapacity for good" means that "throughout the entire range of sinful humanity there is not a single perfectly good action, that is, one that purely expresses the power of the God-consciousness; nor is there one perfectly pure moment, that is, one in which something does not exist in secret antagonism to the God-consciousness" (§ 73.1). Without using the term, Schleiermacher has retrieved the concept of total depravity. Actual sins are actions whose motivation or impetus proceeds from the sensible self-consciousness rather than from the God-consciousness; they are, in the language of the New Testament, deeds of the flesh. Thoughts, too, can be actual sins, as can desire (*Begierde*); thus Schleiermacher retrieves the notion of concupiscence.[12] Actual sin hinges on the question of what is in control of human thought or action, flesh or spirit? – or the lower or the higher self-consciousness? The human ideal is that the God-consciousness permeates the personality and gives the impetus to activity; when this is not the case, actual sins result. "All activities of the flesh are good when subservient to the spirit, and all are evil [*böse*] when severed from it" (§ 74.1).

Schleiermacher's doctrine of sin is marked by both innovation and continuity with tradition. He has defended both original sin and total depravity. His major innovations are his revisionist conceptuality and attendant location of sin in human consciousness, and his alternative account of original sin which holds that sin is the "corporate act and corporate guilt of the human race" (§ 71). By offering a naturalistic explanation and moving away from interpreting human nature through the lens of

Genesis 3, he departs from supernaturalism. By seeking to retrieve the doctrine of original sin at all he breaks with the rationalistic view that human beings are fully capable of the good, and are not in need of redemption.

Sin and evil[13]

For those who took the "Mosaic narrative" literally, the connection of sin and evil was obvious. Weren't pain in childbirth, the reality of toil in order to secure one's existence, and ultimately death itself due to sin? But this interpretative possibility was incredible to Schleiermacher, not only because he had rejected the notion of a literal Fall, but because he regarded the idea of a change in the nature of the physical world to be "fantastic" (§ 82.1). So could a connection between evil and sin still be made intelligible?[14]

Schleiermacher sees a connection: "evil arises only with sin, but given sin, it arises inevitably" (§ 75.1). Why does he say that? Schleiermacher understands evils to be "hindrances" to human life (§ 75). "If ... the pre-dominant factor is not the God-consciousness but the flesh, every impression made by the world upon us and involving an obstruction of our bodily and temporal life must be reckoned as an evil" (§ 75.1). In Schleiermacher's theology of consciousness, evil is a matter of how you look at reality. Given the ideal possibility of a perfect God-consciousness, bodily suffering or even the death of a loved one, while real enough, would not be evils: neither would disturb one's religious consciousness. The "evils" of the world would be experienced as "incentives" (§ 84.4), and the pious response would be "religious submission" (§ 78.2). But given the reality of sin, one's experience of the world is quite different: the "hindrances" of life – death, suffering, want – are experienced as evils. "God has ordained ... that the natural imperfections are regarded by us as evil in proportion as the God-consciousness is not yet dominant within us" (§ 82.2).

Moreover, "all evil is to be regarded as punishment of sin" (§ 76). What could this possibly mean? Schleiermacher rejects the notion that individual misfortunes could be the result of individual sins, as though God punished people, individually, for something they had done. Such an anthropomorphic understanding of the divine causality is irreconcilable with Schleiermacher's position that divine causality is eternal, not temporal, and equivalent in scope to the system of nature (§§ 46, 51–2). While "evil as such is not ordained by God" (§ 48.2), it is ultimately absolutely dependent upon "the absolutely living and active divine causality" (§ 76.1). So, again, it's all a matter of how you look at it: "as man, were he without sin, would not feel what are merely hindrances of sensuous functions as evils, the very fact that he does so feel them is due to sin, and hence that type of evil, subjectively considered, is a penalty of sin" (§ 76.2).

Schleiermacher has managed to retrieve several traditional notions – evil is the result of sin, evil is the punishment of sin – in his thoroughly revisionist framework. But at what price? It is hard not to judge that a subjectivistic reduction of the reality of evil to a phenomenon of consciousness has gone hand in hand with Schleiermacher's conceptual framework.[15] Moreover, Schleiermacher's position has troubling implications for Christian praxis. "The Christian consciousness could never give rise to a moment of activity specially directed towards the cessation of suffering as such … it is a disposition hostile to sin itself that needs to be aroused" (§ 78.2). To combat suffering *per se* would be to be "determined by the interests of the lower side of life," that is, the sensible self-consciousness or flesh. Such an emphasis arouses the further suspicion of dualism: what matters is one's piety, not objective social conditions. Finally, the absence of an exploration of the relationship of sin to moral evil (*das Böse*) is noteworthy and problematic.

REINTERPRETING REDEMPTION

The key to Schleiermacher's "Explication of the Consciousness of Grace" is given in § 87: "We are conscious of all approximations to the state of blessedness which occur in the Christian life as being grounded in a new divinely effected corporate life [*Gesamtleben*], which works in opposition to the corporate life of sin and the misery which develops in it." While this proposition is not, Schleiermacher concedes, "a complete statement of specifically Christian piety," still "all further exposition of what is specifically Christian can easily be attached to this proposition" (§ 87.1). Three themes are introduced: "approximations to the *state of blessedness*" alludes to the experience of redemption; "*Divinely effected* corporate life" points to the condition of the possibility of redemption, Christ; a *corporate life* that "works in opposition to" the "corporate life of sin" provides the answer to the question: *how* does redemption take place?

The meaning of redemption

What is the meaning of redemption? Schleiermacher makes a systematic distinction between *redemption* and *reconciliation*, both of which together constitute redemption in the broad sense. "The Redeemer assumes believers into the power of His God-consciousness, and this is His redemptive [*erlösende*] activity" (§ 100); "the Redeemer assumes believers into the fellowship of his unclouded blessedness [*Seligkeit*], and this is His reconciling [*versöhnende*] activity" (§ 101).

Redemption "in the proper sense" is "the removal of sin" (§ 100.3). Since sin is the inhibition of the God-consciousness, redemption is the "implantation" in human nature of a powerful God-consciousness as "a new vital principle" (§ 100.2). It is the "communication of Christ's sinless perfection" (§ 88), and amounts to the furtherance of the higher life (§ 100.1).[16] Schleiermacher summarizes the "essence of redemption" as follows: "the God-consciousness already present in human nature, though feeble and repressed, becomes stimulated and made dominant by the entrance of the living influence of Christ"; thus "the individual on whom this influence is exercised attains a religious personality not his before" (§ 106.1).

Reconciliation has two aspects, both subsumed under the notion of the assumption of believers into the fellowship of Christ's unclouded blessedness (*Seligkeit*).[17] First, reconciliation means the dissolution of the connection between sin and evil, bringing about "a corporate feeling of blessedness." "All hindrances of life, natural and social" are henceforth no longer evils, but "indications" (*Anzeigen*). Pain and suffering, of course, do not cease, but they no longer mean religious or spiritual misery (*Unseligkeit*), "for they do not as such penetrate into the inmost life" (§ 101.2). Second, "the consciousness of deserving punishment" disappears, replaced by the forgiveness of sins (§ 101.2). If the existential meaning of redemption is a fortified God-consciousness, the existential meaning of reconciliation is blessedness.

The condition of the possibility of redemption/reconciliation

The appearance of Christ in history as the Redeemer is the condition of the possibility of redemption and reconciliation. It is his "sinless perfection" (§ 88) on the one hand and his "unclouded blessedness" (§ 101) on the other that make redemption and reconciliation, respectively, possible. Christ's "sinless perfection" is, of course, the "constant potency of his God-consciousness" (§ 94). Schleiermacher associates the redeeming work of Christ primarily with the prophetic office, as Christ's self-presentation of his God-consciousness (§ 103.2). As far as Christ's "unclouded blessedness" is concerned, it consists in his having no consciousness of sin or guilt, and his not experiencing evil. Schleiermacher associates reconciliation with the priestly office of Christ; although he rejects the notion of vicarious atonement, Schleiermacher, true to his practice of retrieving and reinterpreting the tradition, asserts that "through the suffering of Christ punishment is abolished, because in the fellowship of his blessed life even the evil which was in the process of disappearing is no longer at least regarded as punishment" (§ 104.4). Schleiermacher has much to say about Christ's blessedness in conjunction with the suffering caused by the crucifixion. "His blessedness emerged in its perfect fullness only in that it was not overcome even by the full tide of suffering." Schleiermacher's reasoning is that "robust piety" has as its reward "the almost complete overcoming of physical sufferings in the presence of a glad spiritual self-consciousness" (§ 101.4). The claim seems hardly credible, although Schleiermacher asserts that it is warranted experientially. It does provide some insight into Schleiermacher's thinking about the pious (regenerate) life. This train of thought is crucial to Schleiermacher's rethinking of the doctrine of the atonement: "For in his suffering unto death ... there is manifested to us an absolutely self-denying love; and in this there is represented to us with perfect vividness the way in which God was in Him to reconcile the world to Himself, just as it is in his suffering that we feel most perfectly how imperturbable was His blessedness" (§ 104.4).

This is not the place to unpack Schleiermacher's rethinking of the doctrine of the Atonement, or to purse further the multiple issues raised by Schleiermacher's Christological premises. It suffices to note that Schleiermacher combines liberal revisions with conservative retrievals. The central issue, for our purposes, is this: assuming that someone had them, how are "sinless perfection" and "untroubled blessedness" relevant to anyone else? How does redemption take place?

The means of redemption and reconciliation

Schleiermacher's basic answer to the questions just posed has already been anticipated in § 87: "We are conscious of all approximations to the state of blessedness which occur in the Christian life as being grounded in a new, divinely-effected corporate life [*Gesamtleben*]." Christ's redemptive activity influences human nature by means of a human community which mediates it.

The new corporate life

What is the nature of this corporate life? In the first place, Schleiermacher is thinking of the community of believers in Christ, of those who have been reborn: "all that comes to exist in the world through redemption is embraced in the fellowship of believers, within which all regenerate people are always found" (§ 113). This community constitutes the "sphere of the redeeming activity of Christ" and thus the kingdom of God (§ 114.2). Crucial for our question is the claim: "The new life of each individual springs from that of the community, while the life of the community springs from no other individual life than that of the Redeemer" (§ 113.1). In so stressing the new corporate life derived from Christ as the means of redemption, Schleiermacher has set up a counterweight to the corporate life of sinfulness. But how is it possible for the community to function in a redemptive way?

One can get at this question by considering where the community came from. In the time of Jesus there was no corporate life (at least, none separate from the community of Israel); his first followers experienced Christ's perfect God-consciousness and blessedness directly. The Redeemer "could only enter into our corporate life by means of . . . self-presentation" in word and deed, "thereby attracting men to Himself and making them one with Himself" (§ 101.4). Redemption and reconciliation occurred through a direct (unmediated) relationship to Christ, and the result was the first Christian community. Why is this relevant? "If we start from the principle that our Christianity ought to be the same as that of the Apostles, our Christianity too must be generated by the personal influences of Christ" (§ 127.2). But how is this possible? For, "there is given to us, instead of His personal influence, only that of His fellowship." Schleiermacher answers, "this influence of the fellowship in producing a like faith is none other than the influence of the personal perfection of Jesus Himself" (§ 88.2). The logic of redemption hinges on two claims: (1) Christ redeemed and reconciled others by the direct personal influence of his perfection and blessedness; (2) now that he is no longer present, the community does the same. But how could these claims be true?

Schleiermacher's reasoning is first suggested in the next paragraph (§ 88.3). Here he distinguishes between the individual's "personal consciousness" and the "common consciousness." As far as the first is concerned:

> The individual even today receives from the picture of Christ, which exists in the community as at once a corporate act and a corporate possession, the impression of the sinless perfection of Jesus, which becomes for him at the same time the perfect consciousness of sin and the removal of the misery. *And this is already* in *itself a communication of that perfection.*   [my italics]

The Christian community keeps alive the image of the sinless perfection of Jesus through the prominence it gives to the New Testament (specifically the gospels with their portrayals of Christ), through its witness and especially through its proclamation. "Faith comes from preaching" (§ 121.2); through the ministry of the Word (§ 133), faith is aroused and the living community of the individual with the redeemer is established. "It is always by an influence of Christ Himself, mediated by His spiritual presence in the Word, that individuals are assumed into the fellowship of the new life" (§ 106.2). One may rightly wonder how the impression of the perfection of Jesus' God-consciousness can actually become a *"communication* of that perfection." *How can* a communication *of power* take place through a portrayal of someone? Schleiermacher does not explain. He had no skeptical doubts along those lines: the representation of Christ in preaching is a "spiritual presence" that functions in the same way as did Jesus' physical presence before his first followers. To see Christ's perfection is to become aware of one's sinfulness and to be transformed.

There is more to the means of redemption than the representation of Christ's perfection. In a second argument in § 88.3, Schleiermacher turns to the "common consciousness" (*Gemeinbewußtsein*). No matter how ambiguous the empirical Christian church may be, he claims, there still resides within it a "tendency (*Richtung*) issuing from that [*sc.* Christ's] perfection," the "pure impulse of historical life." Schleiermacher's discussion at this point remains somewhat obscure; I think that he is alluding to his later discussion of the "common spirit" of the community, which he identifies as the Holy Spirit.

> In the Christian Church, as individual influence no longer proceeds directly from Christ, something divine must exist. This something we call accordingly the Being of God in it, and it is this which continues within the Church the communication of the perfection and blessedness of Christ ... Already it is apparent that the communication of the sinless perfection and blessedness which, as an absolute and continuous willing of the Kingdom of God, is the innermost impulse of the individual, must also be the common spirit [*Gemeingeist*] of the whole.
> (§ 116.3)

The common spirit of the whole is, he explains, the Holy Spirit (§ 121). The notion of the Holy Spirit is on the fringes of intelligibility in the modern, post-Enlightenment world; what does Schleiermacher mean by it? Given Schleiermacher's insistence that redemption must be mediated historically (that is, given his opposition to what he calls the "magical" view), the Holy Spirit cannot be a supernatural force.[18] What Schleiermacher says is that the Divine Essence, once "bound up with the human person of Christ," is now "no longer personally operative in any individual, but henceforth manifests itself actively in the fellowship of believers as their common spirit" (§ 124.2). To explain what he means by "common spirit" Schleiermacher mentions in passing the analogy of national character (§ 121.2). But the analogy is not elaborated. Clearly he means something analogous to the corporate life of sin: a group of people with a common disposition, common aims and intentions, share a common spirit. "The new life of each is an activity of this common spirit manifested in the same fashion in all others" (§ 121.2). The lives of the regenerate are transformed, and they re-present the transformed life to others.

Thus Schleiermacher has put forward two mechanisms by which the redeeming and reconciling influence of Christ is transmitted: the biblical picture of Jesus as the Christ and the representation of Christ in preaching, and the common spirit of the community. The shape of Schleiermacher's third alternative to naturalism and supernaturalism is clear. The workings of grace are "supernatural" (because they "proceed from the being of God in the Person of Christ") and "natural" (because mediated historically through the human means of reading, speaking, and personal influence) (§ 108.5). Surely questions arise about the redemptive influence of Christ on his contemporaries, about the power of preaching as the representation of Christ's God-consciousness, and about the influence of the community; one could wish that Schleiermacher had spelled things out more. In the end, redemption (in the inclusive sense) is about the transformation of consciousness; one becomes pious in the presence of piety. If Schleiermacher's explanations are not altogether clear, his intention is plain enough: neither supernaturalism's grace without a mechanism, nor rationalism's religion without the communication of grace, will do. Transforming power is conveyed by the words of the preacher (what could be more classically Protestant than Schleiermacher's emphasis on the Word?) and in the lives of other believers. Surprisingly, the utter dependence of redemption on the mediation of the church seems to fit Schleiermacher's characterization of Catholicism better than that of Protestantism (see § 24). Yet when he turns from the means of redemption to the individual's experience of redemption, to what we might call the phenomenology of grace, Schleiermacher's discussion is consistently and insistently Protestant.

The phenomenology of grace: regeneration and sanctification

How does redemption take place in the experience of individuals? Schleiermacher distinguishes two major issues, which serve to structure his discussion: regeneration and sanctification. Regeneration (*Wiedergeburt,* "rebirth") signifies the "transition from the corporate life of sinfulness to a living fellowship with Christ" (§ 107.1). It designates the "turning point at which the continuity of the old ceased, and that of the new began to be in the process of becoming" (§ 106.1). Sanctification, on the other hand, refers to the "growing continuity of the new life" in which "there is produced a life akin to [the Redeemer's] perfection and blessedness" (§§ 106.1, 110). Schleiermacher's discussion remains quite close to the issues raised in the Reformation. Not only are there numerous citations of sixteenth-century confessions in this section, there are also frequent comments on Catholicism, as Schleiermacher takes pains to differentiate Protestant and Catholic views.

As Schleiermacher analyzes regeneration, the theological categories quickly multiply. First, he distinguishes conversion and justification. Conversion in turn is comprised of repentance and faith (§ 108), two terms central to Protestant–Catholic controversies. In a close phenomenological analysis, Schleiermacher unfolds the psychological stages in the experience of repentance (§ 108.2). If redemption is to be appropriated, the individual must be transformed; conversion is necessary because "no genuine laying hold of Christ is conceivable without such an alteration in the innermost aspirations and endeavors" (§ 108.1). For our purposes, the important point is that, as is the case with other issues, Schleiermacher's position on conversion is the mean between two extremes. Against the pietists he denies that a precisely datable conversion experience is necessary; against those who hold that conversion is unnecessary for those born into the church he puts forth arguments to show that everyone needs conversion (§§ 108.3–4). Thus his discussion of regeneration is both liberal and evangelical.[19]

With the concept of justification Schleiermacher touches upon the central doctrine of the Reformation. He defines it as including "forgiveness of sins" and "recognition as a child of God" (§ 109). In this context he takes up the classic Protestant doctrine of justification by faith. Schleiermacher defines faith as the "appropriation of the perfection and blessedness of Christ" (§ 108); it is "a permanently enduring state of mind" (§ 108.1). His major innovation is to deny that justification is properly understood as a "declaratory act," that is, "an act in time eventuating at a particular moment or an act directed upon an individual" (§ 109.3). Such an understanding would, of course, be inconsistent with Schleiermacher's understanding of the eternal, non-episodic character of the divine causality. Rather, "there is only one eternal and universal decree justifying men for Christ's sake" (§ 109.3). "Justification by faith" means the application of that decree to oneself when one "lays hold believingly on Christ" (§ 109.4).[20] Thus Schleiermacher puts himself clearly in the Reformation camp: justification is not dependent upon works, upon progress in sanctification, but on faith alone.

Sanctification refers to a process, not a finished state, through which the individual approaches the "perfection and blessedness" of Christ. That the transformation of individual lives must be a process is due to "the fact that what have become habitual and therefore often and easily provoked sins have to be countered by the ... power of repulsion, but as the sinfulness of each has a ground in existence prior to him and external to him, his sin cannot be perfectly blotted out, but always remains something in process of disappearance" (§ 110.2). Given Schleiermacher's social and historical understanding of sin, whereby human beings re-present sin to each other, the effect of grace cannot be instantaneous; there is no magical transformation of human life. The life of the redeemed remains a struggle with sin and a series of approximations to blessedness.

One may gain the impression from Schleiermacher's discussion in this section of the *Glaubenslehre* that his agenda has been set more by the sixteenth than by the nineteenth century. Of course, the impression is not altogether just, for his intention is to expound religious experience and he does engage in some subtle revisions of the tradition. But he is throughout in dialogue with the sixteenth-century confessions, and is explicit about the differences between Catholic and Protestant understandings. Thus he claims: "The Roman Church does not count faith as an element in conversion, but puts in its stead confession and satisfaction, in spite of the fact that confession, rightly understood, is included in regret, and that satisfaction is a sheer impossibility" (§ 108.1). Or again: "The Roman Church differs entirely from the Protestant in its use of the expression 'justification' ... faith and justification are kept as far apart as possible, in order the more easily to show man's justification to be dependent on his sanctification" (§ 109.1). If Schleiermacher's discussion of the individual's relation to Christ as contingent upon the relation to the church raises some doubts about whether he meets his own criterion of what constitutes a Protestant view, his discussion of justification and sanctification leaves no doubt where his allegiance on the salient sixteenth-century issues lies.

Redemption as the completion of creation

Schleiermacher's overarching understanding of the human condition, of sin and redemption, is neatly summed up in his statement, "the creation of man is, as it were, divided into two stages" (§ 89.2). The model of a two-stage creation breaks with the Augustinian picture of Fall and Restoration in favor of the Irenaean picture of a developing creation.[21] In the first stage, "God put human nature under the law of earthly existence" (§ 89.3). The sensuous self-consciousness develops first, to the disadvantage of the God-consciousness; "the merely gradual and imperfect unfolding of the power of the God-consciousness is one of the necessary conditions of the human stage of existence" (§ 81.4). In a sense, then, God is the author of sin: "God has ordained that the continually imperfect triumph of the spirit should become sin to us" (§ 81). Yet there is but a single divine decree – to create and to redeem: "the decree that sent Christ forth is one with the decree creating the human race" (§ 109.3). Thus the appearance of Christ is properly "regarded as the completion, only now accomplished, of the creation of human nature" (§ 89), and Christ is appropriately considered the "Second Adam."

POSSIBILITIES AND LIMITATIONS

Schleiermacher's *The Christian Faith* puts forward a sweeping vision of the human condition from the perspective of Christian faith. In some respects it is startlingly revisionist, yet despite his revisionism, Schleiermacher took great pains to show that his new formulas were nothing less than retrievals of the fundamental themes of the Christian faith and of Protestantism, refashioned where necessary to resolve problems of internal coherence and credibility in the changed situation of modernity. It is conventional to call Schleiermacher the father of liberal theology; he saw himself as a centrist, working out a third alternative between the extremes of rationalism and supernaturalism. He has been attacked from both sides: D. F. Strauss took him to task in the nineteenth century for failing to be credible; Karl Barth in the twentieth century charged him with a failure to be appropriate to the Christian faith.[22]

Some contemporary theologians have found Schleiermacher's innovative thinking to be instructive for their own agendas. John Hick effectively exploits Schleiermacher's Irenaean understanding of the human condition in thinking through anew the problem of theodicy.[23] Marjorie Suchocki has recently appropriated Schleiermacher's corporate understanding of sin in her rethinking of the "fall into violence."[24]

If some features of Schleiermacher's thought offer suggestive resources for contemporary thought, other features suffer from what many, from our perspective, must regard as serious limitations. (1) The keystone of the arch, the very condition of the possibility of redemption as Schleiermacher conceived it, his picture of the perfection of Christ's God-consciousness, had already in the nineteenth century been called into question by D. F. Strauss. In so far as the Schleiermacherian Christ not only represents the possibility of redemption but constitutes it, the problem, if verified, is fatal.[25] (2) Schleiermacher's theory of religion is pluralistic, but his soteriology is exclusivistic: Christ is redeemer for all, not just for Christians.[26] Can such a Christian stance be sustained in an age far more sensitive to religious diversity? Is soteriological exclusivism the *sine qua non* of appropriateness? (3) As was suggested earlier in this chapter, Schleiermacher's treatment of evil is problematic. Is seeing evil as a problem of consciousness – how one looks at things – adequate to the problem? Does Schleiermacher's treatment rest upon a dualism of the spiritual life (piety) and embodied, physical life? These questions, in turn, point to a fourth one. (4) Is Schleiermacher's philosophical conceptuality adequate? Has the conceptuality, despite its supposedly purely formal significance, shaped Schleiermacher's theological intentions in problematic ways? To conceive of sin as an inhibition of the higher consciousness and of redemption as its strengthening is to make the Christian understanding of sin and grace center on the issue of piety. Sin is God-forgetfulness and blessedness is pious awareness. The moral dimension of the human condition is apparently neglected – at least in dogmatics.[27] Dualism seems built in by the conceptual framework. Critical questions such as these can and must continue to be raised and pursued as contemporary theologians reflect upon the possibilities and limitations of Schleiermacher's magnum opus.

Notes

1 All in-text citations are to *CF*. Unless otherwise noted, all quotations from the *Christian Faith* are from the Mackintosh and Stewart translation.

2 For credibility and appropriateness as two criteria of theological adequacy, see Ogden 1986, 4–6. For Schleiermacher's commitment to meeting challenges to credibility, see Schleiermacher, *On the Glaubenslehre*, 64.

3 See Schleiermacher, *On the Glaubenslehre*, *passim*; Nowak 2001, 409–19.

4 Hick 1978, 226. John Hick's case in *Evil and the God of Love* that Schleiermacher is best understood as an Irenaean, not an Augustinian, brings into focus the novelty of Schleiermacher's reinterpretation of the doctrine of sin. See Wyman 1994.

5 Mackintosh and Stewart's rendering of *Bezogensein* as "*reciprocal* relation" is misleading. As always "self-identical," the feeling of absolute dependence *cannot* be reciprocally related to the sensible self-consciousness, that is, be itself modified by the relationship.

6 Modern dictionary definitions of *Unlust* include "reluctance," "lack of enthusiasm," "dullness", and "slackness." The *Deutsches Wörterbuch* has seven columns of discussion of the word *Unlust*, and includes synonyms ranging from *Schmerz* and *Leid* ("pain") to *Verdruss* ("dissatisfaction" or "discontent"). This work also supplies the suggestive detail that Luther "loved our word and used it with rich shades of meaning": Grimm 1999, 1145–52; the quotation is from 1148.

7 *Selected Sermons of Schleiermacher*, trans. Wilson, n.d., 38. Von Meding 1992 dates this sermon (P 3 in his bibliography) in 1800, which places it many years

prior to the composition of the *Glaubenslehre*. Thus there may be a methodological problem with using this text for evidence. I am assuming that there is considerable continuity in Schleiermacher's fundamental religious insights over the decades. B. A. Gerrish drew my attention to the significance of this passage (see Gerrish 1984, 65–6 and Gerrish 1993, 162–4).

8 See § 99 Postscript for an important hermeneutical clue to Schleiermacher's procedure: the distinction between propositions which express his views independently and those which connect to traditional doctrines.

9 For a further discussion of this theme see Schleiermacher's sermon, "Christ the Liberator" (DeVries 1987, 43–57), preached in 1820 (von Meding 1992, sermon P 104).

10 In §§ 70–4 Schleiermacher presents his analysis "in closer connection with the accepted forms of the Church," see § 99, Postscript.

11 Ogden 1982. Ogden, of course, uses the term in a Christological sense.

12 Schleiermacher equates the two terms in a footnote to *CF*, § 61.5.

13 See Wyman 2001, for a consideration of some issues raised by Schleiermacher's discussion of evil.

14 There are two terms, *das Übel* and *das Böse*, both of which can be translated as "evil." *Das Übel* refers to such realities as death and suffering; it is a morally neutral term. *Das Böse* refers to moral evil or wickedness. The Mackintosh and Stewart translation does not make a consistent distinction between the two terms. Hudson and Greene's translation of Kant's *Religion within the Limits of Reason Alone* does: it translates *das Übel* as "ills" and *das Böse* as "evil": Kant 1960, book 1. One of the peculiarities of Schleiermacher's discussion of the relation of sin and evil is that he focuses on *das Übel* but says very little about *das Böse*.

15 See the case made in Wyman 2001.

16 The translator of § 100.1 missed an umlaut, and consequently read *Föderung*, "furtherance", as *Forderung*, "challenge." The mistake makes the proper understanding of the paragraph nearly impossible. One can make some sense of the English translation of the first sentence ("the imperfect stage of the higher life, as also the challenge of it") by reading "challenge" as a "challenge to the imperfect stage," and so on throughout the paragraph, but the actual meaning of the German is that the higher life is being "furthered" by the "act of the Redeemer become our own act," not that the imperfect stage is being "challenged."

17 For the most part *Seligkeit* is rendered "blessedness" in the Mackintosh and Stewart translation. But the editors have not rigorously imposed uniformity on the translation, and *Seligkeit* is occasionally rendered as "salvation." See, e.g., *CF*, §§ 137, 137.2.

18 The translators are far too traditional when they use the personal pronoun "He" to refer to the Holy Spirit/*Gemeingeist* in various formulations where Schleiermacher's German does not, in fact, use the personal pronoun or anthropomorphic language.

19 B. A. Gerrish suggests that the term "liberal evangelical" is an apt characterization of Schleiermacher: Gerrish 1984, 31–3.

20 See Gerrish's discussion of this passage: Gerrish 1978, 215, also 111.

21 See note 4.

22 Strauss 1972, 768–73; Strauss 1977, 29: "A sinless, archetypal Christ is not one whit less unthinkable than a supernaturally begotten Christ with a divine and

human nature." Barth 1973, 425–73; cf. 473: "He failed to notice that his result challenged the decisive premise of all Christian theology."

23 See Hick 1978.

24 See Suchocki 1994. Of course Suchocki cannot follow Schleiermacher in his distinctive conceptuality; she finds the principle of the absolute dependence of the world upon God to be incompatible with her process theology. But her thinking about the corporate nature of sin is influenced by Schleiermacher independently of that problem.

25 The distinction between constituting the possibility of redemption and representing it is central to Schubert Ogden's Christology; see Ogden 1982.

26 "He alone is destined gradually to quicken the whole human race into a higher life" (*CF*, § 13.1); "all nations are destined to pass over into the Christian fellowship" (*CF*, § 121.3).

27 What Schleiermacher has to say in his lectures on Christian ethics is, of course, another matter, that cannot be considered here.

8 Christology and anthropology in Friedrich Schleiermacher

JACQUELINE MARIÑA

It is no exaggeration to say that Christological doctrine is the heart of Christian theology. It encapsulates an understanding of God and human nature, as well as how the two relate to each other. How one understands the person and work of Christ depends in part on how one understands the human condition, how it needs to be changed, and what it would take to change it. Moreover, insofar as Christ is understood as the Logos, God's self-revelation, Christology also has implications for the doctrine of God, as well as for the doctrine of how it is that God relates to us. Insofar as a doctrine of the work of Christ has implications regarding how his work changes us and our relations to others, Christology contains the germ of Christian ethics. In the work of Friedrich Schleiermacher, Christology plays no less a central role. As Richard R. Niebuhr has observed, Schleiermacher's theology is Christo-morphic;[1] for him the elements of theology are grounded in the *person-forming* experience of being in relation to Christ and the community founded by him.[2] Both Schleiermacher's dialogue with the orthodox Christological tradition preceding him, as well as his understanding of the work of Christ, are founded on a critical analysis of this fundamental experience and its implications. In this chapter I explore Schleiermacher's understanding of both the person and work of Christ. The chapter is divided into two main parts: in the first I treat Schleiermacher's understanding of the person of Christ, and in the second I treat his view of Christ's work.

THE PERSON OF JESUS CHRIST

Doctrine, for Schleiermacher, is always the result of a reflection on a given *experience* that is presupposed, namely the experience of being redeemed through Jesus Christ. Hence a true appropriation of Christian doctrine cannot be had by proofs or scientific means, rather it can only be brought about "by each man willing to have the experience for himself ... it can only be apprehended by the love that wills to perceive" (*CF*, § 13.2).[3]

Christian doctrines, Schleiermacher tells us, are "accounts of the religious Christian religious affections set forth in speech" (§ 15). They always proceed from a reflection on how the experience of one's self-consciousness has been changed through being in relation to the redeemer.[4] The experience of redemption is grounded in Christ's empowerment of the God-consciousness (the feeling of absolute dependence) to dominate any moment of self-consciousness in which the self stands in relation to the world. Hence the feeling of absolute dependence itself grounds how the world is understood, valued, and felt.[5] It is through the relation to Christ that the self arrives at complete trust in God, who is the ground of both self and world. Through the empowerment of the God-consciousness the self comes to have faith in both God's goodness and power, and this trust itself affects both how the world is viewed as well as what it is that a person desires.

The starting point of Schleiermacher's Christology is the certainty of the *experience* of redemption through Christ. He asks, given this experience, what are the conditions of its possibility? This question prompts him to formulate the four "natural heresies" that must be avoided if the concept of redemption is to be properly understood. The heresies are ways in which the fundamentals of Christian doctrine can be contradicted, while "the appearance of Christianity yet remains" (*CF*, § 22). These are "the Docetic and the Nazarean, the Manichean and the Pelagian" (§ 22). Avoidance of these heresies sets the parameters for both his Christology and anthropology. The first two heresies, the Docetic and the Nazarean, specifically concern the person of Christ. It is to a discussion of these that I now turn.

If Jesus is to be the redeemer, two conditions must be met. First, he must be *like* us, that is, he must have a nature essentially like our own. Second, he must not himself stand in need of redemption, and he must have the requisite power to save those that need redemption. In this regard he must be *unlike* us. The first heresy, which Schleiermacher labels the Docetic, results from thinking of Jesus as so exalted above human nature that he does not partake of it. Schleiermacher notes that "if the difference between Christ and those who stand in need of redemption is made so unlimited that an essential likeness is incompatible with it, then His participation in human nature vanishes into a mere appearance; and consequently our God-consciousness, being something essentially different, cannot be derived from His, and redemption is also only an appearance." The second heresy results from thinking of Jesus as so similar to other members of the human race that "no room is left for a distinctive superiority" (*CF*, § 22). In such a case he himself would stand in need of redemption, and would be powerless to effect the redemption of others. These two

heresies are the Scylla and Charybdis of Christology. They reflect fundamental ways that thinking about Jesus can go wrong. In the Symbol of
Chalcedon of 451 the church laid down guidelines for correct thinking about
Jesus after a protracted Christological controversy. While Schleiermacher
does not directly cite the Chalcedonian Symbol in § 96 where he discusses
the issue of the two natures, it stands in the background of his discussion.[6]
In fact, any serious Christology must come to grips with the problems faced
by Chalcedon. Schleiermacher's own analysis is concerned to avoid the
pitfalls of the one-sided Christologies leading up to the council. He preserves
the upshot of the insights of Chalcedon while at the same time rejecting the
language in which those insights were framed.

The sentence explicated in § 96 reads "In Jesus Christ divine nature and
human nature were combined into one person." The sentence is misleading
in that Schleiermacher ultimately rejects the language of two "natures"
coexisting in one person. He notes that the word "nature" ($\phi\acute{u}\sigma\iota\varsigma$) is used
of finite existences having a particular essence, and remarks that even the
heathens had realized that it was inapplicable to God insofar as God "is to be
thought of as beyond all existence and being" (*CF*, § 96).[7] Hence it makes
little sense to speak of a divine *nature*. But more problematic is the fact that
the requirement that we think of Jesus as having two distinct natures
expressing themselves in one person is analogous to "a formula made up
by combining indications out of which it is impossible to construct a figure."
Schleiermacher notes that:

> Now if "person" indicates a constant unity of life, but "nature" a sum
> of ways of action or laws, according to which conditions of life vary
> and are included within a fixed range, how can the unity of life coexist
> with the duality of natures, unless the one gives way to the other, if the
> one exhibits a larger and the other a narrower range, or unless they
> melt into each other, both systems of ways of action really becoming
> one in the one life ? – if indeed we are speaking of a person, i.e., of an
> Ego which is the same in all the consecutive moments of its existence.
> (*CF*, § 96)

The problem becomes especially intractable if the divine and human natures are thought of as diametrically opposed: the human nature as finite and
capable of suffering, and the divine as infinite and impassible. It was this
antithesis between the passibility of the human and the impassibility of the
divine that led the Arians to conclude that Jesus, who prayed to the Father,
expressed emotions, and suffered on the cross, could not truly be God from
God, but must be, rather, a semi-divine angel. To think that the Son is of the

same essence as the Father, they argued, would be to threaten the divine impassibility.

Leading up to Chalcedon, three ways of trying to come to grips with the doctrine of two natures in one person presented themselves, all of them equally unsatisfactory. Schleiermacher notes that ever since the language of two natures and one person began to be used, the results "have always vacillated between the opposite errors of mixing the two natures to form a third which would be neither of them, neither divine nor human, or of keeping the two natures separate, but either neglecting the unity of the person in order to separate the two natures more distinctly, or, in order to keep firm hold of the unity of the person, disturbing the necessary balance, and making one nature less important than the other and limited by it" (*CF*, § 96). The Symbol of Chalcedon issued parameters eschewing all three results, as well as reaffirming the results of Nicaea, which had laid down, against the Arians, that the Son was indeed God from God. Schleiermacher argues that the language of the two natures in one person led, with almost inexorable necessity, to one of the errors eschewed by Chalcedon. The first is that of the Monophysite Alexandrians, who insisted that after the union between the human and the divine in Christ, there was only one nature, namely, the divine. For all practical purposes this Christology did away with the humanity of Jesus. The irresolvable problem of trying to construct such an impossible figure is solved here, as Schleiermacher puts it, by one nature giving "way to the other." The Symbol of Chalcedon attempted to correct this one-sided construction through its language that "the distinction of the natures is in no way to be abolished on account of this union, but rather the characteristic property of each nature is preserved, and concurring into one Person and one subsistence."[8] It did not, however, explain how this was to be conceived.

Equally problematic was the Antiochene viewpoint, taken to its extreme by the Nestorians, stressing that both natures, the human and the divine, continued to be operative after the union. The problem here was that both natures, each having diametrically opposed attributes, were just about impossible to square with one another insofar as they were to be operative in one person. The result was often a disjointed Christology in which some operations were ascribed to the human nature, others to the divine.[9] This is another possible result of the language of two natures. Schleiermacher notes that the "utter fruitlessness" of such a language is particularly marked "in the treatment of the question whether Christ as one person formed out of two natures had also two wills according to the number of natures, or only one according to the number of the persons." If Christ has only one will, it must have either a divine or a human nature. The human will "always strives for only separate ends and one for the sake of the other"; the object of the divine will, on the other hand, can be "nothing but the whole world in the totality of its development." The attributes of both are mutually exclusive. Whichever is chosen, attributes of the other nature are left out. On the other hand, if Christ had two wills, "then the unity of the person is no more than apparent" (*CF*, § 96). Equally problematic is the character of Jesus' intellect: human reason is discursive; it "knows separate things one after the other," whereas the divine intellect is "omniscient and sees everything at once." The two kinds of intellect cannot co-exist in one and the same person. Antiochene Christology crashed on the shoals of just this problem; while it stressed Christ's two natures, it had a great deal of trouble explaining the union, since the postulation of both natures demanded that Christ act in accordance with the operations peculiar to each. The Alexandrians, in fact, accused the Antiochenes of having a doctrine of two Sons. Chalcedon declared such a position to lie outside the scope of orthodoxy through its language that "the characteristic property of each nature is preserved, concurring into one Person and one subsistence, not as if Christ were parted or divided into two persons, but remains one and the same Son and only-begotten God, Word, Lord, Jesus Christ."[10] Again, how this was to be conceived without contradiction was not explained. Another strategy condemned was that of Eutyches, who seemed to reason that the result of the union was a kind of mixture of the two natures; the Chalcedonian Symbol also rejected this position in noting that the "distinction of natures is in no way abolished on account of the union."[11] Schleiermacher mentions this as the error of "mixing the two natures to form a third which would be neither of them."

It is clear from Schleiermacher's discussion that he is in complete agreement with Chalcedon in regard to the positions it *rejects*. The humanity of Jesus after the union cannot be done away with, yet we must affirm a veritable existence of God in him. Nonetheless the operations of the humanity and the divinity cannot be distributed amongst Jesus' actions, but all actions must issue from a single consciousness. And further, we cannot think that Jesus' nature is some kind of third thing resulting from a mixture of the divine and the human. Nevertheless, Schleiermacher rejects the starting point of Chalcedon, namely the adoption of the language of two natures requiring one to attempt to construct an impossible figure, and leading almost inevitably to one of the aforementioned errors.

Whatever the final assessment of Schleiermacher's Christology, his own strategy has the peculiar virtues of consistency and of avoiding all three pitfalls warned against in the Chalcedonian Symbol. His crucial move to avoid them lies not so much with his rejection of the language of the two natures, however, as with his understanding of the ideal of human nature becoming real in Jesus Christ. Two moves are crucial for his resolution of the Christological enigma. First, the essential character of perfect human nature is just to express the divine. Hence there is no real duality between perfect human nature and the divine. Second, human nature only achieves its perfection in Jesus Christ; in fact the creation of human beings is ordered to perfection in and through Jesus Christ. In the following two subsections I deal with each of these points.

PERFECT HUMAN NATURE AND THE NATURE OF JESUS' SELF-CONSCIOUSNESS

A key problem for Schleiermacher is the question of how the divine can co-exist with the human. Schleiermacher notes that since the Christian faith has never assumed that sin is essential to human nature, "it has always been assumed in Christian faith that a union with God is possible in terms of man's essence" (*LJ*, 100). If the essence of human nature is such that it can be united with God, then there is no contradiction in thinking of Jesus as both fully human and as united with God. The idea of redemption requires that we posit a real existence of God in Christ. Furthermore "to ascribe to Christ an absolutely powerful God-consciousness, and to attribute to Him an existence of God in Him, are exactly the same thing" (*CF*, § 94). God is truly present in Jesus insofar as it is the divine that fully expresses itself in his humanity:

> the existence of God in the Redeemer is posited as the innermost fundamental power within Him, from which every activity proceeds and which holds every element together; everything human (in Him) forms only the organism for this fundamental power, and is related to it as the system which both receives and represents it, just as in us all other powers are related to the intelligence. (*CF*, § 96)

It is in virtue of his absolute dependence on God that Jesus can be the organ for the expression of the divine. It is important to note that all elements of what constitutes a natural humanity are involved in this process, so that for Schleiermacher, Jesus' intellect and will must be fully human. Schleiermacher's is by no means a *logos/sarx* Christology, in which the Logos provides the direct *energeia* to the body of Christ.[12] Rather, all elements of a full and complete humanity are taken up in the process of expressing the divine.[13] As such, Jesus' intellect cannot be an omniscient one, but rather, like ours, proceeds discursively. Likewise his will, like ours, wills one thing for the sake of another; unlike God's it does not will everything at once. As truly human, Jesus is fully enmeshed in all the limitations of embodiment and finite consciousness. Nevertheless, because all the elements of his humanity are fully passive in relation to the divine, his person is able to fully express the divine. According to Schleiermacher's second Christological theorem, "In the uniting of the divine nature with the human, the divine alone was active or self-imparting, and the human alone passive or in process of being assumed; but during the state of union every activity was a common activity of both natures" (*CF*, § 97). In other words, in Jesus each moment of the sensuous self-consciousness expresses the divine in virtue of his absolute dependence upon God. Insofar as Jesus expresses the divine, his self-consciousness is fully active in relation to the world,[14] that is, he imparts his God-consciousness to others and thereby quickens the whole race. For Schleiermacher the Johannine phrase that "the Word become flesh," is fully appropriate in regard to Jesus, since "'Word' is the activity of God expressed in the form of consciousness" (§ 96).

In his *Life of Jesus* Schleiermacher discusses Jesus' God-consciousness and its developmental character in more depth. The divine in Jesus is not a real, discrete consciousness, but is rather "something that lies at the basis of the total consciousness" (*LJ*, 97). In fact, as soon as one conceives of the divine element in him as such a real discrete consciousness co-existing with the human "we clearly put an end to the unity of the personality" (96). On the other hand, if the divine in him is thought of as a vital principle lying at the ground of his consciousness, then we can conceive of it as something that makes its appearance gradually, and whose self-expression becomes stronger as Jesus matures. As such Schleiermacher hopes to make sense of the saying in Luke 2:52 that as a child Jesus "increased in wisdom and in favor with God and man" (98). It is crucial that Jesus' humanity be essentially like our own, for "if we think of him as an absolute model we must think of his action as wholly human, for otherwise I cannot follow him" (84). Nevertheless, while Jesus' humanity is completely like our own in that his consciousness is not an omniscient one, and in that he underwent development just as we do, Schleiermacher stresses that Jesus must be sinless if he is indeed to be the redeemer. He notes that "not only was his moral development progress without struggle, but also his intellectual development was progress without error" (107).[15] His development is that from "complete innocence to an ever more perfect consciousness" (99).

Jesus "was always conscious of being in relation to the divine will" (101) and throughout his development the sensual element never took preponderance over Jesus' God-consciousness (98–9) but rather "nothing was ever able to find a place in the sense-nature that did not instantly take its place as an instrument of the spirit" (*CF*, § 93.4).

Schleiermacher develops a sophisticated analysis of temptation and concludes that Jesus cannot have been genuinely tempted. Everything depends "on determining the point where sin begins." If Jesus' nature was a genuinely human one, he must have been susceptible to the difference between pleasure and pain. However, Schleiermacher does not think that this susceptibility could have involved him in any kind of moral struggle, since "the beginning of sin must lie between the moment at which pleasure and pain exist in this sinless way and that at which struggle begins." Hence, while Jesus felt pleasure and pain, these did not determine his incentives to action (*CF*, § 98). Genuine temptation involves the idea that an object of temptation is an object of desire, that is, that it is genuinely attractive. Temptation also involves the idea of struggle in the self: one struggles with the attractive force of the object of desire. But, Schleiermacher reasons, to think that the sensuous self-consciousness in Jesus was able, of itself, to determine something as attractive or repulsive in such a way that he had to struggle with it, is to posit the origins of sin, even if infinitely small, in Jesus. If the sensuous self-consciousness could, of itself, determine a course of action as *genuinely* attractive for him, this would mean that in him there was a moment of consciousness in which the sensuous self-consciousness was not just the organ of the expression of the Spirit, that is, of his God-consciousness. It is these doctrinal considerations that are the guiding thread in Schleiermacher's understanding of the life of the historical Jesus. As such the reports in the gospels that Jesus was "tempted in all points" are a special difficulty for him (§ 98), and he concludes that the temptation stories do not reflect a genuine temptation of Jesus but are, rather a "parable" of Christ "for his disciples" regarding the "manner in which they should organize their leadership in the office entrusted to them" (*LJ*, 153).

One last point is crucial in understanding the nature of Jesus' God-consciousness and the expression of the divine in him. In Jesus each moment of the sensuous self-consciousness is referred back to his absolute dependence upon the Father; as such each moment of the sensuous self-consciousness is the organ of the expression of this relation, in which his humanity is receptive to the divine power. This power is understood, first and foremost, as love. Hence Schleiermacher notes:

But our canon also compels us to think of the human nature of Christ in such feelings, not as moved for and through itself, but only as taken up into association with an activity of the divine in Christ. *Now this "divine" is the divine love in Christ which, once and for all or in every moment – whichever expression be chosen – gave direction to His feelings for the spiritual conditions of men.* In virtue of these feelings, and in consequence of them, there then arose the impulse to particularly helpful acts. So that in this interrelation every original activity belongs solely to the divine, and everything passive to the human.

(*CF*, § 97.3, italics mine)

This view of Jesus' self-consciousness, and of the mode of the union between the human and the divine in him, is crucial to an understanding of the work of Jesus, which I discuss below.

JESUS AS IDEAL AND THE ORIGINAL DIVINE DECREE

Many of Schleiermacher's critics have concluded that the *Christian Faith* presents an anthropological transcendental philosophy of religion with an amazingly high Christology stuck in the middle. F. C. Baur complained to his brother that if the principle characteristics of Jesus "were derived from religious self-consciousness ... I could think of the Redeemer only as a certain form and potency of self-consciousness ... and the outward appearance of Jesus is not the original fact [from which Christian consciousness is derived]."[16] Such too, was the verdict of Karl Barth, who accused Schleiermacher of an anthropological starting point logically committing him to understanding Jesus as a mere exemplar of human nature. He charges that for Schleiermacher "statements about sin and grace relate to those of the God-consciousness as *predicates* to a *subject*,"[17] that is, sin and grace are viewed as mere modifications of a human nature understood in its own right, from the perspectives of philosophy, psychology and anthropology. As such the revelation given in Jesus Christ cannot function as a supernatural event, that is, as the Word of God against which the natural man must be judged and through which he is redeemed. Rather, Jesus is viewed as functioning inside the parameters of a God-consciousness that is an element of an already given human nature; as such, Barth notes, the advent of Jesus is just about as novel as "the formation of a new nebula."[18] If such is the case, it is hard to understand Jesus as the archetype of the relation between God and persons such that all human relationship to God is rooted in him.[19]

Such judgments cannot be farther from the truth, and can only be the result of a lack of acquaintance with Schleiermacher's *Christian Faith* as a whole. In his lectures, for instance, Barth urged that his students need only read the first twelve sections of the *Christian Faith* in order to come to the conclusion that the rest of the book was not worth the effort.[20] A complete reading of the *Christian Faith*, however, shows that Schleiermacher can quite consistently claim that Jesus must function inside the parameters of what is completely human while still functioning as the archetype in which all human relation to God must be rooted.

According to Schleiermacher, every given state of the God-consciousness in human corporate life is "no more than a mere approximation to that which exists in the Redeemer Himself; and just this is what we understand by His ideal dignity" (*CF*, § 93). In fact, human nature first achieves its perfection in Jesus Christ, whose perfect God-consciousness was destined from the beginning of all time to quicken that of the entire race. Hence, for Schleiermacher "Christ is . . . the completion of the creation of man" (§ 89). From the first moment of its creation the human race was ordered to its completion in Jesus Christ: "For although at the first creation of the human race only the imperfect state of human nature was manifested, yet eternally the appearance of the Redeemer was already involved in that" (§ 89.3). The impartation of the Spirit to both the first Adam, in which this Spirit remains sunk in sensuousness, and to the second Adam, in which its impartation reaches its perfection, "go back to one undivided eternal divine decree" (§ 95). Through this decree it was ordained that the first Adam should reach completion in the second. There is, therefore, according to Schleiermacher, no creation of human nature independent of Jesus Christ, but both go back to a *single establishing action* on God's part. God does not first create the world and then act again to redeem it. That would be to ascribe anthropomorphic characteristics to God's action, since we would then have to posit in God "an alteration of activity and rest in relation to the world." If God first creates something, and must then act again in order to alter what has already been established in creation, then "the world would remain entirely dependent upon God but irregularly, and on divine activities which mutually exclude one another" (§ 38.2).[21] On the other hand, if God's causality is absolute, it cannot belong to the sphere of interaction in which something *independently* existing is acted upon. Rather, God's creative activity itself brings about the existence of what is acted upon. The divine causality is "opposite in kind" to finite causality since it does not belong to the sphere of interaction (§ 51). What God acts upon has no reactive power that is not itself kept in existence through God's activity. As such, God's creative act fully determines the existence of what is brought into being *for the good*. Moreover, given the above considerations, the creative and sustaining activity must be thought of together, so they are really one. God does not first create and then sustain, but rather all action of God upon the world is his enduring sustenance of it, encompassed in the original divine decree through which he orders it to the good.

Schleiermacher's doctrine of the original divine decree, containing the complete destiny of humanity, implies the collapse of the distinction between nature and super-nature. There is a single nature system established by God in the original divine decree, and included in this decree is the way that God relates to the world. Hence everything established through this divine action belongs to nature and is completely natural; God does not first establish nature to exist and relate to him in one way and then establish a second way of relating through miracles and other "supernatural" events. To think of God that way would involve us in the difficulties mentioned above. Hence the impartation of the Spirit to the first Adam (which remained "sunk in sensuousness") and the perfection of the impartation of this Spirit in Christ both form "even in a higher sense, one and the same natural system, though one unattainable by us" (*CF*, § 94.3). Given that the way in which God relates to the world is established through the original divine decree, the creation of humanity is teleologically ordered from its very inception to its perfection in Christ. God relates to humans through the God-consciousness, a "vital impulse" (§ 65) within them that continually undergoes development, but one that remains locked in a state of captivity or constraint aside from the power of Christ. This God-consciousness was destined from the beginning to find completion and perfection in Christ, who alone holds the keys to unlock its power. Schleiermacher notes that

> the uniting divine activity [in the Origin of the Person of Christ] is also an eternal activity, but that, as in God there is no distinction between resolve and activity, this eternal activity means for us simply a divine decree, identical as such with the decree to create man and included therein. (*CF*, § 97.4)

In other words, God's activity of uniting with humanity in the perfect God-consciousness of Jesus Christ is established in the original divine decree; the activity of the God-consciousness in human nature that has not yet been quickened by Jesus is but a prefigurement, in the form of potentiality, of its actualization in Jesus Christ. Therefore, the appearance of the redeemer is already involved in the receptivity implanted in human nature from the beginning (*CF*, § 89.3).

It is true that the God-consciousness can undergo development even if it as yet has no knowledge of the historical Jesus, and as such does not remain at the level of sheer potentiality aside from such historical contact with him. However, when such development occurs, it does so in fits and spurts, so that just as there is a little progress, there is just as much regression to superstition and idolatry. Moreover, whatever progress there is refers back to the original divine decree, in which the teleological perfection of the world is already implanted in the seeds of the world's first beginnings. At this original moment it was already ordained that humanity should be completed in Christ. Hence "the origin of finite existence" is the "source of the whole temporal development," and this is the object of the "divine approval of the world" (*CF*, § 57.2). Moreover, precisely because the coming of Christ is already prefigured in the origin of finite existence, it is appropriate to link "the first consciousness of sin, due to the accession of the God-consciousness, with the first presentiment of redemption" (§ 71.3). Consciousness of sin can be understood as the pangs of creation as it longs for its completion in Jesus Christ.

Important to Schleiermacher's view of Christ as archetype is the difference between the existence of God in Christ and in the rest of the human race. The existence of God in human nature is originally "found nowhere but in Him, and He is the only 'other' in which there is an existence of God in the proper sense." On the other hand, the existence of God in us is only derivative: "it is only through Him that the human God-consciousness becomes an existence of God in human nature" (*CF*, § 94.2). Jesus' relation to God is different from that of all other persons. Only in Jesus is the God relation original and unmediated; the rest of humanity's relation to God must be mediated through him. All these points show that if Schleiermacher's theology is taken as a whole, the charges of Baur, Brunner, and Barth have no basis.

THE WORK OF CHRIST

A clear understanding of how Jesus redeems first presupposes a grasp of what it is that humans need redemption from, namely, sin. Schleiermacher understands sin as the result of inattention to the influence of the higher (transcendental) God-consciousness upon moments of the sensible self-consciousness. The God-consciousness is always present and in relation to the sensible self-consciousness, which is the self's consciousness of itself as related to, and interacting with, the world. Insofar as the God-consciousness is allowed to be effective, it conditions every moment of the sensible self-consciousness. As transcendental, the God-consciousness is like a light that casts its rays on how the world is understood, valued, and felt. As Frank has shown in chapter one in this volume, insofar as the God-consciousness involves an element of *self*-consciousness, it is the consciousness that one is not the author of one's own existence. However, this "gap" in self-consciousness (through which one comes to the consciousness of one's dependence on the absolute) is also the place at which the power of God can shine through, so to speak, into the finite. If this gap remains completely open, so that the power of the divine can pass through it, the body and all the higher functions of the human psyche (such as intelligence, will, and the emotions insofar as they are informed by the former two), become the organs of the spirit. In Christ this is complete, and this is what Schleiermacher means when he notes that in Christ the divine is completely active and the human is completely receptive; in him the human has been taken up completely and become the organ of spirit.

While this gap in the self's consciousness of itself is always present, it can become obscured through the self's thinking of itself as independent. Schleiermacher notes that sin is "an arrestment of the power of spirit due to the independence of the sensuous functions" (*CF*, § 66.2). The "evil condition" from which humans need redemption is an "obstruction or arrest of the vitality of the higher-consciousness, so that there comes to be little or no union of it with the various determinations of the sensible self-consciousness" (§ 11.2). In the state of sin the self shuts itself off from the power of God by thinking of itself as independent, as the source of its own existence. Hence sin is first and foremost "a turning away from the creator" (§ 66.2).[22] Schleiermacher's understanding of the relation of God to human beings, and the results of the sundering of this relation is, at its core, Platonic and Augustinian. There are, of course, important differences. But the similarities are fundamental. The right relation of the soul to God is one in which the soul allows itself to be infused with the power of the divine (the divine love); for Schleiermacher this happens through the feeling of absolute dependence. If the self mistakes itself as independent, it cuts itself off from the source of its true life. All sin is a result of this fundamental mistake, the authority problem in relation to God.

The belief that the self is independent has several important consequences. The first of these is the identification of the self with the body, that is, with the sensuous functions. As Schleiermacher notes, if the self thinks of itself as a body, then it will think that it can be harmed. If what conditions an experience is identification with the "flesh," then "every impression made by the world upon us and invoking an obstruction of our bodily and temporal life must be reckoned as an evil." As such, identification with the body brings fear. Second, as a result of its identification with the body, the self contracts in upon itself; it is ever vigilant lest it be harmed, and it stands in constant competition with others for what it believes are finite resources necessary for the sustenance of the body. If the supremacy of the God-consciousness is done away with, "what is a furtherance to one will often for that very reason become a hindrance to the other." On the other hand, were the God-consciousness determinative of human existence, whatever opposition the world offers to the bodily life of human beings "could never have been construed by the corporate consciousness as an obstruction to life, since it could not in any sense act as an inhibition of the God-consciousness, but at most would give a different form to its effects" (*CF*, § 75.1).

Key to Schleiermacher's understanding of redemption is that the belief system associated with sin is a corporate one having corporate effects. As noted above, this belief system contains three important interrelated elements: first, belief that the self is independent of God; second, identification of the self with the body; and third, belief that the since the self is a mere body, it is inherently independent of others and in competition with them for finite resources. All three ideas are inherently linked. They are not only beliefs of the individual self about the self, but are in general corporate. They are beliefs ensconced and reinforced in communities about what it means to be a self. Moreover, sin is itself always a corporate action. Schleiermacher notes that sin is "in either case common to all." Sin is

> not something that pertains severally to each individual and exists in relation to him by himself, but in each the work of all, and in all the work of each; and only in its corporate character can it be properly and fully understood. This solidarity means an interdependence of all places and all times in the respect we have in view. The distinctive form of original sin in the individual, as regards its quality, is only a constituent part of the form it takes in the circle to which he immediately belongs, so that, though inexplicable when taken by itself, it points to the other parts as complementary to it. And this relationship runs through all gradations of community – families, clans, tribes, peoples, and races – so that the form of sinfulness in each of these points to that present in the other parts as complementary to it . . . and whatever of that power appears in the single unit, whether personal or composite, is not to be attributed to, or explained by, that unit alone. (*CF*, § 71.2)

Sin is never an individual affair, but rather implicates ever-widening circles of community. What the self believes about itself (and hence the actions flowing from such a self-understanding), is never independent, but rather depends, to a great degree, on how the community constructs itself as a group as well as the individuals within it. Hence the sin of one individual is never fully understandable in isolation, but always points past itself. Understanding the corporate character of sin is key to an understanding of the work of Christ; Schleiermacher importantly notes that "the denial of the corporate character of original sin and a lower estimate of the redemption wrought by Christ usually go hand in hand" (*CF*, § 71.3). It is because human beings are so interdependent with one another that the sin of one person implicates the whole race. More importantly, the converse is also true: it is just this interdependence of human beings on one another that makes it possible for the salvation of the whole race to be accomplished in the historical life of one person.

Schleiermacher's understanding of the work of Christ can be broken down into two key moments. First, Jesus strengthens each individual's God-consciousness, enabling it to dominate each moment of the sensuous self-consciousness. In other words, Jesus awakens the God-consciousness and establishes the dominance of spirit over the flesh. Second, Jesus establishes the kingdom of God. Both moments are interdependent, so that the awakening of the God-consciousness occurs through the establishment of the kingdom of God, and the kingdom of God is established through the awakening of the God-consciousness. One is the vertical pole – the relation to God through Christ, the other the horizontal pole – the establishment of a Christian community. Schleiermacher notes that "to believe that Jesus was the Christ, and to believe that the Kingdom of God (that is, the new corporate life that was to be created by God) had come, [are] the same thing" (*CF*, § 87.3). There is no teaching about the kingdom that is not at the same time a teaching about Jesus himself.[23] "The original activity of the Redeemer," Schleiermacher writes, is "that by means of which He assumes us into this fellowship of His activity and His life" (§ 100). This activity is the result of the divine love in Christ, which is communicated to all those who enter into fellowship with him. As a result of the communication of this divine love, "the redemptive activity of Christ brings about for all believers a corporate activity corresponding to the being of God in Christ." The love of Christ is communicated to the believer, and the believer in turn expresses Christ's love to the members of the community of Christ, both those already within the community and those yet to be incorporated into it. Insofar as the believer shares in the blessedness of the being of God in Christ, the "former personality dies, so far as is meant a self-enclosed life of feeling within a sensuous vital unity, to which all sympathetic feeling for others and for the whole was subordinated" (§ 101.2). The love of Christ is a gift to each individual; once received the person is empowered to love others through the love of Christ. As such, the love of Christ for humanity founds the community of the kingdom of God. The "will for the Kingdom of God" is "at once love to men and love to Christ and love to God," which is at the same time "Christ's love working in and through us" (§ 112.3). It is this founding of the kingdom that is the principle work of Christ and the manner in which he redeems humanity.

In entering into the historical life of the human race, and founding a community within it, Jesus communicates the God-consciousness and the activity of divine love. The agency of Christ can only be received as "it appears in history, and can continue to function only as a historical entity." Hence one cannot "share in the redemption and be made blessed through Christ outside the corporate life that he instituted." One cannot "be with Christ, as it were, alone," that is, to be with Christ is to be in the Christian community, and to live out the new way of being towards others that he instituted (*CF*, § 87.3). Our interdependence with other human beings is worked out in history. It is because of this interdependence that the sin of one implicates the whole human community; likewise it is through this interdependence that the perfect divine love of Christ can be mediated historically and redeem humanity.

Important in this regard is that Schleiermacher rejects any understanding of redemption that is not mediated through the community as "magical." Such, in particular, is the Anselmian theory of satisfaction, in which "the forgiveness of sins is made to depend upon the punishment which Christ suffered, and the blessedness of men itself is presented as a reward which God offers to Christ for the suffering of that punishment." According to this theory, the effective element in the forgiveness of sins is that Jesus bore the punishment for the sins of humanity although he was himself innocent; salvation can be principally construed as an individual affair in which the person accepts the sacrifice of Christ on his or her behalf. Schleiermacher notes several problems with this account, in particular the magical character of redemption, in which "something so absolutely inward as blessedness is supposed to have been brought about externally, without any inner basis." Moreover, punishment "is merely the sensuous element in the forgiveness of sins. The properly ethical element, the consciousness of deserving punishment would remain. And this therefore would have to disappear as if conjured away, without any reason" (*CF*, § 101.3). In other words, the

Anselmian theory hardly explains the *ethical* transformation of the individual on whose behalf Christ has worked; it merely represents an exchange
of punishments having to do only with the sensuous self-consciousness.
Contrasted with this is Schleiermacher's own understanding: the individual
becomes blessed through participating in the life of Christ, and this is the
life of love that he imparts to the historical community he founds as he
inaugurates the kingdom. This kingdom is a new way of being in the world,
one that is grasped as one enters the new community and participates in it.
The blessedness that Christ imparts through the historical community is
one that is *person-forming*, "for now all his activities are differently determined through the workings of Christ in him, and even all impressions are
differently received – which means that the personal self-consciousness too
becomes altogether different" (§ 100.2).

For Schleiermacher the passion of Christ, featured so prominently in
the gospels, is not a "primitive element" in redemption and reconciliation.
The primitive element is the foundation of the kingdom and the corporate
blessedness attending it. The suffering, however, does acquire secondary
importance insofar as it exemplifies Christ's perfect obedience and his
steadfastness in his proclamation of the kingdom even in the face of social
evil and sin, that is, the political opposition that would cost him his life. On
Schleiermacher's view portrayals of the life of Christ (a good contemporary
example would be Mel Gibson's *Passion*), focusing mostly on the suffering
are "magical caricature[s]" since they "isolate this climax, leave out the
foundation of the corporate life, and regard this as a giving up of Himself
to suffering for suffering's sake as the real sum total of Christ's redemptive
activity" (*CF*, § 101.3). Rather, Christ's suffering is a result of his having
entered into the fallen human community that had opposed with such
vehemence his introduction of a new mode of being in the world. Only in
this sense can it be said that "His sufferings in this fellowship, if occasioned
by sin ... [were] suffered for those with whom He stood in fellowship, that
is, for the whole human race" (§ 104.4). It is, however, a mistake to think of
his sufferings as the bearing of punishment due to the rest of the race.[24]

Jesus' steadfastness in inaugurating the kingdom (even unto death), the
establishment of which was the only way in which the human race could
arrive at blessedness, is the perfect manifestation of Christ's love. It is therefore in "His suffering unto death, occasioned by His steadfastness" that his
"absolutely self-denying love" is manifest. When the passion is understood in
the context of his establishment of the kingdom, "there is represented to us
with perfect vividness the way in which God was in Him to reconcile the world
to Himself." Through this portrayal of his steadfastness "we see God in Christ,

and envisage Christ as the most immediate partaker in the eternal love which sent Him forth and fitted Him for His task" (*CF*, § 104.4). To sum up, Christ's saving work is his inauguration of the kingdom of God. This kingdom is first and foremost one of divine love. Jesus is perfectly receptive to this divine love in virtue of his absolute dependence on the Father; he expresses this love in his historical presence among human beings. In his communication of the divine love he brings others into fellowship with him, who in turn are enabled to love others as he has loved them. Jesus establishes the kingdom by setting others aflame with the power of divine love.

CONCLUSION

Many contemporary criticisms leveled at Schleiermacher's Christology are the result of too shallow a reading of him. For instance, the charge by Colin Gunton that Schleiermacher's Christology is Docetic, having Apollinarian and Monophysite overtones is unfounded, the result of his having ignored large parts of Schleiermacher's work.[25] The charge is partly a misunderstanding of Schleiermacher's Christology as one "from below" that ignores "those aspects of the tradition which conceive him [Christ] in relation also to past and future eternity."[26] In fact, if taken in the context of the original divine decree, Schleiermacher's Christology is one from above: it is in Christ that the completion of human nature has been ordained, and in this fundamental sense Christ is related to the past and future of humanity. In Christ the fullness of human nature is perfected.

Schleiermacher's understanding of the work of Christ has enormous implications for Christian ethics. It provides a sound basis for liberation theology in its understanding of the principle work of Christ as the founding of the kingdom. Through his inauguration of a new mode of being in the world, Jesus implicitly and explicitly criticizes all forms of domination, exploitation and control.[27] Of course, in Schleiermacher this view is not fleshed out; Schleiermacher does not focus on characterizing the exact nature of social sin. But the basic outlines are there. A close engagement with Schleiermacher's Christology demonstrates both the orthodox tenor of his Christology as well as his relevance for theology today.

Notes

1 On this point see Richard R. Niebuhr's excellent study, especially chapter 5, in which he characterizes Schleiermacher's theology as "Christo-morphic." Neibuhr 1964.

2 Another excellent study of Schleiermacher's Christology is that of Catherine Kelsey. A major emphasis of her study is Schleiermacher's theological starting

point: it is the *experience* of redemption as being in relation to God through Christ. See for example, Kelsey 2003, 46ff.

3 All citations are from the Mackintosh and Stewart translation of *The Christian Faith*.

4 In this regard it is important to note that the analysis of the God-consciousness that Schleiermacher provides in the Introduction of the *Christian Faith* is not an anthropological analysis of self-consciousness that can be understood independently from the context of redemption. As Schleiermacher notes, "There is no general God-consciousness which has not bound up with it a relation to Christ, and no relationship with the Redeemer which has no bearing on the general God-consciousness ... For the former propositions are in no sense the reflection of a meager and purely monotheistic God-consciousness, but are abstracted from one which has issued in fellowship with the Redeemer" (*CF*, § 62). Schleiermacher makes the same point in his second letter to Dr. Lücke. This is key to a proper understanding of Schleiermacher, whose actual views have been obscured by critics such as Karl Barth, who accuse him of basing his Christology on an anthropological starting point.

5 On the transcendental character of the feeling of absolute dependence and how if affects the way that the individual relates to the world, see Mariña, forthcoming.

6 As any student of patristics knows, those controversies are enormously complex, and there can be no doubt that there is a simplifying tendency in Schleiermacher. However, Schleiermacher clearly grasps what are the major pitfalls. On the controversies leading up to Chalcedon, see Grillmeier's excellent study (1975).

7 Schleiermacher may have had Plato in mind, who in the *Republic* at 509b notes that the form of the good (which by many Christian thinkers was taken to be equivalent to God) is beyond even being both in dignity and power.

8 McGrath 2001, 268–70.

9 In a letter written to Nestorius around 430 Cyril of Alexandria condemns just such a position; he notes: "If anyone distributes between two characters or persons the expressions used about Christ in the gospels, and apostolic writings ... applying some to the human being, conceived of separately apart from the Word ... and others exclusively to the Word, let them be condemned." From Cyril of Alexandria, Letter XVII, 12 (Third letter to Nestorius) in *Oxford Early Christian Texts: Cyril of Alexandria: Select Letters*, ed. L. R. Wickham (Oxford: Clarendon Press, 1983), 28.17–32.16.

10 McGrath 2001, 268–70.

11 Ibid.

12 For an excellent discussion of this *logos/sarx* Christology (Apollinarianism) see Grillmeier 1975, 335–9.

13 Moltmann correctly identifies the similarities between Schleiermacher's and Rahner's Christology; see Moltmann 1990, 61.

14 On this point see Mariña 1996, 195–8.

15 That is, while his views concerning the nature of the physical world may have been similar to those of his contemporaries, he never asserted his certainty regarding them since a concern with them was not his task. For Schleiermacher

error "emerges only when the desire for knowing is terminated before the truth is reached" (*LJ*, 110).

16 Strauss 1977, lii.

17 Barth 1982, 205.

18 Barth 1982, 205.

19 Emil Brunner also made similar charges; see Brunner 1924.

20 Barth 1982, 243.

21 While Schleiermacher's discussion here refers principally to the relation between the creative and sustaining activity of God, the idea applies equally to the notion of redemption, which can be thought of as a moment in God's preservation of the creation. Schleiermacher's point is that if God's causality is absolute, divine activities cannot be thought of as limiting one another. For a fuller discussion of this problem see Mariña 1996, 177–200.

22 I provide a more in-depth discussion of the nature of sin in Mariña 2004 and in Mariña, forthcoming.

23 The point is made by Jack Verheyden in his introduction to *The Life of Jesus*, xxxiv–xxxv.

24 Schleiermacher rejects both this "magical" view of Christ's efficacy as well as what he calls the "empirical view." According to the latter view the redemptive activity of Christ occurs principally through teaching and example. The problem here, according to Schleieramacher, is that on this view the work of Christ cannot be understood as something special; Christ is merely another teacher or another good example.

25 Gunton 1997, 98.

26 Gunton 1997, 154.

27 An example of a theology that brings the idea of the kingdom to the forefront is that of Jurgan Moltmann. Moltmann, however, does not acknowledge a debt to Schleiermacher and in fact is quite critical of him for his alleged "anthropocentrism." He critiques Schleiermacher and others for their focus on "the experience of subjectivity." As such, he charges that such theologies are no longer willing "to call into question the social conditions and political limitations of this experience of subjectivity" (Moltmann 1990, 63). My own reading of Schleiermacher shows that such a charge is unfounded, although of course Schleiermacher does not *explicitly* use the idea of the kingdom to judge social and political realities; in him the idea remains only implicit.

9 Schleiermacher's understanding of God as triune

FRANCIS SCHÜSSLER FIORENZA

Christianity is a monotheistic religion along with Judaism and Islam, yet it alone professes that there is one God and three divine persons. The Trinity is integral to the distinctive Christian belief in God. The basic question is whether Christianity, in affirming the Trinity, is still a legitimate member of the trinity of monotheistic religions. Moreover, the affirmation of the Trinity raises epistemological, metaphysical, and theological issues that are central to the interpretation of Schleiermacher's views on the Trinity.

Schleiermacher has been severely criticized for his doctrine of the Trinity, perhaps more than for any other element of his theology. A recent review simply claims: "for Schleiermacher, the Trinity did not fit into the modern conscious concept of experience as the immediate self-consciousness of the believer."[1] Such a judgment reflects a common opinion. The interpretative issues, moreover, are aggravated by the conflicting shifts in Trinitarian theology within the twentieth century.[2] The Neo-Orthodox critique of Schleiermacher emphasized the oneness of God while it argued for the Trinity on the basis of God's self-revelation. Karl Barth, for example, claimed that "the church with its doctrine of the Trinity was defending the recognition of God's unity, and therefore monotheism against the anti-Trinitarians."[3] Today, however, Barth's emphasis on monotheism is criticized. In contrast, Jürgen Moltmann contends that the doctrine of the Trinity served as a critique of a political monotheism, for the belief in a plurality of divine persons undermined the imperial political theology of the monarchy of the one emperor.

The benchmark for interpreting Schleiermacher has drastically changed. If Karl Barth's criticism of Schleiermacher's exposition of the Trinity was a previous benchmark, today theologians as diverse as Pannenberg and Moltmann single out not only Schleiermacher, but also Karl Barth, for unduly emphasizing the unity to the detriment of the Trinity. Pannenberg and Moltmann even criticize major figures of the Western tradition (Augustine, Anselm, and Aquinas) as insufficiently Trinitarian, for emphasizing the oneness of God to the detriment of the Trinity. In addition, they argue for the application of the doctrine of the Trinity to such social issues such as religious pluralism and democratic equality.[4] These shifts affect not only the criticisms, but also the interpretation of Schleiermacher.

CRITICISMS: FROM MARGINAL SIGNIFICANCE TO DENIAL

One charge is that Schleiermacher has marginalized the Trinity. As one author concludes: "The placement of the doctrine of the Trinity at the end expresses the mere marginal significance that the Trinity has for *The Christian Faith*."[5] Schleiermacher's motive, as Claude Welch has suggested, is the "conviction that the doctrine in itself is an unnecessary and unwarranted addition to the faith."[6] His critical remarks about the speculative formulation of the doctrine indeed seem to confirm this reason for its placement at the end. Turning these criticisms on their head, one can ask instead: does Schleiermacher's placement of the Trinity at the end make it the crown of the work? As Richard R. Niebuhr concludes: "Consequently, the doctrine properly belongs at the conclusion of *The Christian Faith*, for its authentic content is nothing else than the body of the theological exposition of the whole of the faith."[7]

Much more serious is Robert W. Jensen's charge that Schleiermacher is an "Arian" who "just drops" the inherited Trinitarian proposition; his "specifically Christian apprehension does not reach to the basic understanding of God at all" because he has "a particularly simpleminded form of the disastrous old distinction between natural and revealed theology."[8] Jensen echoes Johann Adam Möhler's critique, a leading member of the Roman Catholic Tübingen School in the early nineteenth century. Though Möhler's *Einheit der Kirche* shows the influence of Schleiermacher's interpretation of the relation between the Holy Spirit and the unity of the church,[9] his volume on Athanasius lambastes Schleiermacher's treatment of the differences between Athanasius and Sabellius and contends that Schleiermacher has basically a Sabellian view of the Trinity.[10] Möhler contends that Schleiermacher's limitation of human knowledge and his application of divine causality necessarily leads to a rejection of the Trinity. Moreover, his use of the distinction between the hidden and revealed God is evidence of his Sabellian-like view that God is the one eternally unknown monad behind diverse manifestations. These criticisms not only go to the heart of Schleiermacher's understanding of the Trinity, but they also challenge whether Schleiermacher's theological methodology allows him to make any claim about God's very being.

DOCTRINE OF THE TRINITY: AN UNFINISHED CHALLENGE AND TASK

Schleiermacher maintains that the doctrine of the Trinity did not undergo any specific reformulation as a result of the religious impulses of the Protestant Reformation. The traditional doctrinal formulations fail to express this reformation impulse. Moreover, they leave certain conceptual problems unresolved, namely, the unity of the three persons with the one divine essence and the equality of each person with the others. One either considers the unity less real than the Trinity or one considers the three persons less real than the unity. If conceptions of God's relation to the world inevitably contain anthropomorphisms, how much more do descriptions of God's being in God's very self? For these reasons, as Schleiermacher notes, the doctrine of the Trinity vacillates between unitarianism and tritheism as well as between equality and subordination. The doctrine of the Trinity needs to be reformulated to take into account these conceptual issues and, above all, to integrate the Reformation's religious impulses. His *Christian Faith* should be seen as "a preliminary step towards this goal" (*CF*, § 172.2).

Schleiermacher cautiously suggests that the resolution of this question of the unity between the one divine essence and the three persons depends upon the interpretation of the "original and eternal existence of distinctions within the Divine Essence." An appropriate doctrinal formulation should not assert eternal distinctions and yet should exhibit the truth of the union of God with human nature in Christ and with the Christian community. He asks whether the Sabellian interpretation of the Trinity can be placed on a par with the Athanasian. The decree is in eternity but its fulfillment takes place in time. The daunting task is to seek formulations that, while not asserting eternal distinctions, "are yet equally capable of exhibiting in their truth both unions of the Essence with human nature" (*CF*, § 172.2). In his view, the designation of the first person of the Trinity as primary (Father as begetting the other two) establishes unity of essence more than the equality of the persons. Moreover, still unresolved is the question: whether the Son of God is applicable solely to the divine in Jesus and the Father solely to one of the distinctions within the Trinity rather than to the unity with the divine essence? Schleiermacher will seek to resolve these questions, and especially this tension between either prioritizing unity over trinity or trinity over unity, as we shall show, through his interpretation of the Trinity in relation to divine causality.

For Schleiermacher, the central difference between Sabellius and what has become the official church doctrine is this: Sabellius affirms that the Trinity refers to God as ruling general activity as Father, as redeeming as Christ and through the Son, and as sanctifying as Spirit, whereas the church doctrine affirms that the Trinity is something in the Godhead, interior and original, independent of the divine activity. Therefore, the Godhead is in eternity Father, Son, and Spirit.[11] If this is the whole difference, Schleiermacher objects, then the charge of irreligiosity against Sabellius can be challenged and the Sabellian view should be considered alongside the Athanasian view as a possibility for the future development of the notion of the Trinity.

Does Schleiermacher's own constructive presentation of the Trinity coincide with his presentation of Sabellius or are there significant differences between what Schleiermacher labels as Sabellian and what he himself proposes? When Schleiermacher suggests that Sabellius as well as Athanasius should be a resource for future doctrinal progress, he is not making Sabellius the end-point but is suggesting that one should develop an understanding that goes beyond the contrast between Athanasius and Sabellius. Indeed, he suggests, and especially underscores in the second edition, that Christian theology needs to develop the Trinity in a way that takes into account the Reformation impulse, thereby going beyond Athanasius and Sabellius. Rather than simply assuming that he is a Sabellian, interpreters should, therefore, take as their guide the following questions. First, how does Schleiermacher articulate the impulse of the Reformation in his understanding of God as Triune? Second, how does this impulse lead him to structure the whole *Christian Faith* so as to show the soteriological significance of the Trinity? Due to the influence of Töllner and Wegscheider, many eighteenth-century German Protestant theologians (for example, Gruner and Urlsperger) were Sabellian. Therefore, these questions also inquire into what was specific and distinctive to Schleiermacher's views.

LOCATION OF THE DOCTRINE OF THE TRINITY

Traditional treatments of the Trinity entail two significant questions. The first is whether one begins with the one God or with the Trinity. The second concerns how one explicates the Trinity in relation to the unity. The first is more than a pedagogical decision about arrangement, for it is about priorities and foundations. Is the unity of God foundational for the treatment of the Trinity or is the Trinity foundational for the understanding of the one God? The second relates to the very formulation of the Trinity.

Traditional place of Trinitarian doctrine

Thomas Aquinas made two significant changes to Peter Lombard's order of treatment of the doctrine of God that had become standard up until the time of Schleiermacher.[12] The first change involves location: although both place the doctrine of God at the beginning, Peter Lombard begins with the mystery of the Trinity, whereas Aquinas begins with the one God and then moves to the Trinity. It is of enormous significance that his placing of the Trinity after the treatment of the one God became the standard arrangement. The various Lutheran Dogmatics as well as the text-books at the time of Schleiermacher followed this arrangement. For example, a contemporary, K. G. Bretschneider, treats first God's essence, being, and attributes as a philosophical knowledge of God, followed by the Trinity as the dogmatic knowledge based on revelation.[13]

The second change: whereas Lombard treats the operations of God at the very end of the treatise on God, Aquinas places the divine operations between the treatment of the substance of God and of divine persons. This change involves a significant theological difference. Lombard places the divine knowing, willing, and power at the end in order to provide the transition from God's nature to God's external activity, thereby linking the divine activities with the procession of creatures. By placing the operations of God between the substance of God and the Trinity, Aquinas thereby seeks to show the movement from the unity of God to the distinctions within God and then to external activity. The placing of the operations of God before the divine processions links the divine operations and the divine persons. The categories of knowing and willing are the means of understanding the distinctiveness of the divine persons, whereas the category of power is linked to God's external activity or the procession of creatures.

This interpretation of the Trinity should be seen in the context of the influence of Proclus via Dionysius upon the tradition. Proclus maintained that goodness, power, and knowledge constitute the primary divine triad.[14] This primary triad prefigures the triad of the second hypostasis: being, life, and intelligence (proposition 101). This Proclean triad (God as power, eternal Life, and knowledge) appears in Aquinas' *Summa Theologiae.*[15] Power expresses the similarity with the Father, wisdom, the similarity with Son as word, and goodness, the similitude with the divine Spirit that is love. This interpretation of the Trinity within the context of divine operations and its Neo-Platonic background provides a context for demarcating Schleiermacher's placement of the Trinity and his view of divine causality.

Schleiermacher's placement of the doctrine of God and the Trinity

The charge that Schleiermacher has marginalized the doctrine of the Trinity by placing it at the end of the *Christian Faith* overlooks

Schleiermacher's innovative treatment of God. There is no special place for the doctrine of God within the *Christian Faith*. Nor is there a separate treatise on the nature, existence, and attributes of God followed by a separate treatise on the Trinity. Instead, Schleiermacher distributes the divine attributes and thereby the doctrine of God throughout the whole *Christian Faith*. He links the distinct divine attributes with specific themes of the Christian faith. Moreover, as his *Sendschreiben* explain, the divine attributes of wisdom and love are deliberately placed at the end of the *Christian Faith* in order to express the specifically Christian consciousness of God. The concluding doctrine of the Trinity, then, articulates this explicitly Christian consciousness of God. The attributes of God, spread throughout the *Christian Faith*, culminate in the Christian consciousness of God as wisdom and love. The Trinity follows then not as an appendix but as a "conclusion" (the first edition even refers to it as the "crown") that explicates this specifically Christian consciousness of God.

A parallel exists between the understanding of God and the divine attributes and the understanding of the Trinity. Just as the experience of the divine causality in various modulations leads to the consciousness of the diverse attributes of the one God, so too does the Christian experience of the being of God in Christ and in the church lead to an understanding of God as triune. It is the distinctively Christian experience of the divine causality that experiences and understands God not as power, but primarily as love (with wisdom the perfection of love) – so much so that God's very being is love. Schleiermacher has thereby transformed the traditional Neo-Platonic triad of power, goodness, and wisdom. The consciousness of God as love perfected in wisdom is the heart of the Christian faith, whereas the consciousness of God as power is an abstraction from the Christian experience of God as love.

DIVINE CAUSALITY AND TRINITY

The relationship among the divine causality, the divine attributes, and the Trinity is central to understanding the Trinity. Philosophical conceptions about causality are the implied background theories. In the period of Christian antiquity, the philosophical categories of essence, power, activity, and product were used to describe causal relations. The interpretation of these categories became central to the understanding of the Trinity among classical Christian authors and within the Trinitarian controversies of the fourth century. These presumed specific accounts of the divine causality; Schleiermacher's understanding of divine causality is likewise central to his view.

Causality as an epistemological, ontological, and theological category

The notion of causality has epistemological, ontological, and theological significance. Plato notes that every being that exists has the power to produce an effect and this provides a means for knowing what exists. Knowledge of the effects leads to knowledge of the cause. Power as an expression of an essence is the source of knowledge of an essence. Moreover, higher beings that arc of themselves inaccessible to the knowledge of lower beings are known through their causality. The Stoics distinguished a synectic and procatarctic cause. A synectic cause is one in which when present the effect remains, but when not present, the effect ceases. The causal sequence used in the medical (Galen) and philosophical (Iamblichus) traditions distinguished essence, power, activity, and product. Iamblichus remarks that a "power is a median between an essence and an activity, put forth from the essence on the one hand, and itself generating the activity on the other."[16]

Causality is theologically significant because causality has been used not only to understand the divine activity and creativity, but also the relation between the persons of the Trinity. Power describes a causality that is a natural expression of the divine essence; it inheres in the divine essence and makes the divine essence knowable. Differences in the conception of the sequence (essence, power, activity, and product) were decisive to the ancient Trinitarian debates. Whereas Gregory of Nyssa underscored power as connatural and a source of knowledge of the common nature, Eunomius rejects the connaturality of the causality and hence for him, the Son and God the Father are dissimilar. In short, the understanding of divine causality was essential to the interpretation of the Trinity and relation among the persons.[17] Moreover, Gregory uses the images of fire and heat to show that power and nature are inseparable.[18] The Son and Spirit manifest the same causality because they have the same nature; they all give heat and light because they are the same fire.

Schleiermacher's understanding of the divine causality

When Schleiermacher uses the term "causality," he is very much aware of its inadequacy when applied to both divine and human activity because of the distinction between divine causality and finite causality. Finite causality is partial and involves both activity and passivity. Divine causality, however, does not entail passivity. Schleiermacher interprets divine causality as living vitality.[19] As living vitality, God's causality is experienced as redeeming love in the Christian consciousness of the divine attributes of love and wisdom. The divine attributes express modulations in the way in which divine causality concretely comes to consciousness. For Christians, it comes to consciousness primarily as the experience of redemptive love resulting from the being of God in Christ and in the Christian community; in contrast the experience of God as power is an abstraction from this Christian experience.

Schleiermacher's understanding of divine causality should be seen in relation to his understanding of causality. He discusses causality within the context of knowledge and the specificity of judgment against the background of the distinction between judgment and concept.[20] A knowledge that takes place exclusively within the form of concept would lead to an understanding of being as unchanging and always the same. When being is viewed under the form of judgment, then it becomes flowing and changing. The relation between necessity and freedom is associated with the distinction between concept and judgment as well as between power (*Kraft*) and causality. Whereas empirical knowledge based on judgment seeks beings under the notion of necessity in its causal relations, speculative knowledge brings everything under the form of freedom. When it is a question of the transcendent, then there are two limits of thought: the absolute communality of being and the absolute subject. "All our formulas for the transcendental are incomplete, though they have a true content," namely that the absolute subject is identical with the absolute powers of which all powers are appearances.[21] Within religious feeling and human self-consciousness, the transcendent ground is present but one needs to be conscious that the limit of our thought is approached. Consequently in language and reflection about the divine attributes and divine causality, there is both the consciousness of the transcendent ground and our awareness of the limits of our anthropomorphic thoughts.[22]

Divine attributes and God as triune

Schleiermacher's understanding of the divine attributes is both complex and nuanced. Since in God there is no distinction between essence and attributes, he cautions that one should not understand the divine attributes as an aggregate of attributes. Likewise, he criticizes the distinction between the active and inactive attributes: the activity of God is such that it cannot be separated from the being of God. Schleiermacher's intention is to overcome the distinction between the economy of salvation and the metaphysical conception of God. Moreover, the lack of a distinction between essence and attributes "also implies, that insofar as anything true is predicated of God by means of what we posit as a divine attribute, what is thus truly predicated must also express the Divine essence itself" (*CF*, § 167.1). Schleiermacher treats the attributes in dialectical pairs, underscoring their polar distinction in order to unite them. The divine attributes of utter inwardness, holiness, and love express God's distinction from the world, whereas the utter livingness, justice, and wisdom articulate God's relation to the world. The distribution of the divine attributes throughout the *Christian Faith* shows that God is related to all aspects of the human experience of the world and that "the world is a complete revelation of the attributes of God" (*CF*, § 92.3).[73]

The *Christian Faith* culminates in love and wisdom. The prime attribute is love, and love alone is the attribute that constitutes the divine essence. The concluding section, prior to the Trinitarian conclusion, presents the divine causality as love and wisdom. Love is the divine imparting, whereas wisdom is the right ordering of the whole sphere of redemption. Divine wisdom is a perfecting of the divine impartation, self-presence, and revelation of God as love. Love is not the perfection of wisdom, but wisdom is the perfection of love. The analysis makes clear that redemption is the key for Schleiermacher's understanding of God.

Several cautions, however, are necessary in interpreting the divine attributes. First, love and wisdom are separable in human life just as human will and understanding are distinct.[24] Often understanding or volition lag behind one another. However, Schleiermacher emphasizes that it would be highly anthropomorphic to apply such a separation or division to the divine essence, where each is "intrinsically contained" in the other (*CF*, § 165.2). Traditionally, the operations of understanding and will are used to illustrate the Trinity. As noted above, in Aquinas the operations of understanding and of will are keys to understanding the distinct divine persons. In contrast, Schleiermacher argues that it is anthropomorphic to separate understanding and will in God; therefore, in God they are "intrinsically contained" in each other (*perichoresis*).

Second, Schleiermacher interprets divine love as more than self-communication and as the very essence of God: "Love and wisdom alone, then can claim to be not mere attributes but also expressions of the very essence of God" (*CF*, § 167.2). He is not maintaining that love and wisdom are merely the revealed manifestations of a hidden unknown monad. Instead, Schleiermacher is making a claim about the very essence of God. Since Schleiermacher conceives of wisdom as the perfection of love, God is then absolute wisdom. The divine love is directly experienced in the Christian consciousness of redemption and on the basis of this experience the consciousness of God is built up. The relation that Schleiermacher establishes in regard to the attributes speaks against the claim that he has made omnipotence the basic attribute of God in the sense of "perfectly real causality" (*CF*, § 165.2). In the Second Letter to Dr. Lücke, Schleiermacher argues that the attribute of omnipotence is abstracted not only from the doctrine of preservation, but also from the attributes of wisdom and love. Only in the exposition of the attributes of divine love and wisdom in the second part of the *Christian Faith* does Schleiermacher explicate the distinctively Christian religious consciousness of God as love and wisdom containing the essentials of what is expressed in the doctrine of the Trinity.[25]

Third, in interpreting Schleiermacher's understanding of the attributes of love and wisdom in relation to the divine causality, several caveats should be kept in mind. The divine causality should not be divided among the persons, even though it might be natural to think of Father alone as creator and preserver, Son alone as redeemer, and Spirit alone as sanctifier.[26] On this point Schleiermacher is distant from a Sabellian identification of personhood with specific salvation–historical manifestations. The causality belongs to the one divine essence. The other caveat is the avoidance of anthropomorphisms. The activities of willing and knowing are distinct activities in humans where a difference exists between the activity itself and the result of the activity just as there is a distinction between means and ends. These finite dualisms, however, are not present in the one divine essence. To introduce them into the divine essence is to introduce an anthropomorphic view of God and God's activities. These cautions contrast with the more classical view where the Proclean triad of being, intelligence, and goodness is interpreted in terms of power (Father), wisdom (Son as word), and good (love, divine Spirit) and where the intellectual operations of knowing and willing are introduced between the unity of God and the Trinity to illustrate the internal relations of the Trinity; but power illustrates the divine external activity.

CHRIST AND SPIRIT AS KEY TO THE CHRISTIAN CONSCIOUSNESS OF GOD AS TRIUNE

Although Schleiermacher affirms that the Trinity is not an object of immediate religious consciousness, it would be incorrect to conclude from this that what is religiously affirmed as Christian in the Trinity is not essential to Schleiermacher's theology. Instead, Schleiermacher sees the doctrine of the Trinity as "a combination of several utterances." For Schleiermacher, the "essential element" is "the doctrine of the union of the Divine Essence with human nature, both in the personality of Christ and in the common Spirit of the Church; therewith the whole view of Christianity set forth in our Church stands and falls" (*CF*, § 170.1). Without the being of God in Christ, redemption could not be concentrated in his person and, unless there was the union of the Spirit with the church, the church could not continue the redemption. The doctrine of the Trinity was established in the defense of the Christian conviction that in Christ and in the Spirit indwelling in the church is nothing less than the divine essence.

Schleiermacher grounds the Trinity neither through speculation nor through direct immediate experience, but rather in terms of the Christian community's historical experience of the presence of God's being as "person-forming" in Christ and as "community-forming" in the Christian community. The Trinity is not based upon a Hegelian conception of God as Spirit that grounds the Trinitarian differentiation of God in God's self-consciousness. Instead, it is the Christian consciousness of the deity of the Son and the Spirit that necessitates a threeness of God as Father, Son, and Spirit. Schleiermacher's reformulation of the two-nature and one-person doctrine through the notion of the person-forming presence of the being of God in Jesus Christ links Christological and Trinitarian doctrine.

Person of Christ

The specific character of Christian piety refers to the redeemer and understands the redeemer in relation to the divine essence. It is not only in poetic, rhetorical, and apologetical language, but also in the strictest doctrinal formulas that the divine being is in Jesus in a special way. The Christian view of the redeemer distinguishes Christianity from Judaism and paganism. Judaism acknowledges the oneness of God, but God in God's oneness is not present in historical human nature. Hellenism has God present in human nature, but denies the oneness of God. The Christian vision stands between the two: union between God and human nature and yet the oneness of God. This specifically Christian belief provides the starting point of the belief in the Trinity.

Holy Spirit and church

Though the ecclesial tradition emphasizes the equality of the third person to the other two, Schleiermacher complains that the third person has not been treated with the equal accord of the first two persons.[27] Therefore, he seeks to overcome this deficit and to, so to speak, bring the Holy Spirit out of the margins. He makes the Holy Spirit central to the Christian community and suggests that the Holy Spirit should be understood not individualistically but as the common spirit.[28] His conception brings together the twofold root of the notion of spirit, namely, the analogy to the spirit of a people *and* the relation to Christ.

What is decisive for Schleiermacher is that the divine causality and activity united with the Son unites with the community. The person-forming activity in Jesus becomes the community-forming activity of the Spirit in the community. Moreover, the being of God in Christ and the being of God as the Spirit of the Christian community are not only distinct from one another, but the latter is dependent upon the former. The experience of the reality of the Christian community is the presupposition for the consciousness of and language about the third way of God's being. Sabellius had referred to a succession of the manifestations of God as three successive "prosopa" (persons). Schleiermacher links the presence of God in Christ and the community in relation to God's gracious being to God's decision. The Holy Spirit as the common spirit of the Christian community is the present reality of the love of God in Christ and as such is the organ or instrument of God's wisdom that gradually brings God's love into history. As an instrument of activity this love works its way out into the future of the world and to the increased experience of the presence of God's being.

The unconditional divine decree and the divine essence

For Schleiermacher the Christian experience of God's causality as wisdom and love is the Christian experience of the perfection and power of God's redeeming activity. From this experience the Christian abstracts to the power of God. It is the consciousness of divine grace that constitutes the Christian experience of God as wisdom and love, and in this sense the ending of the *Christian Faith* is the culmination of the Christian experience. The consciousness of grace is such that the Christian experience is not as such an experience of "utter dependency" but rather an experience of the power of our redemption. Consequently, the centrality of the being of God in Christ and the church has implications for our understanding of the divine essence and the unconditional divine decree via the experience of grace.[29] Christians should have an understanding of God that correlates with their consciousness of divine grace (*CF*, § 90.2). God should not be understood simply as an aggregate of the divine attributes as if these were the sum of divine decisions. The divine decision and election is not an expression of immediate self-consciousness. Instead, when one is fully conscious of what has been occasioned in the world through redemption, then one is conscious of the totality of divine decisions as an unconditional decision of love. The experience of God as love within the Christian community, not just individually but collectively, makes one conscious of the being of God as gracious love.

CRITICAL RECEPTION

The immediate reception of the *Christian Faith* after its publication involved both a defense and criticism of Schleiermacher's views. Schleiermacher's students followed his path. Rather than the Hegelian emphasis on God as spirit and the Trinity as the differentiation of God's self-consciousness, they argued that it is the full divinity of the Son and Spirit, to which the Scriptures attest, that leads to the affirmation of God as triune.[30] However, what remained in dispute was whether the biblical affirmation of the Father, Son, and Spirit as divine necessitated a speculative doctrine about the inner differentiation within God.

Early reception: students and critics
One year before the appearance of the second edition of the *Christian Faith*, Carl Immanuel Nitzsch published his *System der christlichen Lehre*, in which he concurred with Schleiermacher's emphasis on the specifically Christian consciousness of redemption. However, the Christian belief in Jesus as the Son of God presupposes a self-differentiation in God's essence and necessitates the doctrine of the immanent Trinity. Nitzsch, however, does not explicate how this self-differentiation should be understood. Eight years later, in his dogmatics, August Twesten criticized the traditional placement of the Trinity at the beginning of systematic theology after the treatment of the one God.[31] Instead, following Schleiermacher, he contends that the Trinity should flow from the Christian experience of Christ and the Holy Spirit. Nevertheless, Twesten also maintains the necessity of the immanent Trinity.

Against these critics, Friedrich Lücke, a student and friend of Schleiermacher, makes the case that the immanent Trinity is not biblically grounded, not even in John's gospel.[32] Schleiermacher's study, as he underscores, historically went only as far as Athanasius. However, the speculative Trinitarian developments occurred afterwards. Systematically, Lücke points out the weaknesses of the different starting points. If the Trinity is grounded on God's self-knowledge and self-love, then the result is much more readily a triad or trinity of revelation than an immanent Trinity. If the distinction between the hidden Father and the expressed God (the Son) and remembering God (Spirit) is the starting point, then the result is a conception in which the hidden God is only a monad. The distinction is not so much in God as it is in the contrast between God's self and God's self-revelation in relation to the world as Father, Son, and Holy Spirit.[33] Carl Immanuel Nitzsch responds to Lücke by defending the necessity of interpreting this threeness within the concept of God in contrast to deism and unitarianism. The triad of revelation is a revelation of the "triuneness" or Trinity of God's very being.[34] Schleiermacher's assertion that the Trinity should be understood as a consequence of the Christian experience of redemption in Christ was indeed influential, but the theological reaction turned on the immanent Trinity, with Nitzsch and Twesten for the immanent Trinity, and Lücke defending Schleiermacher's view. The crucial point of the ensuing discussions focused on personhood. An exchange takes place in *Theologische Studien* in which Delbruck criticizes Schleiermacher; Lücke responds, and Christian Weisse defends Delbruck against Lücke. Isaac Dorner joins in this criticism: only by defending an immanent understanding of the Trinity could one defend the personhood of God.

There is clearly a difference between Schleiermacher and traditional theology. The adequacy of an anthropomorphic notion of personhood was a central issue at the time due to the influence of Spinoza.[35] At the same time the atheism controversy surrounding Fichte came to the fore precisely over his critique of the application of the anthropomorphism of personhood to God.[36] In a letter to Schleiermacher, Jacobi observes that the major difference between Schleiermacher and himself is the radical way that Schleiermacher is aware of the limitations of applying anthropomorphic language to God, such as the distinction between will and understanding.[37] For example, Aquinas is aware that intellect and will are distinct in humans and that an anthropomorphic transferal of the operations of the human mind to God is inadequate. His solution is that the operations of the mind within human beings become within God subsistent ways of being. In contrast, while Schleiermacher distinguishes between wisdom and love as distinct human activities, he understands the divine wisdom as the perfection of love and maintains that love is the essence of God while cautioning against an anthropomorphic interpretation of these attributes.

Reception despite critique

Wolfhart Pannenberg and Jürgen Moltmann develop Trinitarian theology in a way that shows Schleiermacher's influence even though they affirm a plurality of persons in a way that goes contrary to his very views. For example, Pannenberg maintains that any deduction of the plurality of persons from the essence of God, whether spirit or love, falls into either a modalism or a subordinationism that fails to do justice to Trinitarian dogma.[38] Pannenberg's critique of Karl Barth echoes a Schleiermacherian theme when he notes that Barth "bases his own doctrine of the image of the Trinity in the human soul, and not as he demanded, on the content of the revelation of God in Jesus Christ."[39] Although Pannenberg's starting point, which is the relation of Jesus to the Father, is closer to Schleiermacher's Christological starting point, nevertheless his conclusion is quite different in the way he moves from the relation of Jesus to the Father to intra-trinitarian mutuality. Hence he notes: "we see a mutuality in their relationship that we do not see in the begetting."[40] Although Moltmann likewise begins from a Christological starting point, he underscores the threeness so much that Walter Kasper discovers the danger of a tendency toward tritheism.[41] These authors represent a conception of the Trinity opposed to Schleiermacher, although they have been influenced by his starting point and his attempt to link the economy of salvation with the immanent Trinity.

CONCLUSION: PERSONHOOD OF GOD AND THE DOCTRINE OF THE TRINITY

Any evaluation of Schleiermacher's understanding of the Trinity depends on one's understanding not only of Trinitarian doctrine, but also of the person of God.[42] It is obvious that Schleiermacher elucidates the divine causality in a way that seeks to overcome any anthropomorphic conception of willing and knowing as separate operations in God. The medieval tradition sought to overcome an anthropomorphic conception of intellect and will as internal operations by making them into distinct subsistent relations (influenced by Boethius' understanding of personhood). Schleiermacher attempts to avoid any anthropomorphic conception by linking the divine activity and the divine being so that he specifically identifies God as love. Consequently, the distinct being of God in Christ and in the Christian community is not simply a manifestation of an unknown monad or God, but is the very essence of God and the perfection of God's creative activity.

Schleiermacher has two modes of working. On the one hand, he wants to think the Trinity from an understanding of the divine presence in Christ and the community, which pushes him to a distinctive interpretation of each person. God's causal redemptive activity is the very being of God by which God's creativity comes to perfection as a redemptive creativity in Christ and in the Spirit of the Christian community. On the other hand, Schleiermacher's understanding of the divine causality and his epistemological strictures lead him to shy away from speculations about the interior relations of the Trinitarian persons.

Second, an analysis of the reflection on the being of God in Christ and within the church indicates a conception of the Trinity that should not be equated with Sabellius' view as is usually done. Schleiermacher insists that the one God is creator, redeemer, and sanctifier, and that this should be applicable to all three. His emphasis on the being of God in Christ and the community leads him to make the being of the Spirit in the community dependent upon and flowing from the being of God in Christ. Such an interpretation is closer to the traditional *filioque* than it is to Sabellian modalism.

Schleiermacher's understanding of Trinitarian doctrine should be located within his understanding of the notion of person in relation to God. Not only does he note that church doctrine uses the notion of person quite differently in the doctrine of the Trinity and in Christology, but he has to face the challenge of whether God should be conceived anthropomorphically in terms of personhood. The influence of Spinoza and the atheism conflict that Fichte's critique generated made central to contemporary discussions the extent to which the application of the category of personhood to God is anthropomorphic. These discussions also bear upon Trinitarian language. In the Western tradition, Augustine was reluctant to call the three hypostases three persons and he tends to take the Latin *substantia* as the equivalent of *hypostasis*. In the twentieth century, Karl Barth's formulation of three modes of existence is taken up by Karl Rahner but reformulated as three modes of subsistence.[43] Karl Rahner underscores the distinction between the modern concept of person as self-consciousness and the ancient understanding of person. In the face of contemporary theological social interpretations of the Trinity, the patristic scholar André de Halleux cautions that the use of concepts such as intersubjectivity and dialogue (along with modern subjectivity) for understanding the Trinity has the "great danger of anachronism when read into patristic conceptions."[44]

In the face of the contemporary conflicts about the Trinity, Schleiermacher appears much more cautious due to his awareness of the inadequacy of applying an anthropomorphic idea of personhood to God. The question remains whether the credal metaphors of light from light express more than a relation of begetting but also a mutuality of persons.[45] Whereas many conceptions of the Trinity assert the mutuality of persons, Schleiermacher underscores much more strongly the interconnection between the being of God and the Christian experience that the one living and loving God as activity and causality is present in the being of Christ, and through him the love of God becomes present in the being of the Holy Spirit in the Christian community that perfects the order of creation.

In summary, against the criticism that Schleiermacher marginalizes the Trinity, it has been noted that Schleiermacher does not have a separate treatment of the doctrine of God but develops it through the whole *Christian Faith*. The divine attributes culminate in wisdom and love. God's essence is love. This Christian understanding of God is based upon the Christian community's experience of God's redemptive causality and God's presence in the community and in Christ. Whether this is sufficiently Trinitarian remains a question that Christian theologians will continue to debate but not without the influence of Schleiermacher's critical questions and constructive proposals.

Notes

1 Meeks 1982, 373.
2 For an analysis of Moltmann and Pannenberg, see Murrmann-Kahl 1997, 163–225.
3 Barth 1936, I.I, 351.
4 Moltmann 1981, 129–50.
5 Axt-Piscalar 1990, 96.
6 Welch 1952, 5.
7 Niebuhr 1964, 156.
8 Jensen 1982, 134.
9 Möhler 1996, pt I, 79–205.
10 Möhler 1827, 305–33.
11 Schleiermacher, "Über den Gegensatz zwischen der Sabellianischen und der Athanasianischen Vorstellung von der Trinität," in *KGA*, I.10. English trans. by M. Stuart, "On the Discrepancy between the Sabellian and Athanasian Method of Representing the Doctrine of the Trinity."
12 Hankey 1987, 19–56.
13 Bretschneider 1914.
14 Proclus 1963, *Th. P.* I.xvi.
15 See also *Summa Theologiae*, 1.39, 8, obj. 3, and Aquinas' exposition dealing with causality and the similitude of power, wisdom, goodness to persons of the Trinity.
16 See Iamblichus, 1973, 74–5.
17 Both Eunomius of Cyzicus and Gregory of Nyssa interpret the unity on the basis of a different pre-understanding of causality. See, e.g., Barnes and Williams 1993, 217–36 and Barnes 2001.
18 This is a classic convention of Platonism (used by both Plato and Plotinus): see Rist 1967, 69.
19 The second edition of the *Christian Faith* has an increased use of the term "divine causality": see Takamori 1991, 265–78.
20 Schleiermacher, *Vorlesungen über die Dialektik* (ed. Arndt), vol. I.257–72; vol II. 542–90.
21 Schleiermacher, *Vorlesungen*, I.575.
22 Schleiermacher, *Vorlesungen*, II.583–6.
23 Cf., as power, *CF*, § 57. 1; as justice, *CF*, § 84, 2; as wisdom, *CF*, § 169.3. See Ebeling 1970, 159.

24 On the relation between wisdom and love, see Schleiermacher, "Über die wissenschaftliche Behandlung des Tugendbegriffs," in *Schleiermachers Werke*, vol. I.349–77, esp. 362ff.

25 Schleiermacher, *On the Glaubenslehre: Two Letters to Dr. Lücke*, 55–6.

26 Today, seeking to avoid gender-based terms such as "Father, Son, and Holy Spirit", some correlate between individual activity and individual divine person (hence: creator, redeemer, and sanctifier). Schleiermacher follows the tradition that divine activity *ad extra* flows from the one Divine Essence and is shared by all. For a historical critique of the relating of the individual divine persons to specific activities, see Wiles 1976, 1–18.

27 Schleiermacher, "Über den Gegensatz zwischen der Sabellianischen und der Athanasianischen Vorstellung von der Trinität," *KGA*, I.10, 573.

28 Brandt 1968, 108–86.

29 Lessing 1979, 450–88, esp. 477ff.

30 Lücke 1840, 63–112.

31 Twesten 1837.

32 Lücke 1840, 63–112.

33 Lücke 1840, 99.

34 Nitzsch 1841, 295–345 and Weisse 1841, 345–410.

35 On this point see Lamm 1996.

36 Fichte 1977, 347–73.

37 See Schleiermacher's letter in response, Cordes 1971, 195–211.

38 Wolfhart Pannenberg notes that love is closer than the idea of a divine self-consciousness and leaves more room for plurality. Pannenberg 1991, 297–8.

39 Pannenberg 1991, 304.

40 Pannenberg 1991, 313.

41 Kasper 1984, 379, n. 183.

42 For an execellent analysis of Schleiermacher's understanding of theism, see Niebuhr 1970, 176–205.

43 Rahner 1970, 73–6.

44 Halleux 1986, 290.

45 Beierwaltes 1977, 75–111.

10 Providence and grace: Schleiermacher on justification and election

DAWN DeVRIES AND B. A. GERRISH

> There is only *one*, eternal and general decree to justify humans for Christ's sake. This decree is identical with the decree to send Christ ... and this again is simply *one* with the decree to create the human race, seeing that in Christ human nature is first brought to completion.   (*CF*, § 109.3)

In any presentation of Christian theology that aspires to be systematic, the order of topics is by no means a matter of indifference: the sense of a doctrine is, at least in part, a function of its location. Anyone who has looked into some of the leading works of Protestant dogmatics may be puzzled to find "providence," "justification," and "election" linked in a single discussion. At first sight, they seem to make an odd association of three theological terms that belong in different parts of a system. ("Grace," the second term in our title, is likely to be ubiquitous in Protestant theology rather than reduced to a particular locus.) *Providence* has always appeared early in the order of topics, under the doctrine of God, and *justification* comes much later under "soteriology," the subjective appropriation of the redemption won by Jesus Christ. The placement of *election* has varied. In the definitive edition of his *Institutes* (1559), John Calvin took the unusual step of moving the discussion of election (or predestination) from its customary attachment to the doctrine of God's providence and attached it instead to justification by faith and prayer as the principal exercise of faith; there it served to answer the question why one individual comes to faith, another doesn't. Friedrich Schleiermacher, though he placed providence and justification in their conventional systematic locations, postponed election still further than Calvin, placing it under ecclesiology, the doctrine of the church. Why, then, Schleiermacher on providence, justification, and election?

The dogmatic importance of treating election as a part of the doctrine of the church will be readily apparent. It is warranted by Paul's argument in the Letter to the Romans (chs. 9–11) about the election of Israel, and it illustrates Schleiermacher's determination to avoid individualism in the presentation of Christian doctrines. Less obviously, it needs to be shown that what Schleiermacher thought about both justification and election was formed, in part, by his understanding of God's providence. The first part of the *Christian Faith*, which contains the doctrine of providence, regulates what can be said in the second, in which Schleiermacher dealt with the distinctively Christian themes of sin and grace. His thoughts on the relation of divine to natural causality in part one necessarily called, in part two, for some recasting of Christian beliefs about the subjective experience of redemption and the divine good pleasure that draws a line between the elect and the non-elect. The operations of divine grace in justifying the sinner and gathering the church are determined by the mode of God's providential activity, which, for Schleiermacher, could only be understood to work naturally and to be directed to the world and humanity as a whole; providence could not be taken piecemeal, divided into a multitude of supernatural interventions on particular occasions or distinct decisions about the lives of particular individuals. Hence this chapter begins by examining Schleiermacher's conception of divine providence, or (as he preferred to say) God's "preservation," and only then attempts to interpret his account of justification and election.[1]

PROVIDENCE, OR DIVINE PRESERVATION

From the first, Schleiermacher's understanding of the God–world relationship was suspected of pantheism. And yet, it would be easy to overestimate the extent to which his understanding of creation and providence departs from Protestant orthodoxy. In his treatment of these doctrines, he carefully attempted to appropriate suitable language from the evangelical confessions while excluding misleading concepts and the unwarranted inferences many church people drew from them. The doctrine of preservation, as he reinterpreted it, attempts to resolve what he took to be a conflict in the thinking of the older divines: a conflict between their understandings of the divine "decree" and of the divine causality. The idea of a single divine decree or plan that encompasses the whole is undermined, he believed, by a concept of divine causality as occasional or arbitrary. The orthodox divines, however, flirted with just such a limited concept of divine causality, especially in their implication that providence relates to individuals in and for themselves, and in their arguments for the possibility of miracles conceived as breaches in the nature system.

The discussion in the *Christian Faith* begins (§ 36) with attention not to an evangelical confession but to the Roman Symbol, precursor of the so-called Apostles' Creed. Schleiermacher notes that this creed confesses belief in God the *pantokrator*, the almighty, an expression that perfectly captures the awareness of absolute dependence out of which every religious feeling takes rise. This designation of God is superior to the later term "Creator," because it applies to every part and every moment of finite existence, not just to the beginning. In fact, the question of origins does not arise from the religious self-consciousness at all, but from general human curiosity, and it is more properly the subject of scientific exploration. Unfortunately, because Christian theologians took up the mythological accounts of creation in Genesis, there has been confusion about what is really at stake in creation and preservation. Schleiermacher insists that these doctrines do not commit the Christian faith to a particular account of how the world began, but rather define the relationship between the world and God that is presupposed by Christian faith. Everything that exists is continuously sustained by divine preservation (*Erhaltung*). The division of this theme into two separate doctrines – creation and providence – is merely traditional. There is no reason to retain it from the subject matter itself, since the consciousness of God as the Almighty does not imply any such division. If either doctrine is correctly expounded, it contains within itself all that is implied by the other (§ 38). Nonetheless, Schleiermacher chooses to retain the traditional division for purely pedagogical reasons, using the doctrine of creation as the place to clear away "alien" elements that have crept into the Christian presentation of the God–world relationship, and allowing the doctrine of preservation to explicate this relationship as it is intuited in the feeling of absolute dependence.

Why does Schleiermacher prefer the term "preservation" to "providence?" It seems that he discovers this to be the preferred term in what he deems to be the best of the evangelical confessions – those whose language is closest to the Roman Symbol.[2] Much later, however, in his discussion of the divine attributes of love and wisdom, he gives a further explanation for his preference. Preservation is a concept abstracted from the Christian consciousness of the divine world-governance (*Weltregierung*) that is forming the world into the kingdom of God. Everything in nature – and especially human nature – is created and directed towards one purpose: the self-imparting of the deity. He writes:

> Because there is no division or opposition anywhere in the divine causality and we can only regard the governance of the world as a *unity*, directed towards a *single* goal, the church or the kingdom of God ... is the *one* object of the divine world-governance. ... [W]e stray

from the right path as soon as we assume that for the individual thing there is a special divine causality somehow separate from its connection with the whole.   (§ 164.3, emphases in the original)

Theologians who use the term "providence," however, seem to fall into just this error, especially in their distinction between "general," "special," and "most special" providence. According to this reasoning, it would seem that some things are more especially the effect of divine causality than others. But that cannot be so. If the divine decree is one, then every single thing in nature and history must be construed within the perfect realization of that decree.

> Everything in our world – human nature first, then *everything* else (all the more surely the closer the connection with human nature) – would have been differently arranged, and the whole course of human happenings and natural events would thus have been different, if the divine decree had not been for the union of the divine essence with human nature in the person of Christ and, consequently, the union of the divine essence with the fellowship of believers through the Holy Spirit.   (§ 164.2)

The word "providence," then, is liable to an individualistic or atomistic interpretation of the divine activity and threatens to undermine the unity of the divine decree. Almost as an afterthought, Schleiermacher notes that the term "providence" (*Vorsehung*) does not appear in the normative texts of the Christian religion, anyway. It is a foreign term that was first taken from pagan authors by later Jewish writers and then adopted by Christian theologians. It would be better to stick with the Scriptural terms "predestin-ation" or "foreordination" (*Vorherbestimmung, Vorherversehung*), precisely because they are far more apt for clearly expressing the relation of each individual part to the connected whole and representing God's governance (*Weltregiment*) as an inwardly coherent plan.

   But what is the content of the doctrine of preservation for Schleiermacher? The primary explication of the doctrine is found under proposition 46: "The religious self-consciousness, in virtue of which we relate everything that stimulates or affects us to absolute dependence on God, completely coin-cides with the view that these same things are conditioned and determined by the interconnectedness of nature." Schleiermacher notes that it is quite common to oppose events sharply as being *either* natural *or* caused by God. On inspection, however, this way of thinking will not do. Otherwise, "with the completion of our knowledge of the world [of nature] ... the development of the devout self-consciousness in normal life would cease ... [and] the love of religion would resist every inclination for research and any extension of our knowledge of nature" (§ 46.1). The apparent opposition of the interests of piety and the interests of science, however, is in fact a misunderstanding.[3] Piety takes its rise from the awareness that all finite being depends absolutely on God, or the Infinite, for its existence. If this proposition is thought through in a way that avoids anthropomorphic conceptions of God's activity or deterministic understandings of human agency, then the only recourse is to the idea of the interconnectedness of the nature system. God does not work alongside natural causes, as one agent among the many; rather, God works through natural causes, as the One in All.

> In this "All-One" of finite being, then, is posited the most complete and most universal interconnectedness of nature; and if we feel ourselves, as finite beings, to be absolutely dependent, then these two completely coincide: the most complete persuasion that everything is wholly determined and grounded in the totality of the system of nature [*in der Gesamtheit des Naturzusammenhanges*] and the inner certainty of the absolute dependence of all finite being on God. (§ 46.2)

Schleiermacher's allusion to Spinoza's "All-One" might suggest that he has finally left behind the thought-world of Protestant orthodoxy. But, citing the orthodox Lutheran theologian Johannes Andreas Quenstedt (1617–1688), he notes that all the strictest dogmaticians have understood divine preservation and natural causation as "one and the same thing, only seen from different viewpoints" (§ 46.2). If philosophy does not provide a generally accepted formula for expressing the relation of God and the world, then dogmatics can only vacillate between formulas that approach identification of the two and formulas that place them in opposition. But Schleiermacher thinks this problem can be solved in another way: by focusing not on *being* but on *causality*. The question is not, What distinguishes God from nature? but rather, What distinguishes God's general or universal (*allgemeine*) causality from a particular (*besondere*) cause set in motion by finite beings? And in answer to this question, an absolute distinction can be drawn. Finite beings have a particular and partial causality, because they are connected with all other finite beings in the web of natural causation. They do not have absolute, but only relative, freedom to realize their powers in actions. But God's causality is universal: it is that on which the totality of particular and partial causality is dependent. Divine preservation is the upholding or sustaining (*Erhaltung*) of the entire nature system.

In his discussion of the divine attributes corresponding to creation and preservation, Schleiermacher lands on a formula that aptly expresses how universal and particular causality can be understood to co-exist, and he further specifies divine causality as not only universal but also absolute – unconditioned or non-reciprocal. God's absolute causality (*schlechthinnige Ursächlichkeit*) is equal in extent (*dem Umfange nach*) to the natural order, but it is different in kind (§ 51.1). Thus, while God is active in every part of finite existence, from the smallest to the largest, and from the beginning to the end, God acts in God's own unique way. Omnipotence implies that God is powerful in everything that occurs. But divine causality does not replace the causality of finite agents. On the contrary, God sets in motion and continually sustains the powers that are given to each and every part of the created order, and all of these act in concert to realize a divinely appointed goal. As the "whence" of the feeling of absolute dependence, God is related to everything. The deity acts, not like a finite agent who must choose between a limited range of interactions with other parts of the nature system, but as the absolute cause that always and everywhere relates to everything.

Of course, this conception of divine causality has immediate consequences for the way in which one conceives of the meaning of divine providence. Schleiermacher is critical of much of the traditional dogmatic language. As we have already seen, he takes the divisions between general, special, and most special providence to be useless. God does not act more in relation to some parts of the system of nature than others (§ 46, postscript; cf. § 164.3). Similarly, the distinctions older dogmaticians made between preservation, cooperation, and governance cannot be maintained. To speak of divine "cooperation" could imply that there are aspects of finite activity that go on independently of the divine sustaining activity. But that would destroy the proper distinction between universal and particular causality. The divine government must mean "that everything happens and can happen only as God has originally and always willed, by means of the forces distributed and preserved in the world" (§ 46, postscript). If one takes it to mean that while some things occur that are not really willed by God, God overrules to direct them towards his purposes, that introduces a distinction among finite things that is not included in the feeling of absolute dependence. Thus only the notion of divine preservation is strictly required.

Under the next three propositions (§§ 47–9), Schleiermacher discusses some false inferences that people characteristically draw from the notion of God's providence. One such mistaken notion is that hindrances to life, which most of us would call "evils," are not so dependent on God as life-enhancing events. Schleiermacher is consistent in arguing that God is the author of all that is – even sin and its consequent evils (§ 48; cf. §§ 75–8). God does not will sin and evil as particular things, however, in and for themselves (God does not will *any* particular things in and for themselves!), but only in relation to the divine decree for the whole. To exempt evil from the divine causality would be to raise the specter of a cosmic dualism, a metaphysical position ruled out for Christian faith with its rejection of Manicheanism.

Another mistaken notion is to distinguish between "free causes" and "natural causes," and to imply that the former are somehow less dependent on God than the latter (§ 49). The details of Schleiermacher's rejoinder need not detain us here. Briefly, he asserts that human freedom is not an illusion, but neither is it something that distinguishes human agency from so-called natural causes. On the contrary, all living things have some freedom to act in relation to their particular kind of being. And such relative freedom is not in contradiction to absolute dependence, either in the case of humans or in the case of other living things.

More important for our purposes is the final mistaken notion (which Schleiermacher actually addresses first in the course of his argument): that miracles occur as breaches of natural causality (§ 47). Schleiermacher was well aware of the reasons why an appeal to miracles, so understood, had been prominent in Christian dogmatics. For some theologians, miracles were proof of the divine omnipotence and of a divine governance that could counteract the bad effects of free causes. But neither of these claims will stand. If God needed to interfere in the course of nature, that could only be because God did not get it right the first time – a notion inconsistent with the divine perfection. And if so-called free causes could so thwart God's plan that an intervention was necessary, God would not be truly omnipotent. Other theologians argued that neither prayer nor regeneration would make sense if there were no possibility of something new occurring as the result of them, something other than what would have happened without them. But Schleiermacher answers that prayer and its effects are part of God's original plan, and regeneration can be understood in analogy to the incarnation of Christ as the supernatural becoming natural. Miracles, understood as interruptions in the course of nature, are simply not required to explain these experiences.

But miracles are not only unnecessary; they are actually destructive of the feeling of absolute dependence. If natural causes were overridden even in a single case, Schleiermacher argues, it would "completely abrogate the concept of nature" (§ 47.2). A supposed miraculous event would be separated from the sum total of all other finite causes that led up to it and were thwarted when the necessary effect did not occur, or from the later causes and effects that followed it, all of which would be different because of this novel interruption in the causal nexus. Divine causality as absolute and universal would be similarly compromised, for now God would relate to at least one event or thing in a different manner than all the rest. And piety's fundamental intuition – that God is all-sovereign – would be undermined. Schleiermacher identifies the "one great miracle" as the coming of Christ into the world (§ 47.1; cf. §§ 13–14). But even this miracle is not a breach of the nature system. Christ himself does not have a different relation to the order of nature than do other free causes. In the miracle of the redeemer's appearance, the supernatural becomes natural.

Schleiermacher's reconstruction of the doctrine of providence, then, moves away from the older theology at several points. God is not conceived of as an extremely powerful particular cause, but rather as the absolute and universal cause. Hence, divine causality must be understood as fundamentally different from finite causality. Schleiermacher envisions God's unique causality as active in everything – co-extensive with the entire nature system, yet absolutely distinguishable from it in kind. Such a move rules out a view of God as an agent who occasionally (perhaps very frequently) interacts with particular agents in the nature system. That God, in Schleiermacher's view, would be finite. But it is precisely such an image of God that enabled the older theology to make distinctions between general and special providence. The "most special" kind of providence was seen as divine intervention on behalf of particular persons. Further, Schleiermacher's understanding of the coincidence of divine causality and the interconnection of nature turns attention away from the individual and towards the whole. The individual relates to God only as a part of the whole, which is the actual object of the divine preservation. This thought was not unknown to Protestant orthodoxy, but more common was Calvin's notion that the hand of providence was especially to be seen in divine action on behalf of the individual.[4] Finally, Schleiermacher's rejection of miracles marks a major departure from earlier theology. He is clear that he is making no philosophical judgment about the possibility or impossibility of miracles *per se*.[5] He is simply saying that if such interruptions in the causal nexus were to occur, piety would be impossible, for there would be no adequate ground for the feeling of absolute dependence. At the same time, science and morality would be equally impossible, for one would have no basis for confidence in the consistency of nature or of human agency. Thus, Christian faith presupposes that God acts in relation to the whole, and that everything that has ever existed or will exist in the future is called forth and sustained by God for the purpose of realizing the divine decree to redeem humanity in

Jesus Christ. Perhaps the best summary of Schleiermacher's understanding of preservation occurs in one of his sermons, "The Power of Prayer in Relation to Outward Circumstances." He states that in prayer we should approach God as the Unchangeable One,

> in whom no new thought, no new decision, can arise since he said to himself, "All that I have made is good." . . . If, because of the web of events [*den Zusammenhang*] that he has ordered you must do without your wish, you have a substitute for it in all the good you see in the world . . . . But the Wise One is also kind. He will not let you go without and suffer only for the sake of others. His will is that for the justified everything should serve their own good (cf. Rom. 8.28). So arises trust that notice has been taken of us, too, within the whole, however small a part we may be.[6]

JUSTIFICATION AND ELECTION

What, then, are the implications of this revised doctrine of providence for evangelical Christian beliefs in the justification of the sinner and the predestination of the elect? In his presentation of both beliefs Schleiermacher made a critical move from the customary focus on the individual to his distinctive perspective on the whole, and he sought to reinterpret the traditional accounts in harmony with his persuasion that the divine activity works "naturally" – in accordance with the law-governed course of nature. This not only required him to revise the inherited doctrine of justification by faith; it also enabled him to propose a solution to the problem of double predestination bequeathed to him by the teaching of his Reformed or Calvinistic school.

Justification by Faith

Recent studies of Schleiermacher's theology have shown less interest in his doctrine of justification by faith than in his Christology. True, his reflections on the person and work of Christ are the heart of the *Christian Faith*. But neglect of the sections he devotes to conversion and justification, placed together under the heading "regeneration" or "rebirth," may say more about recent Protestant theology than it says about his. Justification, Martin Luther's "article of a standing or falling church," was certainly not forgotten in the last century: it earned an important section in Karl Barth's *Church Dogmatics*, for example, and it figured prominently in ecumenical negotiations between Roman Catholics and Lutherans. But few today would wish to argue anymore that justification is the center of Protestant theology. Barth himself insisted that not justification but the confession of Jesus Christ is the true article of a standing or falling church. Paul Tillich's well-known verdict seemed to move justification still further from the center: "[I]t is so strange to the modern man that there is scarcely any way of making it intelligible to him."[7] In actual fact, Tillich was a master at retrieving the language of justification by viewing it in the context of other threats to human existence, more characteristic of our times than the anxiety of guilt and condemnation. But mainline Protestant theologians since Tillich have, with few exceptions, hardly been inclined to place reaffirmation or reconstruction of Luther's "chief article" at the center of the theological task; and where it is not neglected, the treatment of it may lack the depth of the older theology.

Schleiermacher, by contrast, without adopting justification by faith as his chief article, took pains to give it close attention, as the Lutheran and Reformed theological traditions required of him. In form, if not always in substance, the *Christian Faith* preserved connection with the great dogmatic systems of Protestant orthodoxy. From a letter of Schleiermacher to his friend Joachim Christian Gass (May 11, 1811) we know that the first time he gave the lectures out of which the *Christian Faith* emerged, he consulted the theological system of Quenstedt, and subsequently the nine-volume loci of Johann Gerhard (1582–1637) – both of them orthodox Lutheran divines, and both cited several times in the *Christian Faith*. In addition, Schleiermacher brought with him to his dogmatic labors something of his youthful experience among the pietists, for whom conversion was always of paramount concern. It is no surprise that his section on conversion is among the most perceptive discussions – theologically and psychologically – in the *Christian Faith*. He argues that conversion is by no means superfluous for those born and baptized in the church, but need not always be a datable crisis-experience; and he insists that, although a lively receptiveness on the part of the hearer is presupposed, consent to the word of the gospel can only be ascribed to the prevenient work of grace, not to some natural cooperation of the will. There must, in any case, be a *turning point* in the passage from the old life of sin to the new life in Christ, and this turning point is what is meant by "regeneration" (§§ 106– 7), which, along with "conversion" (§ 108), includes "justification" (§ 109). The *growth* of the new life begun in regeneration is "sanctification" (§§ 110–12), and this means not just the cultivation of personal holiness but a deepening commitment to the kingdom of God: for all Christ's activity rested on his will for the kingdom of God (§ 110.3), and communion with him is inconceivable apart from sharing in his mission to the world (§ 111.4).

Our concern is with the main lines of Schleiermacher's intricate thoughts on justification, although, as indicated, it is a fragment of a larger, complex discussion on the way in which communion with the redeemer comes to expression in the individual; and this entire discussion is itself strictly a sequel, corresponding in systematic detail to what Schleiermacher has previously said about the person and work of Christ. In the first division of his overall theme "The Consciousness of Grace" he has shown how, by virtue of this consciousness, we are to think of the *redeemer*; in the second, he must show how, on the same basis, we are to think of the *redeemed* (§ 91.2). He moves on in sections 106–12, then, to what we may call his profile of the Christian, adopting traditional rubrics but noting inconsistency in their use by the Reformation confessions and the old Protestant divines. First, however, before turning directly to the doctrine of regeneration, he pauses to offer a prefatory remark, important for our discussion, on his order of topics (§ 106.2). Ought he not to consider the *community* of the redeemed before the redeemed *individual*? Everything he has said so far must surely incline us to expect that the community will come before the individual, the church before the Christian. In fact, he follows the reverse sequence. Why?

The strength of Schleiermacher's interpretation of sin was his insistence that sin must be understood collectively as a social phenomenon, a contagious disease and not just an individual transgression (§ 71.2), and he has described the work of Christ as the establishment of a *new* "common life" (*Gesamtleben*) that works against the "common life" of sin (§§ 87–8). Hence, he has maintained that there is no such thing as a solitary Christian (§§ 24.4, 87.3), and he now repeats the point: the call to fellowship with Christ comes only from the new common life, and the sanctification of each comes from the influence of the whole. But, of course, the whole is made up of individuals. He could begin, then, either way: with the individual or with the community. One reason he offers to justify his choice of beginning with the individual is particularly interesting (missed, unfortunately, by the English translators). The gospel now comes through the preaching of the Christian community, which in this sense is superordinate to the convert. Still, just as in the days of his earthly ministry the call of Christ ("Follow me!") laid hold of individuals, so today it is by an act of Christ himself, mediated through his spiritual presence in the word, that the individual is taken up into the fellowship of the new life (§ 106.2; cf. § 108.5). The word of Christ, though proclaimed in the community, singles out the individual, and to the consciousness of someone in the grip of conversion all human instrumentality vanishes and Christ is immediately present (*Christus sich ... unmittelbar vergegenwärtigt*) in all his redeeming and reconciling activity (§ 108.5). It remains true, however, that the individual convert is simultaneously drawn from the "outer community" of listeners into the "inner community" of the regenerate (§ 113), and we will find that Schleiermacher's presentation on the justification of the individual requires him, in actual fact, to adopt the perspective of the whole: it is *humanity* that is justified for Christ's sake.[8]

What, then, is justification as one aspect of regeneration, and how is it related to conversion, the other aspect? Schleiermacher defines and distinguishes the two in proposition 107: "To be taken up into life-giving communion [*Lebensgemeinschaft*][9] with Christ, considered as a person's changed relation to God, is justification; considered as a changed form of life, it is conversion." Schleiermacher asserts that both justification and conversion are effects of union with Christ, and that you cannot have the one without the other. Though the terms differ, the assertion is reminiscent of John Calvin's presentation of the same theme in the 1559 *Institutes*. Calvin again comes to mind when Schleiermacher proceeds to discuss conversion before justification. Somewhat surprisingly, he can even say in one place that his presentation *derives* justification from conversion – the changed relation from the changed form of life (§ 109.3). But this cannot mean that, in the order of being, justification itself *depends on* conversion, as though God's activity were in recognition of human activity. That would bring Schleiermacher too close to the Roman Catholic view, which he rejects, that a person's justification depends on his sanctification (§ 109.1). Conversion – the gift of repentance and faith – is a work of God on, rather than in, the sinner; and on the human side the actual turning point is only what Schleiermacher calls the initial "*in*activity" of one confronted by the arresting vision of the perfection and blessedness of Christ (§ 108.2; cf. § 109.3). Justification and conversion are simultaneous, and the foundation of both is communion with Christ.

The changed relation to God that justification describes has to do with removal of the consciousness of guilt and deserving punishment (§ 107.1). But, like Calvin once again, proposition 109 distinguishes two aspects of the new relation: "That God justifies the one who turns to him [*den sich Bekehrenden*: the convert] includes two things: that he forgives him his sins, and that he recognizes him as a child of God." Schleiermacher designates this proposition a *Lehrsatz*, by which he usually means an official church doctrine (rather than a "theorem," as the English version translates it), open to dogmatic criticism and revision (§ 27.1–2; see, for example, §§ 96.3, 118.3). But he admits that the double aspect of justification does not in fact have symbolic authority in the Lutheran and Reformed confessions, even if the dogmatic theologians do often speak of adoption.[10] He wants to insist that justification is something more – more positive – than the remission of sins. Nevertheless, justification must, he thinks, *include* forgiveness, and it is precisely in regard to forgiveness that the doctrine of divine providence qualifies what can be said. For what can it mean to speak, as the official church doctrine does, of a particular act of God that justifies an individual, forgiving him his sins?[11]

In the language of Christian devotion, the sinner is pictured standing before the judgment seat of God the Father and awaiting the divine verdict of acquittal or condemnation. As Schleiermacher remarks, the picture often includes the intercession of Christ, who points out a person in whom he has effected faith and commends him to the Father for forgiveness and adoption (§ 109.3). The Father then pronounces the verdict "not guilty." In the crucial passage, Schleiermacher comments:

[I]f we want to speak, as far as possible, without picture language [*Versinnlichung*] and with dogmatic sharpness, we can as little here as elsewhere allow a temporal act [*Akt*] occurring in a particular moment or directed to an individual. There can only be an individual and particular *effect* of a divine act or decree, not such [an act] itself. That is to say, only insofar as every dogmatic discussion starts from the self-consciousness of the individual, as the present discussion begins from consciousness of the change in the individual's relation to God, can we think of the justifying divine activity [*Tätigkeit*] in its connection with the individual.[12]

The moment of a person's justification, in Schleiermacher's view, is strictly the breakthrough of God's eternal decree *for humanity* into the consciousness of the individual. Although, then, he has decided to begin with the manifestation of Christ's work in the individual, the treatment of justification leads him, as usual, to the perspective of the whole. Justification has nothing to do with averting God's anger or punishment from this or that particular sinner, much less with any legal fiction by which God pronounces the unrighteous righteous (cf. § 107.2) . Earlier, Schleiermacher has already relegated divine punishments and the image of God's "wrath" to a primitive stage of religious development at which the deity was still thought of as irritable and not above feeling insulted (§ 84.3). The "forgiveness of sins" in the ecclesiastical formula, then, could only be cessation of the consciousness of guilt in the mind of one who is drawn into communion with the redeemer and accordingly strives against sin as "something foreign" in him (*ein Fremdes*), an alien intrusion (§ 109.2–3; cf. Rom. 7:17, 20, one of Schleiermacher's favorite Pauline texts). In short, God's justifying activity is one with his governance of the *whole*,[13] and justification by faith occurs as the divine decree for humanity is appropriated by an individual who turns to Christ (§109.3–4). This presentation of the subject, Schleiermacher assures us, is *not* liable to the misunderstanding that each individual justifies himself,[14] since it traces everything back to the action of Christ (§ 109.3) – and of course to the divine decree, to which we turn next, albeit more briefly.

The election of grace

Lack of interest in Schleiermacher's doctrine of justification has been matched in the recent theological discussion by neglect of his doctrine of election – all the more surprising because, in part, he anticipated Karl Barth's controversial attempt to revise the Calvinist dogma of predestination.[15] Schleiermacher was not necessarily deviating from Calvinist orthodoxy when he spoke of a single, *general* divine decree. The Reformed or Calvinist divines frequently used "decree" (singular) as the comprehensive term for the plan by which God ordains everything that comes to pass. Even when they argued about the order of the *particular* "decrees" (plural) included in the divine plan – the decrees to create the world and humans, to permit the fall, and to predestine the salvation of the elect – they freely acknowledged that the plurality cannot refer to any real distinctions in the will of God, which (like God himself) is absolutely one; it refers to the logical relations between the things decreed or the temporal sequence in which they come about.[16] Nor did Schleiermacher dissent from the orthodox Calvinist view that the execution of the divine decree in the preaching of the gospel divides humanity into two groups. The question, for him, was *how* and *why* the division is effected.

Calvin did not invent the doctrine that is regularly associated with his name. Along with the other Protestant reformers, including Luther, he revived it in its strict Augustinian form to counter the alleged tendency to semi-Pelagianism in late medieval theology. But Calvin is the right point of departure for our present theme, because it was Calvin's treatment of election that Schleiermacher undertook to defend against the strictures of a Lutheran critic, Karl Gottlieb Bretschneider. Calvin began his discussion of election in the 1559 *Institutes* (book 3, ch. 21) with the observation that the covenant of life is not preached to everyone, and among those to whom it is preached it does not meet with the same reception. In agreement with the later Augustine, he thought himself constrained by Scripture to attribute this diversity to God's election, by which salvation is gratuitously offered to some while others are excluded from it. The doctrine of election, he believed, is the final proof that the gift of grace really *is* gratuitous – a totally free act of God by which he gives to one what he denies to another, without regard for the merit of either. Undeterred by the "great and difficult questions" that the doctrine occasions, Calvin arrived at this formulation of it: "We call 'predestination' God's eternal decree by which he determined in himself what he willed to become of each individual [*de unoquoque homine*]. For all are not created in a like condition, but eternal life is foreordained for some [the elect], eternal damnation for others" (sec. 5).[17] Calvin was of course aware that Scripture speaks also of the election of Israel, or a remnant of Israel. But the way he defined "predestination" indicates that the destiny of the individual was in the forefront of his mind. As the Scripture says, "I have loved Jacob, but I have hated Esau" (Mal. 1:2–3; Rom. 9:13). Calvin inferred that the eternal decree of election divides the human community irrevocably into two fixed groups of individuals. And it was just this dualism that Schleiermacher, despite his professed defense of Calvin, set out to overcome. Once again, his understanding of divine preservation comes to his aid: the appearance of divine caprice in election is set aside if we avoid "atomistic" thinking (§ 120.2, 4), and if we recognize that the execution of the divine decree conforms to the laws of nature.

Though characteristically dense in some of the details, in outline Schleiermacher's account of election and predestination in the *Christian Faith* (§§ 117–20) is straightforward enough. Fundamental to his entire understanding of redemption is the conviction that the incarnation of Christ inaugurated an entirely new stage in the history of humanity: it began the regeneration of the human race (§ 116.2). Sooner or later every nation will become Christian, and every individual may thus be said to bear within himself the "predestination to blessedness." The total efficacy of Christ's high-priestly dignity is demonstrated only when all are included in this predestination to blessedness, which must be taken as completely universal: God sees all humankind only in Christ (§ 120, postscript). In sum, there is only the *single* decree of predestination to blessedness (§§ 119.2–3, 120.4): it is *humanity* that is elected in Christ, a thought that reappears in Barth's doctrine of election (along with other thoughts peculiar to him).[18] It was not wholly novel even in Schleiermacher. It bears a resemblance to what Calvin called the "absurd invention" of his Roman Catholic adversary Albert Pighius.[19] But Schleiermacher was unwilling to concede, as Pighius did, that it is possible to deprive oneself of the benefit of universal election.[20]

Schleiermacher could not evade Calvin's observation concerning the inequality of the gift of Christ's grace, which is given to some and withheld from others. He agreed with Calvin that the inequality can be traced only to the divine good-pleasure, not to any meritorious advantage that one individual may have over another, since all are absolutely equal only in sin (§§ 116.2, 118.1, 2). But we are not prevented from asking by what this divine good-pleasure is determined (§ 117.4). The answer is that the execution of the divine decree takes place under the conditions of the divine governance of the world, which is strictly governance according to law. And one obvious law is that what starts from a single point spreads only gradually over an entire area (§ 117.1). This "law" enabled Schleiermacher to acknowledge that there is indeed a division in the human community, but to insist that it is only a "vanishing contrast" between the regenerate – the "elect," who have been picked out of the world – and the *not yet* regenerate (§§ 116.1, 117.3, 118.1, 119.2). Even the fact that some who hear the gospel do not receive it *now* must be attributed to the divine governance and means only that their time has not come. "For although the power of God's Word and of the love that seeks the salvation of humans is constant in the inward great act of preaching, there is a difference of effect grounded in varying states of receptiveness, and this depends on the circumstances in which the divine governance of the world places each person" (§ 114.2).[21] "It could not be otherwise if the supernatural in Christ is to become nature, and the church to develop as a natural historical phenomenon" (§ 117.2).

It has not been our purpose in this chapter to judge Schleiermacher's wrestling with the traditional Christian doctrines of justification and election, only to show its coherence with his idea of providence or preservation. Clearly, the result is the achievement of an acute and profound theological mind. Anyone who wishes to take the next step of *evaluation* may not judge his performance on the two doctrines to be of equal systematic worth. Despite his adherence to the old language, Schleiermacher ends with a justification by faith that seems to be a far cry, not only from naïve piety, but from the best thoughts of the old dogmaticians, too. Whether to conclude that this is a good thing or bad, would require a different kind of discussion than is offered here. As for the doctrine of election, Schleiermacher's revision may win more general approval insofar as he rescued it from the dualism that had always plagued the Calvinist dogma of double predestination. But there, too, difficulties remain for further discussion. His "vanishing contrast" between the regenerate and the unregenerate drives him necessarily toward universal salvation and the hope for a second chance after death (*CF*, § 118), and that has never been the majority opinion among Christians. And perhaps even *his* treatment of the divine decree remains incorrigibly anthropomorphic. His disciple, Alexander Schweizer, at any rate, decided that predestination is simply an improper representation of the Christian consciousness of grace.[22]

It may of course be objected that Schleiermacher's reinterpretation of the old beliefs was bound to go wrong because it was methodologically flawed to begin with: he let part one of the *Christian Faith* regulate the content of part two.[23] But it could well be argued that he was doing no more than some of the most eminent Christian theologians have done for two millennia. The fact that part one rests on philosophical and scientific principles current in Schleiermacher's day doesn't automatically make the *Christian Faith* bad theology, but it does open it to scientific and philosophical criticism. He lived at a time when, for many, the old image of God no longer worked. But he showed how it was possible to believe in a divine activity that does not disrupt the regularity of nature but directs the total course of nature uninterruptedly to God's ends.

Notes

1 The first part of this chapter was drafted mainly by Dawn DeVries, the second by B. A. Gerrish, but we are jointly responsible for the final version. Our main primary source is the second edition of Schleiermacher's *Christian Faith* [*Der christliche Glaube*, 1830–31]; all internal references are to this text. The word "proposition" is used to denote the summary sentence (*Leitsatz*) with which Schleiermacher introduced each section. Unless otherwise indicated, translations in this chapter are ours.

2 The Bohemian and Scots' Confessions, cited in the introductory note to *CF*, § 37. Interestingly, none of the confessions cited in this note uses the term "providence" or "provider." The preferred term is *conservatio* or *conservator*.

3 Schleiermacher argued elsewhere that in the theology of the Reformation there was the basis for an "eternal covenant between the living Christian faith and completely free, independent scientific inquiry, so that faith does not hinder science and science does not exclude faith." Schleiermacher, *On the Glaubenslehre: Two Letters to Dr. Lücke*, 64.

4 To illustrate the thesis that "by government all things are so guided by God that they serve the purpose of the world whole and thereby achieve their own purpose," Heppe cites the *Leiden Synopsis* (1581), which states, "[W]e shall be more correct in saying that it does not belong to Providence that by it each separate thing should be guided to the particular end suited to it, but absolutely to the end congruent with the whole work." Heppe, 262. Compare John Calvin, *Institutio Christianae Religionis* (1559), 1.16.4–6: in Calvin 1926–59, III, 194–7.

5 "We do not here have to pass judgment on the possibility [of miracles] in itself, but only on the relation between a hypothetical acceptance of miracles and the feeling of absolute dependence" (*CF*, § 47.1).

6 Schleiermacher, *Kleine Schriften und Predigten*, 1.173–4. A piety directed towards the goodness of God manifested in the whole, however, may have a dark side. In the prayer that Schleiermacher delivered at the graveside of his young son Nathanael in 1829, he implored, "Let me not only submit to your omnipotence, not only resign myself to your inscrutable wisdom, but also discern your fatherly love" (*Kleine Schriften und Predigten*, III.341). In the face of the evil that individuals experience, it is easier to believe in the omnipotence than in the love of God.

7 Tillich 1951, 193.

8 See the epigraph, taken from *CF*, § 109.3, at the head of this chapter.

9 Like so many of Schleiermacher's compound technical terms, *Lebensgemeinschaft Christi* is difficult to put into English. More than "fellowship," such as the association between two friends, *Lebensgemeinschaft* suggests having life in common: one might venture to translate the expression *Lebensgemeinschaft Christi* as "participation in the life of Christ." But it needs to be borne in mind that Schleiermacher also uses *Gemeinschaft* for a "community," which is what he takes the Christian church to be.

10 His catena of quotations does not include the Westminster Confession (1647), which expressly follows the chapter on justification (ch. XI) with a chapter on adoption (ch. XII). In Calvin, the connection of reconciliation with adoption is explicit, but not so formally stated as by Schleiermacher.

11 Some mental gymnastics are required of Schleiermacher, especially when he tries to accommodate the fact that the evangelical church "views the divine act of justification as declaratory," which seems to imply that there must be a multitude of such acts (*CF*, § 109.3).

12 *CF*, § 109.3 (emphasis ours). Our epigraph at the beginning of this chapter follows. Note that, though his usage is not entirely consistent, it was more natural for Schleiermacher to speak of the divine "activity" (*Tätigkeit*) than of a divine "act" (*Akt*).

13 Schleiermacher discusses the other pertinent aspect of God's justifying activity, its conformity to the natural *laws* of the world order, when he turns to the doctrine of election. As we will see, the actual moment when regeneration occurs is determined by the personal identity and particular circumstances of the individual, and these are given by the general divine governance of the world, which Schleiermacher does not hesitate to call "divine predestination" (*CF*, § 119.1).

14 The negative in the German expression *nicht leicht* ("not readily" or "hardly") was apparently missed by the English translators, who perhaps were predisposed to think that the presentation really *was* liable to the "misunderstanding" Schleiermacher dismisses!

15 It has become the custom to speak of the Calvinist doctrine of *predestination*. Some Reformed theologians, among them Schleiermacher and Barth, take *election* as the preferred rubric. The topic is introduced in Calvin's 1559 *Institutes* as "The Eternal Election by Which God Has Predestined Some to Salvation, Others to Destruction."

16 On the question whether creation and the fall were decreed solely as the means to carry out God's actual goal – to display the glory of his mercy by saving the

elect – Schleiermacher shows at least an affinity with the supralapsarians, since he asserts that sin is ordained by God for the sake of redemption (*CF*, § 81.3).

17 Calvin 1926–59, IV.374.

18 Barth 1957, II.2, ch. 7; see 116–17, 149, 163, 167, 195, 310, 313, 450. The absence of any discussion of Schleiermacher in these passages is curious.

19 See Calvin 1956, 27–8, 45, 71.

20 Barth, too, acknowledged this possibility but without absolutely excluding the other possibility: that, in the freedom of divine grace, the circle of the elect may finally coincide with the world of humanity as such (*Church Dogmatics*, II.2:41/–18). In any case, "Not every one who is elected lives as an elect man" (321), though the life of a rejected person is "objectively impossible" (346).

21 Schleiermacher notes the parallel with the "elect" Christ himself, who was chosen in the fullness of divinely determined time (*CF*, §§ 116.1, 120.2–3).

22 On Schweizer and his critical review of earlier attempts, before Schleiermacher, to mitigate the Calvinist dogma of double predestination, see Gerrish 1978, ch. 4. Schleiermacher himself points out that "a proposition that articulates a divine decree is not an expression of the immediate self-consciousness" (*CF*, § 90.2).

23 He asserts this most explicitly with regard to the divine attributes (see *CF*, § 56, postscript), but the procedure is implicit throughout.

11 Schleiermacher's *Christian Ethics*

EILERT HERMS

(translated and condensed by JACQUELINE MARIÑA and
CHRISTINE HELMER)

A proper grasp of Schleiermacher's *Christian Ethics*[1] presupposes an understanding of the following: the relation between ethics and faith (the two parts of dogmatic theology), the relation of historical theology to philosophical theology, and a correct understanding of theology's place in the theory of human knowledge as a whole.

THE PLACE OF CHRISTIAN ETHICS IN THE CONTEXT OF HUMAN UNDERSTANDING[2]

In his introduction to the *Christian Ethics*, Schleiermacher notes the relationship of Christian ethics to Christian faith (*CE*, 2) and to philosophical ethics (*CE*, 24). To understand properly these relationships we must first reflect upon the conditions of the possibility of knowledge in general and how these conditions affect how we are to understand: (1) the place of theology in relation to possible knowledge as a whole; (2) the place of dogmatics in theology; (3) especially in relation to philosophical theology; and, (4) in light of the relationship between Christian faith and Christian ethics (as the two parts of dogmatics). Finally, given these considerations, we must reflect upon the relation of Christian ethics to philosophical ethics.

Making use of the transcendental philosophy inaugurated by Kant, Schleiermacher reflected upon the conditions of the possibility of knowledge and how these conditions determined the kinds of knowledge possible. However, he moved beyond Kant in noting that these conditions must be of such a kind as also to reveal the possibility of transcendental knowledge itself. Moreover, Schleiermacher noted that knowledge is a mode of human activity and has its place in the totality of human activity. As such, the conditions of its possibility are nothing other than the conditions of the possibility of all human activity.

Since his early period Schleiermacher understood these conditions as the "ensoulment of nature through reason"[3] – that is, the direction of natural processes in light of the self-development of individual members of the human race, in other words, in light of the human condition. The contingent character of such a condition is grounded in the effect of nature on human rationality (natural processes) and the effect of human rationality on nature (historical processes). Schleiermacher reflected on these conditions in his theory of complete humanity during his early period in the *Monologen* (1800) and in his later period in his lectures on psychology (1818).[4]

Insight into the human condition is *a posteriori* insofar as the existence of such a condition is *given*. However, knowledge of this condition involves a description of the enduring elements conditioning all human activities such as knowing. As such this insight is the *a posteriori* knowledge of the conditions of the possibility of all human activity, which are as such *a priori* valid for all human actions. These transcendental conditions ground the possibility of human activity and are known through reflection upon it. Schleiermacher described this state of affairs as "feeling" and the "immediate self-consciousness" (*CF*, § 3). The conditions making human activity possible have the character of an unavoidable impulse towards the individual's own activity, and as such are characterized by an inner determination of the immediate self-consciousness through a determination of its modes of activity. In its determined character the immediate self-consciousness is an impulse for . . . , an interest in . . . , a striving for a given mode of activity of symbolizing or organizing.

There are two kinds of activity determining the immediate self-consciousness. In Schleiermacher's writings up to 1816 they may be understood as "symbolizing," and "organizing" in the ethical texts; after 1818 they are characterized as "knowing" and "doing" in the psychology,[5] as well as in the *Christian Faith* and the *Christian Ethics*. "Doing" and "organizing" have an organizing effect on the individual's relation to the world. On the other hand, what is symbolized and known is simply grasped without the intention of having such an effect. Both are modes of human activity that mutually condition one another: without doing and organizing there is no expansion of knowledge, and without symbolizing and knowing there is no reflection on doing (*CF*, § 3.3).

Schleiermacher divided interest in knowing into two kinds. First is the interest in knowledge for its own sake. Here the object of knowledge is the nature of knowledge itself and the practice of knowing; Schleiermacher calls this "pure" knowledge. The second is the interest in knowledge of the nature and actual state of practical affairs, and which knowledge can be systemized. Schleiermacher called this "positive knowledge." Because the object of theology has to do with these practical matters, Schleiermacher characterized theology as a "positive" discipline.

A science is "positive," according to Schleiermacher, if it comprehends a number of disciplines belonging together because they are "required for the resolution of a practical task" (*BO*, § 1, postscript).[6] Like law and medicine, theology is a "positive" science (*Wissenschaft*). However, it differs from them because it is oriented to the governing of religious communities, in Schleiermacher's case, the Christian church (*BO*, §§ 3, 5).

What belongs to theology's core of scientific knowledge? Because theology is a positive science, it proposes general rules that are applied to the contemporary church's situation. These rules are determined by the demands of the church and the tasks before it. Knowledge of what these demands and tasks are presupposes theoretical knowledge of the particular contemporary situation of Christian life, a Christian life having a particular essence and history. As such, while practical theology is the goal of all theology and concerns the knowledge of rules, it presupposes two other areas of theology: philosophical and historical theology.[7] While philosophical theology has to do with theoretical insight into the *essence* of Christian life (*BO*, §§ 32–68), historical theology concerns the way in which the contemporary situation of Christian life has developed historically (*BO*, §§ 69–256). Both philosophical theology and historical theology constitute an inner unity given the identity of their subject matter: the actual history of the Christian life. Yet they approach this subject matter from two different perspectives. Historical theology investigates the continuous change in Christian life as it manifests itself in concrete historical moments. Philosophical theology investigates those characteristics that remain the same throughout these changes and which, as such, constitute the uniqueness and identity of the Christian life. What is essential to Christian life manifests itself in particular historical moments. However, each moment also contains variations peculiar to it alone. What is unique to each moment can only be grasped in relation to an understanding of what is essential to Christian life; hence both perspectives arrive at completion only in and through one another (*BO*, §§ 65, 67).

The essence of Christianity encompasses life in a religious "pious" community. The community is unified through the "conviction of the truth of its manner of believing" and the corresponding ways of living together in community (*BO*, § 39). At each point of their development, both are historical manifestations of communal life. Hence, an understanding of the current situation requires an understanding of the history leading to the present moment (*BO*, §§ 103–48). As such, historical theology consists of three parts: exegetical theology, church history, and knowledge of the present situation, containing dogmatics and statistics. Exegetical theology explores the foundational historical moments of Christian communal life through interpretation of the New Testament Scriptures (*BO*, §§ 83, 103). These documents record the workings of Christ on his disciples, and the workings of both on the early Christian community (*BO*, § 105). The effects of these workings on the present historical moment are not immediate, but are, rather mediated through history. Investigation of this mediation belongs to church history; it is, as such, "the middle member in the three parts of historical theology" (*BO*, §§ 149–94). The third member, knowledge of the present situation, consists of two parts: "church statistics" (*BO*, §§ 232–50), taking stock of the current state of the church, and dogmatic theology, which is "the knowledge of the currently valid doctrines of evangelical theology" (*BO*, § 195; cf. *CF*, § 19). Historical theology thereby describes, in each of its parts, "the formation of doctrine, or the bringing to clarity of the pious self-consciousness" as well as the "shape of the communal life," that is, of the ethos, cultus, and organization of Christianity throughout its changing circumstances (*BO*, § 166). As such, theoretical doctrines can also be viewed as practical ones (*BO*, § 183).

DOGMATIC THEOLOGY

Dogmatic theology consists of a definite set of expressions of the pious self-consciousness. Consciousness of belonging to the community of persons confessing their certainty of having been saved through Jesus Christ (*CF*, § 14) comes to clarity in and through these expressions (*BO*, § 166). Dogmatics is a *historical* discipline since it does not *construct* doctrines but merely *reflects* the essential expressions of Christian consciousness at each moment of its history (*BO*, §§ 177, 180). As such, it is the life of the church, and not dogmatic theology, that is decisive as to which dogmatic utterances have validity. Dogmatic theology has an influence on the life of the church insofar as it systematizes these utterances and weeds out contradictions (*CF*, § 17). Hence although dogmatic theology is a historical discipline, its task is a systematic one. As scientific knowledge, the task of dogmatic theology is given in the context of the Christian community for the purpose of church government (*CF*, § 18). This task is to connect all descriptive–didactic statements of faith in such a way that they are directed to one and the same object: membership in the Christian community, a community grounded in the certainty of redemption through Christ (*CF*, §§ 19, 28).

DOGMATIC AND PHILOSOPHICAL THEOLOGY

Historical theology cannot make headway in its subject matter without presupposing the concept of the essence of Christianity developed by philosophical theology. Philosophical theology is the critical investigation (combining speculative insights and empirical findings) of the essential conditions of being human in relation to the essential characteristics of life within the Christian community. In them lie the conditions grounding their manifestation in any given historical moment.

Just as historical theology offers no *a priori* proof for the Christian faith, neither does philosophical theology. The essential features of what it means to be human manifest themselves only in concrete historical appearances; hence, religion is to be found only in its historically conditioned variations. The interdependence of philosophical and dogmatic theology must be understood in the following way: both are directed towards the same object. In no way does philosophical theology ground historical theology. Schleiermacher's reference to the essential conditions of being human takes place in the context of his exposition of the Christian faith and expresses the idea that Christianity exists under the universal conditions of being human, as these conditions are understood from within the standpoint of Christianity.

CHRISTIAN DOCTRINE AND CHRISTIAN ETHICS

Dogmatic theology is the complete systematization of all statements of faith. It encompasses two parts: Christian doctrine and Christian ethics. Christian doctrine systematizes ontological (cosmological and anthropological) expressions of the Christian faith; Christian ethics systematizes practical expressions of the Christian faith. Both are oriented to the same object: pious Christian states of mind (or the certainty of faith [*CF*, § 14]) as the redemptive work of Christ. Because dogmatic theology includes both Christian doctrine and Christian ethics, Schleiermacher needs to determine the way in which both are integrally related yet distinct from one another. Their integral relation is effected by the identity of their subject matter: the linguistic articulation of the pious Christian life (*CF*, 26). Both Christian doctrine and Christian ethics reflect the character of dogmatic theology as a historical discipline. Their task is limited to systematizing non-contradictory statements of faith having a descriptive–didactic character.

The distinction between both disciplines reflects a difference within the unity of their subject matter. This distinction is anchored in the Christian determination of the immediate self-consciousness and its ground. As long as it is not perceived, we cannot distinguish between the two parts of dogmatic theology, namely Christian doctrine and Christian ethics. The difference is discussed in three texts: The *Brief Outline, Christian Ethics,* and *Christian Faith.* In the *Brief Outline* Schleiermacher speaks only of the difference between the two classes of statements but does not explain it (*BO,* § 223). Both the *Christian Ethics* and the *Christian Faith* are in agreement that the difference rests on the psychic state of Christian piety as a determination of immediate self-consciousness effected by the redemptive activity of Christ (*CE,* 16ff.; *CF,* § 26). Schleiermacher's return to fundamental anthropology in the psychology lectures of 1818 influenced this view.

The most detailed view is provided in the *Christian Ethics,* itself based on the third foundational paragraph of the *Christian Faith.* Here Schleiermacher describes the relations between piety in general as a determination of feeling or immediate self-consciousness vis-à-vis knowing and doing. This description was fundamental for Schleiermacher as early as the *Speeches* (1799) and was later reinvestigated in the lectures on psychology. The view picks up on the idea of the ensoulment of nature through reason. It establishes that the *koinos logos* that is, the rationality constitutive of human nature, only manifests itself in two irreducible ways (*CE,* 442). In the "Introduction" to the *Christian Ethics* they are called "representation" (*Vorstellen*) and "action" (*Handeln*); in the Introduction to the *Christian Faith* they are called "Knowing" and "Doing." What Schleiermacher has in mind becomes clear when the two texts are compared. Doing and Knowing are two different manifestations of human doing taken in a wider sense. As such, they are manifestations of human reason. In the *Christian Ethics* Schleiermacher notes that both representing and acting are the effects of a preceding motive that grounds them both. Representing is based on a preceding "*interest*"; acting is based on a preceding "*incentive*" (*CE,* 22). This motive precedes representing and acting and is, as such, not their effect. Rather it is effectively given as the implication of the piety that precedes and grounds the activity of reason (understood as a determination of the immediate self-consciousness). Hence a person's religion (piety) must always be distinguished from his or her Knowledge/Representation and Doing/Action, although only in such a way that these two modes of human activity are understood as having a preceding religious interest or incentive and are never separated from it (*CF,* § 3.4). What is true of religion in general is also true of Christian piety: it is characterized by a double motive. It grounds the desire for knowledge and representation, that is, the desire to symbolize, since it encompasses an interest. At the same time it also grounds the desire to act, since it encompasses an incentive.

Determination of the immediate self-consciousness making up piety includes this double motive. This is because the pious determination of the immediate self-consciousness contains an effective motive insofar as it is the certainty of a person's *becoming*, a becoming that must include the person's relative free cooperation with it (*CF*, § 4.1). This certainty contains two poles corresponding to the double motive. On the one hand, it is the certainty of existence that is given to the person to *know*; on the other hand, it is the certainty of a life that is given to the person to *shape*.

The object of certainty of the immediate self-consciousness is what makes piety take an interest in knowledge and moves it to action. Schleiermacher makes this point clearly in the "Introduction" to the *Christian Ethics*: "What then is the object that sparks the interest of the pious, and what is it that incites them to action? It is God, the highest Being" (*CE*, 23). However, not God in Godself, but rather, God as the *telos* of the human world, and furthermore, God not as the mere creator of the present moment, but God as the one who is effective in Christ, who saves humanity from domination by the world (*CF*, § 11.2–4). The same idea is expressed in the *Christian Ethics*: God is the ground and guarantee of the beginning and completion of the journey towards blessedness: the triumph of "spirit" over "flesh" (*CE* 42–51; 293–319; 516–21; cf. *CF*, §§ 116–121). Insofar as the Christian certainty of redemption is directed to what is given to it to *know* concerning God's relation to the world, it involves an *interest*. All expressions of the Christian faith that speak to this interest belong to Christian doctrine. Insofar as this certainty is directed toward human cooperation in *becoming* blessed, Christian piety is an *incentive* to action. All expressions of faith having to do with this incentive belong to Christian ethics (*CE*, 23).

Schleiermacher's *Christian Ethics* answers the question: Given that there *is* a religious self-consciousness, how must it develop itself, and what must come of it? (*CE*, 23). Schleiermacher provides a description of those actions that are the result of "power of the religious self-consciousness as determined by Christ" (*CE*, 1, 7, 12, 15). The "rules of life" portrayed in the *Christian Ethics* are primarily descriptive and are normative only in a derivative sense. They have the character of a hypothetical imperative: If and because you are Christ, act that way.

Christian ethics and Christian doctrine cover the same breadth of subject matter, but from two different perspectives. In the *Christian Ethics*, Schleiermacher tells us that "Christian ethics is also Christian doctrine," since membership in the Christian church presupposes knowledge regarding the nature and essence of such a community. Moreover, "Christian doctrine is also Christian ethics" since an essential element of Christian doctrine is the idea of the "kingdom of God on earth." Schleiermacher notes that "expression of the idea of the kingdom of God on earth is therefore nothing other than the expression of the art and manner of Christian life and action, and that is Christian ethics" (CE, 12). While Christian ethics and Christian doctrine may differ in their *contents*, they mutually presuppose one another. Christian ethics presupposes an interest in *self-knowledge*, and an interest in the existence and character of faith (*Glaubenslehre*) is possible only through the free *activity* demanded by the incentive of faith.

The pious determination of the immediate self-consciousness consists in two relations: the relation of the self to God (absolute dependence) and the relation of the self to the world (relative freedom and relative dependence). The difference between Christian ethics and Christian doctrine depends upon which relation of the immediate self-consciousness is being understood. If the immediate self-consciousness is understood in relation to the existing relation between persons in the world to God, the result is Christian doctrine. If it is understood in terms of the existence of faith as active in the world, the result is Christian ethics.

CHRISTIAN ETHICS AND PHILOSOPHICAL ETHICS[8]

The locus of Schleiermacher's philosophical ethics is the historically grounded essence of Christianity. It investigates the enduring conditions of all possible historical life given to the *conditio humana*, and it seeks to grasp these conditions in accordance with scientific rules through a speculative procedure. The enduring structural moments valid for all human ethical states of affairs on account of the *conditio humana* can also be found in the *Christian Ethics* (CE, 27, 176–7). Just as human ethics has to do with the rule of the spirit over the flesh, that is, of the *koinos logos* over the physical constitution of the world, so too, Christian ethics consists in the rule of the higher self-consciousness redeemed by Christ over the lower (CF, § 5). Just as the form of virtue pertains to human ethics, so too, it pertains to Christian ethics. Just as ethical activity under human conditions reveals the irreducible aspects of representation (symbolization) and action (organization), so too, does the ethical activity of faith. And as all possible ethical activity takes place in the community, the same is true of Christian ethical activity. In short, there is no contradiction between Christian and philosophical ethics (CE, 25–8). And this is so, because Christian life is a specific form or variety of human life in general.

This does not mean, however, that the *Christian Ethics* organizes its material according to the structure of philosophical ethics: the good, virtue, and duty. While this possibility is explicitly recognized (*CE*, 77–81), Schleiermacher does not take this position. This is because although Christian and philosophical ethics do not contradict one another, they are formally distinct. Their objects and methods are different (*CE*, 28–34). As a part of dogmatic theology, Christian ethics is not a speculative discipline, but rather, a historical–empirical one. Its direct object is the self-expression of faith concerning the incentive of pious Christian feelings, and its indirect object is reflection upon this self-expression. The scientific form of the *Christian Ethics* is not due to its following the form of the philosophical ethics, but is given, rather, through its material: the expressions of faith regarding the incentives of faith. So Schleiermacher, "It [Christian ethics] must be the portrayal of communion with God as it is conditioned by communion with Christ the redeemer, insofar as this is the motive for all Christian actions. It can be nothing other than a description of those ways of acting having their origin in the reign of the Christianly-determined religious self-consciousness" (*CE*, 26). The goal of Christian ethics is to systematize the self-expressions of faith through an exploration of the incentive of faith. Schleiermacher asks, "How does it [the Christian self-consciousness] become an incentive, and how does it pass over to action? We must next explore whether the Christian consciousness is a simple incentive, which first becomes a multiplicity as it is expressed, or whether it is in itself multiple" (*CE*, 35).

THE ONE OBJECT AND THREE THEMES OF THE *CHRISTIAN ETHICS*

The nature of the incentive of the Christian pious consciousness must be explored in order to know whether or not it is a multiple one. The starting point is the viewpoint of the pious Christian condition of the soul as a determination of immediate self-consciousness. Our first question is: under which condition does the feeling state of the immediate self-consciousness as determined by Christ's redemptive activity become an incentive to action? All action presupposes a lack and serves to overcome it, so that only the state of *emerging* blessedness, which implies that the goal of blessedness has not been achieved, can be an incentive to action. The starting point of this emergence is the claim that the dominion of the higher God-feeling has over the sensuous world feeling. Its goal is the state of "absolute blessedness" (*CE*, 36, 40), that is, the state of totally actualized communion with God. All moments in between these two limits can be characterized in terms of pleasure or pain: as pain, insofar as the flesh (sensuous consciousness) strives against the reign of the God-feeling, and as pleasure insofar as the flesh willingly becomes the organ of the higher consciousness (*CE*, 42, 45).

Our second question is, how does this emergent blessedness (*werdende Seligkeit*) become an incentive to action? (*CE*, 35). Given that the moments of this emerging blessedness can take the character of pleasure or pain, it can become an incentive in two different ways. Insofar as the striving towards complete blessedness is characterized by pain, it is an incentive to action that *re-establishes* the flesh as the organ of the spirit. This condition corresponds to the (at bottom) already actualized reign of the spirit over the flesh, even when it might be hindered by the refractoriness of the flesh. As such the incentive is one to a "re-establishing action" (*wiederherstellendes Handeln*) (*CE*, 44). On the other hand, the emerging blessedness can be pleasurable insofar as the flesh is willing to be the organ of the spirit. Insofar as it is this, it is an incentive to action that strives to extend the dominion of spirit over those areas not yet grasped by it. Such action is thereby an "expansive action" (*erweiterndes Handeln*) (*CE*, 45).

There is yet a third kind of incentive that manifests itself in the emerging blessedness. Emerging blessedness always manifests itself in two ways: as a *becoming* (as such, a movement that is still incomplete, still attacked by the refractoriness of the flesh), but also as a movement towards *blessedness*. As such, it is in its essence what complete blessedness will also become: the decisive reign of the spirit over the flesh, and thereby also a foretaste or analogue of complete blessedness. It manifests itself when the expansive action comes to a temporary halt, and when the re-establishing action is about to begin. These are the "enduring" (*CE*, 49) conditions of the possibility of a transition from pain to pleasure. As a state of indifference between pleasure and pain, it is free of both. Since this indifference between pleasure and pain can be an incentive to action, it is another incentive to a third kind of action.

The indifference between pleasure and pain *can* be an incentive to *action* because it is an analogue of complete blessedness (*CE*, 47). As the enduring condition of the possibility of pleasure and pain and the incentives to action rooted in them, this indifference still belongs in the emergence of blessedness. Its belonging here is demanded by the character of human becoming, namely as the being of an individual in community (*CE*, 509). For Schleiermacher the human being "is only something when s/he is connected to the whole in a living way, as developing from earlier moments and transitioning to later ones, that is, when in a certain sense s/he is an enduring being" (*CE*, 49). This connection does not occur through human activity alone, but requires an action. This consists in nothing other than

(1) the fixing of the particular manner of *becoming* through redemption, through the establishment of an enduring way of being, and at once; (2) the manifestation of this particular way of being (*CE*, 49). This action aims at being in community and brings it to consciousness (*CE*, 513). It does so insofar as it completes being in community, but also always presupposes it.

Being in community is effected through the redemptive work of Christ, through the communication of his Spirit as that of all those who receive him. This grounds the putting on of Christ (*Christsein*) and as such the beginning of blessedness, which is the "brotherly love" uniting all Christians. The action whose incentive is to become like Christ aims at nothing other than the expression of this brotherly love. As such, it is an action that consists in nothing but the expression of being in the community of the redeemed; it is a "representing" or "expressive" action (*darstellendes Handeln*) (*CE*, 50).[9]

The specific difference between this action and the "re-establishing" and "expansive" actions is that it does not refer back to the incentives of pleasure and pain. It refers rather to an impulse that grounds a state of consciousness, which is the possibility of the transition between the two, the equilibrium between them, and is indifferent to them (*CE*, 51). It is the precondition to the incentives of both re-establishing and expansive actions, since it portrays the reign of Spirit over the flesh.

Each religious determination of the immediate self-consciousness is an incentive to a representing or expressive activity, since it is a determination of life in community. This implies that the pious Christian state of mind urges actions having two characteristics: (1) the experience of redemption (through being grasped by the piety of Jesus) is one that each person has individually; (2) at the same time it is common to all Christians. It is the communal Christian spirit that grasps each person individually and manifests itself variously in each. Human actions can have a predominantly "individual" character (insofar as they express variation) or they may have an "identical" character (insofar as they express this common communal character) (*CE*, 55–68). Life in community is such that the action of one individual on another influences the community as a whole, and the action of an individual is always the action of the community through that individual, who represents it. The interplay between the actions of the community on individuals, and individuals on the community is the condition of the historical forward movement of the common Christian life.

These three incentives to the three kinds of action equally have their origin in the religious determination of the immediate self-consciousness. As Schleiermacher notes, "there is no moment in life in which there would not be a ground for each of these determinations [understood as religious feeling as an incentive in itself] and each of their corresponding actions" (*CE*, 54). Each of the three incentives exists only in *relation* to the other two, so that a complete description of all three incentives must show how one moment preponderates over the other two. The three moments must appear in a given order.

Despite their common origins, the three moments stand in an asymmetrical relation to one another. This is true from a transcendental perspective. Given its transcendental character as a feeling of the relation between the God-feeling and the world-feeling (flesh and spirit), the immediate self-consciousness includes all modifications of pleasure and pain that the felt relation can itself take. As such, the representing activity portraying the blessed life is always one that *precedes* and *follows* re-establishing or expansive actions. The joy of the Lord leads to a representing activity (*darstellenden Handeln*) so that pleasure and pain can arise, in turn leading to re-establishing or expansive actions. All effective actions have a representing (or expressive) activity as their ground and partake in this expressive activity.

The starting point of the *formation* of self-consciousness is the ensoulment of nature through reason; for the history of the formation of each Christian life, the starting point is being grasped by the Christian "joy of the Lord." What kind of action leads to the living continuity of the Christian life? The first element of continuity is the re-establishing action; with the entrance of the Christian joy of the Lord, the refractoriness of the flesh is first felt. All else "follows by itself" (*CE*, 86). Given the effectiveness of the re-establishing action, an expansive action follows. Through the expansive action both the individual and the community achieve the perfected state of being a Christian. The transition between both modes of action leads through a state of indifference between pleasure and pain, implying the impulse to action of the representing mode.

THE RELATION OF THE CHRISTIAN LIFE TO THE PRE-CHRISTIAN LIFE

Both the *Christian Ethics* and the *Christian Faith* have as their material the Christian condition of the soul that is formed by the redemptive activity of Christ. This condition presupposes the universal human conditions given in creation. The activity of Christ completes or re-shapes, but does not annihilate, the universal conditions of humanity presupposed by it. Through the orientation of humanity to Christ's redemption, humanity achieves the goal for which it was created. All expressions of faith concerning Christian life always presuppose expressions about created humanity, and as such, about the fact that the Christian life continuously co-exists with the common human life. In the *Christian Faith,* some of these statements can be found in the expressions regarding creation as the arena for salvation (*CF,* §§ 59–60), and some are integrated with the complex of statements having to do with the communal Christian life (*CF,* §§ 113–56). In the *Christian Ethics,* the *pneuma hagion,* the common Christian spirit, is understood as a form of the *koinos logos,* the ensouled human life and its universal creaturely conditions (*CE,* 58–62). The Holy Spirit (*pneuma hagion*) shapes creaturely life by orienting it from its beginning to its completion (*CE,* 314), potentially first, and then actually.

Systematization of the foundational characteristics of all actions grounded in faith involves not only statements having to do with Christian activity in the "inner" sphere of the Christian common life (*CE,* 516), but also with those having to do with the "outer" sphere of the common life shared between Christians and those yet to become Christians (*CE,* 620). This outer sphere is also characterized by the three kinds of actions enumerated above: re-establishing action, expansive action, and representing action. Through this systemization, the *Christian Ethics* as well as the *Christian Faith* make valid the claim of the self-consciousness and self-expression of the Christian faith that faith is not so much redeemed from the created world as freed to live together with all created beings under the conditions given to it from its beginning to its holy *telos.*

THE EFFECTIVE CHARACTER OF THE RE-ESTABLISHING ACTION

The purifying or re-establishing action presupposes that human life has been grasped and determined by the Spirit of Christ and the Holy Spirit, and it effects the re-establishment of the reign of the Christian spirit over the flesh. The refractoriness of the flesh consists in these incentives of the pre-Christian life still effective in Christian life. Given the enduring relation between the conditions of the Christian and the pre-Christian life, the re-establishing action is necessary (*CE,* 43–5).

The pre-Christian life, as the ethical life in need of redemption, contains the enduring preconditions and context of the Christian ethical life as *redeemed* ethical life. For Schleiermacher, both the pre-Christian and the Christian are both forms of *ethical* life. This is an implication of Schleiermacher's fundamental anthropology: the relation of the world-feeling and the God-feeling is given through the ensoulment of the pre-human physical world through reason. As Schleiermacher notes in the "Introduction" to the *Christian Faith,* the feeling of absolute dependence undergoes an inner historical development dependent upon how clearly the distinction between self and world is held in view. Religious self-consciousness moves from fetishism, to polytheism, and henceforth to monotheism, which itself has aesthetic and teleological forms (*CF*, §§ 5–11). In contradistinction to Kant, for Schleiermacher there can be no genuine ethical life, as the reign of the spirit over the flesh, without genuine positive religion. The kind of ethical life that develops is dependent upon the kind of positive religion in place. From the point of view of higher forms of religious life, some ethical forms of life appear as extremely deficient manifestations of it, that is, as forms of ethical life in need of redemption. They await the predominance of the God-feeling over the world-feeling, and from the Christian point of view are all "flesh" (*CE*, 97–100). The introduction to the first part of the *Christian Ethics* presupposes these points rather than developing them explicitly, but they are key to understanding the need for the purifying actions in Christian life.

The fact that all individuals have only a partial and individual location in communal life is the reason why each individual has only a partial grasp of Christ's spirit. Hence the individual continues to be assaulted by the refractoriness of the flesh, purification from which is a principle condition of an individual's consummation (*CE*, 108). Schleiermacher understands the nature of sin as conditioned by the social character of human nature (*CF*, §§ 66–72). The grasping of the individual through Christ's spirit does not remove these conditions but makes it possible to defend the God-feeling from the attacks that result from the demands of incompletely redeemed communal life.

The purifying activity of the Christian community on the individual is directed at the individual disrupting participation in the common Spirit of Christ. This threat can be one to either the individual or the community, and elimination of the threat can take place through either the individual or the community. If through the latter, then this is "church discipline" (*CE*, 139). For this the following is required: first, communal institutions that further knowledge of dangerous, one-sided positions, hence forms of mutual "admonition" (*CE*, 170–2); second, institutions that help conquer one-sided manifestations of the flesh's refractoriness, such as the church's pastoral care and activity of love (*CE*, 151, 154, 157); and third, communal institutions that purify the Christian spirit of the individual, particularly the "self-active" and "edifying" parts of the worship service, the sermon and sacraments (*CE*, 151–72). Here the purifying activity invites the individual rather than excludes him or her. It also preserves the purity of the community by permitting church doctrine to be taught only by those in whom "there is no tendency to alter God's word" (*CE*, 164), and by requiring the Lord's supper to be celebrated in a worthy manner, that is, not received by those openly living in sin (*CE*, 164). The church, on the other hand, can also stand in need of purification. Against the Roman Catholic position that the church must itself be the agent of its own purification, Schleiermacher advocates the evangelical position that an individual can act to purify the church. As such, this is the impulse to "church improvement," of which the Reformation of the sixteenth century is an example (*CE*, 178–205).

Given the enduring relation between Christianity and the pre-Christian life, re-establishing or purifying actions must also take place in contexts pre-existing Christianity: the family and the state (*CE*, 217). They are already forms of ethical life, since they participate in the ensoulment of nature through reason, and as such, to some degree in the reign of spirit over flesh. The Christian life, the reign of Spirit over flesh, is nothing other than a developed form of natural ethics, one that both encompasses and surpasses all preceding states in an inner-historical way. Christian life thereby partakes in the ethical life of the family and state (civil society), modifying it in specific ways. In relation to the household the main concerns are the relations between spouses and those between parents and their children (*CE*, 219); the civil state is characterized through the order of right (*CE*, 243).

The Christian household is an integral part of the Christian community (*CE*, 217). The *Christian Ethics* does not characterize all forms of re-establishing actions in the household, but focuses on purifying activity relevant to the education and up-bringing of children. It focuses on the time frame spanning "the awakening of conscience" (*CE*, 222) up until "religious maturity" (*CE*, 239). It includes all those actions that strengthen and purify the awakened conscience in order to achieve the complete dominion of the Christian spirit over the flesh. These actions are "gymnastics" (*CE*, 230) and "self-control" (*CE*, 227); they are encouraged by the experience of joy, and not rewards and punishments, which only strengthen the sensuous self-consciousness. The practice of family devotions is hence central in the Christian formation of the household (*CE*, 223–30).

The constitution and task of civil society (the state) is different from that of the family. Civil society regulates all relations through right (*CE*, 243).[10] As the ground and preserver of the conditions of right, the state defends the freedom of all its citizens through external order (*CE*, 235). The family also belongs to the state since it requires this order for its preservation. Conversely, the state also depends upon the civil attitude of its citizens. Just as the family can become the organ of the church's education of human conscience, so too, participation in the care for rights protecting freedom can assume a Christian character. Nevertheless, the state cannot assume power over the church's life. Statements of faith are limited to the "if" and "how" of Christian participation in political activity having as its goal the re-establishment of the order of right (*CE*, 243).

THE EFFECTIVE CHARACTER OF EXPANSIVE ACTIONS

Schleiermacher describes the specific goal of Christian activity aiming at expansive actions in the second section of the first part of the *Christian Ethics*. The real differences in the ends of Christian actions (representing or expressive actions, re-establishing actions, and expansive actions) are grounded in the character of the reign of the Spirit over the flesh. In it can be found the complex goal of Christian expansive activity: the formation of the disposition for the sake of the up-building of talent, and the up-building of talent for the sake of the formation of the disposition (*CE*, 304–5).

Schleiermacher provides an analysis of the Christian relation of Spirit to flesh in its concrete structure as its becoming is characterized by the work of Christ. The state of becoming blessed – the blessedness that is on its way towards completion – is the *constitutive* spirit of humanity, the *nous* or *koinos logos* (*CE*, 302–4; 313–15). However, the reign of the Spirit over the flesh is only set in motion through the Spirit of Christ. In light of this fact, Schleiermacher's statements in the *Christian Faith* and the *Christian Ethics* stand outside the controversy between naturalism and supernaturalism. The kernel of truth in rationalism is that the *pneuma hagion* (Holy Spirit) is qualitatively similar to the *koinos logos*; it is more like a higher potency of it. The kernel of truth in supernaturalism is that this lower potency is not the genesis of the higher power (*CE*, 303). As such this higher power is "grace." Its work can only be set in motion through the coming of Christ and his work, which cannot be accounted for in terms of preceding circumstances. As such, Christ's coming appears as something foreign to the development of nature. The faithful, however, understand this foreignness as a mere appearance, since the difference between the creation of human nature and its redemption is merely a relative one circumscribed by the unity of the divine will (*CE*, 314).

The *pneuma hagion* (Holy Spirit) alters the relation of spirit to flesh given at creation. What is given at creation is the desire for the spirit's dominion over the flesh. Through the Holy Spirit, this desire is fulfilled and dominion is realized. To the created spirit corresponds the *koinos logos* as that which seeks the dominion of spirit over flesh (*CE*, 305). As such the flesh, which is to become the organ of the *pneuma hagion* comprehends *nous*, that is, the "organ of intelligence," as well as the *psyche*, the "organ of the different functions of the individual's sensuous nature" (*CE*, 305–7). The former (*nous*) is the site of the disposition, the "unity of direction of the will"; the latter is the site of talent, understood as the "skill already at the disposition of the will" (*CE*, 307). There is no disposition without striving after talent, and no talent without disposition. However, neither talent nor disposition can be reduced to one another, since each develops in accordance with its own laws. As such, the goal of expansive actions can only be to build up both: a disposition productive of talent, and a talent supportive of disposition.

Schleiermacher's view of disposition and talent formation implies that there are two interrelated forms of community. Expansive actions *presuppose* one kind of community and *found* another (*CE*, 291–2). Both communities co-exist with one another. The communal life presupposed by these expansive actions is the purely created state in which the dominion of spirit over flesh exists only as a desire. The communal life awakened by the Holy Spirit is the Christian community, the church, in which the spirit has achieved true dominion over the flesh and is brought onto the path of completion. These two forms of community are the same insofar as Christ's spirit is presupposed (*CE*, 300), although admittedly in the first case Christ's spirit is presupposed only as an unfulfilled *desire*. The community founded by expansive activity is the same one presupposed by it, but as a redeemed community whose desire has been fulfilled (*CE*, 303).

Expansive actions found not only the church community but the civil community as well, and each in relation to the other. The church's common life is an extensive and intensive "formation of disposition for the sake of talent formation," and the civil community is an extensive and intensive "building up of talent for the sake of the building up of the disposition" (*CE*, 326). The task of expansive activity is to build up both forms of communal life.

The goal of the expansive action taking place in the church is the formation of the disposition for the sake of talent formation. The goal of this activity is the historical extension of the Holy Spirit through the entire human race, or the kingdom of God on earth. In between the beginning and end of this expansion, expansive activity takes place in two communities. The first community exists throughout the whole process of this extension. This is marriage as the community of sexuality and the education of children. The second community is the ecclesial community. Through the influence of the Holy Spirit, marriage and the family are characterized by expansive actions (*CE*, 217). Through the Christian formation of the family, church organization arrives at its completion (*CE*, 336).

Expansive action in the church principally takes shape through the awakened spontaneity of its members (in which the Spirit already reigns), and the up-building effects of their activities. These take place *extensively* through Christian mission and Christian pedagogy (*CE*, 373). Expansive action is *intensive* when its goal is the deepening of Christian piety, which takes place through Christian communication. Included in its goals is the furthering of religious independence and skill in communication. One of its principle institutions is the school (*CE*, 388–90).

The goal of expansive action taking place in civil society is the formation of talent for the sake of the disposition. The Christian spirit aims at making use of the inner relation between reason and the sensuous consciousness for its expansion. The inner dimension of this relation is the disposition; its outer dimension is talent. The Christian spirit integrates both, but in such a manner that actions whose goal is the formation of talent are subordinated to those building up the disposition (*CE*, 444–5). Christian action not only presupposes civil life, but must shape it in a Christian manner. The Christian principle "empowers" civil life and "changes it" (*CE*, 441, 449). The process of the formation of talent is ordered to the universalization of the Christian disposition, that is, the kingdom of God (*CE*, 461). Faith shapes and empowers talent and natural processes for the sake of the "expansion of the kingdom of God according to the Christian idea" (*CE*, 461).

From the point of view of the Christian faith, individual communities are necessary since they ground essential differences between individuals (*CE*, 452). Peace between such communities is achieved through entrance into the state. Right rules in and among these states; it limits war through the re-establishment of the conditions of right among states (*CE*, 444–6). The Christian faith supports the shaping of talent and natural processes through the external preservation of the forms of right valid for ownership and commercial exchange. Moreover, it recognizes and furthers the civic disposition (i.e., the community spirit and charity within the civil community) of all, including non-Christians. In such a way, the Christian impulse "sanctions" the purely civic disposition, but also reorients it in subordinating it to the impulse that motivates "the expansion of the kingdom of God on earth" (*CE*, 461).

REPRESENTING OR EXPRESSIVE ACTIONS

The Christian determination of the immediate self-consciousness grounds both re-establishing and expansive actions and is, as such, the intermediary between the two. It is the incentive to expressive actions that do not alter the Christian state of mind, but rather portray or express the emergence of blessedness. Through them an inner state is expressed, and the immediate being-for-self becomes a being-for-others. This becoming-for-others is unavoidable, since redemption of the human spirit through the spirit of Christ is merely the completion, and not the annihilation of the created human condition. As such, this expression or portrayal of the emergent blessedness is nothing other than the "realization of human nature itself" (*CE*, 517). It is therefore an action that presupposes and grounds community, making it an "object of consciousness" (*CE*, 515).

The idea of the church is first discussed in statements regarding the expressive Christian life, even though it is presupposed in re-establishing and expansive actions. The redemptive work of Christ equally sets all who receive it on the way towards blessedness and binds them in brotherly love, wherein they are all equal. This state of affairs is the direct effect of representing or expressive actions. The church can only develop through communication of the spirit of Christ. This spirit is the incentive to the expressive actions of the redeemed that "work upon each other" and that perfect the community in such a way that it is visible as a community to both the faithful and the world (*CF*, § 121). These expressions are evangelical statements on the constitution of the church.

What is expressed in this activity is the fact that believers redeemed through the work of Christ become organs of God. Expression is a "service of God" in the sense of a "service of witness": the witness that one has been taken by God to serve and hence to express oneself as an organ of God (*CE*, 525–6). The use of language, through which inner states are outwardly expressed, is key to this expression. Christian expression includes the entire range of effective actions. This entire range of actions can be subdivided into two spheres: "the service of worship in the narrow sense" and "the service of worship in the wider sense" (*CE*, 530–5). The service of worship in the narrow sense is the worship service itself through which the congregation is built up (*CE*, 566). The service of worship in the wider sense includes all those activities generated by the incentive towards blessedness; it is an expression of the entire life of the Christian as it is held in common with others (both Christians and non-Christians) (*CE*, 599). Each form demands the other: the worship service becomes mere superstition when it is not related to the service of worship in the wider sense; the service of worship in the wider sense loses its ethical significance if it is not related to the worship service in the narrow sense (*CE*, 535–7).

CONCLUDING REMARKS

For Schleiermacher all of dogmatics is a historical discipline that empirically investigates the statements of faith that are "valid" in the church. There is a certain sense, then, in which all dogmatic statements are historically contingent. It is clear that many of Schleiermacher's systematic statements in the *Christian Ethics* are no longer valid today since they relate to the no-longer-existing social conditions of his own day, for instance, the structure of national communities. However, statements of faith not only reflect the reality of the past, but also the enduring essence of faith. This essence encompasses certainty regarding the process of human- and world-becoming, a process grounded in the divine decree. Statements of faith not only contain empirical knowledge regarding a determined inner-worldly situation, but also offer insight into the essence and goal of the world process as a whole. These are "speculative" statements. As such, they make truth claims that surpass the context in which they were first expressed. These truth claims are relevant to us today. And it is our duty to engage and take a position vis-à-vis these claims.

Notes

1 The standard edition is still *Die Christliche Sitte nach den Grundsätzen des evangelischen Kirche*, edited by Ludwig Jonas (Berlin, 1843) in *Friedrich Schleiermacher's Sämmtliche Werke*, I.12. All future references to the *Christian Ethics* will be provided internally as *CE* with the page number following.

2 For the origins of this view see Herms 1974; the view is further developed in Herms 2003, 6, 7, 13, and 14.

3 See Herms 2003, 2.

4 See Herms, "Historische Einführung," in *KGA*, I.4, xx–xxxiv.

5 *SW*, III.6.

6 References to the *Kurze Darstellung (Brief Outline)* are to the second edition of 1830. All future references will be internal to the text, indicated by *BO* with the paragraph number following.

7 This is pointed out by Schleiermacher in the first edition of *BO*, § 31).

8 On the relation between the two see the groundbreaking study by Birkner 1964.

9 Translator's note: Schleiermacher's expression is "darstellende Handeln" which includes both representing and expressive activity.

10 Schleiermacher openly follows Kant's concept of the state as developed in paragraph 45 (Kant 1996, Ak. VI.313). The idea is fully developed in Schleiermacher's *Vorlesung über die Lehre vom Staat*.

12 Schleiermacher's exegetical theology and the New Testament

CHRISTINE HELMER

When compared to the intense study of his theological and philosophical works, Schleiermacher's contributions to exegetical theology have enjoyed relatively little scholarly attention. One reason might be the towering status of the theological works, the *Christian Faith* and *Brief Outline*, as well as the philosophical texts, the *Dialectic* and the *Hermeneutics*, works which have dwarfed Schleiermacher's own detailed interpretations of specific New Testament books and passages. Another reason might be the cool reception of his published exegetical works. Soon after his death, critical voices raised concern about Schleiermacher's imposition of dogmatic categories onto his hermeneutical efforts. Yet another reason might be the small number of exegetical works chosen for publication in Reimer's *Sämtliche Werke* or in the current *Kritische Gesamtausgabe*.[1] Although Schleiermacher lectured almost every semester on the New Testament between 1804 and 1834,[2] only a fraction of his exegetical works have been published.

In spite of the marginalized posthumous reception, Schleiermacher was considered to be at the forefront of New Testament scholarship in his time. In conversation with the nascent early nineteenth-century research on the Synoptics, Schleiermacher proposed a theory of Synoptic dependence resting on orally transmitted stories about Jesus prior to their redaction by the New Testament authors. In regard to I Timothy, Schleiermacher showed that the apostle Paul was not its author, thereby paving the way for critical deuteropauline scholarship. Similarly, Schleiermacher's research on the parallel structure of Colossians 1:15–20 set the literary parameters for research on this text well into the late twentieth century. Furthermore, he was the first theologian to offer public lectures on the life of Jesus, lectures which were unfortunately published in 1864, right before D. F. Strauss' devastating critique the following year.[3] Last but not least, for the English-speaking world, Schleiermacher's *Commentary on Luke* was his first work to be translated into English.[4]

Although Schleiermacher's individual exegetical works stand as achievements in their own right, it is my intention to view them in the systematic context of Schleiermacher's theological and philosophical thought. Schleiermacher's exegetical contributions will be contextualized both in relation to his understanding of the tasks of exegetical and dogmatic theology, and as products of an exegetical methodology informed by the critical disciplines of hermeneutics and dialectic. In the first section, I discuss Schleiermacher's approach to exegetical theology by taking a close look at the new way he configures the Christ–Scripture relation against the backdrop of Protestant orthodoxy's position on the canon. Schleiermacher determines Christ's priority over Scripture in such a way as to establish a non-competitive relation between an ecclesial use of the Bible and a scientific investigation of the New Testament canon. In the second section, I define Schleiermacher's determination of the task of exegetical theology as the investigation of the canon. For Schleiermacher, the literary New Testament canon fixes apprehensions of Christ at an original historical proximity to the source; the search for the idea of the canon involves proposing a solution to the Synoptic problem in order to combat Reimarus' charge against the New Testament "hoax." In the third section, I explain Schleiermacher's exegetical methodology as an application of hermeneutics to New Testament texts. I also show how Schleiermacher complements hermeneutics with dialectic in order to make exegetical knowledge claims. In the fourth section, I describe the allegedly controversial relation between exegetical and dogmatic theology in Schleiermacher's thought, and propose to read Schleiermacher charitably in view of the relation between conceptual and empirical reason. Although a treatment of Schleiermacher's exegetical theology should address his practical theology, particularly his commitment to both the study of Scripture as formative of the cleric's and the theologian's life and the homiletical focus on a biblical text, such detail is beyond the scope of this chapter.

EXEGETICAL THEOLOGY AND SCHLEIERMACHER'S THEOLOGICAL SYSTEM

In the late eighteenth and early nineteenth centuries, the face of exegetical theology was rapidly changing. With the increasing Enlightenment demand to read the Bible like any other book, the discipline changed by reconfiguring both the methodology applied to the subject matter and the object under scrutiny. The developing field had, as its point of departure, the doctrine of Scripture as laid out in the dogmatic manuals of seventeenth- and eighteenth-century Protestant orthodoxy.[5] In these manuals, the doctrine of Scripture secured the infallible epistemological source of dogmatic theological truths by the doctrine of divine inspiration; real, verbal, and personal types of inspiration justified the canonical determination of the Old Testament, the New Testament, and some deuterocanonical works. It was the pietist tradition which mediated the transition from reading the Bible as a source of doctrinal knowledge concerning divine mysteries to a record of historical biblical religion. By emphasizing a personal engagement with and study of Scripture, the pietists individualized the Reformation's *sola Scriptura* principle, and paved the way for the modern critical study of the Bible.[6] As a consequence of this development, the intimate link which Protestant orthodoxy forged between dogmatics and exegesis by the *dicta probantia* method of proving theological doctrines was loosened. Biblical texts were viewed as documents of positive religion, and were not to be semantically flattened to suit the prescriptions of dogmatic-theological propositions. Johann David Michaelis' (1717–1791) historical treatment of the religions of the ancient Near East, Johann Salomo Semler's (1725–1791) work on the canon's formation, Johann Philipp Gabler's (1753–1826) proposal for the new field of biblical theology, and Johann Gottfried Herder's (1744–1803) literary study of Hebrew poetry all contributed significantly to post-Protestant orthodox scientific approaches to the Bible.

In order to retain the dogmatic interest of biblical interpretation, the object of biblical study was reconfigured against the backdrop of the sciences. Schleiermacher took seriously the challenge posed to theology by the natural and historical sciences. If these sciences exposed the six-day creation to be a non-literal flourish or the biblical text to be the historical expression of human authorial intention, then doctrines that had relied on biblical warrants for their truth were particularly vulnerable to erosion. In his famous *Second Letter to Friedrich Lücke*, Schleiermacher wrote that the supernaturalism of orthodox Christology and a pneumatologically inspired Bible could no longer be supported by historical research on the Bible (*KGA*, I.10, 345–59). In order to withstand the inevitable erosion as well as to advocate non-competition between doctrine and scientific development, Schleiermacher relocated theology's justification from the written letter to the religion's "inner power" (*KGA*, I.10, 354). Christianity's inner power was to be identified with neither metaphysics nor morals, but with faith's certainty located in pre-reflective immediate self-consciousness (*CF*, § 14.1). Based on this new experiential foundation for theology, Schleiermacher reversed the Christ–Scripture correlation without detriment either to the scientific investigation of the Bible or to the integrity of the Christian faith. Scripture was grounded in Christ and not the other way around (*CF*, § 128). The literary fixing of experienced perceptions and apprehensions

(*Auffassungen*) of Christ were the result of an encounter with Christ, rather than its presupposition.

In orienting theology to its object "behind the text," Schleiermacher's theology embodied both a scientific and an ecclesial spirit. It is constituted by an idiosyncratic mixture of an ecclesial spirit, which has as its interest the promotion of spiritual health in the contemporary church, and a scientific spirit, which has as its interest the study of the subject matter in dialogue with the wider academic community (*BO*, §§ 9–13). Both interests balance perfectly in the idea of the "prince of the church" (*BO*, § 9). In view of the specific requirements for exegetical theology, the distinction between the ecclesial and scientific mind-sets is significant. On the one hand, the distinction relieves the scientific study of Scripture from its responsibility to bear the weight of proving doctrines from the text. The text can be studied critically as the "first member" (*CF*, § 129) in a historical series, without detriment to either personal faith or to the normative status of Scripture for doctrine and morals. On the other hand, the unity between both mind-sets secures Scriptural intentionality for scientific study. The ecclesial interest orients the scientific gaze to the historical appearances of Christianity's essence. At its original site, the essence of Christianity is embodied in the person of Jesus of Nazareth. Guided by the ecclesial designation of the subject matter, the scientific mind-set takes as its exegetical object the texts to be studied as reflecting the documentation of this person. The texts are products of what Landmesser calls a "Christological preference criterion."[7]

The ecclesial interest serves to organize the subfields of theology, including exegetical theology, into a "theological whole" (*BO*, § 8). In distinction to Schelling and Fichte, Schleiermacher deems theology a positive science because, like jurisprudence and medicine, its organizing principle is a practical task. Theology, itself ordered to ethics as the "science of the principles of history" (*BO*, § 29), is organized as a task with sub-roles for the purpose of serving the contemporary church's government (*BO*, § 5). The tasks of the theological subfields are determined by theology's practical orientation (*BO*, §§ 24–31). As the first of three sub-disciplines, philosophical theology is given the speculative task of minimally fixing the concept of the essence of Christianity for subsequent material determination. The second sub-discipline, historical theology, has the empirical task of determining the essence's appearance in the church's history to the present day. Within historical theology, exegetical theology forms the first part of a triad. To exegetical theology is allocated the task of investigating the original documents recording the origins of the essence's historical manifestation. At its origin, the essence of Christianity is to be grasped in the period of Christ's "action and effect ... both on and with his disciples" and that of "his disciples toward the establishing of Christianity" (*BO*, § 105).[8] Although this period cannot be definitively divided from the following period of church history, Schleiermacher lays down the development of doctrine as the tentative boundary between the two periods (*BO*, § 87). As the period following the original appearance of Christ and his disciples, church history forms the second subfield. The third subfield of historical theology, church statistics, has as its object the knowledge of the present state of Christianity, respectively as the church's doctrine and as its social conditions. To use the organic metaphor Schleiermacher himself proposes in the first edition of the *Brief Outline*, philosophical theology is the root and historical theology the "corpus" of theological study (*BO*, 1st edn., I, § 26, and I, § 36). Theology's third and final sub-discipline, practical theology, uses the knowledge of Christianity gleaned from both philosophical theology and historical theology in order to develop rules for application in the church.[9] In this sense, practical theology is the "crown" of theology (*BO*, 1st edn., I, § 31). As a whole, the theological organism works to promote the church's health and to eliminate its diseases.

EXEGETICAL THEOLOGY AND ITS TASK

If the task of theology as a whole is to determine the historical appearances of the essence of Christianity with the intention of improving the present condition of the church, then exegetical theology is given a sub-task in this constellation. For Schleiermacher, exegetical theology has as its specific task the determination of the canon. In *BO*, § 104, Schleiermacher writes, "Thus, the correct understanding of this canon is the unique, essential task of exegetical theology." In Schleiermacher's system of theological science, the canon is a key concept that particularizes one dimension of the essence of Christianity. As a philosophical–theological concept, the canon represents the self-identical essence preserved through its diverse historical shapes and through its "expression in the production of ideas" (*BO*, § 47). Once the formal definition of canon is given, Schleiermacher gives it material determination in the exegetical sense of a historical document. The canon is expressed in the collection of New Testament texts.[10] It is, however, not to be identified with the literary form of the Christian Bible. For Schleiermacher, the term Bible is an ecclesially pragmatic one. It denotes the unity of Old and New Testaments used by the church since its earliest traditions (*BO*, § 115). In contrast, the canon is composed of those

New Testament texts that represent the literary fixing of the essence of Christianity's original manifestations. As such, the canon includes those documents, the "*evangellion* and *apostolos*" (*BO*, § 105), which are historically most proximate to Jesus of Nazareth's immediate sphere of influence. As the expression of Christ's person and his activity in calling disciples to found the church, the canon is restricted to the New Testament.

Given Schleiermacher's distinction between the canon as an essence concept and its historical expression in literary texts, the exegetical–theological task becomes one of infinite searching for more true expressions of the essence. For Schleiermacher, the canon as literary text represents the "purest"[11] manifestation of Christianity's essence at its origins. Nevertheless, the New Testament texts are still liable to criticism because they contain both accurate and false apprehensions of that essence (*BO*, § 103). Given the historical distance between oral sources and the New Testament's literary fixing of apprehensions of Christ, false elements have entered into the process. In its determination of the canon, exegetical theology must identify and excise those false elements, and conversely, it must identify true elements fixed in extra-canonical literature in order to include them within the critically reconstructed canon (*BO*, §§ 108–14). The search for the critical canon begins by closing the gap between the original appearance of Christ and the later apprehensions recorded in the New Testament.

It was Hermann Samuel Reimarus (1694–1768) who pressed the question concerning the distance between Christ and the canon. It was this question and Reimarus' devastating solution that motivated two centuries of biblical scholarship to investigate the Synoptic problem.[12] In the fragments published anonymously by Gotthold Ephraim Lessing (1729–1781), Reimarus attacked the attempts to harmonize the four gospels – from Tatian's *Diatesseron* into the sixteenth century – and argued that the contradictions between the gospels gave evidence for the disciples' falsification of Jesus' original intentions.[13] By accusing the disciples of twisting Jesus' moral intention and tainting it with supernaturalist elements, Reimarus' criticism exposed the church's very biblical and by extension doctrinal foundations as built, not on solid rock, but on sinking sand. In response, scholars, most notably Lessing, Johann Gottfried Eichhorn (1752–1827), and Johann Gottfried Herder (1744–1803), attempted to fill in the gap between Jesus and the New Testament by positing lost sources behind the gospels to explain commonalities and to account for differences. Lessing argued for several versions of an Aramaic *Urgospel*, which were later translated into Greek as the Synoptic gospels. Eichhorn built on Lessing's *Urgospel* theory by positing four intermediate documents explaining the complex relations among the Synoptics. For Herder, the *Urgospel*, like the Homeric epics, was oral. It was gradually fixed in literary forms, each arranging Jesus' sayings and deeds around a "schema defined by the three 'heavenly signs,' baptism, transfiguration and resurrection."[14]

Like his predecessors, Schleiermacher's exegetical goals were spurred by Reimarus. In the *Life of Jesus* and the *Christian Faith*, Schleiermacher alludes to Reimarus, both criticizing his argumentation for its implausibility, and pressing the exegetical desideratum to fill in the gap between Christ and the canon (*LJ*, 23–4, 445, 474; *CF*, § 99.2). For Schleiermacher, a history of the formation of the gospels would not only demonstrate exegetically that the church was founded on truth, but would also assure historically the link between Christ and the church for dogmatic purposes. For its soteriological stability, Schleiermacher's Christology itself requires such an exegetical anchor, securing the continuity of the person of Christ with untainted apprehensions of his redemptive work. Schleiermacher's own work was explicitly in dialogue with Eichhorn, Heinrich Eberhard Gottlob Paulus (1761–1851), Johann Jakob Griesbach (1745–1812), and Johann Leonhard Hug (1765–1846), and he made use of Wilhelm Martin Leberecht de Wette's and Friedrich Lücke's synopsis of the gospels.[15] Schleiermacher offered his own original solution to the problem of Synoptic dependence with his commentaries on Luke (1817) and the *Papias-Fragment* (1832). In contrast with Eichhorn's *Urevangelium* hypothesis and Hug's theory on Matthew as the oldest gospel source, Schleiermacher proposed that a collection of Jesus' sayings (Matthew 5–7; 10; 13:1–52; 18; 23), together with a narrative source, "proto-Mark," was behind Matthew.[16] On the basis of the *Papias-Fragment*, Schleiermacher made this historical argument by locating two authors, Matthew and Mark, in the eyewitness period (*KGA*, I.8, 230ff.).[17] The canonical Synoptic gospels were later compilations of these original sources, collected "without change" (*KGA*, I.8, 180) or theological imposition by their authors into increasingly larger units of original sayings and stories about Jesus (*KGA*, I.8, 16–19). As a result, Schleiermacher concluded that Matthew was the first gospel, informed by both the *logia* collection in Aramaic and proto-Mark, and Mark was the final gospel, borrowing from both Matthew and Luke. With regard to the canonical gospels, Schleiermacher agreed with Griesbach who had also proposed Matthew as the earliest and Mark as the final gospel.[18] Nevertheless, through his appeal to the sayings and to patristic evidence, Schleiermacher differed from Griesbach, although the latter enjoyed the greater reception history. In 1853, the Matthean priority was challenged by Karl Lachmann (1793–1851), who argued that Mark was the original gospel.[19]

Although Schleiermacher attempted to fill in the historical gap between Christ and the Synoptics, he unfortunately opened up a rift between the Old and New Testaments. Since the first review of his *Brief Outline*, Schleiermacher rightly came under fire for his problematic view of both the canonical status of the Old Testament and Old Testament warrants for Christian dogmatic propositions.[20] On the one hand, he retained the Old Testament in his pragmatically defined Christian Bible, but on the other, he identified the Christian canon exclusively with the New Testament (*BO*, §§ 103–5). The key reason rests with the conceptual discontinuity Schleiermacher advocates between Judaism and Christianity. The New Testament's "Christological preference criterion" represents the central perspective of Christianity, which is, for Schleiermacher, conceptually discontinuous with that of Judaism.[21] Discontinuity is achieved by the historical appearance of Christ, which, for Schleiermacher, eliminates the need to base Christian faith and theology on the Old Testament (*CF*, § 27.3, 132.3). Conceptual difference, rather than historical continuity, seems to play again into the argument of *Christian Faith* (§ 12), where Schleiermacher argues that both Judaism and Hellenism are equidistant from Christ in their need for redemption and in their reconciliation with God through Christ. In *Christian Faith* (§ 10), however, he can argue for conceptual similarity, where both Judaism and Christianity are identified as monotheistic teleological types of religion, in distinction to Islam, which represents aesthetic monotheism. At stake for Schleiermacher seems to be the historical relationship between Judaism and Christianity, which cannot according to his viewpoint be understood in a way that compromises the integrity of each religion's central perspective.

Nevertheless, Schleiermacher's view also seems to acknowledge the continuity between the two religions in order to address the hermeneutical question of how the new arises from the old. Although in the *Speeches*, Schleiermacher mentions this historical continuity between Judaism and Christianity with vitriol,[22] in the *Christian Faith* (§ 12) he writes of the "special historical connection" between them. This connection serves to argue for the Old Testament as a necessary aid for exegetical theology. What the Old Testament can deliver is hermeneutical, philological, and historical information for the purpose of understanding the production of Christianity's new ideas within languages and concepts of the "old" paradigm (*BO*, §§ 127–31, 140–4). Schleiermacher's understanding of the Old Testament, the Septuagint, and the deuterocanonical corpus as auxiliary texts aiding the interpretation of the New Testament should be understood from the hermeneutical perspective of individual novelty that cannot be explained from, but is contextualized in, the religion that bears it.

EXEGETICAL THEOLOGY: HERMENEUTICS AND DIALECTIC

Although post-Reformation efforts to formulate rules for textual interpretation began with Flacius in the mid-sixteenth century, Schleiermacher is credited for systematizing the rules of a general hermeneutics into a coherent whole and giving hermeneutics its place as a technical discipline within his system of science. By consolidating the initial efforts of Friedrich A. Wolf, Friedrich Ast, and Johann August Ernesti (1707–1781) to formulate rules applicable to the interpretation of any text, Schleiermacher gave hermeneutics the scientific status of a methodology indispensable for the Bible's critical investigation. With Schleiermacher, the significance of hermeneutics as the handmaiden to exegetical theology (*BO*, §§ 132–9) is made uncontroversial.[23] If, however, the goal of exegetical theology is to study the documents of early Christianity "correctly" (*BO*, § 88), then that older handmaid of theology, philosophy, cannot be discarded entirely. If hermeneutics has as its task to understand the speech of an author correctly, then the claims to knowledge concerning that speech belong in the domain of dialectic. Hermeneutics and dialectic, as Schleiermacher claims, mutually presuppose each other.[24] In this section, I discuss Schleiermacher's appeal to hermeneutics and dialectic in order to show how knowledge claims about the subject of exegetical theology can be made. The first part discusses Schleiermacher's hermeneutics in view of individual apprehensions of Christ as they are fixed in the New Testament. The second part shows how exegetical theology presupposes the epistemology and adopts the method of the dialectic.

The subject of history, as is the specific case of historical (and exegetical) theology, is a historical event. What Schleiermacher means by historical event, however, is not positivistic in the sense of a physical entity. History is ordered to ethics as the science of its principles, not to physics. For Schleiermacher, history is constituted by the intersubjective context in which humans externalize for each other individual apprehensions of an event in non-discursive and discursive forms of expression (*CF*, § 6.2). Multiple perspectives shape, as well as are influenced by, the event, which is a unity in which many participate. Furthermore, participative interplay introduces novelty into history. Through the process of human interaction, which makes up an historical event, new meaning is added to the old. Humans are the bearers of history, as well as its meaning-makers.

As the "art of understanding particularly the written discourse of another person correctly,"[25] hermeneutics is the auxiliary discipline for the study of history. The historical object of hermeneutical study is twofold. The first task is to reconstruct the intersubjective context constituting the historical event. Through grammatical analysis, access to the context is gained by investigating the objective features of language and the history of the era, as well as the individual author's particular use of language. Through technical interpretation, the work is put into its biographical context. The second hermeneutical task is to reconstruct the unity underlying the author's speech. Authorial intention is, for Schleiermacher, the individual participant's apprehension of the event in its totality. It is the pre-discursive "fact in the mind"[26] that is then expressed in speech, the unique apprehension of the total event as the tendency (*Tendenz*) underlying discursive articulation and constituting the whole. The pathway of understanding the utterance "better than its author"[27] methodologically reconstructs the incipient unity from the discourse produced by it. Hermeneutics is an "art" of infinite approximation that grasps the production of the new from the old through grammatical analysis, technical interpretation that studies authorial style and divination (which Schleiermacher always connects to comparison). History is accessed by hermeneutics.

In the case of the New Testament, the event lying behind the text is the historical appearance of Jesus of Nazareth. For Schleiermacher, this event is constitutive of the literary production of New Testament texts, which are the object of exegetical theology. In order to make this claim, Schleiermacher identifies Christ's appearance with his influence. The person of Christ is intimately related to the apprehension (*Auffassung*) of his person by those in his proximity. Christ's appearance is perceived as the "total impression" (*CF*, § 14, postscript and § 99, postscript) of his person, which calls forth a distinct modification of immediate self-consciousness. Precisely this modification is the constituent element of Christian consciousness, which attributes the removal of the need for redemption to Jesus. Jesus' person elicits a realignment of sensible and immediate self-consciousness (*CF*, § 11.2–4), which is expressed as individual apprehensions of Christ's person. The original eyewitness accounts of Jesus' person are produced under the impact of his redeeming presence. Although the later redactional stages subsume the original stories into larger units written by those who did not experience the immediate bodily proximity of Jesus, his spiritual presence, operative in the community, is still effective to evoke the same impact in later generations (*CF*, § 14.1).

For Schleiermacher, the hermeneutical object of the New Testament texts is the individual author's apprehension of Christ. The tendency (*Tendenz*) underlying the author's text as a whole is constituted precisely by individual experiences of Christ's person. In his own work, Schleiermacher uses literary coherence as the criterion for measuring historical proximity to Christ. Deemed an "immediate eyewitness" (*LJ*, 171), John writes a unified literary composition in clear view of a precise tendency: the tension between the catastrophic outcome of Jesus' life and the nature of his activity (*LJ*, 159).[28] As later redactors, the authors of the Synoptic gospels betray no clear tendency in their works, which are more collections of distinct narratives than coherent literary unities (*LJ*, 158–9).

Schleiermacher's hermeneutical privileging of grammar as the discursive access to history is evident in his meticulous philological and grammatical analysis of two New Testament texts. As he claims in his commentary on Colossians 1:15–20, the text's meaning is gleaned from an analysis of the "logical and grammatical relationships among the sentences in which [the formal elements] occur";[29] a hermeneutical analysis must be undertaken independently of dogmatic interest in order to unearth what the author originally intended by the speech.[30] It is the study of this Christological hymn which led Schleiermacher to discover the literary parallel between verses 15–16 and 18–19, thereby tilling the ground for 200 years of scholarship on this text. For Schleiermacher, the literary parallel cannot be interpreted in a way that divides up the Son according to two metaphysical natures: the pre-existent Son in whom all things were created (vv. 15–16), and Jesus of Nazareth as head of the church (vv. 18–19).[31] Rather, the two passages are semantically equivalent in view of one referent. As head of the church, Jesus Christ is the one in whom all creation is established. Gleaned by careful philological study of the original Greek, this meaning dovetails with what Schleiermacher deems to be Paul's tendency to locate Christ's work against the backdrop of God's universal redemptive activity.[32] In another text, the *Commentary on I Timothy* (1807), Schleiermacher also applies philological analysis together with a linguistic–literary study of the book's expressions and epistolary genre with results that call into question its apostolicity. By comparing the letter with Paul's speeches in Acts, as well as with two other letters attributed to Paul, Titus, and 2 Timothy, Schleiermacher concludes that 1 Timothy cannot have Paul as its author, but is a compilation of Titus (ch. 1–3) and 2 Timothy from chapter 4, dated to the end of the first century C.E. (*KGA*, 1.5, 153–242). With this denial of apostolic authorship, Schleiermacher set another exegetical precedent, this time for deuteropauline scholarship.[33]

Hermeneutical rules regulate the investigation of authorial intention from its literary fixing in speech. The path by which the text's meaning is established by exegetical–theological claims to knowledge is regulated not by the hermeneutics, but by the dialectic. The question regarding the reciprocal relation between Schleiermacher's hermeneutics and dialectic has recently been posed by Manfred Frank. Frank notes that there seems to be an apparent discrepancy in Schleiermacher's position between the linguistically relativistic perspective of the hermeneutics with its stress on individuality, and the dialectic with its stress on the unalterability and universality of knowledge.[34] The relation between the two disciplines is, however, not as contradictory as it seems. Both are inextricably related to Schleiermacher's fundamental insight that thought comes to completion in language.[35] While the hermeneutics reconstructs the pathway from speech to authorial intention, the dialectic reconstructs the production of discourse from an initial thought and regulates the process from thinking to knowing. Furthermore, both are allocated the role of technical or "rule-prescribing" disciplines in Schleiermacher's system of science because they determine the rules, gleaned from critical knowledge, to be applied to a particular given sphere of human activity (i.e. the state) in order to shape that particular area.[36] As such, both are "doctrines of art" (*Kunstlehren*), meaning that the application of the rules to a state of affairs cannot be governed by other rules. Yet each has its distinct field of operation. Dialectic provides the rules of the "identical symbolization"[37] of knowledge as the goal of intersubjective discourse, while hermeneutics explores an individual participant's perspectival understanding of an event. If hermeneutics isolates unique authorial intention, then dialectic prescribes how claims to knowledge common to research participants can be made. For Schleiermacher, dialectic stipulates two rules for knowledge: (1) the correspondence of thought with being; and (2) the construction of the totality of knowledge.[38] When the hermeneutics is seen in relation to these two rules, then any suspicion of linguistic relativism is blocked. The intentionality of thought together with its relation to claims made in other scientific areas are conditions that secure the fact that progress in knowledge, even though discursively constituted, can be achieved.

Although Schleiermacher's own *Dialektik* has primarily physical realities in view, its conditions and rules for knowing can be applied to the ethical reality determined as the hermeneutical object of exegetical theology. If exegetical theology's goal is to distinguish the canonical from the uncanonical, then the procedure of supplementation and elimination can be regulated by the dialectic's procedure for arriving at knowledge. For Schleiermacher, the dialectic's procedure is epistemologically determined by the relation of predicates to a concept in a judgment. Thinking has two forms, concept formation and judgment formation, and a judgment is made by combining two (or more) concepts (*Dial* O, 187ff.). The predicates are themselves gleaned from sense-experience through the organic function. From the organic pole, individuality is introduced into thinking, while uniformity is controlled by the intellectual pole. In a dialogical context, however, the difference in predicates becomes the source of controversy. In order for disagreement to be at least penultimately resolved, agreement concerning the identity of the object must be pre supposed (*Dial* O, 22 [1833 Introduction]). Judgment formation then proceeds by testing the possible predicates in view of the object and by eliminating those predicates that have arisen due to false schematization (*Dial* O, 332–6, 369ff.). According to Schleiermacher's intentional logic, true possible predicates are contained in the concept as "inauthentic judgments," while true actual predicates remain the subject of "authentic judgments" (*Dial* O, 206ff.). In view of the New Testament, the controversial predicates arise through individual schematizations of Jesus' appearance. These predicates are the object of exegetical–theological testing which, through a process of hermeneutics and criticism, determines if those predicates belong essentially to Christ's original appearance, and by extension to the facts of Christian consciousness. Schleiermacher's privileging of John's structural narrative over the Synoptics reflects such an exegetical decision. The concept of the essence of Christianity at its original manifestation is determined by certain predicates constituting the continuity of Christianity's essence in all its subsequent forms. Which further predicates are added to the concept is the task of church history and dogmatic theology. At its original point in history, however, exegetical theology determines those predicates belonging inherently to the original facts of Christian self-consciousness.

How the predicates enter into the process of concept formation is explained by the dialectic's minimum/maximum continuum between image (*Bild*) and concept (*Begriff*). For Schleiermacher, the image results from the organic function, while the concept systematizes those impressions by distinguishing between them (*Dial* O, 172ff.). The epistemological continuum between the two functions guarantees, at least theoretically, the correct entrance of sense-data into their corresponding concept. When Schleiermacher discusses Jesus' appearances, he appeals to the image pole in order to underscore the idiosyncrasy of a religious experience (*CF*, §§ 88.2, 105.1). The "total impression" of Christ is a religious experience because the image perceived through the organic pole is directly related to the modification of immediate self-consciousness. Schleiermacher's understanding of image does not preclude a key point regarding the circulation of Christ in the church's preaching (*CF*, § 14.1). By virtue of its communication, the total impression is fixed discursively, as is the case with the New Testament writings. The image has been transferred into the concept.

As a key condition for knowledge, the correspondence between thought and being also plays a role in exegetical theology. When carried into his theology, the realism of Schleiermacher's *Dialektik* lays the groundwork for a correspondence theory to be adapted to the intentionality of the New Testament. Textual intentionality is precisely the anchor into reality that Schleiermacher needs to combat Reimarus. This anchor guarantees not only the non-fictional status of encounters with Christ, but also provides the basis for undertaking a formation history of the gospels. Although on the merits of the dialectic alone, Schleiermacher's realism could explain the impact of Christ in purely physical terms, as a theologian, his interpretation of that impact is a soteriological one. The correspondence between the text as an apprehension of Christ and the reality of Christ's redemptive presence is constitutive of the New Testament's production. A right alignment between sensible consciousness and God-consciousness is the transformative effect of Christ's sinless perfection and potent God-consciousness (*CF*, §§ 97–8), conveyed by a total impression of his person. Even at the most original layers of the New Testament, Christ's transformative activity compels discursive apprehensions. Exegetical theology has as its task to determine which historical events in Christ's life are constitutive for calling forth apprehensions of his person with soteriological implications. In his own work, Schleiermacher deems the resurrection, ascension, and last judgment to be accidental to the original facts of Christian consciousness (*CF*, § 99). Thus exegetical theology is at once exegetical because it proposes those original events that are part of Christ's biography, and theological because it judges those events to be soteriologically constitutive for the Christian consciousness in the church's history.

In this section, I have discussed how both hermeneutics and dialectic feed into Schleiermacher's conception of exegetical theology's task. On the one hand, dialectic presupposes the hermeneutical task of understanding the individual ways in which the New Testament authors apprehended Christ. On the other hand, hermeneutics presupposes the text's intentionality by way of the dialectic's realism and epistemology. Furthermore, hermeneutical statements must themselves adhere to the dialectic's rules in order to be claims of knowledge. Through this reciprocal relation, exegetical theology maintains its scientific interest while also holding on to the experiential dimension that compelled the texts' production in the first place.

EXEGETICAL THEOLOGY AND DOGMATIC THEOLOGY

The final topic to be treated is how Schleiermacher views the relation between dogmatic and exegetical theology. On this front, he did not escape severe criticism, although his reviewers tended to articulate their misgivings after his death. Not even his friend and colleague, Friedrich Lücke, spared him the remark that Schleiermacher read his own individuality into the New Testament, thereby "transforming the apostle [Paul] into his likeness."[39] It was D. F. Strauss who also pinpointed the problem that with his *Life of Jesus*, Schleiermacher "betrays his standpoint as more dogmatic than historical."[40] And the readers of that text will note that its biographical reconstruction dovetails nicely with the Christological sections of the *Christian Faith*.

The common view of Schleiermacher is informed by a bias favoring the objectivity of historical impartiality against the subjectivity of dogmatic imposition. When Schleiermacher's own theological system of science is considered, however, a decisively non-dualistic picture of the epistemological continuum undergirding his theological method emerges. For Schleiermacher, exegetical and dogmatic theology are two sub-disciplines of historical theology. Although the move to relegate dogmatic theology to historical theology was a controversial one,[41] Schleiermacher intended to make a key point. By defining dogmatics as the "knowledge of doctrine that now has currency in the evangelical Church" (*BO*, § 195), Schleiermacher stresses the historical location of all doctrines, thereby reflecting the conditioned character of his own theological conviction. Knowledge of the contemporary state of the church culminates in the historical–theological project as the empirical observation of the church's history from its origins to the present day. The objects of religious faith are not to be derived from reason, as is the case with the idealist concept of God against which Schleiermacher contends in the *Christian Faith* (§ 4.4), but are observations concerning the historical expressions of Christian self-consciousness. By this privileging of empirical reason to arrive at historical–theological claims, Schleiermacher applies his dialectic to his theological method of gleaning the predicates of lived religion from the stage of history. Nevertheless, empirical reason is seen on a continuum with speculative reason; the latter is charged with the task of conceptually defining the self-identical essence and the former fills in the concept with historical content. Mutual reciprocity between empirical and speculative reason epistemologically determines Schleiermacher's method of oscillation between conceptual, philosophical theology and empirical, historical theology. As a result, Schleiermacher's *Life of Jesus* inevitably makes soteriological claims concerning Christ's person, and his erroneous privileging of John as the historically original gospel contains a seed of theological truth about Christ redemptively effecting the coherence of self-consciousness.

With his system of theology, Schleiermacher configures the relation between exegetical and dogmatic theology in a way differing from the *dicta probantia* method of Protestant orthodoxy. The orthodox strategy presupposed the self-sameness of spiritual realities and assumed that discursive articulation did not introduce historical difference into those realities. The methodological result was to semantically flatten the referents of biblical texts to accord with doctrinal claims. For Schleiermacher, however, ethical realities are metaphysically rooted in a self-same essence, which is speculatively, never empirically, defined. The object of empirical study is the essence's discursive manifestation, changing through time, differing in linguistic articulation, and situated in particular cultural–historically determined sites. The consequence of this position is that, for Schleiermacher, dogmatic theology must be verified (*bewährt*), but can never be proven by Scripture (*BO*, § 210). This means that historical and linguistic difference need not be reduced to transculturally identical terms and then collapsed into an eternal truth. Rather, difference is prized as individual perspectives of a feeling identical throughout Christianity's history. Constituting identity through time is the "certainty of each person's own immediate religious self-consciousness" (*BO*, § 209). This transcultural sameness of feeling, not the identity of a religious object or theological words, provides the content for dogmatic propositions that are to be tested in view of the parameters stipulated by the canon. It is, once again, the privileging of Christ over Scripture, which determines "personal conviction" (*BO*, § 196) that is then verified by New Testament authorial intention to determine if the experience of Christ has, in fact, been established as a possible experience at the origins of Christianity. And again, this verification process is one of infinite approximation because it proceeds in dialogue with the endless exegetical searching for the canon.

Although Schleiermacher envisioned a relation between exegetical and dogmatic theology that is yet to be explored in all its rich detail, there remains the nagging problem of his execution of his own method. Are the historical–critical results overshadowed by his theological commitments? Rather than discrediting outright Schleiermacher's theory along with an application deemed problematic from a positivist historical research perspective, the following words of Friedrich Lücke can still be appropriated.

Even "where he erred by virtue of the surpassing strength of his unique spirit, [Schleiermacher] was able to stimulate more scientific life and [intellectual] striving than a hundred others, who, lacking both spirit and peculiarity of character did not even err once."[42]

CONCLUSION

Although not an uncontroversial element in Schleiermacher's thought, his exegetical contributions to the developing field in the early nineteenth century and to the theory of exegetical theology remain landmarks in theology. Although contested, Schleiermacher's search for the New Testament canon remained a task designated by his own understanding of exegetical theology within his system of theological science. The canon was one concept threaded through his formal encyclopedia's systematic connections and epistemologically accessed by an oscillation between speculative and empirical reason. The scientific spirit wedded to the ecclesial spirit was not only a theoretical requirement for the exegetical theologian, but was one embodied in Schleiermacher's own practice of lecturing on the books of the New Testament throughout his professorial career and in his lifelong preaching activity. Yet the clear insight informing systematic complexity was Schleiermacher's privileging of the subject "behind the text," the one whose personal presence motivated the production of the New Testament texts in the first place, and the one whose impact still creates the continuity of Christian self-consciousness through to the present day.

Notes

1 The works in Reimer's *SW*, 1.2 are now available in *KGA*, 1.5 and 1.8. *KGA*, 1.5 includes Schleiermacher's "Commentary on 1 Timothy" ("Über den sogenannten ersten Brief des Paulos an den Timotheos. Ein kritisches Sendschreiben an J. C. Gaß [1807]," 153–242). *KGA*, 1.8 includes the "Commentary on Luke" ("Über die Schriften des Lukas: ein kritischer Versuch, Erster Theil [1817]," 1–180); the previously unpublished "Introduction to Acts" ("Einleitung in den geplanten zweiten Teil über die Schriften des Lukas [Über die Apostelgeschichte, 1817]," 181–93), the "Commentary on Colossians 1:15–20" ("Über Kolosser 1, 15–20 [1832]," 195–226), and the "Commentary on the Papias-Fragment" ("Über die Zeugnisse des Papias von unsern beiden ersten Evangelien [1832]," 227–54). For the excellent introduction to Schleiermacher's exegetical work, see Patsch and Schmid, "Einleitung," in *KGA*, 1.8, vii–lvii. *SW*, 1.8 contains Schleiermacher's *Introduction to the New Testament* [*Einleitung ins neue Testament* (1845)]. Slated for future publication in the *KGA* [= *SW*, 1.6 (1864)] is *Das Leben Jesu*. It is currently available in the English as *The Life of Jesus* (1975). Subsequent references to this translation will be referred to as *LJ*, with the page number following.

2 For a list of all the New Testament lectures Schleiermacher delivered, see Arndt and Virmond 1992, 300–30.

3 See Verheyden's "Introduction" in *LJ*, xi; Strauss' 1865 criticism is translated into English in Strauss 1977.

4 The English translation of the 1817 text appeared in 1825 without explicit mention of the translator, Connop Thirlwall. See Patsch and Schmid, *KGA*, 1.8, "Einleitung," xxxii. Thirlwall's translation is available in *Luke: A Critical Study*, 1993. Cf. Ellis 1980, 417–52.

5 For the Protestant orthodox doctrine of Scripture, see Schmid 1961, 38–91 (= §§ 6–12), and Heppe 1978, chs. 2–3.

6 See Wallmann 1994, 30–56.

7 Landmesser 1999, 459–79.

8 Translations of the *Kurze Darstellung* are from Schleiermacher, *Brief Outline of Theology as a Field of Study*, trans. Tice.

9 For Schleiermacher, practical theology is the theory *for* praxis, rather than *of* praxis. Its application is an art in the Kantian sense that the application is a matter of individual talent, not a subsumption under another rule. See *BO*, § 265 as well as Schleiermacher, *Hermeneutics and Criticism and Other Writings*, 11.

10 In the first edition of the *Kurze Darstellung* or *Brief Outline* (1811 edn.), Schleiermacher uses the term "idea of the canon." See *Kurze Darstellung*, 1st edn., 1, §§ 1–2. This is a regulative idea in Kant's sense as the object of infinite approximation. Cf. *Kurze Darstellung*, 1st edn., 1, § 10. In the second edition of the *Kurze Darstellung* (1830 edn.), Schleiermacher refers to the canon as the "collection of those writings which contain the normative presentation of Christianity" (*BO*, § 104).

11 *BO*, § 83. For Schleiermacher, the origins are relatively "pure" or free from foreign influences entering into the historical trajectory of a religion once that religion becomes extensive over subsequent generations and other cultures.

12 Kloppenborg 2000, 275.

13 Lessing published the *Fragmente des Wolfenbüttelschen Ungenannten* between 1774 and 1778. The fragments are translated into English in Talbert 1985. For a detailed summary of Reimarus' position and the ensuing discussion of the Synoptic problem, see Kloppenborg 2000, 275–328.

14 Kloppenborg 2000, 279.

15 See de Wette and Lücke 1818.

16 See figure 23a in Kloppenborg 2000, 296. Kloppenborg writes that Schleiermacher's *logia* collection theory was preceded by Herbert Marsh's proposal.

17 Kloppenborg 2000, 295.

18 Kloppenborg 2000, 279–83 for a discussion of Griesbach's hypothesis.

19 Kloppenborg 2000, 295–7.

20 Schwarz 1812, 526–7. Cf. the following voices critical of Schleiermacher's view of the Old Testament: Kraeling 1955, 59–67; Kraus 1988, 170–3 (§ 45); Steiger 1994, 305–27; Smend 1991, 128–44; Trillhass 1991, 279–89.

21 See the fifth speech in *OR*, Crouter, 113–23.

22 Schleiermacher notes, "I hate that type of historical reference in religion": *OR*, 114.

23 Between 1805 and 1833, Schleiermacher worked out his hermeneutical theory, which was published posthumously as *Hermeneutics and Criticism* in *SW*, I.7. *BO*, § 137 mentions "special hermeneutics" as the application of general hermeneutics to the New Testament.

24 *Hermeneutics*, 7–8.

25 *Hermeneutics*, 3. Schleiermacher's claim that hermeneutics involves "correctly" understanding the speech of another ("die Kunst die Rede eines andern richtig zu verstehen" [*SW*, I.7, 7–8]) is a significant point often overlooked in interpretations of Schleiermacher's hermeneutics.

26 *Hermeneutics*, 23.

27 *Hermeneutics*, 23. The formula is articulated prior to Schleiermacher by the romantics Friedrich Schlegel and Novalis. See Schleiermacher, *Hermeneutik und Kritik*, ed. Frank, 55.

28 Schleiermacher disagreed with Karl Bretschneider on the historical priority of John. Bretschneider published *Probabilia* in 1820, assigning a late date to John. On this point see Verheyden's "Introduction," to *LJ*, xxxi.

29 Schleiermacher, *On Colossians*, translated by Reed and Braley, 51. Schleiermacher assumed that Paul wrote Colossians as well as the Christological hymn in Col. 1:15–20.

30 *On Colossians*, 51.

31 *On Colossians*, 51.

32 *On Colossians*, 69, 73–4.

33 For two historical introductions to this work, see Patsch, "Einleitung," in *KGA*, I.5, lxxxviii–cxxiii, and Patsch 1991, 451–77.

34 Schleiermacher, *Dialektik*, ed. Frank, vol. 1, 34–40.

35 *Hermeneutics*, 7.

36 Birkner 1964, 35. Other technical disciplines are pedagogy, politics, and practical theology.

37 Birkner 1964, 41.

38 Schleiermacher, *Dialektik*, ed. Frank, vol. 1, 63–5.

39 Lücke 1834, 771, cited in Patsch and Schmid, "Einleitung," in *KGA*, I.8, xlvii. Patsch and Schmid document other reviews of Schleiermacher's work in their "Einleitung."

40 Strauss 1977, 36.

41 Fischer 2001, 74.

42 Lücke 1834, 771, cited in Patsch and Schmid, *KGA*, I.8, xlvii. Translation mine.

Part III

Culture, Society, and Religion

13 Culture, arts, and religion

DAVID E. KLEMM

THE QUESTION CONFRONTING SCHLEIERMACHER

How should religion relate to culture? Schleiermacher's famous book, *On Religion: Speeches to its Cultured Despisers* (1799), presents an epoch-making answer to this question, which I will analyze and interpret in some detail in this chapter.[1] In so doing, I will focus on tensions between Schleiermacher's stress on the relative and culturally conditioned character of historical religions and his attempt in the *Speeches* to identify what is common to all religions. I will also consider whether or not Schleiermacher's understanding of Christian revelation enters into his evaluation of religion in relation to culture within the context of his contribution to comparative religion. Finally, I will briefly assess the role of culture, in particular that of the arts, in fostering spirituality. I begin with some notes about the meaning of "culture" in Schleiermacher's time, and then I proceed to its relation to religion.

The term "culture" (*Kultur* in German) refers originally to the sphere of agriculture and husbandry, where one cultivates plants and animals in order to improve them or make them better.[2] By extension to the human realm, a cultured person is one who has improved herself or himself by developing the highest capacities of the mind or talents. In both domains of meaning, culture is an achievement of human purposiveness, which transforms what is given naturally according to the refined and reflected value of goodness.

The term *Kultur* was of course closely related to the term *Bildung*, but with a difference. The German sense of culture was applied primarily to social groups and referred to the highest goods of society, especially its intellectual, artistic, and spiritual achievements.[3] *Bildung*, by contrast, referred primarily to the cultivation of the individual. In his study of *Bildung* in relation to culture, Hans-Georg Gadamer stresses that the intentionality of *Bildung* (culture) moves from the particular elements of culture and personality in the direction of the universal.[4] He writes that

Promotion to the universal is not something that is limited to theoretical *Bildung* and does not mean only a theoretical attitude in contrast to a practical one, but covers the essential determination of human rationality as a whole. It is the universal nature of human *Bildung* to constitute itself as a universal intellectual being. Whoever abandons himself to his particularity is *ungebildet* ["unformed"], e.g., if someone gives way to blind anger without measure or sense of proportion. Hegel shows that basically such a man is lacking in the power of abstraction. He cannot turn his gaze from himself towards something universal from which his own particular being is determined in measure and proportion.

Bildung is a task that requires the sacrifice of particularity for the sake of the universal. This sacrifice entails the restraint of desire and hence freedom from the object of desire and freedom for its objectivity.[5]

Given the drive within culture and *Bildung* to universal meanings and standards of goodness, the question about how religion should relate to culture was, at Schleiermacher's time (as it is today), hotly disputed. Religion, of course, is part of culture, and many people want to know how to relate the teachings and practices of their particular religious community (for example, a specific Christian church) to the complex cultural world around them. The problem is that religion is sufficiently different from other parts of the culture that this makes its relationship to culture as a whole questionable. How so?

The historical religions typically claim to possess some divinely revealed, material knowledge on matters of metaphysics and morals that, if true, would be of utmost importance to the project of human culture. Such purported knowledge includes insights concerning who or what God or the ultimate reality is, what kind of human life is justified in God's eyes, and how humans may be redeemed from sin, evil, or ignorance into some kind of eternal life or salvation. Through the influential writings of Rousseau and others, the historical religions have been called "revealed religions" or "positive religions," and I will use these terms interchangeably here. According to Rousseau, positive or revealed religion is *particular* in the nature of the case: it is religion based on particular revelations of God that are entrusted only to particular people within particular traditions, teaching people particular ways in which God purportedly wants to be worshipped.[6] Revealed religion is also intolerant and exclusive; each particular religion claims that it is the one true religion, and that all other religions are false. It is understandable that members of such particular religious traditions would believe that (their) religion should attempt to shape and influence common cultural understandings so as to make them correspond to the substance of their religious beliefs.

When Schleiermacher wrote his *Speeches* in 1799, Europe was well familiar with the problems that attend this attitude about the superiority of revealed religion over culture in determining how to shape fundamental human values. Contention, strife, hostilities, and warfare continued to erupt among different groups following the Thirty Years a War (1618–48) for reasons that can be traced back at least in part to religious and cultural differences between groups. The French Revolution was the determining event for Schleiermacher's generation of "89"-ers," and in many ways the revolution was about who would have control over the cultural institutions, especially educational institutions – the Catholic church or a civil state.

Enlightenment thinkers criticized the historical religions from the standpoint of universal philosophical principles and the necessary conditions for a civil state. Partly to escape devastating religious strife, and partly to expose the self-contradictions in revealed religion, various forms of "natural religion" were posited. In dramatic contrast to the particularity of the revealed religions, the truths of natural religion are held to be in principle universally accessible to any rational being whatsoever. Natural religion promulgated tolerance on the basis of a set of elements common to all particular religions. Rational deductions of the existence of "God" as a universal highest principle of design and order in the universe, the existence of the soul as evident in immediate self-consciousness, and the finite freedom of the self over against the universe, constituted essential elements of different versions of natural religion.

The high point in the development of philosophical approaches to the problem of relating religion and culture came in Kant's philosophy. In the Preface to the first edition of the *Critique of Pure Reason*, Kant wrote: "Our age is the genuine age of criticism, to which everything must submit. Religion through its holiness and legislation through its majesty commonly seek to exempt themselves from it. But in this way they excite a just suspicion against themselves, and cannot lay claim to that unfeigned respect that reason grants only to that which has been able to withstand its free and public examination."[7] Criticism (or "critique") is the capacity to negate any immediate relationship to reality insofar as it claims truth for what is established in that relationship. The revealed beliefs of particular religious traditions are of just such a kind. While it is often the case that sacred texts are understood as they are received and interpreted through the community (and is in this sense that they are mediated), this reception remains uncritical insofar as the process of reception and interpretation itself, as well the original formation of sacred texts remains unanalyzed. Critique suspends believing immediacy; it does not accept things as they appear, but rather submits all appearances to tests of critical reflection – including appearances of divinely revealed truths in sacred texts and traditions.

For the modern thinkers of the Enlightenment, including Schleiermacher's generation of cultured thinkers, critique, not religious belief, was the highest cultural value. For them, religion, if it was to survive at all, had to give up particularity and become universal natural religion. Historical criticism of biblical texts had successfully challenged immediate belief in the truth of sacred texts, and rational criticism of dogmatic theology called into question all material knowledge of God and the soul. What was (and is) at stake in the choice between positive religion and natural religion?

Positive religions offer people some very powerful satisfactions that come with particularity: a strong sense of identity in belonging to a special community of the faithful, a set of secure beliefs by which to live one's life, and certainty of redemption from a fallen world. These things satisfy some very basic human desires, but the cost of these satisfactions is high. In light of universal critique, revealed religions appear as blind and arbitrary in the naïveté of their pre-critical beliefs; they also appear as exclusivistic and contentious in their mutually competing claims to be the one true religion. In choosing particularity over universality, the revealed religions sacrifice the infinite demand for universal truth for the concrete assurances of particularity. They appear to be opposed to the demands of culture.

By contrast to positive religions, natural religion offers philosophical indifference to particularity, grounded in an interest in universal truth. One gives up the sense of identity based on "our" group and identifies with the universal and formal idea of humanity as such. One gives up claims to material knowledge of God and God's ways and instead engages in infinite criticism armed with abstract forms and principles. One gives up the certainty of redemption in favor of the openness to the objectivity of not-knowing. The cost of this choice is also high. In choosing universality over particularity, natural religion sacrifices the immediacy of believing in images from sacred sources for the indifference of the scientific mind. Schleiermacher, in writing his *Speeches*, was highly aware of facing precisely this difficult decision: positive religion or natural religion? As we shall see, Schleiermacher's answer refuses this dilemma.

Schleiermacher presents his answer to the question in *On Religion: Speeches to its Cultured Despisers (Über die Religion: Reden an die Gebildeten unter ihren Verächtern)*. It is a work of philosophical theology, which is difficult to understand partly because of its rhetorical form. Schleiermacher has not written a philosophical–theological treatise about religion (as in the first sense of the ironical title, *Über die Religion*). Rather, he has composed five persuasive speeches, which nonetheless contain a logical argument about the essence of religion. These speeches are addressed to the "cultured despisers of religion," who hold themselves to be above religion (as in the other sense of the ironic title, *Über die Religion*).

THE ESSENCE OF RELIGION

The first speech, "Apology," begins in direct address to his audience with an appeal to listen to him speak about religion and its essential nature, in spite of the fact that "Especially now, the life of cultivated persons is removed from everything that would in the least way resemble religion" (*KGA*, I.2, 189; *OR*, Crouter, 77/3). Schleiermacher initiates his argument with reference to the unity in difference of two opposing forces or ontological principles, from whose interaction each definite being is composed. These forces are precisely the principles of universality and particularity to which we have just alluded: "The one," which we could call particularity, "strives to draw into itself everything that surrounds it, ensnaring it in its own life and, wherever possible, wholly absorbing it into its innermost being." "The other," which we could call universality, "longs to extend its own inner self ever further, thereby permeating and imparting to everything from within, while never being exhausted itself" (*KGA*, I.2, 191; *OR*, Crouter, 80/5). Applied to religion, we can understand positive religion and natural religion to occupy "the extreme ends of this great series" (*KGA*, I.2, 192; *OR*, Crouter, 81/6).

In the second speech, "On the Essence of Religion," Schleiermacher writes that, "Religion's essence is neither thinking nor acting, but intuition and feeling. It wishes to intuit the universe, wishes devoutly to overhear the universe's own manifestations and actions, longs to be grasped and filled by the universe's immediate influences" (*KGA*, I.2, 211; *OR*, Crouter, 102/22). Intuition is immediate perception of something in the form of an image (*KGA*, I.2, 215; *OR*, Crouter, 105/26). Feeling is immediate consciousness of how the self is affected by something (*KGA*, I.2, 218; *OR*, Crouter, 109/29). Religion is intuition and feeling of the action of the universe on the self. Image and inwardness combine in religion at the "center of our being," prior to their separation in reflection and prior to producing action, in a "first mysterious moment ... where sense and its objects have, as it were, flowed into one another and become one" (*KGA*, I.2, 221; *OR*, Crouter, 112/31), there "to make everything holy and valuable" (*KGA*, I.2, 218; *OR*, Crouter, 109/29). Religion produces an image of the living universe, the vibrant whole, interacting with the self in its deepest feelings.

As such, religion's essential nature is not to be confused with either metaphysics or morality; nor is it a mixture of the theoretical and practical

(*KGA*, I.2, 209; *OR*, Crouter, 99/20). It is "something integral" in itself that is an ingredient in human nature: "Praxis is an art, speculation is a science, religion is the sensibility and taste for the infinite" (*KGA*, I.2, 212; *OR*, Crouter, 103/23). Intuition and feeling of the universe, says Schleiermacher, is always something individual – "the immediate experiences of the existence and action of the universe" – each of which is a self-contained work without necessary connections to other intuitions and feelings, prior to and distinct from a set of concepts or principles for action (*KGA*, I.2, 215; *OR*, Crouter, 105/26).

SCHLEIERMACHER'S AUDIENCE: RELIGION'S CULTURED DESPISERS

Schleiermacher addresses his audience as "you" who have "raised yourselves above the herd, are saturated by the wisdom of the century" (*KGA*, I.2, 189; *OR*, Crouter, 77/3). The "you" are the young intellectual elite of his day, the brilliant philosophical and literary minds driving the development of culture in the early German romantic movement, who are thoroughly at home in the world of critical thought. The problem Schleiermacher sees in his audience, and which he wants to cure, is that these *virtuosi* of culture despise religion so much that it is damaging their own ability to think clearly and therefore to shape culture with integrity. Contempt, hatred, and disdain distort the mind and twist the will. Nothing good comes from them.

Schleiermacher presents his *Speeches* as a therapy for the diseased souls of religion's cultured despisers. Schleiermacher understands how his audience could have such contempt for religion, for he and they are aware of the absurdities of particular religion (*KGA*, I.2, 199–200; *OR*, Crouter, 89/12). Presumably, his audience has already sacrificed the particularities of religion in favor of the universal: "When you declaim against religion, you do so usually in the name of philosophy; when you reproach the church, you speak in the name of the state" (*KGA*, I.2, 279; *OR*, Crouter, 175/83). But the declamations and reproaches of his audience are infected with passions opposed to religion, which in fact have become indistinguishable from religion's own passions. He asks them to be properly informed about their contempt (*KGA*, I.2, 198; *OR*, Crouter, 88/11). He claims, "I do not wish to arouse particular feelings that perhaps belong in its realm, nor to justify or dispute particular ideas. I wish to lead you to innermost depths from which religion first addresses the mind. I wish to show you from what capacity of humanity religion proceeds, and how it belongs to what is for you the highest and dearest" (*KGA*, I.2, 197; *OR*, Crouter, 87/10–1).

Why does Schleiermacher so address his audience? Because to comprehend the essence of religion with the dispassionate indifference and openness of a philosophical attitude can save the mind from the particularism and exclusivism into which its cultured despisers themselves have fallen through their disdain. What, then, does Schleiermacher want his audience to do relative to understanding religion and its role in culture? Let us first consider the possibility of recovering the role of positive religion within culture.

SCHLEIERMACHER ON POSITIVE RELIGION

Clearly, Schleiermacher does not advocate returning to or rehabilitating the historical, revealed religions as such. For Schleiermacher, philosophical and historical critiques of revealed religions have effectively negated their claims to be recipients of divine revelations. Schleiermacher is himself a philosopher who stands above these claims (*Über die Religion*). He knows that religion is neither metaphysics nor morals, neither thinking nor acting, but intuition and feeling of the universe. He understands that as such religion cannot give material knowledge about God or God's intentions for human beings; each religion provides one possible intuition of the universe among an infinite set of possibilities (*KGA*, I.2, 299; *OR*, Crouter, 195/100). Schleiermacher knows that revealed religion is capable only of offering opinions and beliefs, whereas it claims to have revealed knowledge.[8]

In the fourth speech, "On the Social Element in Religion," Schleiermacher addresses the special contempt that the cultured despisers have for religious organizations (*KGA*, I.2, 266; *OR*, Crouter, 162/72). Schleiermacher argues that their disdain for particular religious communities (churches) is actually directed not toward the historical religions as such, but toward a false church that is an inversion of true religious community. Schleiermacher says that actual ecclesiastical societies are not truly societies of religious people (*KGA*, I.2, 283; *OR*, Crouter, 180/87). In fact, an inverse relationship exists between an individual's participating in church groups, on one side, and knowing the concept of religion and having a genuine intuition and feeling of the universe, on the other side. Those who know and have religion shun the churches, and those who embrace the churches lack religion (*KGA*, I.2, 275–6; *OR*, Crouter, 172/80).

A false church is a society in which one person (the religious leader or priest) actively imparts opinions and the others passively receive them (*KGA*, I.2, 276; *OR*, Crouter, 172/81). For Schleiermacher, the people who are attracted to such communities lack religion in its essential nature; at best they are seekers of religion and not those who "have become conscious of their religion" (*KGA*,

1.2, 273; OR, Crouter, 169/78). Schleiermacher goes so far as to say that if these people did acquire a concept or intuition of religion, they would leave the (false) church, because the false church substitutes dogmas and rituals for intuition and feeling of the universe. Schleiermacher holds that these false churches, or "sects," in fact contradict the essential nature of religion in promoting ideas such as the utter difference between priesthood and laity, the need to convert outsiders, and the exclusive claim for salvation. Such positive religion is actually nothing other than "sectarianism" (KGA, 1.2, 297, 301; OR, Crouter, 193/98–9, 197/102). In no way does Schleiermacher advocate that such sectarianism should assume a privileged role within the developing culture of his day.

Schleiermacher's negation of the claims of revealed religion nonetheless includes an element of affirmation. Religion necessarily and essentially includes a social element, because those who do have a genuine sense and taste for the infinite in the finite naturally seek to express and communicate what they see and feel in their relationship to the living universe (KGA, 1.2, 268; OR, Crouter, 164/73). They do so in word and in symbolic actions (KGA, 1.2, 276; OR, Crouter, 172–3/81). Hence Schleiermacher distinguishes the "true" church from the "false" church. The true church is made up of those people who self-consciously have religion and live it in mutual communication (KGA, 1.2, 276–7; OR, Crouter, 173/81). The true church focuses on an individual image and feeling of the universe, makes no exclusive claims to truth, displays no trace of tyrannous hierarchy between lay people and priesthood, and feels no need to convert others to the one true religion. It is a free-flowing, mobile group with no hard lines between priests and lay people, and no strong divisions between itself as a group and other groups. In it, each individual openly proclaims religion, knowing that the boundaries of the community shift and change in time, and that its very existence is transitory and temporary (KGA, 1.2, 287–8; OR, Crouter, 184/91).

SCHLEIERMACHER ON NATURAL RELIGION

How does natural religion fare for the author of the Speeches? In addressing his audience, Schleiermacher says "in spite of all your aversion to religion generally," and your "quite exquisite hatred" of the existing historical religions, "you have always endured ever more easily and have even spoken with esteem of something else, which is called natural religion" (KGA, 1.2, 296; OR, Crouter, 192/98). Schleiermacher's response is, "I for my part protest most vehemently against this preference ... I declare this preference for natural religion to be the grossest inconsistency and the most obvious self-contradiction" (KGA, 1.2, 296; OR, Crouter, 192–3/98).

According to Schleiermacher, natural religion is merely abstract and formal reasoning. It has no basic intuition and feeling of the universe of its own and therefore contradicts the essence of religion. When taken to an extreme, as in Hume's skepticism, natural religion deconstructs itself and leaves critical thinking with nothing at all except the permanent condition of self-criticism. Natural religion ends up being "merely an indefinite, insufficient, and paltry idea that can never really exist by itself" (*KGA*, 1.2, 298–9; *OR*, Crouter, 195/100). In Schleiermacher's words, "The essence of natural religion actually consists wholly in the negation of everything positive and characteristic in religion and in the most violent polemic against it." It is "a bristling against everything definite and real" (*KGA*, 1.2, 310–1; *OR*, Crouter, 207/110).

However, there is an element of affirmation in Schleiermacher's critique of natural religion. Schleiermacher's own articulation of the essence of religion participates in the project of natural religion to articulate the common, necessary structure of the historical religions. What exactly is Schleiermacher's alternative proposal to both positive religion and natural religion?

SCHLEIERMACHER'S PROPOSAL FOR PHILOSOPHICAL THEOLOGY

Schleiermacher wants his audience to rise above both the historical religions and natural religion in order to ascend to *philosophical theology* as a self-conscious and reflexive way of thinking about and experiencing religion in its truth. I propose to examine Schleiermacher's conception of the relations among positive religion, natural religion, and philosophical theology by reference to Plato's explanation in *The Republic* of the levels of human thinking in relation to the corresponding orders of being. In the analogy of the divided line, Plato distinguishes between opinion (*doxa*) and knowledge (*epistēmē*). Plato also discusses the conversion of mind that is necessary to move from contentment with opinion to the search for knowledge: one must be able to give up attachment to the visible realm of things as they present themselves to the mind in order to think the truth of things according to invisible concepts, causes, and principles. The purpose of education (*Bildung* as part of culture) is to enable insight into the idea of the good – the principle of principles, and standard of standards, that makes possible any true thinking about being.

Schleiermacher's assessment of positive religion clearly belongs at the level of opinion on Plato's divided line.[9] Plato divides opinion into "illusion" (*eikasia*), where we can place those people who passively learn the biblical stories and church teaching, and who perform the rites in a rote way, and "belief" (*pistis*), where people additionally form and express their own opinions about the stories, teachings, and rites. In both cases, people believe immediately in what we could call concrete, particular, mythological meanings presented in sacred narratives and ritual actions. These meanings are thence interpreted and elaborated as objective, dogmatic truths about the universe in pre-critical theologies. At this level, we have particularity without reference to universality, that is, opinion that has not submitted itself to critical reflection.

Natural religion is the result of making the conversion from belief to critical or reflective thinking that intends knowledge. With natural religion, we rise to the lower level of knowledge that Plato calls mathematical reasoning (*dianoia*), which comprehends underlying principles that make phenomena possible. At this level the mind looks beyond visible realities by the power of critical reflection to grasp the intellectual principles underlying them. Now the focus is on testing the truth of particular appearances in the light of universal principles. In so testing, the critical reflection exemplified in natural religion draws a basic distinction between objectivity and subjectivity. Beliefs that cannot be reflected as truly objective are relegated to the domain of subjectivity and lose their status. For natural religion, the universal forms that are common to the historical religions – such as the form of a design in the universe and form of a rational being – retain their objectivity. The particular content of different revealed religions is considered subjective and is negated.

Philosophical theology belongs at the highest level of knowledge,[10] which Plato calls intelligence (*noēsis*) or dialectic – a term that Schleiermacher uses first to denote philosophy. Dialectic encompasses thinking about thinking; it understands the truth about truth. It rises to what we could call reflexive thinking by thinking the activity of thinking itself as it critically reflects upon its objects. In this way, dialectic thinks the first principle of all thinking about being, which Plato calls the form of the good as the absolute identity of subjectivity and objectivity in their difference. Schleiermacher asserts the same thing – namely, that all human thinking is grounded on a first principle of absolute knowing that itself cannot be known in its truth as such. Schleiermacher in the *Speeches* writes that religion has an intuition and feeling for this absolute principle ("the universe"); dialectic *knows* what religion *intuits*. The point is that only from the standpoint of dialectic can thinking grasp what Schleiermacher calls the essence of religion.

Philosophical theology is thus necessarily above both the historical religions and natural religion, respectively, on a divided line, just as dialectic is above both belief and critical reflection. Schleiermacher is asking the cultured despisers of religion to ascend beyond the critical reflection of *dianoia* to dialectic, where they can comprehend the strengths and weaknesses of: (1) positive religion as belief; (2) natural religion as critical reflection; and (3) dialectical knowledge of the absolute (the "good").

Very importantly, Schleiermacher agrees with Plato's Socrates that the philosopher should serve culture as a whole by embracing not only the ascending dialectic, but also the descending dialectic. Recall Socrates' advice "to live with your fellows in the cave and get used to seeing in the dark."[11] The reason for descending is that "you will see a thousand times better than they do and will distinguish the various shadows, and know what they are shadows of, because you have seen the truth about things admirable and just and good." Likewise, Schleiermacher advocates that true mediators of religion should remain in the false church to serve the seekers there who lack "the true principle of religion" (*KGA*, 1.2, 278; *OR*, Crouter, 174/83). Their purpose would be "promotion to the universal," as Gadamer discussed it in relation to *Bildung*. What can philosophical theologians bring to positive religion and natural religion?

Philosophical theologians can understand the positive religions in their truth – what they are and what they are not. For example, they understand that the historical religions do in fact proceed from a living intuition of the universe – that is the strength of positive religion. They also understand that the historical religions do not comprehend themselves as such. Historical religions take their intuition to be a revelation of true knowledge about God or the absolute reality, which is impossible. Because philosophical theologians understand the essence of religion, they can understand the corruption that creeps into positive religion. Moreover, philosophical theologians are in a position no longer to see the field of positive religions as they struggle among competing truth systems, but rather as an array of complementary religious intuitions. Philosophical theologians are free, by the power of imagination and understanding, to enter into the intuitions and feelings of the universe found in the historical religions, while being free from their particular claims to truth. In addition, philosophical theologians can show others within the historical religions, those with eyes to see, how they too can assume this twofold freedom for and freedom from the positive religions.

Likewise, philosophical theologians understand that natural religion stands above positive religion, where it can grasp the principles that are common to the historical religions. Natural religion thus stands beyond the bitter contentions that divide historical religions. Such is the strength of natural religion. Philosophical theologians also understand the weakness of natural religion, namely, believing it can ground religion in metaphysics or morals. Natural religion has lost the concrete, particular embodiment of religion in intuition and feeling. Thus philosophical theology is a gift both to culture, which it grasps in its differentiated wholeness, and to religion. It rightly comprehends both the historical religions and natural religion from the inside, as human phenomena that constitute real forces within culture, while criticizing one-sided attachments to particularity (in positive religion) or universality (in natural religion).

THE RELATION BETWEEN CHRISTIAN REVELATION AND PHILOSOPHICAL THEOLOGY

Schleiermacher was a Christian minister who served the evangelical church throughout his life. Does Schleiermacher's understanding of Christian revelation enter into his evaluation of religion in relation to culture within the context of his contribution to comparative religion? In the *Speeches*, Schleiermacher lauds pluralism in religion as something necessary and desirable, and for its sake he advocates separation of church and state (*KGA*, I.2, 287; *OR*, Crouter, 183/90). A plurality of religions is, he says, rooted in the concept of the essence of religion itself. The systematically basic types of religion each involve a vision of the whole of things. Minimally these views include: (1) universe as chaos; (2) universe as system; and (3) universe as unity in multiplicity (*KGA*, I.2, 301; *OR*, Crouter, 197/102). Each of these types can undergo other modifications in form and appear as personalism, pantheism, naturalism, polytheism, deism, etc. According to Schleiermacher, we gain from a plurality of religions, because different manifestations of religion enable different kinds of people to find the religious expression that is most appropriate to them (*KGA*, I.2 294–5; *OR*, Crouter, 190–1/96–7).

Schleiermacher says that the content of the basic intuition in Christianity is "the intuition of the universal straining of everything finite against the unity of the whole and of the way in which the deity handles this striving, how it reconciles the enmity directed against it and sets bonds to the ever greater distance by scattering over the whole individual points that are at once finite and infinite, at once human and divine" (*KGA*, I.2, 316; *OR*, Crouter, 213/115). In other words, the basic intuition is of the universe as composed of contending parts which struggle against the whole, and of the action of the whole on the parts to bring them into harmony and mutual correspondence. Expressed in the narrative form of the Bible, the basic intuition of Christianity is one of rebellion and reconciliation. Through the fall of humanity, the world has departed from its original harmony and has given itself over to self-centered corruption; yet all this happens for the sake of redemption worked through the providence of God by his mediators (*KGA*, I.2, 317; *OR*, Crouter, 214/116).

In addition, Schleiermacher understands the basic form of Christian intuition to be permanent, unremitting critique of idolatry. Because Christianity, "in its most characteristic basic intuition," treats religion itself as material for religion, Christianity is religion "raised to a higher power" (*KGA*, I.2, 317; *OR*, Crouter, 214/116). Christianity, in this sense, is absolute religion; it is in principle polemical in attacking irreligion (*KGA*, I.2, 318; *OR*, Crouter, 215/117). In Christianity, the finite ever wishes to intuit the universe perfectly, in infinite holiness; yet it necessarily fails. The feeling associated with this intuition is a feeling of unsatisfied longing, directed towards an infinite reality that is understood to be infinite and thus ultimately unknowable and unattainable by finite humans. Thus the mood of "holy sadness" determines the tone of all Christian religious feelings (*KGA*, I.2, 320; *OR*, Crouter, 217/119).

Is Schleiermacher's philosophical theology the same as his view of Christianity as a positive religion? They both display a systematic whole made up of parts, in which there is tension among parts yet mutual belonging of parts to the whole. They both know that the absolute is necessary to the system, that nothing is known or knowable without the absolute, yet that a knowing of the absolute is impossible. They both exist as a self-critical and unrealizable search for the absolute. What does this similarity mean? Rather than suggesting that Christian revelation somehow grounds Schleiermacher's view of religion in its highest expression, the similarity explains the historically contingent circumstances under which Schleiermacher's thinking emerged from Christianity as a positive religion into his form of philosophical theology. However, I see no necessary connection between Christianity and Schleiermacher's philosophical theology. Plato's dialectic pre-existed Christianity, and Schleiermacher's philosophical theology bears even more striking resemblances to Plato's system.

SCHLEIERMACHER'S LATER SYSTEM OF THOUGHT

A wealth of corroborating evidence exists in the structure of Schleiermacher's later system of thought for my argument that Schleiermacher recommends philosophical theology to his audience of cultured despisers of religion. The first piece of evidence relates to the fact that Schleiermacher, who is best known as the author of the *Christian Faith*, assigned systematic (dogmatic) theology to the historical disciplines in the *Brief Outline of Theology*. The reason he did so is that Schleiermacher does not consider religion to be the foundation of culture. Dialectic is the foundational philosophical–theological discipline for the entire system, with its articulation of the structure of culture. The second piece of evidence refers directly to the fact that Schleiermacher's dialectic presents the systematic, conceptually rigorous form of the philosophical theology presented in the *Speeches*. Let me elaborate this point.

Dialectic for Schleiermacher is an investigation into the first principles of knowing by inquiring into the nature, structure, and rules of all actual thinking that aspires to become knowing (*Dial* O, 66–7). Schleiermacher approaches dialectic with reference to the art of leading a dispute to a successful agreement. There are two fundamental conditions of the possibility of resolving dispute in knowledge, which are systematically related to one another. First, for dispute to arise at all, we must postulate an original absolute identity of thinking and being (*Urwissen*) as the condition of the possibility of recognizing that differences exist in thinking about being (actual differences presuppose a logically prior unity). This is *the idea of God*, defined as the principle of the wholly undifferentiated origin point of thinking that relates to being. Second, for successful resolution of dispute, we must postulate a wholly differentiated totality of all thoughts as the condition of relating different thoughts to some third thought. This is the *idea of the world*, defined as the principle of the wholly differentiated totality of thinking about being. Together the idea of God and the idea of the world constitute the limits of all finite thinking about being. God is the idea of an origin point, and the world is the idea of a goal, for any thinking about being. Readers of the *Speeches* can identify these two interrelated ideas as the philosophically rigorous forms of the "two opposing forces" he enunciates in the first speech.

For Schleiermacher, dialectic provides the grounding principle for both theoretical reason (whose principle is nature) and practical reason (whose principle is freedom). Dialectic hence grounds both natural science and ethics. Ethics has a wide meaning here; it is the universal theory of the human world, and thus it provides the framework for all of the human sciences. A brief consideration of the ethics shows how Schleiermacher relates religion to culture in precisely the way I have suggested on the basis of reading the *Speeches*.

SCHLEIERMACHER'S PHILOSOPHICAL ETHICS AS A PHILOSOPHY OF CULTURE

Schleiermacher's philosophical ethics are at heart a philosophy of culture, which divides the entire cultural realm into distinct, relatively autonomous spheres of culture according to their appropriate goods.

Schleiermacher divides the cultural spheres according to two systematic principles. The first division is between the *organizing* capacity to shape nature according to the human spirit, and the *symbolizing* capacity for the spirit to be shaped by the expressive power of nature. The second division is between forms of organizing or symbolizing that are either *identical* in all people (public) or *different* among people (private). The resulting fourfold division looks like this:[12]

	Organizing	*Symbolizing*
Identical (public)	law/state	science, academy
Different (private)	sociality, household	religion, art

Law and state are institutions in which people impose uniformity of thought, language, and action on all members of society; whereas in forms of hospitality (friendships, domestic life), people order their lives differently according to individual decisions of social association. In institutions of science and the academy, people respond to the world around them according to universal forms and methods; whereas in religion and art, people respond differently to the world around them, according to individual taste and disposition.

The meaning of "religion" that Schleiermacher locates as a different (private) symbolizing function of culture is, of course, positive (revealed) religion that is expressed through the churches. This sphere of culture belongs squarely in the domain of belief on Plato's divided line. Natural religion falls under the identifying (public), symbolizing function of culture, as a product of science and the academy. It belongs to the lower level of knowledge (mathematical reasoning) on Plato's divided line. Philosophical ethics provides the capacity to mediate between particularity (in the "different" spheres of culture) and universality in the "identical" spheres of culture). It is part of dialectic on Plato's divided line. Within this differentiated framework, how does Schleiermacher understand culture generally, and the arts in particular, to contribute to an individual's *Bildung*? I begin by considering the goal of spiritual development toward the highest good.

THE ROLE OF CULTURE AND THE ARTS IN FOSTERING SPIRITUALITY

Schleiermacher's ethics intends to demonstrate the rational structure underlying the differentiation among cultural spheres. By distinguishing among cultural spheres, he does not thereby seal off each one from the others. The cultural spheres remain related to one another as distinct parts of one whole. At the center of Schleiermacher's ethics is the doctrine of the highest good as the totality (*Inbegriff*, or unity and difference) of the goods from all four cultural spheres. The highest good is the whole human being, which has achieved balance and harmony among its parts precisely by participating in all four cultural spheres. The highest good prescribes what is truly reasonable for human beings; it is the ideal of completed morality actualized in history.

The aim of the ethics is to guide a human being to its wholeness through its appropriative participation in all four cultural spheres. The highest good is to manifest spiritual freedom by actualizing one's own individuality such that you yourself become "a compendium of humanity" in which "your personality embraces the whole of human nature, and in all its versions this is nothing but your own self that is reproduced, clearly delineated, and immortalized in all its alterations" (*KGA*, 1.2, 232; *OR*, Crouter, 124/41).[13] To actualize as many possibilities as one can, in a unique configuration of humanity, is to become a whole individual. The cultural spheres are the forms and functions of such self-actualization in culture. To become whole in this way is the highest spiritual task.

Religion – in the sense of positive religion – has a place as a different symbolizing function within the cultural whole for Schleiermacher. To integrate religion into a fully actualized individuality would include these ingredients: (1) producing out of one's own inner consciousness an intuition and feeling of the infinite in the finite (the universe); (2) communicating one's intuition and feeling with others; and (3) understanding the place of religion as a private (differentiating) spiritual function of symbolizing reality that is not confused with science, law, or other spiritual functions. Art, like religion, belongs to the different symbolizing sphere of culture. What role does art play in cultivating one's individuality?

In the third Speech, "On Self-formation (*Bildung*) for Religion," Schleiermacher says, "Religion and art stand beside one another like two friendly souls whose inner affinity, whether or not they equally surmise it, is nevertheless still unknown to them" (*KGA*, 1.2, 263; *OR*, Crouter, 158/69). Schleiermacher recognizes that people with the artistic sense (*Kunstsinn*) can come to intuit and feel the universe through great and sublime works of art, but he professes not to understand it himself. For Schleiermacher, art provides a medium of expression for feeling; feeling and intuition can objectify themselves in art. Art, however, is not religion and it cannot replace religion, as was suggested by some of Schleiermacher's audience.

Clearly, for Schleiermacher art is a medium for religious communication, but it is distinct from the substance of religion itself as intuition and feeling of the universe. Art, therefore, plays its appropriate role in culture by evoking and sustaining religious apprehensions.

CONCLUSION

I have posed the question to Schleiermacher, how should religion relate to culture? At Schleiermacher's time, two basic possibilities presented themselves: either one could affirm the claims of positive religion to submit cultural forms to the authority of particular religious belief, or one could support the arguments of natural religion that the culture of universal criticism should curtail the influence of the historical religions. I have argued that in the *Speeches*, Schleiermacher rejects this dilemma. Schleiermacher presents an alternative to the cultured despisers of religion in philosophical theology (or dialectic). Philosophical theology comprehends both positive religion and natural religion better than they do themselves, by understanding the essence of religion as intuition and feeling of the universe. From its self-critical standpoint, philosophical theology rises above and cools the passions on both sides of the dispute between positive religion and natural religion. It sets one free for the truth that is resident in both positive religion and natural religion, while freeing one from their one-sided and false claims. I argue that Schleiermacher's own understanding of Christian revelation is not a necessary condition for his articulation of philosophical theology. Finally, I explain the role of culture in fostering a spirituality that is appropriate to philosophical theology by referring to Schleiermacher's philosophical ethics. The genuinely spiritual person is the one who appropriates the meanings resident in all four cultural spheres from the dialectical standpoint.[14]

Notes

1 Citations to the German text of *Über die Religion: Reden an die Gebildeten unter ihren Verächtern* in *KGA*, I.2 are followed by references to the standard English translation of the first (1799) edition of *On Religion* by Richard Crouter. The first set of page numbers refers to the 1988 first edition of this translation, the second set to the 1996 second edition. All English translations are from Crouter.

2 Tanner 1997, 4.

3 Tanner 1997, 9.

4 Wilhelm von Humboldt, Schleiermacher's colleague at the University of Berlin, is quoted by Gadamer 1975, 11.

5 Gadamer 1975, 13.

6 Rousseau 1983, 231–300, esp. 271–89.

7 Kant 1998, Axi, note.

8 On this point, see Mariña 2004, 125–43. Schleiermacher's brand of experiential expressivism allows him to assert that while all religion must be positive in the sense of being historically situated (hence he eschews the option of "rational religion") all are expressions (varying in regard to their success) of the "inner fire." They are all however, culturally mediated expressions of an original experience, and are, as such, historically conditioned appearances.

9 Plato 1987, 249–55.

10 For a different view of Schleiermacher's understanding of the relationship of philosophical theology to theology, see Eilert Herm's discussion of the topic in chapter 11 on the *Christian Ethics* in this volume. According to Herms, the perspectives philosophical theology and historical theology "arrive at completion only in and through one another."

11 Plato 1987, 263.

12 See Schleiermacher, "Über den Begriff des höchsten Gutes. II," *SW*, III.2, 470–95. For excellent commentary on the fourfold division, see Scholtz 1995, especially chapter 3, "Ethik als Theorie der modernen Kultur. Mit vergleichendem Blick auf Hegel," 35–64. The chart is on p. 36.

13 In the *Monologen* of 1800, Schleiermacher puts it this way: "Each man is meant to represent humanity in his own way, combining its elements uniquely, so that it may reveal itself in every mode, and all that can issue from its womb be made actual in the fullness of unending space and time" (*KGA*, I.3, 18; translation in Schleiermacher, *Soliloquies*, trans. Friess, 31.

14 I would like to thank Gary Bailey for helpful comments about this chapter and for a long-standing critical conversation about Schleiermacher's thought.

14 Schleiermacher and the state[1]

THEODORE VIAL

INTRODUCTION

On Christmas Day 1808 Friedrich Schleiermacher looked forward to his appointment as pastor of Trinity Church in Berlin, a chair in theology when the new University of Berlin opened, and his wedding. He wrote to his fiancée, "If I also came into any activity on behalf of the state, even if merely temporary, then I would really not know how to wish for more."[2] Schleiermacher's personal correspondence and journals are full of references to the importance for him of the state, Prussia, Germany, and politics. Wilhelm Dilthey writes of Schleiermacher, "he belongs to those great men who first found a way from their private circumstances to live for the state without an official position, without ambition for political adventure, in the sure self-confidence of the citizen. Without this self-confidence life does not appear to us to be worth living any more. And yet it is not more than a half century since these men struggled and acquired it."[3] Through his academic lectures and his sermons he became what we might call today a public intellectual. Schleiermacher lived in the era of the construction of the modern nation. To discuss Schleiermacher and the state means to go beyond Schleiermacher on church–state relations, and beyond the political context and implications of his theology. It means also to take up his role in envisioning a modern Prussia and a modern Germany.[4]

Schleiermacher served Prussia directly in many capacities beyond his posts as professor and pastor (both of which were state positions). From 1808 to 1810 he was director of the Berlin Academic Deputation. In 1809 he began working under the minister of education Wilhelm von Humboldt to organize the new University of Berlin. He served as dean of the theological faculty four times (1810–11, 1813–14, 1817–18, 1819–20) and as rector of the university in 1815–16. The last five years of his life he served on Berlin's Poverty Directorate (*Armendirektion*). Furthermore, Schleiermacher lectured on "The Theory of the State" ("Die Lehre vom Staat") six times: 1808–9 (a subscription series in Berlin), and 1813, 1817, 1817–18, 1829, and 1833 (courses at the University of Berlin). He also presented two lectures on the state to the Royal Academy of Sciences in Berlin in 1814.

But Schleiermacher's interactions with and contributions to Prussia and Germany extend beyond official service and lectures. In the first two sections I will set the context in which his thought and activity took place, and show the theological and philosophical principles that underlie and tie together his very diverse activities. In the third section I discuss Schleiermacher's active participation in a subversive plot to stage a popular uprising against the French armies that occupied Prussia in the years 1806–13. The fourth section takes up a series of influential political sermons he preached during these years. These sermons led Dilthey to call him the greatest political preacher in Germany since Luther. The fifth section covers Schleiermacher's editorship of a political newspaper, the *Prussian Correspondent* (*Der Preussische Correspondent*) in the pivotal year 1813. In the sixth section I discuss Schleiermacher's activities on behalf of the church governance in Prussia, working sometimes with and sometimes against King Friedrich Wilhelm III (ruled 1797–1840) to unify Prussia's Reformed and Lutheran churches.

SETTING

Prussia remained neutral in European imperial struggles leading up to 1806. Napoleon's increasing demands on Prussia finally prompted Friedrich Wilhelm III to send his troops out against the French. On October 14, 1806, Napoleon and his troops crushed the famous Prussian armies in battles at Jena and Auerstadt. Prussia held on to only four provinces, all occupied by French troops, and agreed to pay huge reparations to France. The king and his court left Berlin and took up residence in Königsberg, the farthest point east in Prussia.

French troops occupied Halle, where Schleiermacher was a professor at the university, on October 17, 1806. Napoleon closed down the university on October 20. When Napoleon made Halle part of the kingdom of Westphalia, ruled by his brother Jerome, Schleiermacher left for Berlin. On December 31, 1807 he wrote to Charlotte von Kathen, "I cannot accommodate myself to this government and must live under a German prince, so long as there is one."[5]

A movement to reform Prussia gathered momentum. Karl Freiherr vom Stein, chief minister to the king, was the central figure.[6] He fought to modernize and rationalize Prussia's government and took steps to develop a culture of political participation in Prussia, to move from a model of subject to that of citizen. Stein took steps to abolish hereditary serfdom and to open the military's officers' corps to men of merit from all social classes. He created provincial legislative bodies. Stein's hope for these was "the animation of the common spirit and sense of citizenship, making use of the sleeping or misguided powers and scattered knowledge, the accord between the spirit of the nation, the reanimation of the feeling for the Fatherland, independence and national honor."[7] He wanted all classes of Germans, even those who traditionally did not bear responsibility for government or the army, to be willing and able to take a hand in the defense of Prussia against the French.

The defeat of Napoleon at Leipzig in 1813 and the king's adoption of reforming rhetoric in establishing an army and declaring war were the high points of the reform movement. The king had twice promised a constitution to Prussians. But with Napoleon's defeat the major pressures for reform disappeared. The king became an enthusiastic supporter of the Karlsbad Decrees, formulated by Metternich in August 1819. These decrees called for close supervision of universities so that professors could not spread "harmful ideas which would subvert public peace and order and undermine the foundations of the existing states."[8] During this time Schleiermacher frequently had undercover police attending his lectures and sermons.

LINK TO THEOLOGY

For Schleiermacher, dogmatic theology is a description of the redemptive experience of Christians in particular communities. One fails to understand Schleiermacher's theology if one overlooks its relationship to his political community. The "Introduction" to the *Christian Faith* outlines his theory of what a community is, and what sets the Christian community off from any other.

Individuals both act on the world and are acted on by the world. "Thus in every self-consciousness there are two elements, a – so to say – self positing, and a not-from-self-posited" (*CF*, § 4.1).[9] We act on and are acted upon by the various communities in which we find ourselves. Schleiermacher identifies the family, the church, and the state as the most important of these. He explicitly rejects the idea of the origin of communities as a kind of social contract between rational individuals. The basic unit that creates any community is not the individual but the household. "[T]he state is a community, but not the original community, rather it presupposes a few already; that is a multitude of individual humans, by which we must take notice of that which nature has set apart and bound together, and that is the two sexes. Without them there is no state because a state presupposes a succession of generations."[10] There is no form of social organization without the household that produces generations of humans.

Larger communities are formed from households, either linked genea-logically (tribes) or accidentally. In both cases, "there must the people live together, and finally get along; have a language and also conduct a common way of living."[11] Households that live together in close proximity will eventually forge a common way of living and a common language because of the reciprocity that defines human consciousness.

The process by which humans communicate and influence one another is described in Schleiermacher's hermeneutics. Each individual speech act is a combination of a common language and the particular personality of the speaker. Of course the totality of language on which we must rely to under-stand one another and so forge a common life is made up entirely of just such individual utterances.[12] So the style of each individual's speech, shaped by her or his personality, in turn shapes the very language in which we ourselves have ideas and try to express them. Others with whom we are in contact influence us, and we in turn exert an influence on them, and after a period of interaction a common life and language begin to take shape.

A conglomeration of households with similar customs (*Sitte*) and lan-guage is not yet a state. Schleiermacher defines a state as "the opposition of authority and subject."[13] The limiting cases are anarchy and despotism. In a state of anarchy there is no such distinction of authority and subject. But neither is there in the master–slave relationship of despotism, for the slave is not a subject; the will is located entirely in the master. There is no reciprocity; the slave is treated not as a human subject but as a machine.[14]

Groups do not establish an authority to facilitate working together, since working together precedes the state and in fact is its presupposition. Nor can it be for common defense. In that case states would disband when a given threat passed. States do facilitate working together, and they do provide defense, but neither activity gives rise to states.[15] Rather, "history gives evidence that humans cannot go beyond a certain point of develop-ment without building a state. Thence it is also clear as day that progress in the pre-state condition in contrast to a situation with a state was exponen-tially smaller." A state, for Schleiermacher, is a healthy development of a social organism that occurs when that organism establishes laws that sanction and express its customs. It furthers the ends of that organism and helps express that organism's individual personality.[16]

Schleiermacher's view of the state is in stark contrast to the dominant Enlightenment view of the state as machine, a view that leads to the principle that "that government is best which governs least" (Thomas Paine). For Schleiermacher it would be "one-sided" to wish for the day when the state was no longer necessary because the state is not a necessary evil but represents the completion (*Vollendung*) of human life and the maximum of the good.[17] In fact Schleiermacher blames this Enlightenment view as one of the factors in Prussia's defeat, since it caused detachment in individuals from their national community.

Schleiermacher's theory of the state is intimately connected to his Christology. In the wake of the Enlightenment, models for understanding the redemptive work of Christ seemed limited to irrational supernaturalism (what Schleiermacher calls "magical") or the deistic view that Jesus was no more than a great teacher and moral exemplar (what Schleiermacher calls "empirical"). Schleiermacher proposed a third model. He argued that any community, from a family to a nation, formed around the distinctive personality of its founders. When someone has had a particularly profound idea or experience, he or she is driven to share it. "[H]e should express and communicate everything that is in him, and the more vehemently something moves him, the more intimately it penetrates, the stronger is the drive to look upon the power of the same outside himself in others" (*Über die Religion; KGA*, I.2, 267).

Because religion is an intuition of the infinite, people who have had a profound religious experience are driven not only to tell others, but also to listen to what others have experienced. Religion naturally forms social groups. "They are conscious of encompassing only a small part of it, and that which they cannot reach directly they will at least perceive through a foreign medium. Therefore he is interested in each expression of the same, and seeking to supplement himself he listens intently to every sound that he perceives of it [of such an expression]" (*Über die Religion, KGA*, I.2, 268). It follows that one's highest religious duty is to cultivate one's individuality. "Each person should represent humanity in his own way, in a singular mixture of its elements, so that it reveals itself in each way, and everything that can come forth out of its womb can become real in the fullness of infinity" (*Monologen, KGA*, I.3, 18).

The exchange of experiences in these groups will not leave the participants unchanged. "So feeling ... is not exclusively for oneself, but becomes external originally and without definite intention or reference through facial expression, gesture, tone, and indirectly through speech, and so becomes to others a revelation of the inner. This mere expression of feeling ... passes over ... into lively imitation, and the more the perceiver ... is able to pass over into the same state, the more easily will this state be brought forth through the imitation" (*CF*, § 6.2). One expresses feelings in speech, gesture, and expression, and these are then imitated by, taken up into the personalities of, those with whom one comes into contact.

This is why groups of households thrown together eventually forge a common life and language.

The Christian church is the community that gathered around and was shaped by the personality of Jesus. What made Jesus' personality so compelling was "the constant strength of his God-consciousness" (*CF*, § 94). His followers gradually imitated his words and thoughts, his very gestures and expressions. And these in turn were adopted by later members of the community. In the conversations, mutual influence, and gestures of the members of that community, the effects of Christ's personality are still present. In joining a church, then, one is confronted in a very real sense by the personality of Jesus, by the strength of his God-consciousness, and it is this experience that is redemptive.

Note that this model of the redemptive work of Christ does not require the violation of any laws of nature, yet it does not reduce Jesus to merely an important teacher or example. *More importantly, this model presupposes specific views of what communities are and how they function.* The requirement that each develop in his or her own way places certain requirements on a healthy community. Schleiermacher writes, "[E]ach should grant to the other the freedom to go where the spirit drives him or her ... In this way each would find in the other life and nourishment" (*Monologen, KGA,* I.3, 32). Restrictions on the self-expression of individuals in any community, whether a church or a nation, tend towards despotism. If the interactions of a community's members are externally constrained, they will not pass along their words, gestures, and expressions in unmutilated form.

In explaining the redemptive work of Christ, Schleiermacher uses an analogy that makes the link between the church and national states.

> Let us now suppose the case that a group that naturally belongs together is united into a civil society by an individual. ... So in this one the idea of the state first comes to consciousness, and this idea takes possession of his personality as its direct dwelling place. He then takes up the rest of the community into the life of this idea by bringing them to clear awareness of the unsatisfactory nature of their condition up to now, through his effective proclamation. In the founder the power of the idea establishes itself to form in them the idea that is his innermost living principle and to take them up into the community of this life. By means of this not only does a new common life come into being among them in complete contrast to the earlier common life, but also each becomes for him or herself a new person, that is, a citizen.
>
> (*CF*, § 100.3)

The link between Schleiermacher's Christology and his political thought and activity lies in the necessary conditions for communities (families, churches, nations). Healthy communities provide an arena for free mutual interaction. These interactions result in a common life, which the community then tries to further. Anything that begins to constrain the free expression of individuals and their impact on each other skews these interactions. In the sphere of the church it is the very presence of Christ and the possibility of his redeeming activity that is at stake. In the civic sphere it is the common way of life and modes of thought that are the source of strength of the people. The program of the reformers and Schleiermacher's Christology share this same view.

Schleiermacher played a significant role in German political history for being one of the most public of intellectuals in his calls for a modern nation made up of participating citizens under a constitutional monarchy rather than passive subjects under an aristocracy. The theological roots of his "imagining" of a modern Prussia and Germany must lead us to refine current scholarly assumptions about religion, secularization, and modern nations.

CONSPIRACY

In April and May of 1808 secret societies began to organize a popular uprising against the French. Schleiermacher became involved with the Berlin group, and undertook a mission for them in August and September 1808. Apparently on the theory that a clergyman would raise fewer suspicions, Schleiermacher was sent to Königsberg to make contact with the king and his advisors. Schleiermacher met with the highest members of the king's inner circle, including the queen and crown prince, as well as Stein, general chief of staff Neithardt von Gneisenau, and minister of the war department Gerhard von Scharnhorst. Although he did not have a private meeting with the king, the king did request to hear him preach, which he did on September 4.

Schleiermacher had worked out a complicated system of codes for protecting information he sent back to Berlin.[18] The system proved too cumbersome. Schleiermacher's friends in Berlin wrote to him after receiving his first letter dated August 30, "The exemplariness of your letter did not want to shine on any of us, at least it suffered from the consequences of immoderation."[19] The conspirators then apparently tried invisible ink with no better results.

This was not the only occasion on which Schleiermacher tried to play a direct role in some sort of military action. In 1813–14 Schleiermacher tried through various channels to get an appointment as field preacher to the military (his applications were never successful), and he drilled with the Berlin militia (*Landsturm*).

Such activity is not unexpected given his political thought. If the key to a healthy civil (as well as ecclesiastical) community is the free and active interaction of all its members, then the prescription for Prussia's ills was to get the vast majority of Prussian subjects, accustomed to centuries of passively accepting the rule of an aristocratic elite, to become active citizens. Schleiermacher and the other reformers saw a popular uprising and a citizen army as far more than a way to gather enough troops to confront the huge French army. The real value would be to enfranchise the Prussian masses, who had up to this time been excluded from any important role in what traditionally was Prussia's most important institution, the army. Napoleon's occupation, while clearly an undesirable burden, also offered an opportunity to rethink the nature of political participation in Prussia, to make it a modern constitutional monarchy.

POLITICAL SERMONS

Schleiermacher's greatest contribution to the resistance against the French was his preaching. Under French occupation political assemblies were banned and the press was heavily censored. Worship services, however, continued.

In general Schleiermacher thought that politics did not belong in the pulpit. But in unusual circumstances, to ignore major disturbances means that worshipers would not find the peace they sought, the elevation of piety, which is the goal of Christian worship.[20] Napoleon's occupation of Prussia was a major disturbance. "[T]hrough an unusual occurrence we find our series of talks on the suffering redeemer interrupted, and our gathering today dedicated to a completely different subject. How we all were moved to the core through the events of last week!"[21]

In these sermons one can see the full range of Schleiermacher's political thought, presented in a popular way designed to move the Prussian and German people in the direction of resistance and reform. Schleiermacher saw in Prussia's disaster an opportunity for his congregation to reflect on the true state of their faith. If one's love for God, strong in good times, becomes limited in hard times, then this is not love for God but love for the world.[22]

One thing we have learned, Schleiermacher argued, is the close connection between the character of a people and the character of its leaders. "The whole and the part had one life, one destiny – also the same virtue and ethos." "Many say, it is not my mistake [referring to the disaster at Jena and Auerstadt], but the generals, or the soldiers, or those who hold the reigns of power. This is to make a new mistake, to make a sharp distinction between the individual and the whole." The sins of the leaders are the sins of the people: "Where fearlessness and contempt for danger, love of order and faithful obedience are the character of the members of a people, their lack of courage and independence cannot reveal themselves in great quantities, when only through the former virtues can the community be saved" (*SW*, II.I, 251–2).

I want to focus on two sermons that specifically address the Christian roots of the political reform program. On August 24, 1806 (roughly two months before Jena and Auerstadt) Schleiermacher preached a sermon in Halle entitled, "How Greatly the Dignity of a Person is Enhanced when One Adheres with all One's Soul to the Civil Union to which One Belongs."[23] Schleiermacher warned of the danger of the lack of public spirit, "in which there is no lively care for public affairs, no eager taking part in the destiny of the community." The problem stems from the common view that the state is an artificial machine designed to protect the individual in his or her personal activities against external threats and internally from "mistaken inclinations" (*SW*, II.I, 218). From this view love of fatherland seems limiting; it is much better to be a "world citizen."

Schleiermacher, in contrast, argued that Christian faith encourages devotion to the fatherland. He took as his text Ephesians 2:19: "You are no longer guests or aliens, but citizens with the holy and God's fellow tenant." Paul's use of the metaphor of citizen to argue for equality of Jews and gentiles in the church indicates that Paul held citizenship in high esteem (*SW*, II.I, 220).

Schleiermacher argued that states are the organic expression of a people's highest strivings. "When such an institution is founded, it is one of the greatest steps forward possible for our race. Never has culture reached such a high point that such an association is disbanded – they always disband through disturbances" (*SW*, II.I, 221). "Everything great requires a great mass of powers, which humans only have in connection with one another ... Whoever scorns such associations can only accomplish what an individual can accomplish on another individual" (225). "It is not need that binds men but an inner air and love, a given common existence, an indestructible common voice" (232). Because nations offer the chance for the greatest historical advances, he concludes that "[t]hese associations belong to the house of God. It follows that patriotism is good, and those who think it is not for them are like guests or aliens" (222).

Nationalism does make some people xenophobic, "but," Schleiermacher asked, "is this not the imperfection of humans and not the mistake of the thing itself? Do we reckon the failings of love to love itself?" Patriotism should, in contrast, awaken appreciation for other peoples. "He who is not inspired by the determination of his own people cannot know the characteristic calling of other peoples, and cannot take proper pleasure in the greatest achievements of mankind and the correct love towards those who work for these achievements" (*SW*, ii.i, 228).

Schleiermacher explicitly linked his theology to the reformers' vision of Prussia and Germany in a sermon in Berlin on January 24, 1808, the birthday of Friedrich the Great, entitled "On Proper Respect for Civil Greatness from an Earlier Time."[24] Conservatives had argued that it was precisely the modernizing changes since the time of Friedrich the Great that had weakened Prussia. Schleiermacher's text was Matthew 24:1–2, in which Jesus prophesies the destruction of the temple. If the temple is a monument to the greatness of Jesus' people, what can we learn from its destruction? The Jews were wise enough, Schleiermacher argued, to hope not for a return of David, but for a descendent of the same line who belonged to the time in which they had their need (*SW*, ii.i, 356–7). In other words, the messianic hope is not for a return to the past, but for a new greatness that embodies the spirit that made the past great. "Others wish, if not for Friedrich, then to return to the external arrangements and the whole state of an earlier gleaming time, in the belief that in these lived the happy and elevating power ... But there is never a return in human affairs" (358–9).

Schleiermacher argued that Friedrich's greatness was based not merely on his own talent, but on his people's spiritual power and Friedrich's skill in making use of all the sources of knowledge available among his people (*SW*, ii.i, 357). Friedrich extended freedom of faith because he wanted subjects worthy of being ruled (369). When Schleiermacher looked at the history of Friedrich's reign he saw precisely the time when sharp distinctions of rank began to break down, when people won respect not by virtue of birth ("external rank") but "through their mental gifts and ways of thinking." "Further, do not forget that it was a fundamental law of the government of that great king that all citizens were equal before the law, and how loudly he stressed that each individual had worth only insofar as he was obedient and loyal and through his activity worked for the good of the whole" (367).

For Schleiermacher the principle that leads to the formation of healthy and strong nations is the freedom of individuals to cultivate their talents and interact with each other in a way that allows for the formation of a common life from the bottom up. This freedom entails a responsibility, too. Citizens must act not selfishly but for the good of the whole, and further they must exercise their political maturity through active participation.

Schleiermacher attributed Friedrich's greatness to his willingness to put this principle into place. This principle formed the basis of the reform program proposed by Stein and others. Surely, Schleiermacher argued, the renewal of Prussia also lies in these same principles.

THE PRUSSIAN CORRESPONDENT

From July 1 to September 30, 1813 Schleiermacher served as editor of the political newspaper *The Prussian Correspondent* (*Der preussische Correspondent*). Benedict Anderson has called our attention to the role of newspapers in the creation of modern national identities.[25] Schleiermacher's goals as editor were to build national resistance to the French occupiers, and to build a critical public opinion. The hoped-for result was the creation of political citizenship in Germany. Matthias Wolfes has identified three themes that appear in *The Prussian Correspondent* under Schleiermacher's leadership far more than any others.

The subject treated in most detail is the plans to create a militia and reserve army. King Friedrich Wilhelm III had refused to do either, but the events of 1813 largely took the decision out of his hands. On March 17 he issued the address "To My People" ("An Mein Volk") that called for a militia. Orders to form a reserve army followed in April.

The second dominant subject under Schleiermacher's editorship was the attack by the French general Colombe on Lützow's volunteer battalion. When a cease fire with France was signed in 1813, all Prussian troops were to be on the right side of the Elbe by June 12. Lützow was not, but when he met French troops on June 17 he told them that he was trying to get back peacefully. The reported reply of French general Normann was, "the armistice is for everyone but you," whereupon the French opened fire. Schleiermacher used the event to whip up anti-French fervor. In the August 8 issue he reported that Lützow's corps had been re-established stronger than ever, and he interpreted this as an allegory of the rise of Prussia.[26]

The third theme important to Schleiermacher the editor was the French general Moreau. Moreau had helped Napoleon take power, and was a successful and famous general. He was also a staunch republican. This, in addition to his fame, earned him Napoleon's hatred. In the spring of 1813 he accepted an invitation from the Russian emperor to switch sides and fight against Napoleon. On August 10 he entered Berlin as a war hero. Schleiermacher used his joyful reception in Berlin as an example of a good form of nationalism that was not based on hatred of the French (in general

Schleiermacher was always careful to distinguish his own hatred of Napoleon from his admiration for the French people and what they, as a modern nation, had tried to achieve).

Schleiermacher, like all the reformers, was critical of the June 1813 armistice with France. He believed that Prussia could not learn from its past and achieve its full potential without carrying through the war to the very end. On June 11, 1813, King Friedrich Wilhelm III ordered his censors to keep the Berlin newspaper editors on a tight leash. Schleiermacher criticized the armistice in *The Prussian Correspondent* on July 14. He wrote that while some "want to recover from their exhaustion," others "believe that from the results of the war to this point no peace is to be expected . . . and that if such a peace could be concluded between the individual powers, Germany in general and our state in particular require an enormous development of strength, as is only possible under the exertions of war, to arrive at a worthy state out of which health and well-being could develop."[27] The king was infuriated. He read Schleiermacher's piece as, at best, a criticism of his government as weak, at worst as a call for a violent change of government. On July 17 the king issued a cabinet order to the interior ministry to fire Schleiermacher from his state positions (pastor, professor) and banish him from Prussia. The order was watered down by Karl von Hardenberg (Stein's successor as chief minister) before being sent on to minister of the interior Kaspar Friedrich von Schuckmann, who read it as an order to warn Schleiermacher to tread very carefully lest he be faced with these consequences.

Schleiermacher argued to Schuckmann that he was not calling for a violent overthrow but urging that Germany and Prussia could only be unified under Prussia's present government in time of war. Schleiermacher was investigated for high treason in October 1813, but nothing came of the investigation. Schleiermacher turned over the editorship of *The Prussian Correspondent* to Achim von Arnim on October 1, 1813.

CHURCH AND STATE

Prussia was in the unusual position of having a majority of Lutheran inhabitants but a Reformed ruling family (the Hohenzollerns). In 1804 Schleiermacher published an essay in which he argued that the continued separation of the two Protestant confessions in Prussia was harmful. Most subjects no longer knew the dogmatic basis of the separation. The result was a partisan spirit and a clinging to external words and formalities that bred superstition, apathy, and works righteousness.[28] Schleiermacher argued that, rather than splitting the creeds of the two confessions down the middle, it would be enough for them to participate in the Lord's supper together.

These essays earned Schleiermacher a reputation as a proponent of church unification. King Friedrich Wilhelm III, whose wife was Lutheran and with whom he wished to celebrate the Lord's supper, had long had an interest in unifying the two confessions in Prussia. The king created a post for Schleiermacher as the first Reformed theologian and university preacher on the faculty of the Lutheran University of Halle, rather than lose a potential ally in the effort to unify the church to a university in another territory.

Plans for church union were largely put on hold during the French occupation and Wars of Liberation. In 1814 the opportunity arose again. On September 17 the king established a commission to look into unification. We have seen how the king and Schleiermacher eventually fell out over differing political visions for Prussia. Although both worked for the unification of the Protestant confessions, they now worked at cross-purposes. The issues were three: the source of the unifying impetus, the institutional shape of the unified church, and the desirability of a church constitution.

The king's commission defined its task as one of liturgy reform. Schleiermacher attacked the commission, arguing that the commissioners had put the cart before the horse. The problem was that the commission "came together not of itself, by virtue of a divine inner call," "rather was sought after and established by an authority which, though universally honored and also recognized for its pious views, is nevertheless worldly" (*KGA*, I.9, 64). Reform of the liturgy, and church reform in general, should come from an inner impetus from the church community itself, and not be imposed by the worldly authorities external to it. Once again we see the importance for Schleiermacher of the free interaction of individuals as the basis of a healthy community.

Such an internal reform, Schleiermacher believed, should result in an appropriate form of ecclesiastical government. This authority would be grounded in a constitution that protected the church from meddling by the secular government (while the church remained supported financially by that government). The form of the ecclesiastical government would be a synod that included freely elected representatives, both clergy and layperson, from both Reformed and Lutheran congregations (*KGA*, I.9, 107–72). The general mood of the government in the wake of Napoleon's defeat was reactionary. Such an ecclesiastical government smacked too much of popular legislative bodies. The king on April 30, 1815 had issued an order that churches in the Prussian territories should be governed by consistories.

In October 1817 the Berlin churches decided in celebration of the 300th anniversary of the Reformation to have a joint celebration of the Lord's supper. This coincided with a call by the king to unify the confessions. The celebration occurred on October 30 in the Nicolai Church, led by Schleiermacher and his Lutheran friend and colleague Philipp Marheineke. The king was present. This common celebration of the Lord's supper did not, of course, resolve the questions of the form a unified church was to take. Schleiermacher continued to oppose the plans of the government.

The final chapter in Schleiermacher's struggles over the relationship of church and state began in 1821. The king, desiring a liturgical renewal and dismayed at the wide variations in liturgies in Prussia, created his own order of worship (with the help of Job von Witzleben) and sought to impose it on the Prussian church. It was modeled on Luther's service of the mass.

Schleiermacher attacked the new order of worship. He argued that the order of worship was entirely a matter for the congregation to decide, not the external civil authorities. Furthermore, when the order of worship was controversial, to force it onto the church was to oppress the church. "For when a significant part of the clergy must be dismissed to put a liturgy into motion (of which there are examples), then that is already an oppression of the whole church" (*KGA*, I.9, 218 n. 8). Nowak writes, "That was bold. Such a manner of expression could only be used by a man who in the fight over the sovereignty of the liturgy was also leading a fight for the political rights of Christians and citizens."[29]

The king took up the pen personally in 1827 (with co-author Neander) to attack Schleiermacher's essay. He appealed to Luther's authority as the force for liturgical renewal. Schleiermacher's response mocked the new liturgy as a "[c]omposition of a roll of the dice" (*KGA*, I.9, 395), argued that Luther's liturgy was in fact still heavily under the influence of Catholicism, and pointed out the irony of trying to base a Reformed renewal on an appeal to tradition. It is in this essay that Schleiermacher's famous phrase "the Reformation still goes on!" appears (*KGA*, I.9, 471).

In the end the king simply ordered the adoption of his new order of worship in 1829, with only minor compromises. He allowed certain regions to maintain particular liturgical traditions. Schleiermacher was allowed to face the congregation rather than the altar while praying, and was freed from the requirement to make the sign of the cross and to recite the Apostles' Creed. At the end of this long period of struggle with the king there was a reconciliation of sorts, the king awarding Schleiermacher the order of the Red Eagle (third class) in July 1830.

CONCLUSION

Schleiermacher's willingness to battle the king over church–state relations was based on his view that, while the state needed the church and
should support it, the church could only flourish without external interfer-
ence from the state. Why this is the case is clear from his Christology. The
very presence of Christ's personality depends on the ability of individuals in
the church to develop freely and interact without artificial constraints from
the outside.

This is the model of a healthy community that Schleiermacher tried to
promulgate in his sermons during the Napoleonic occupation and Wars of
Liberation. Prussia's weakness stemmed from apathy bred by too little
participation on the part of most social classes, and an Enlightenment
model of the state as a necessary machine on the part of some of the elite.
Prussia's defeat was a providential call to awaken, for all Prussians to take an
active role in their national community. These were the goals of the reform
movement headed by Stein. In other words, Schleiermacher called for
Prussians to become citizens of a modern nation, perhaps even a unified
Germany, rather than subjects. Just as individuals must cultivate their
individuality, so the world needs each nation to develop in its own way.
This is precisely why Schleiermacher saw Napoleon's campaigns as not
merely political crimes, but crimes against God. Some of Germany's greatest
contributions had been religious, and Schleiermacher believed that
Germany still had many contributions to make to the rest of the world
because of the particular spirit or personality that bound its citizens
together. All of Schleiermacher's political activities – lecturing, preaching,
trying to stage a popular uprising, editing a political newspaper, drilling
with the militia, defending the autonomy of the church against the king –
were dedicated to fostering the kind of national community that could play
its role in the providential unfolding of history.

Notes

1 The research for this chapter was funded in part by an Individual Research
   Grant from the American Academy of Religion, and a Faculty Summer
   Development Grant from Virginia Wesleyan College.
2 In *Friedrich Schleiermachers Briefwechsel mit seiner Braut*, 272. All translations
   in this chapter are mine unless otherwise indicated.
3 Dilthey 1960, 1–2.
4 Schleiermacher is one of the first, after the fall of the Holy Roman Empire, to
   envision a unified Germany, on a confederate model. In an 1813 letter to
   Friedrich Schlegel that scholars refer to as his "political credo," he writes,

"My greatest wish after liberation, is for one true German Empire, powerfully representing the entire German folk and territory to the outside world, while internally allowing the various *Länder* and their princes a great deal of freedom to develop and rule according to their own particular needs." Cited in Sheehan 1989, 379.

5 *Aus Schleiermachers Leben. In Briefen.* Band 2, 106, cited in Wolfes 2002, 150. Wolfes' exhaustive work is the most complete and insightful discussion of Schleiermacher's political thought and activity available to date.

6 Among the many links between Schleiermacher and the reformers, one of the most interesting is Stein's January 9 1809 letter to his wife, written as he fled Prussia under sentence of death by Napoleon, who had discovered the plot to organize a popular uprising. In this letter Stein recalled that eight days previously they had read together Schleiermacher's sermon entitled "On What We Should and Should not Fear" (preached New Year's Day 1807 and published in a collection of Schleiermacher's political sermons in February 1808), and that this sermon gave him strength and confidence as he fled. See Wolfes 2002, 162.

7 Karl Freiherr vom und zum Stein, "Über die zweckmässige Bildung der obersten und der Provinzial, Finanz und Polizey Behörden in der Preussischen Monarchie," the so-called "Nassauer Denkschrift," in Stein 1931, vol. II 227.

8 Cited in Sheehan 1989, 408.

9 Translations from the *Christian Faith* are my own.

10 Schleiermacher, "Vorlesungen über Politik gehalten von Schleiermacher im Sommer 1829: Nachschriften von Hess und Willich," in *KGA*, II.8, 499–500. I cite this manuscript as *Die Lehre vom Staat* (HeWi), following the abbreviations of the editor. Schleiermacher's own notes on which his lectures were based I cite simply as Schleiermacher, *Die Lehre vom Staat* (1829).

11 *Die Lehre vom Staat* (HeWi), 515.

12 Schleiermacher, *Hermeneutics and Criticism*, ed. Bowie, 8.

13 *Die Lehre vom Staat* (1829), 69.

14 *Die Lehre vom Staat* (HeWi), 503.

15 *Die Lehre vom Staat* (HeWi), 507–8.

16 *Die Lehre vom Staat* (HeWi), 511, 512.

17 *Die Lehre vom Staat* (HeWi), 509.

18 Raack 1964, 209–23.

19 Letter from Reimer dated September 5, 1806, cited in Raack 1964.

20 Schleiermacher, *Die praktische Theologie nach den Grundsätzen der evangelischen Kirche im Zusammenhange dargestellt*, SW, I.13, 212, 211.

21 Schleiermacher, *Predigten*, SW, II.4, 69–83, preached on March 28, 1813. Sermon title: "For the Benefit of those Mustered for War." On March 17, Friedrich Wilhelm III had ended a long period of wavering and issued a call for troops to join the Russians in attacking Napoleon.

22 Schleiermacher, *Predigten*, SW, II.1, 246–61. From a sermon held in Halle on November 23, 1806 entitled, "On Making Use of Public Disasters," given soon after the enemy had occupied the city of Halle.

23 Schleiermacher, *Predigten*, SW, II.1, 218–33.

24 Schleiermacher, *Predigten*, SW, II.1, 353–70.

25 Anderson 1991.
26 Wolfes 2002, 370–1.
27 Schleiermacher, *Der Preussische Correspondent*, 60 (July 14, 1813), col. 7.
28 In this discussion I follow the section in Nowak 2001, entitled, "Kirchenreform, Reformatsionsjubiläum, Kirchenunion," 356–71. Here see 141.
29 Nowak 2001, 387.

15 Schleiermacher, feminism, and liberation theologies: a key

THANDEKA

To explain the current impasse in scholarship on Schleiermacher and feminism, a key is needed. Contradictory conclusions have hindered the advance of Schleiermacher research in this area. For example, some scholars emphasize Schleiermacher's high valuation of women's moral and religious character and his 1798 "Idee zu einem Katechismus der Vernunft für edle Frauen" (*KGA*, I.2, 153–4).[1] They therefore correctly deem him a friend of contemporary feminist issues.[2] Other scholars point to his stands against the political, educational, and social liberation of women and rightly call him an opponent of women's civil rights.[3] Most accurately, those scholars who realize that his "feminine impulses" and "anti-feminist exclusion of women from public life" are not easily separated wisely call for more research because something seems amiss.[4]

These disparate judgments can be explained by investigating the ideas in Schleiermacher's work on which they are based. Most significant is what Schleiermacher called his "doctrine of the soul,"[5] consisting of his analysis of how the human spirit organizes human feeling and thereby gives rise to human consciousness. Schleiermacher used male and female gender images and concepts to describe this unitive structure of human consciousness. His descriptive and prescriptive use of the same set of terms created a structural confusion in his work. The key to unraveling this structural confusion is found in Schleiermacher's "doctrine of human affections," which included the art of the use of music to stir the affections. In this "doctrine of human affections" Schleiermacher created a set of gender images that moved beyond the restrictive gender biases of his own Prussian, Protestant, religious world.

Schleiermacher, like most eighteenth- and nineteenth-century German pietists, affirmed the division between the civil society (*die bürglicher Gesellschaft*) and the religious community (*die religiöse Gemeinschaft*).[6] Men had an active life outside the family, while women were restricted to family household affairs and were defined by the receptive religious attributes of the laity (*PS*, 400). Schleiermacher affirmed these socially sanctioned patterns and cultural beliefs in his advocacy of educational and civil restrictions on women's activities so that the "natural," "female disposition" of the woman to attend to her household, her marriage, her children, and her religious sentiment could be enhanced rather than "damaged."[7] However, Schleiermacher also described a proto-gender (the original state of the self) that preceded these gender biases.

EXPERIENTIAL ROOTS OF SCHLEIERMACHER'S THEORY

The source of Schleiermacher's theorizing about this "other" gender, which cannot be defined by male and female terms, is found in his own experiences of music and his subsequent theorizing upon these experiences. The roots of his doctrine of the soul and human affections lie here as well. His personal life was deeply enmeshed in music. While he was a theology professor at the University of Halle (1804–6), he spent Thursday and Friday evenings talking about and listening to music at the homes of friends. Here, discussions of music and religion blended together with musical performances.[8] Schleiermacher's vocabulary for music came of age in these settings.[9] In 1805 he had been devastated by the news from Eleanore Grunow that she would not divorce her husband and marry him and it was music that had regenerated him, in particular that of Friedrich Ludwig Dülon, the preeminent flautist of Europe.

In Schleiermacher's time the hope was pervasive that music would regenerate the listener's sentiments, moods, feelings, and dispositions. The art and science of the use of music to stir the affections was called "the doctrine of human affections" (*Affektenlehre*). The term *Affektenlehre* was coined by the German composer Johann Mattheson (1681–1764), who believed that different major and minor scales evoked different affective states within the listener.[10] The basic claim of this doctrine was that music was resonant and thus stirred and altered dispositions.

A grief-stricken Schleiermacher had attended the solo performance of Friedrich Ludwig Dülon on December 2, 1805. The experience was regenerative, and as a result he felt an explosion of creative energy. Three weeks later he sent his *Christmas Eve*[11] dialogue off to his publisher. In his letter of February 6 to Reimer, he remarked upon the relationship between his experience of Dülon's music and his production of the *Christmas Eve* dialogue. The dialogue had something of "an artwork resemblance to it."[12] Schleiermacher deemed that the dialectic form of the work, with its continuous interjections of musical surprise, contrastive narrative and reflective standpoints, taken collectively, was adequately crafted for the expressive, festive, celebratory, and incarnational reality of Christmas among friends and family.[13] Schleiermacher believed that his deadened feelings were re-enlivened through music.

HOW MUSIC MOVES FEELINGS: SCHLEIERMACHER'S DOCTRINE OF HUMAN AFFECTIONS

Schleiermacher, in keeping with his cultural era, believed that music moves human feelings. Music, to use Schleiermacher's term, consists of "moments of affection" (*Affectionsmomente*).[14] These moments are the result of the actual impress of sensations upon the ear and thus within the self. The internal result of the impress of sensations is an affect, a moment of sensible self-consciousness. Music, according to Schleiermacher, is thus quite literally, affect attunement (*Stimmung*). This transformation of physical impulses (sound) into rhythmic feeling (music) is a nonconceptual activity of human consciousness. It is an act of understanding by the human spirit (*Geist*) explained from the standpoint of that which it orders: human affect (*Affekt*).

Accordingly, Schleiermacher analyzed music in order to understand human consciousness from the perspective of physical, organic human experience, that is, human affections. Thus, the first level of his doctrine of the soul consists in Schleiermacher's analysis of how music moves human affections and thereby shifts human consciousness. This foundational stage of his doctrine of the soul can be called his doctrine of human affections because it is an explanation of how music moves human affections. Schleiermacher uses this analysis of human feelings to identify the organic "material" the human spirit mentally organizes through acts of making sense (*Besinnung*) of one's own stirred and agitated affections. This sense-making activity of the human spirit together with the affective "senses" is a moment of human consciousness as a created and creative unity of thoughts and feelings.

A key to Schleiermacher's analysis of human consciousness can thereby be found by focusing on his study of human affections. Basic to this construction is his definition of "affect." This definition is found in his work on aesthetics, rather than in his theological work, because aesthetics, for Schleiermacher, is the study of how the physical movement of human feeling becomes art. Art is the creative external expression of an internal state of human consciousness. Thus theology is a particular study of human consciousness as expressive, creative activity. Theology, in other words, is the study of external human expressions that have emerged from *pious* states of human consciousness.

Schleiermacher's redefinition of "affect"

Schleiermacher used the term "affect" (*Affekt*) to identify the purely physical, emotively empirical, organic condition of a person's spiritual life. By so doing, he created a new vocabulary for Protestant thought, one that could describe the organic material and physical facts of one's own personal and communal spiritual life. The results of his innovative work were two-fold. First, he succeeded in bringing theology back from its rational, "metaphysical wastelands."[15] Second, when he tried to make his discovery the foundation of Christian doctrine and theology, he was roundly condemned as pagan, papist, Gnostic, pantheistic, and self-contradictory.[16]

Schleiermacher began a revolution in nineteenth-century Protestant thought by redefining human consciousness so as to include organic human "affect." His innovative use of this term is best understood by placing the word in its immediate, cultural, and etymological context. This context was created in the seventeenth century when Germans began to use the Latin-based term *affectus*.[17] As Karl Bernecker notes, the terms "affect" (*Affekt*) and the "movement of the disposition" (*Gemütsbewegung*) of a person very quickly became equivalent terms. The German term *Affekt* was used to describe the spiritual condition (*vestige*) of a person. This term, however, was almost never used to describe the physical condition of a person (*körperliche Befinden*). Schleiermacher broke this rule. He moved beyond his own era by using the term "affect" and its related terms "being affected," "affection," a "moment of affection," and "affected" (*Affiziertsein, Affektion, Affectionsmoment, afficiert*) to refer to the physical, empirical, and organic condition of the individual's emotive and spiritual life. Schleiermacher, in short, defined *affect* as a biological fact of the human spirit. To "care for souls," in Schleiermacher's lexicon, meant to attend to their human affections (*CC*, 100).[18] Schleiermacher's innovative, systematic use of the term as a reference to an organic, psycho-spiritual state of human nature not only moved him beyond his own era, but put him on the cutting edge of the field of affective neuroscience that is transforming the way in which the psychological sciences conceive of human experience today.[19]

Schleiermacher described what contemporary terminology would call a "feeling state," a physical disposition of the self that has arisen from the biochemical activation of signal systems that have physiological causes within the human organism.[20] Two centuries ago, Schleiermacher identified human affections as foundational to the organic experiences of internal human, psychological experience.

The musical temperament of human affections

Schleiermacher believed that the movement of affect by music is part of the native constitution of the human being. The human body was constructed in such a way that strong surges of affect must be expressed through bodily movement and gesture (*PT*, 81). As Gunter Scholtz notes, for Schleiermacher the beginning point "is the anthropological fact that the agitated/excited feeling, the affect, will express itself directly in a somatic reaction, in sounds, gestures, and actions."[21] In other words, the human body is anatomically designed so that strong surges of affect produce external physical expressions such as ordered sounds (music), physical gestures such as facial expressions, and bodily motions such as "flight or fight" reactions.

The way the affections are moved depends upon the skill of the musician and the active receptive ability of the listener. Music begins as movements of sounds impressed upon the ear. These movements are ordered internally by the self into measure, rhythm, melody, and harmony and emerge in self-consciousness as the movement of sound, that is, music (*AO*, 179–80). Music, from this perspective, is our own self-conscious awareness of feeling moved. What has been moved within us is *affect*.

We hear one note and then another. To hear them as harmonic or sequential is to combine internally and connect the sounds into melodious tones. This internal activity of combination and connection is the foundation of Schleiermacher's doctrine of human affections. The initial physical, ordering principle is the impress of the sound upon the ear transmitted by the musician. This impress, however, is actively received by the listener. Thus the listener is a creative coordinator of this first movement of raised affection. The listener's affections are moved (impressed upon) and thus moving (expressive).

The original impulse or "affect" is thus not a measured movement. It is sheer agitation (*UK*, 192). Music transforms this agitated state of human affect into a conscious act of creation: art (*UK*, 192). The difference between the original impress and the subsequent expression is the space created by the human spirit, that is, the soul's mental act of understanding the shift in affect that has just occurred. Spirit and affect are thereby linked. The link between the act of understanding and the shift in the affect is, for Schleiermacher, the creation of a conscious moment of awareness, that is, human consciousness. Human consciousness *is* this lived experience. It is the human experience of coherence as a being who both thinks and feels (*UK*, 182). The link *is* the self.

In sum, the difference between initial agitation and the ordered arrangement of affections is the work of the human spirit and human affect.

The difference between the act (of thinking) and the shift (of feelings) is the expanse of human self-consciousness. It is the transition point between a particular act of understanding and a particular shift in affect. This transition, from a purely physical standpoint, is expressed in physical terms. It is, for example, the transition in human consciousness from the awareness of sound to the awareness of a musical note. This transition is a movement of the listener's own physical state of consciousness, a movement of human affections. Human consciousness does this work physically as altered states of human affections.

Schleiermacher's use of gender images and concepts

Schleiermacher used gender images and concepts to describe how human consciousness constructs the harmonic transition from sound to music. Specifically, his first reference to harmony involves the difference between the male and female voice. He thereby used the language of gender to describe the foundation of this movement of human affection. His use of male and female gender terms, as such, was not a foundational aspect of his work. Rather, the terms were descriptive. Accordingly, Schleiermacher's reference to a dimorphic division of human genders into male and female is insufficient to grasp the most elemental structure of his doctrine: the state of the self that precedes the human awareness of gender division and, concomitantly, the awareness of harmony.

The awareness of harmony presupposes the awareness of difference or division. This awareness of difference is achieved by comparison. This comparative difference is not the same as the transition point of shifts in human consciousness discussed in the previous section. The shift itself, as noted there, is a *state* of self-consciousness. A comparative awareness of difference is, by contrast, a reflective *act* of understanding.

Thus, the first basis for harmony, Schleiermacher argued, is the reflective awareness of the difference in tone between male and female voices when singing the same note. Our awareness of this difference is the foundational stage of harmony (*AO*, 181). However, the actual difference between the two voices is, itself, neither male nor female. It is neither harmonic nor disharmonic. Rather, the distinction is the space of difference between the two voices that links them together as a unitive experience. This link, as noted above, is the self.

The original human gender: "artist"

Schleiermacher gave this difference between male and female genders a gender of its own. He called it "one gender," and named it the "artist."

According to Schleiermacher, "artists are an acutely sensitive gender" ("die Künstler überhaupt, ein reizbares Geschlecht sind": *UK*, 223). They respond immediately to what is going on around them. This one gender, Schleiermacher argued, is the original state of the self (psyche or soul) before it is split into male and female genders.

Music, Schleiermacher concluded, enables each person to become whole again through an experience of the person's original gender, which is neither male nor female nor androgynous (since the use of these gender, dimorphic terms represents the split self and thus cannot be used to define the self before it is split). In this moment of musical creation, the gender of the self is one.

According to Schleiermacher, every human being is an artist because our very being, like the rest of the natural world, is an act of divine creation by the first artist (God). Therefore, our original gender is "one" with all creation. Experience of the unity of the self, from this perspective, is a mystical moment. Here the self at one with all of life is an act of divine creation. The rediscovery of the soul's original gender is the regeneration of the self and thus, for Schleiermacher, is quite literally an act of divine creativity. When Schleiermacher listened to music, he believed that he was moved rhapsodically into the place within himself that was neither male nor female but was the place where they are originally one. Listening to music, for Schleiermacher, meant feeling the movement of his own affections at one with life itself, before they are sorted and ordered into discrete thoughts.

Schleiermacher's way of listening to music was described by one of his friends as "sinking" into the musical tones. Schleiermacher would then "awaken" during the breaks in the musical performance and describe his experience of music rather than offer "learned discourse" about music.[22] Schleiermacher, when in this state, described his feelings rather than critiqued them. He felt himself to be an artistic creation at the moment of its birth.

Schleiermacher described this life-sustaining and creative moment in the first edition of his *Speeches on Religion* as the "natal hour of everything living in religion" (*KGA*, I.12, 90; *OR*, Crouter, 113). The unity of mind and body, understanding and affections, were quite literally for Schleiermacher the "holy essence" of the universe. Here Schleiermacher used male/female, dimorphic gender images to describe rather than define the unitive state of the one human gender. He used male and female images of sexual play and intercourse to describe the experience of the one artistic gender of creativity at the moment of its creation. This moment, however, is fleeting:

With the slightest trembling the holy embrace is dispersed, and now for the first time the intuition [*Anschauung*] stands before me as a separate form; I survey it, and it mirrors itself in my open soul like the image of the vanishing beloved in the awakened eye of a youth; now for the first time the feeling [*Gefühl*] works its way up from inside and diffuses itself like the blush of shame and desire on his cheek. This moment is the highest flowering of religion. (*KGA*, I.12, 89–90; *OR*, Crouter, 113)

When the original unity is sundered, human experience is split. A purely mental form of awareness (*Anschauung*) and a purely internal feeling of awareness (*Gefühl*) appear. The human spirit is thus split into a mental form and an affective form. The content of the unitive experience is originally empty of thoughts and images (*Anschauung*). It is, rather, filled with feeling that is the receptivity of the self to life itself, without any affective determination defined (*Gefühl*). But this moment splinters into: (1) a mental form distinct from the entirety of its feeling-based content; and (2) a moment of raised affect, which must be determined, ordered and arranged by pious feelings.

From this sundered unity, a blush or some other facial expression or bodily gesture necessarily appears as the organic, external, affect-based expression of the prior moment of union. A mental form also must appear. The initial content of this form is images and then concepts as the re-presentation (*Vorstellung*)[23] of a unitive event that has just occurred but is now gone. These two splintered forms are now defined, rather than described, by Schleiermacher's male/female gender terms. It is here, with this shift from the state of wholeness to the state of a split consciousness that the confusion in Schleiermacher's use of gender terms begins. Schleiermacher now uses reason (images and concepts) to define the content of the male and female gender terms of split consciousness. Reason thus replaces affect as the actual content of the gender experiences he describes. By so doing, the original gender of self-consciousness is elided. The space of genuine difference is omitted. Schleiermacher's use of male/female gender terms becomes prescriptive rather than descriptive.

SCHLEIERMACHER'S THEOLOGICAL DOCTRINE OF THE SOUL

The shift from description to prescription marks Schleiermacher's mature theological enterprise. Schleiermacher's Christology, as explained in the *Christian Faith*, is thus the most abstract aspect of his doctrine of the human soul, and is generally known and studied as his theology of redemption wrought by Christ. He uses concepts, definitions, and their logical relations to make his points. Gender terms do not define his theology. Rather, they simply exemplify what the male element in the split in consciousness (from Schleiermacher's perspective) does when left to its own structures: it reasons.

Schleiermacher's Christology thus consists of propositions and claims rationally presented and argued. He readily acknowledges the impossibility of proving experientially that his theological claims are correct. In this realm of human experience, he says, there is no mathematical proof to demonstrate that things must be so and not otherwise (*CF* [1830], § 100.3). The only test, Schleiermacher concludes, is personal experience. And so he calls upon his readers to examine the structure of their own piety, that is, their own "immediate self-consciousness." They must use this self-evidence, Schleiermacher insists, to determine the veracity of his claims. They must find the affective (female) side of pious experience in order to complete, through description, his (male) definitional claims.

Accordingly, in the *Christian Faith*, Schleiermacher shows that the penetrating presence of Christ in human nature is a creative act. However, the most concrete context for his analysis of Christ's activity as *creative*, and its relationship to human feelings, is his doctrine of human affections. But this embodied, non-cognitive, unmediated, affective context is absent in his theological work. This is the case because feeling's native expression is movement and gesture, rather than speech (*PT*, 81).

Instead, in his theological work Schleiermacher elaborates in conceptual terms the affective experiences the concepts presuppose: Christian pious affections. He uses logic to make points about the redemptive activity of Christ. For instance, one of his arguments can be reconstructed in the following way:

Premise One: If in the formation of the Redeemer's Person the only active power was the creative divine activity, which established itself as the being of God in Him, then also His every activity may be regarded as a continuation of that person-forming divine influence upon human nature.

Premise Two: The only active principle is the creative divine activity.

Conclusion: Christ's every activity may be regarded as a continuation of this person-forming divine activity.

As a correlate to this argument, Schleiermacher can claim that the "penetrating" activity of Christ cannot establish itself in an individual without becoming person-forming in him (*CF* [1830], § 100.2). This means that all of the activities of Christ are first determined in and as human affections. Thus when Christ has penetrated human affections and become their vital principle "all impressions are differently received – which means that the personal self-consciousness too becomes altogether different."

Christ's activity is thus known through the human dispositions. Christ, Schleiermacher concludes, reconciles the disparate parts of a person so that they act in tandem as one harmonious whole. Christ is the condition of the union. He is its ground. How is His presence known? It is felt as the wholeness of the self. His presence is known through the sustained feeling of wholeness that is expressed and experienced as the music, facial expressions, gestures and tones of a religious community (*CF* [1830], § 101).

Schleiermacher's theological definition of imaginative improvisation (*Fantasie*)

The rational complement to Schleiermacher's theological reasoning is his imaginative theological improvisation. This is the case because imaginative improvisation (*Fantasie*) is the first cognitive expression of the way in which human affection has been altered. Imaginativeness is concrete thinking, a schematization of human consciousness (*UK*, 208–9). The imaginative expressions are imaginative movements of sustained human consciousness, measured, ordered, and displayed. They are the mental expressions closest to the experience of altered human affections. They are affect-near. Concepts, by contrast, are affect-distant.

Schleiermacher's theological fantasies will thus be closer to female rather than male gender-defined images. This is the case because imaginativeness, for Schleiermacher, is always accompanied by affection. Schleiermacher called this link between feeling and imaginativeness their "living association" ("lebendigen Zusammenhang"). The link itself is their-attunement one to the other. Feeling and imaginativeness are thus the multiple sides of a moment of sensitive self-consciousness. Their interplay creates the moment of lived experience as a sustained moment of affection. Each act of imagination is an expression of a discrete aspect of the sensate moment that had been mentally grasped and elaborated. Schleiermacher, we might say, uses the term *Fantasie* (imaginativity) as concrete theological thinking.

Accordingly, Schleiermacher composed his sermons as acts of imagination. They are vivid displays of concrete, affective thinking. A fine account of his multi-perspectival, improvisational sermonic style is presented in the personal reflections of one of Schleiermacher's closest friends in Halle, Henrik Steffens. Steffens, Schleiermacher, and two of their friends went on a weekend excursion that ended just in time for Schleiermacher to deliver a Sunday morning oration in honor of the memory of the queen. The friends awakened "after a few hours sleep, and still had a walk of a mile and a half before us." Schleiermacher walked in front of his friends, who "perceived that, in spite of his swift pace, he was sunk in deep mediation." They did not disturb him. Steffens describes what happened when they arrived at church:

> Schleiermacher went up into the pulpit . . . His discourse gave evidence of the careful artistic arrangement of all the parts, which was his distinguishing characteristic as a preacher . . . The idea that he who had delivered extemporaneously, and with perfect self-confidence, so well-digested, artistically arranged, and lucid a discourse, could have spent the preceding hours in frivolous and dissipated frolic, must have appeared to all as perfectly absurd.[24]

This description and the extended passage that follows it touch on three factors at play in Schleiermacher's artistic creations as preacher. First, spontaneous invention: Schleiermacher delivered his sermon extemporaneously. This was his standard style for sermons. Second, multi-perspectivalism: Schleiermacher's delivery displayed multiple perspectives and diverse ideas. Third, friendship and its immediate religious context: what goes on between friends is the place where regeneration begins and redemption occurs.

SCHLEIERMACHER'S PIOUS *FANTASIE* OF GENDERED IMAGES AND CONCEPTS IN THE *CHRISTMAS EVE* DIALOGUE

Schleiermacher sustained the affections regenerated by Dülon's concert by determining them piously as images (*CF* [1830], § 3.4). The *Christmas Eve* dialogue is a sustained, sermonic, imaginative, improvisational act. It predominantly consists of mental constructions linked to pious affections that are displayed (images) from multiple perspectives. His *Christmas Eve* dialogue is his most concrete expression of his Christology since it is an improvisational orchestration of the vast array of his pious affections ordered and sustained as images. The human soul is displayed as the back-and-forth movement between pious affections (female) and pious reflections (male). The soul is neither the affections nor the reflections. The "plotline" thus becomes that of determining who can give and be the closest approximation of the wholeness of the human soul. The soul in the narrative is split because it is represented as male and female. The representations thus refer to something that they themselves are not: the unitive experience of the human soul, which all images and concepts presuppose.

The women and men speak their native gender tongues as seemingly split selves: images (female) and abstract concepts (male). The highest value is given to the pious affections (female) and any move away from them (male) will create an awareness of the need to return to them. Friedericke plays the piano, sings lyrics from the poems of romantic poets, and improvises melodies to accompany or as interlude to the conversation among the friends. Sophie also plays and sings. The host explains the link between music and religious feeling, saying "every fine feeling comes completely to the fore only when we have found the right musical expression for it." And further, "it is precisely to religious feeling that music is most closely related . . . What the word has declared the tones of music must make alive, in harmony conveying it to the whole inner being of its hearers and holding it fast there" (ChrEve, 46).

The second level of the play is images, the first mental expression of human affections religiously configured. Accordingly, Schleiermacher's women provide the group with the definitive content of the imagination. Ernestine describes a lady, seated on a church pew, as she and a small child peer into each other's eyes, transfixed. Although she could see the disposition of the mother shift, what was communicated throughout was "a sense of affable serenity" (ChrEve, 58). Agnes describes the image of an infant who was not interested in his Christmas gifts because he was "still completely oriented toward his mother . . . His consciousness [was] still united to hers." Only she "could cherish and gladden it" (ChrEve, 61). Karoline describes an infant who lay dying in his mother arms but gains new life after all had lost hope. The mother thus feels blessed twice because a special gift of grace had given her two heavenly children: her son and the Christ child. The dominant image throughout the stories and comments by the women is that they are closer to Christ than men because women have never broken the continuity of childhood within them. Like Christ, they are not in need of conversion because they never broke away from the divine human nature. Their affections, we would say, have not been split.

Next come the concepts. Leonhardt, the rationalist, affirms Christianity as a "vigorous social force," locates its meaning in symbolic expressions of God's eternal decree rather than in a historical Jesus, and deems the main object of Christmas celebration to be children (ChrEve, 71–5). Ernst believes that Christmas represents the mood that the festival is designed to incite: joy

(*ChrEve*, 77). The cause of this joy is the redeemer, because "there is no other principle of joy than redemption." The festival makes persons conscious of "an inner ground out of which a new, untrammeled life emerges" (*ChrEve*, 79).

The final speaker is Josef, who arrived while the men were speaking. He pronounces the men's speeches tedious, cold, and joyless: in short, affection-less. Christmas, he confesses, creates within him a "speechless joy, and [he] cannot but laugh and exult like a child." All human beings are children for him on this day, "and all the dearer on that account." He confesses that he has become "just like a child again" (*ChrEve*, 85). The pain from Schleiermacher's own broken relationship with Eleanore Grunow is expressed in Josef's confession that Christmas joy does not cancel his pain. Josef's confession of speechless joy in the midst of a non-cancelable pain is in keeping with Schleiermacher's statement to his friend Georg Reimer on December 21, four days before he completed his manuscript: "What I must give up, as Eleanore must, is marriage, the forming of a wholly undivided life ... Thus I cannot but keep on saying that I shudder at my life as before an open wound that cannot be healed, but peace dwells within my heart, dear friend, whole and unalloyed – a peace which, wherever it comes, is by its very nature eternal and cannot wither away."[25]

Schleiermacher had discovered a way to have, affirm, and sustain joy in the midst of his own non-cancelable pain. His affections, which were initially moved by Dülon's musical fantasies, are now sustained (in the mental "fantasies") by images of women and Christ. The structure of Schleiermacher's peace of mind is thus linked to these images, which he has reproduced in *Christmas Eve*. He makes its images definitive, concrete facts of human experiences.

THE KEY

The key to Schleiermacher's use of male and female gender concepts and images is his understanding of consciousness as split. This way of reading Schleiermacher focuses attention on his use of male and female images and concepts: (1) to describe what has been lost: the sustained and sustaining human experience of wholeness; and (2) to define what remains: sundered, gendered souls.

This decoding process reveals a paradox in Schleiermacher's use of male and female gender terms: his use of these terms reifies the split in human consciousness that they are designed to resolve. In other words, the original gender "artist" in Schleiermacher's analysis of human consciousness is not and cannot be defined by a split, dimorphic consciousness that uses the terms of its schism to define its wholeness. Three results follow from this way of decoding Schleiermacher's analysis of human consciousness:

(1) Schleiermacher's analyses and discussions of male and female human experiences will always express only a part of the human experience of wholeness.

(2) In Schleiermacher's conceptual scheme, it is impossible to be a male or female human being and be complete without reference to the opposite gender.

(3) Autonomous gender experiences are impossible in Schleiermacher's practical scheme of things because male and female experiences, in their own respective terms, are states of split consciousness: Man cannot be complete alone; Woman cannot be complete alone. Each requires the other for completeness.

Scholars in the field of Schleiermacher and feminist studies thus determine Schleiermacher's value for contemporary feminist issues and concerns based on whether these investigators focus on

(1) the equality of functions Schleiermacher establishes between the male and female genders;

(2) the unitive experience of wholeness (and the female as closer to this unitive experience than the male);

(3) his reification of these gendered distinctions as a split consciousness that reduces the other (female) to terms that complement and complete male deficiencies.

Using this key, readers in Schleiermacher and feminism studies can sort through the plethora of claims and order them. In what follows I discuss two of these claims. In each discussion, I focus on the author's evaluation of *Christmas Eve* and conclude with references to wider perspectives broadening the discussion

In her book *The Feminine Soul*, Marilyn Massey assesses Schleiermacher's use of gendered images and concepts and his ideas about women's civil rights from the standpoint of principle (3): his reification of gendered distinctions for male benefit. Massey can thus conclude that Schleiermacher granted women a special function in religion for the benefit of male autonomy.[26] She carefully identifies the nineteenth-century gender coding Schleiermacher uses to describe the women in his play. Massey draws on ample evidence from Schleiermacher's own views to support her claims.

Massey's own standpoint is clear. She seeks to give women a special status by giving them the superior soul. She thus rejects Schleiermacher's fundamental claim that humanity, when whole, is one gender. The major problem with Massey's critique of Schleiermacher is her own agenda: she strives to prove the feminine soul superior to the male soul. She has written her book to affirm "the unique spiritual qualities" of women as superior to those of the male soul and salvific for the world.[27] Massey thus commits the same fallacy for which she indicts Schleiermacher: gender superiority. The core level of the error for both Massey and Schleiermacher, however, is not gendered arrogance but a constricted cultural imagination. Their work displays "a presumed natural law of dimorphism, encoded in cultural reasoning, that assigns all things sexual to biological types, male and female."[28]

Anthropologist Gilbert Herdt, when defining this problem of a presumed ontologically two-valued determination of sexual identity as either male or female, vividly identifies the central problem: culturally defined gender traits are biologized. This is done by *both* Massey and Schleiermacher. Contemporary anthropological fieldwork on sexual cultures around the world challenges this dominant Western bias exemplified by both Massey and Schleiermacher. "Gender-identity development across cultures," Herdt notes, has led anthropologists and social scientists into the area of "fuzzy sex and gender categories of individuals who seemed to be neither clearly male nor female."[29] The solution to Massey's particular "feminist" critique of Schleiermacher is thus not necessarily a "feminist" solution, since feminism is not a univocal perspective on gender-definitions and designations.

In her groundbreaking book, *The Role of Women in the Life and Thought of the Early Schleiermacher (1768–1804)*, Ruth Richardson focuses on principles (1) and (2): the complementary equality of the male and female and the unitive experience of wholeness in Schleiermacher's work. Richardson's work is the "first monograph-length study in any language on gender relations and the role of women in the life and thought of the early Schleiermacher."[30] She demonstrates Schleiermacher's consistent use of gender images and concepts in works written during the same general period in which he wrote *Christmas Eve*: his *Monologen* (*KGA*, 1.3), *Confidential Letters on Friedrich Schlegel's "Lucinde,"* and his *Brouillon on Ethics*.[31] Richardson notes that since in all of these works Schleiermacher

> ardently professes the limitations of gender and the importance of the fusion of the male and female *Geschlechtscharaktere* [gender-based characteristics] (and even their eventual extinction as separate

entities), it would also seem that any interpretation of *Christmas Eve*
that focuses on the women's stories or solely on the men's discourses
would be working at variance with Schleiermacher's own intent. [32]

Richardson thus affirms the position set out in section (2) of our key:
discussions of male or female are not complete without reference to the
opposite gender.

Richardson's review of two centuries of scholarship on Schleiermacher's
Christmas Eve also reveals a stunning fact: a "restrictive focus (on either the
male or female experiences) has characterized the entire history of the
interpretation of *Christmas Eve*, an interpretation that has covered two
centuries and included lengthy analyses by scholars such as Friedrich
Wilhelm Joseph von Schelling, David Friedrich Strauss, Wilhelm Dilthey,
Emmanuel Hirsh, and Karl Barth."[33] Leading Schleiermacher scholars, in
short, have failed to understand the importance of the co-determinate
relationship between male and female gender terms in Schleiermacher's
work. Emphasizing the nonconceptual "single" gender aspects of
Schleiermacher's work, Richardson coins the term "psychological androgyny" to refer to this unitive human experience. Richardson's choice of
the term *androgyny* is, however, unfortunate since it refers to someone
with both male and female sexual organs. Schleiermacher, on the other
hand, refers to the one gender, "artist," as someone who is not defined by the
male/female split. Schleiermacher does not use male and female terms to
define this one gender.

Richardson makes this misstep in terminology by overlooking
Schleiermacher's own language of music and logic. Schleiermacher
believed that language has two sides, which he referred to as the logical
side and the musical side of language (*UK*, 208–9). Richardson, instead,
makes gender as male/female the defining term for the unitive experience
of consciousness. Schleiermacher, as we have seen, referred to the gender
of the person in this state as "artist." He did so because creativity in its own
terms is neither male nor female, nor both. Schleiermacher's doctrine
of human affections is thus the place where he moves beyond the
dimorphism that informs his more pervasive, prescriptive use of gender
images and concepts.

Richardson concludes that Schleiermacher was a *Mensch*, a human(e)
being, someone who actively embraced and affirmed the full humanity of
self and others. Richardson can reach this conclusion because she does
not emphasize principle (3): Schleiermacher's reification of his gendered
distinctions as a split consciousness that reduces the other (female) to

terms that complement and complete his male deficiencies. Massey, as we saw, paid pointed attention to this latter aspect of his work and dismissed the part of Schleiermacher's work that Richardson admires: his affirmation of human experience as a state beyond the isolated male or female soul.

The work of Richardson and Massey, together, demonstrate the folly of any attempt to read Schleiermacher from a "feminist" perspective, as if there is only one such perspective in feminism *or* Schleiermacher. The use of our key makes evident the reductionism that occurs when scholars fail to use a multi-perspectival approach to assess Schleiermacher's work in general or his work in relationship to feminist studies.

CONCLUSION

Schleiermacher's doctrine of human affections is more advanced than his own gender-based, theological constructions and images of his doctrine of the human soul. The key to Schleiermacher's work on gender issues thus points to two different aspects of his work: the theory (of how human affections move) and the practice (of how reason dictates these affections). The link between these two aspects is praxis. Schleiermacher's praxis restricted the civil rights of women.

It is here, at this point of praxis, that contemporary feminist and liberation theologians can help further Schleiermacher studies. They can help reconstruct the terms needed to liberate men and women from the contemporary implications entailed in his constrictive civil rights policies for men and women. They can find and identify the legacies of androcentrism and sexism his work produced in the academy, the church, and in civil society. This is the case because the hallmark of feminist and liberation theologies is attention to the link between images and concepts, and their paradigmatic effects on human freedom.

Rosemary Radford Ruether made this point decades ago in her groundbreaking book, *Sexism and God-Talk: Toward a Feminist Theology*. Feminist theologians, she argued, demand change of all theological claims that "contradict human experience in significant ways."[34] Liberation theologian Juan Luis Segundo makes a similar point in his book *Signs of the Times: Theological Reflections*, when noting that liberation theology is a liberative theology because of its insistence upon "a richer conjunction of practice *and* theory." It attempts "to verify the 'praxis' of faith." Liberation theologians focus on the "impact of theological concepts or beliefs on dehumanizing practices."[35] Schleiermacher's extraordinary work in music and affect theory created a new vocabulary for an embodied, liberative theology. Feminist and liberation theologians can use this aspect of his work to advance the embodied, theological revolution Schleiermacher's work began but could not sustain.[36]

Notes

1 "Idea for a Catechism of Reason for Noble Women." Richardson provides an English translation in Richardson 1991, 60–1; another translation can be found in Schlegel 1971, 220–1.

2 Richardson's work is outstanding in this area; see Richardson 1991.

3 See Massey 1985 for a vivid presentation of this perspective.

4 Guenther-Gleason 1992, 127. Her essay provides a strong summary of the textual incongruities in Schleiermacher's work.

5 See Schleiermacher, *Über den Umfang des Begriffs der Kunst in Bezug auf die Theorie derselben* [*On the Scope of the Concept of Art in Relation to its Theory*], in *SW*, III.3, 181–224, esp. 183; future references to this text will be provided internally as *UK* with the page number following.

6 Schleiermacher, *Pädagogische Schriften I* (1826 *Lectures*), 145. Future references will be given internally as *PS* with the page number following.

7 See Guenther-Gleason, 113–27.

8 Börsch 1957, 355–6.

9 See Scholtz 1981 for a fine overview of the entire topic of the development of Schleiermacher's interest in music and its function in his life and work. See also Blackwell 1985, 446.

10 See Sadie 1990, 171–2 and Buelow 1983, 393–407.

11 References in this chapter are to the 1826 second edition (Schleiermacher, *Christmas Eve*, trans. Tice). References to this translation will be provided internally as *ChrEve* followed by the page number.

12 Schleiermacher, *Aus Schleiermachers Leben*, ed. Dilthey, vol. IV. 122.

13 *Aus Schleiermachers Leben*, 122.

14 *Friedrich Schleiermachers Ästhetik*, ed. Odebrecht, 52. Future references will be provided internally as *AO* followed by the page number.

15 For a fuller discussion, see Thandeka 1995.

16 Schleiermacher, *On the Glaubenslehre*, 34–6.

17 Bernecker 1915, 1–3.

18 Schleiermacher, *Die praktische Theologie nach den Grundsätzen der evangelischen Kirche*, in *SW*, I.13, 28. Future references will be given internally as *PT* followed by the page number. English translations of selections from this work have appeared in Duke 1988. References to these translations will be indicated internally by *CC*.

19 See Panksepp 1998, for a detailed delineation of this "revolution" in contemporary approach to the study of human nature.

20 Clore and Ortony 2000, 27. See also Panksepp 1998.

21 Scholtz 1995, 217.

22 Letter of A. Müllers, December 2, 1805, cited by Börsch 1957, 356.

23 For Schleiermacher, the term *Vorstellung* (representation) refers to images and concepts rather than to sounds and movements (*AO*, 95).

24 *Life of Schleiermacher*, ed. and trans. Rowan, 18n.–19n.
25 Schleiermacher, *Aus Schleiermachers Leben*, ed. Dilthey, vol. II. 47.
26 Massey 1985, 146.
27 Massey 1985, 5–9.
28 Herdt 1999, 245.
29 Herdt 1999, 244, 246.
30 Richardson 1991, iii.
31 Schleiermacher, *Brouillon zur Ethik (1805–6)*, ed. Birkner.
32 Richardson 1991, 150–1.
33 Richardson 1991, 151.
34 Ruether 1983, 12, 16.
35 Segundo and Hennelly 1993, 94.
36 Parts of this chapter are based on my paper "Schleiermacher's View of Human Affections," presented to the Schleiermacher group at the 2002 meeting of the AAR. I would like to thank Walter Balk and Jack C. Verheyden for their invaluable critical reviews of an earlier draft of this chapter and their refinement of translations of German passages included in it. I would also like to thank my research assistant Danielle Gerrior for her assistance in this project. Special thanks to my partner Naomi King for her review and critique of the work throughout the various stages of its development. Special appreciation to Constance L. Grant for her critical review and invaluable editorial assistance.

16 Schleiermacher yesterday, today, and tomorrow

TERRENCE N. TICE

In the early nineteenth century, Schleiermacher contributed substantially to the birth of the modern age (including some features that are oddly dubbed "post-modern" today). The foregoing chapters are designed chiefly to present accounts of certain major areas of Schleiermacher's activity. My task here is to focus on problems and prospects within contemporary Schleiermacher studies.

SCHLEIERMACHER'S SCHOLARLY IDENTITY AND ACHIEVEMENT: A SUMMARY OVERVIEW

Although Schleiermacher's work outside theology deserves to be better known, thus far he is much more reputed for what he produced in theology, still strikingly contributive with respect to both general method and content. Of particular importance currently are the following elements. First is his thoroughgoing use of only generally applicable hermeneutical and historical–critical procedures in every area. Second is his philosophical-mindedness[1] (while eschewing any intrusion of philosophical content anywhere, though he does occasionally "borrow" from philosophical method and content to establish a frame for concepts like "religion" and "ethics"). Third is his assignment of interactively "scientific" and "ecclesial" functions to all three essentially interlocking parts of theology that he designated. Fourth is his consistent focus on support of leadership for church practice as the sole aim of theology; he defines church practice as both congregational service in all places and governance at all levels. Fifth is his centering on one historical locus for all that theology directly attends to (in his case, the evangelical church in Germany, a locus that he would doubtless greatly broaden today). With respect to the content of doctrine, he divides his presentation into two parts: that which expresses the relation of grace to sin in the process of redemption and that which contains presuppositions for what is contained in Christian religious self-consciousness. Although his Christian ethics is differently organized, it too describes the Christian life solely in terms of God's preparatory grace and redemptive grace in Christ, the latter passed down by the divine Spirit that constitutes the community of faith. Finally, in his account of Christian faith he uses three forms of dogmatic propositions. All three forms refer to God's relationship in Christ to individuals in the community of faith, so that in both parts of the systematic presentation of doctrine each is an expression of Christian religious self-consciousness with regard to components in that relationship, respectively self, world (including church), and God. Thus, the doctrine of God is present in every section, not only in those emphasizing the divine attributes. Underlying all these features, moreover, are two requirements: first, that all theological work reflect the relationship with God that shapes distinctively Christian religious self-consciousness (what he calls "faith"), and that, in doing this, every doctrinal account of faith and life reflect solely "the redemption accomplished in Jesus of Nazareth," passed down through the generations of interpersonal witness and receptivity to God's grace continually made available through that succession within Christian communities of faith.[2]

In consequence, no introduction (or propaedeutic) from outside and no natural theology are acceptable, nor is any hierarchical authority for faith and life. The experience of faith and life in relationship to Jesus' own perfect God-consciousness as it impressed itself on Jesus' companions, contained (albeit imperfectly) in the New Testament witness, is alone authoritative. Even creeds and confessions are imperfect guides only, subject to theological examination and subsequent revision. Ultimately, Schleiermacher trusts in the ever wise and loving God alone, thus revealed. In every aspect of church life, he seeks to exercise a corresponding love and wisdom;[3] therefore anathemas and schism are wholly out of place. He counsels meeting both conflict and historically inevitable separation in that same spirit, and his sermons, ecclesial writings, and participation in controversy evidence his remarkably earnest endeavor to do so throughout his forty-year career as a minister.

Recently a colleague who teaches practical theology, a discipline that Schleiermacher once called "the crown of theology" and that, in effect, he invented, said to me that his main purpose is to move beyond Schleiermacher so as to highlight the ministry of the laity. I responded that he could not possibly move so far beyond Schleiermacher's intent as to accomplish that end. In his own time, it was a great achievement for him to insist on a fully integrated theological education for clergy, almost the only leadership that the evangelical churches had. To me, to read closely what he was led to affirm regarding the relationship of clergy and laity is to see that he emphasized planting the seeds of proclamation[4] in each other, thereby fostering the ministry of each and every layperson. This includes service in the church plus outreach into the family, social–cultural engagement and politics. Fostering these ministries is the primary task of every ordained clergyperson.

In these respects Schleiermacher tends still to be way ahead of most of us. Moreover, he repeatedly averred that Christian faith is essentially a matter of feeling, especially "feeling absolutely dependent" on God, not of adherence to thoughts or to rules for action. Therefore, doing theology does not itself either create or guarantee faith. Furthermore, he also knew in his bones that it is the genuine faith of the laity, whom the clergy are called to serve, that constitutes the community of faith. It is the laity, brought together and nourished by the Spirit of God, that both constitutes and advances the true church from generation to generation.

In the end, then, this service of shared leadership is what authentic Christian theology is all about, and it lies at the heart of Schleiermacher's continually renewed contributions to modern theology as its reputed founder. The intellectual aspects, including his undoubted contributions to the development of philosophical theology, exegesis, and historical studies, as well as to philosophy of religion and other studies on religion, he meant to lie essentially in service to "faith" as he experienced and then came to understand it.

In short, Schleiermacher was not only prescient, he was accomplished in numerous ways that are still relevant today. In those respects, his achievements can readily be evaluated as far broader and potentially more long-lasting that those of all but a few philosophers and theologians before or since. Given this general outline, I now proceed to the three remaining considerations of this chapter.

STAGES OF SCHLEIERMACHER RECEPTION, ESPECIALLY IN THE ANGLOPHONE AND AMERICAN DOMAINS

For brevity's sake, the history of Schleiermacher reception in English-speaking domains can be divided into five periods.

1 Ignorance and rejection (1799–1899)

In the early nineteenth century a mere handful of English-speaking theologians and not many philosophers knew German at all well. One of them was Connop Thirlwall, who in 1825 issued Schleiermacher's 1817 critical work on Luke in translation. This act proved to be a serious detriment to Thirlwall's career, for in England the book was generally thought to be diabolical. Years later, however, Lord Melbourne called Thirlwall to his bedroom where he lay ill and, when Thirlwall entered, held up this book saying "I am making you a bishop!"

Except for rather isolated instances like this one, for a century Schleiermacher's thought was either totally ignored or resoundingly rejected. A few other translations appeared over succeeding decades – in Scotland *Brief Outline* (1850) and *Christmas Eve* (1890), and in the United States his 1822 Trinity essay (1835), but all went quickly out of print and were lodged in but few libraries. Before Mary Wilson issued a large volume of twenty-seven translated sermons in England (1890) her highly reputed academic guide warned her against doing this, for it would ruin her career. Schleiermacher's reputation throughout the century was that of being a heretically "liberal" interpreter of the Bible and of having sacrificed Christian faith to secular trends.

2   Awakening awareness and limited respect (1900–1939)

Indirect knowledge of what Schleiermacher had done advanced slowly during the early twentieth century, notably through Dilthey, Harnack, Troeltsch and others in Germany, and thence through students who came to Germany for advanced study. These influences bore fruit mostly in the awareness of theologians' scathingly negative critiques. Those coming most prominently from Barth and Brunner (but not Bultmann or Tillich), added to his being known chiefly at second hand, despite translations by John Oman of *On Religion* (1894), and by Horace L. Freiss of *Soliloquies* (1926), the joint translation of *Christian Faith* by several noted theologians of Scots Reformed lineage from Scotland and the U.S.A. (1928), and a slight growth of literature in English. The rise of liberal–progressive movements, especially in America served to augment this trend.

3   Neo-Orthodox enmity and new reappraisals (1949–1959)

By this time, very little was known or discussed regarding Schleiermacher's philosophy. In the late 1930s the parents of Richard Brandt, later a leading analytic philosopher, sent him to Germany to study philosophy. There he encountered Schleiermacher and produced *Schleiermacher's Philosophy* (Yale University Press, 1941), the first comprehensive work on the subject. Now out of print, it must be adjudged inaccurate and greatly out-of-date, as are the translations of *On Religion*,

Soliloquies, and *Christian Faith* (all still in print nonetheless). Yet, it is a significant overview, and its appearance signals a time-delayed sea change in Schleiermacher reception that actually began almost two decades later.

Meanwhile, after the Second World War a broader flow of students began to study abroad. On both sides of the Atlantic numbers of seminary teachers were preaching the Neo-Orthodox party line, experienced by the present author in the 1950s when my own scholarly life began constantly to intertwine with Schleiermacher's fortunes. In the 1950s there were no courses on Schleiermacher, but there were occasional comments, mostly derisive or dismissive. In 1956, at Princeton Theological Seminary, the Scotsman Norman Victor Hope taught a course on the history of modern theology in which he argued, "Oh, by the way, there is Schleiermacher, who is reputed to have been the father of modern theology. He was a liberal, and we will say no more about him here; but in case you think 'liberal' is all a bad thing, let me tell you what one of my teachers told us. He said: 'A liberal is one who accepts the truth from whatever quarter of the sky it may come'." This advice had a strong effect on this author, one that led to my first reading of Schleiermacher's *Christian Faith* over a period of several days, and that proved to be a life-changing experience.

In England and Scotland, this period continues, for the most part, to the present. During a 1997 journey to both countries, where I led sessions on Schleiermacher's *Christian Faith* and *On Religion* in a number of theology seminars, I found professors and students who were very positive about his thinking in each place. Parts of both books are on the syllabus in theology there.

4 The "Schleiermacher Renaissance" begins in the Americas (1960–1984)

Richard R. Niebuhr's very thoughtful book *Schleiermacher on Christ and Religion* (1964) helped open a new era in Schleiermacher scholarship. In 1961 my "Schleiermacher's Theological Method" appeared, a dissertation widely circulated and consulted though never published. Since 1966 my successive general bibliographies on the Schleiermacher literature (1985, and in *New Athenaeum* 1989, 1991, 1995, 1998, and forthcoming) have chronicled a constantly burgeoning attention to Schleiermacher's actual work, mostly in German or English, though Italian and French scholars were also catching on. Graduate seminars were introduced in several places, including the major influence of Brian Gerrish in Chicago, Michael Ryan at Drew, and R. R. Niebuhr at Harvard. In 1966–9 my translations of *Brief Outline, Christmas Eve,* and *On Religion* were published, only to be taken out of print soon after, however. In 1967 there was a major gathering of scholars interested in Schleiermacher at Vanderbilt (see Funk 1970). By the early 1980s Schleiermacher was attracting attention in the American Academy of Religion's nineteenth-century theology group, out of which grew the formation of a Schleiermacher seminar, then group, which has continued to this day. An important volume evaluating Barth's criticisms of Schleiermacher, edited by Robert Streetman and James Duke (1988), was one of the early fruits from that enterprise.

5 The Americans take a significant part in international dialogue and research (1986 – the present)

By far the largest growth of activity in Anglophone and American Schleiermacher scholarship has occurred over the past twenty-five years. The International Congress held in Berlin on the occasion of the 150th anniversary of Schleiermacher's death (1984) led to several outgrowths apart from activities already mentioned. Since 1985 nearly annual meetings of translators have been held for Edwin Mellen Press's Schleiermacher Studies and Translations series, in which almost all of its two dozen volumes, mostly of translated texts thus far, have been accompanied by monographs, and both major international conference volumes and festschrifts have appeared under its auspices. In 1988 a journey to Schleiermacher's haunts was arranged by the series director, Ruth Richardson. Since then, six volumes of *New Athenaeum/ Neues Athenaeum*, edited by her and devoted chiefly to Schleiermacher research, have seen the light.

The International Schleiermacher Society, a collegial organization that I have led from its founding in the mid-1980s, has organized or co-sponsored several international conferences: recently in England at York (a section in 1999), in the U.S.A. at Drew (2000), earlier in Italy and Germany and in 1994 one in the former East Germany (Gosen) with the University of Berlin. In addition to Edwin Mellen Press, several other publishers have also helped to sustain a growing stream of translations and other volumes to accompany a comparably huge body of articles and essays over the past twenty-five years. Schleiermacher is, at last, coming into his own in English-speaking domains, and with these scholars there is an increasing involvement of scholars from Italy, France, Scandinavia, the Netherlands, India, Japan, Korea, Turkey, and elsewhere. Dozens of book-length projects are currently in process, including translations of most of the remaining major works by Schleiermacher. Four volumes of sermons have appeared since 1988, and many more are in process.

In America today, we do not find a particularly strong tendency to reach into the past for assistance in present tasks; yet, growing numbers of scholars are finding Schleiermacher to be their contemporary, often to be beckoning to them from some place ahead on the routes they are taking. Therein lies a reasonable expectation of further influence by Schleiermacher, thus a continuing growth of Schleiermacher-related scholarship in America, the United Kingdom and around the world today.

RECENT GROWTH OF SCHLEIERMACHER SCHOLARSHIP

By my last count, at least forty-three volumes on Schleiermacher, excluding translations, sets of papers given at the American Academy of Religion after 1998, and multiple essays by English writers appearing in books issued in Germany or Italy, were published in English during the twenty-five years from 1978 to 2003. Lengthy monographs attached to translations are not however included in this total. Articles and chapters from this period, many of them based on original research, numbered in the hundreds and dissertations in the dozens. Over that period graduate-level courses and seminars also continued to grow, to two dozen or so by 2003.

The bibliography to this volume contains a list of items available in English translation. In addition to these translations, over eighteen more volumes of translation are well advanced, including Schleiermacher's early essays and reviews, the "Jewish Housefather" essay (1799), his lectures on psychology and on practical theology, a volume comprising all three editions of *On Religion*, *Soliloquies*, his monographs on election and Trinity, and occasional essays on confessional issues. A new critical edition and translation of *Christian Faith* is to be followed by the 1826 lectures on *Christian Ethics*, as well as more material on hermeneutics and dialectic, the critical essays on 1 Timothy and on academia, and academy essays on criticism, philology, and translation.

Other high priority translation projects include the 1803 account of all previous ethical systems, the lectures on aesthetics and on education, the church–political writings, selections from Schleiermacher's vast correspondence, more academy essays and addresses, *Heraclitus* (1807), other pieces on Greek philosophers, Plato notes, and many volumes of sermons.

SOME AREAS FOR FUTURE EXPLORATION IN SCHLEIERMACHER SCHOLARSHIP

Finally, I wish in closing briefly to indicate some areas where huge gaps remain, not only in English-speaking domains but especially there. All of the areas that I have chosen to list are of considerable significance for cutting-edge inquiry beyond Schleiermacher scholarship itself. I start with philosophy, which as a bridge to other disciplines as well as a foundational one, covers an immense territory in Schleiermacher's own production; then I conclude with theology, as before.

Some areas in philosophy where lacunae in interpretation of Schleiermacher's thinking are to be found include the following:

1. Schleiermacher's psychology overall warrants much closer attention.[5] This is especially true in practical areas of philosophy and science where its theories could be used fruitfully, viewing them as a basis for work in all other areas of philosophy.

2. Dialectic, hermeneutics, and criticism are already gaining widespread treatment. It will be gratifying to move beyond typical epistemological inquiries into the details of use. It can sensibly be claimed that without such practical attention consideration of these disciplines would remain seriously incomplete at foundational and theoretical levels.

3. Schleiermacher's aesthetics is still under-examined. Beginning with his accounts of sensory consciousness, it would be valuable then to look particularly at his use of resources available to him in his own time, especially in music and the visual arts. An amply annotated and illustrated edition of his aesthetics lectures would serve handsomely to advance this work, if placed in historical context and compared with later developments in aesthetics (notably by way of Croce and Collingwood).

4. Philosophy of science never received systematic treatment at Schleiermacher's hands (partly because of Fichte's misconceived and abortive attempt, which he chose not to challenge directly). However, he had in fact the lineaments of a highly developed, complex view, one possibly more mature in its general features than is to be found in most quarters of philosophy or science today.[6] This view is radically historical, contextual, and systematic in its makeup. It can still help serve admirably for a critique of many current views and practices. In historical terms, some basic aspects of it are allied to what have come to be called "pragmatic" approaches. These links, I believe, would well repay investigation.

5. As usual, there has long been sufficient historical information and corresponding texts to accurately follow Schleiermacher's political thought and activities. Now that the thick *KGA* volume containing his lectures on "The State" has appeared (1998), there is no excuse, and there is much to explore.

6. Most of the time, Schleiermacher's sixty-five years were extremely engaged and fertile, quite apart from his professional production. One highly effective way to lay out the cycles of engagement and retreat in his life, for which much documentation is available, would be to sort out the several major social institutions that he treated in his ethics and to let his life and writings illumine each other. For example, in the *KGA*, and in translations and monographs, the domains of academia, church and confessional affairs, and free sociality are already being nudged toward such fuller treatment. The family, child-rearing, education of the young, friendship and development through the life cycle have barely begun to obtain such treatment in English. Among this latter set, only education has a substantial literature in German, and even there much remains to be done. (In Germany Schleiermacher is renowned for his lectures on education, for they inspired major progressive moves in that arena.) In all these social domains, he will warrant a claim to be our contemporary, even at the present great distance from the society he knew. The late Kurt Nowak's recent 400-page life of Schleiermacher (2001) provides fine background for such interests.

7. As I have tried to show elsewhere,[7] translation, as one of the most demanding aspects of the hermeneutical endeavor, is a philosophical art. Recently Manfred Frank remarked that translation is a powerful way to get to know another's thought intimately. I am sure that Schleiermacher, who translated several volumes of English sermons by Fawcett and Blair before he began a twenty-five-year career translating Plato, would agree. Herewith I simply issue a call to learn the craft by working on Schleiermacher's writings. Despite the current disvaluing of such work in some quarters, I can testify that good translation is among the finest, most demanding, stimulating, and gratifying scholarly employments possible. Not many oeuvres, I dare say, could so repay a scholar's investment as Schleiermacher's, especially if it is done with the aid and critical discipline afforded by a community of translators. Much opportunity lies open here.

8. Although Schleiermacher flourished during the hey-day of German idealism, strictly speaking he is not an idealist as was long contended. Even his earliest writings display inquiries in alternative directions. Likewise, in several early works he significantly contributed, in general cultural terms, to early German romanticism, but atypically in many respects. His overall outlook in both philosophy and theology largely displays independent roots. The directions he was to take in

both philosophy and theology can already be detected in the years before he came to Berlin in 1796 and then took part in that budding movement. Thematically, the birth of modern theology, of which he was the "father," is already present in his sermons from 1789 to 1807, before he served with Wilhelm von Humboldt as co-founder of the University of Berlin in 1808–11. Strictly speaking, moreover, Schleiermacher never belonged to a distinct school of thought, nor did he ever attempt to form one for students to follow. In lectures he did present his own ideas quite pointedly and systematically, based on critical examination of alternatives and carefully developed through argument. As he often said, his chief aim withal was to get students and readers to think for themselves. All these historical matters need to be fully brought to light and clarified. As the above essays will no doubt have helped to show, Schleiermacher's reputed place in history needs drastic reappraisal.

9. For one thing, it is now clear that although he is regarded to be one of the greatest theologians of all time, the immense, if sensible, demands that Schleiermacher places on theological education and scholarship have still received minimal notice even to the present. Wide-reaching interpretative generalities tend to leave the most promising particulars of detailed investment and integrative endeavor in the shadows within Anglophone and American arenas, as they often do elsewhere. Mimicking other academic fields, the tendency in theology still is to compartmentalize departments. Especially through his *Brief Outline of Theology as a Field of Study*, Schleiermacher can still help us move beyond that tendency into more interdisciplinary pursuits.

10. Remaining gaps in studies of Schleiermacher's theology are as follows. In English-speaking areas his practical theology, his sermons (nearly 600 of which are already available for study and translation; 503, mostly in the form of detailed outline, are as yet unpublished),[8] his remarkably creative attention to church music, and his own forty-year practice as a pastor and leading churchman are wide open for study. His exegetical and hermeneutical work is already in no small part accessible through the sermons, though the courses in exegesis that he taught nearly every term at Berlin are yet to be transcribed from the archives. Since he regarded philosophical theology to be a discipline as yet barely developed, he never lectured on this subject. However, numerous signs of what he would have said are available in *Christian Faith, On Religion* and other writings. The overarching aim was to carve out "the distinctive nature of Christianity," particularly

regarding the mainstream churches that stem from the Reformation and in contrast with other modes of faith. There is still much work to be done here in Schleiermacher scholarship. Next to no attention has been given to the work he did in church history, history of doctrine, and history of Christian ethics. Finally, Christian ethics itself has only recently begun to get the comprehensive treatment it deserves.[9] Beyond all this would be attempts to trace how Schleiermacher's own activity, interactive as it was among all these disciplines of theology, might provide some models for activity in the third century since his pioneering activity in the field began.

Notes

1 See my essay "Schleiermacher's Use of Philosophical Mindedness in Theology," in Helmer, Kranich and Rehme-Iffert 2003.
2 Kelsey 2003.
3 See Tice 2002, 21–32.
4 See Tice 2003a.
5 See Tice 1991b, 509–21.
6 See Tice 1991a, 45–82.
7 See Tice 1998, 115–28.
8 See Tice 1997.
9 See Brandt 2001.

Schleiermacher: bibliography of works, editions, and translations

I first list the volumes available so far of the *Schleiermacher Kritische Gesamtausgabe*, edited by H. J. Birkner, G. Ebeling, H. Fischer, H. Kimmerle, and K. V. Selge. Berlin: Walter de Gruyter, 1980–. (In the 1990s major changes took place in the editorial board of the *KGA*: Hans-Joachim Birkner died in 1991 and Gerhard Ebeling and Heinz Kimmerle resigned their editorial positions. These members were replaced by Günter Meckenstock [1994] and Ulrich Barth and Konrad Cramer in 1997.)

The historical–critical edition of the complete works of Friedrich Schleiermacher, as well as his unpublished writings and correspondence, are divided into five sections: I. Writings and drafts; II. Lectures; III. Sermons; IV. Translations; V. Correspondence and biographical documents.

The following volumes have appeared thus far or are in preparation:

I: *Writings and drafts*

KGA, I.1: *Jugendschriften 1787–1796*, ed. Günter Meckenstock, 1983.

KGA, I.2: *Schriften aus der Berliner Zeit 1796–1799*, ed. Günter Meckenstock, 1984.

KGA, I.3: *Schriften aus der Berliner Zeit 1800–1802*, ed. Günter Meckenstock, 1988.

KGA, I.4: *Schriften aus der Stolper Zeit 1802–04*, ed. Eilert Herms, Günter Meckenstock, and Michael Pietsch, 2002.

KGA, I.5: *Schriften aus der Hallenser Zeit 1804–1807*, ed. Hermann Patsch, 1995.

KGA, I.6: *Universitätsschriften. Herakleitos. Kurze Darstellung des theologischen Studiums*, ed. Dirk Schmid, 1998.

KGA, I.7: parts 1 and 2: *Der christliche Glaube nach den Grundsätzen der evangelischen Kirche im Zusammenhange dargestellt (1821/22)*, ed. Herman Peiter, 1980.

KGA, I.7: part 3: *Marginalien und Anhang*, ed. Ulrich Barth, 1983.

KGA, I.8: *Exegetische Schriften*, ed. Hermann Patsch and Dirk Schmid, 2001.

KGA, I.9: *Kirchenpolitische Schriften*, ed. Günter Meckenstock, 2000.

KGA, I.10: *Theologisch-dogmatische Abhandlungen und Gelegenheitsschriften*, ed. Hans-Friedrich Traulsen, 1990.

KGA, I.11: *Akademieabhandlungen*, ed. Martin Rössler, 2002.

KGA, I.12: *Über die Religion*, ed. Günter Meckenstock, 1995.

KGA, I.13: *Der christliche Glaube nach den Grundsätzen der evangelischen Kirche im Zusammenhang dargestellt (1830–31)*, ed. Rolf Schäfer, 2003.
KGA, I.14: *Kleine Schriften 1786–1833*, ed. Matthias Wolfes and Michael Pietsch, 2003.
KGA, I.15: *Register für die I. Abteilung*, ed. Lars Emersleben, 2005.

II: Lectures
KGA, II.8: *Vorlesungen über die Lehre vom Staat*, ed. Walter Jaeschke, 1998.
KGA, II.10: *Vorlesungen über die Dialektik*, ed. Andreas Arndt, 2002.
KGA, II.16: *Vorlesungen über die Kirchliche Geographie und Statitik*, ed. Simon Gerber, 2005.

III: Sermons
Twelve volumes of approximately 600 pages each will be devoted to Schleiermacher's sermons.

IV: Translations
Schleiermacher is particularly famous for his translations of Plato's writings into German; he also published a number of translations of English sermons and travelogues. Preparations have not yet started for this section.

V: *Correspondence and biographical documents*
KGA, V.1: *Briefwechsel 1774–1796*, ed. Andreas Arndt and Wolfgang Virmond, 1985.
KGA, V.2: *Briefwechsel 1796–1798*, ed. Andreas Arndt and Wolfgang Virmond, 1988.
KGA, V.3: *Briefwechsel 1799–1800*, ed. Andreas Arndt and Wolfgang Virmond, 1992.
KGA, V.4: *Briefwechesel 1800*, ed. Andreas Arndt and Wolfgang Virmond, 1994.
KGA, V.5: *Briefwechsel 1801–1802*, ed. Andreas Arndt and Wolfgang Virmond, 1999.

In preparation:
KGA, V.6: *Briefwechsel 1802–1803*, ed. Andreas Arndt and Wolfgang Virmond, 2005.
KGA, V.7: *Briefwechsel 1803–1804*, ed. Andreas Arndt and Wolfgang Virmond, 2005.

Other editions:
The older edition of Schleiermacher's writings is: *Sämtliche Werke*, Berlin: G. Reimer, 1834–64. This edition was divided into three sections: (1) theology; (2) sermons; and (3) philosophy, and comprised thirty-one volumes.
Another frequently cited edition of selected texts is: *Schleiermachers Werke. Auswahl in vier Bänden*, edited by Otto Braun and Johannaes Bauer, 4 vols., Leipzig: Meiner, 1927–8. Reprint, Aalen: Scientia Verlag, 1981.

Select editions of individual works:
Friedrich D. E. Schleiermacher, *Die Allgemeine Hermeneutik*, ed. by Wolfgang Virmond. Schleiermacher-Archiv, vol. I.1271–310. Berlin: Walter de Gruyter, 1985.

Ästhetik (1819–25). Über den Begriff der Kunst (1831–32), ed. Thomas Lehnerer. Philosophische Bibliothek, vol. 365. Hamburg: Felix Meiner, 1984.
Ästhetik, ed. Rudolf Odebrecht. Berlin, Leipzig: Walter de Gruyter, 1931.
Vorlesungen über die Ästhetik. Berlin: Reimer, 1842.
Aus Schleiermacher's Leben. In Briefen, ed. Wilhelm Dilthey. Berlin: Reimer, 1860.
Briefe bei Gelegenheit der politisch theologischen Aufgabe und des Sendschreibens jüdischer Hausväter. Berlin: Evangelischer Verlagsanstalt, 1984.
Briefwechsel Mit Joachim Christian Gaß, ed. W. Gaß. Berlin, 1852.
Briefwechsel mit seiner Braut, ed. Heinrich Meisner, 2nd edn. Gotha: F. A. Perthes, 1920.
Brouillon zur Ethik (1805–6), ed. Hans-Joachim Birkner. Philosophische Bibliothek, vol. 334. Hamburg: Felix Meiner, 1981.
Der Christlicher Glaube, 7th edn., ed. Martin Redeker. 2 vols. Berlin: Walter de Gruyter, 1960.
Die christliche Sitte nach den Grundsätzen der evangelischen Kirche im Zusammenhange dargestellt, aus Schleiermachers handschriftlichen Nachlasse und nachgeschriebenen Vorlesungen, ed. Ludwig Jonas, Friedrich Schleiermachers Sämtliche Werke, I.12. Berlin, 1843.
Dialektik (1811), ed. Andreas Arndt. Philosophische Bibliothek, vol. 386. Hamburg: Felix Meiner, 1986.
Dialektik (1814–15). Einleitung Zur Dialektik (1833), ed. Andreas Arndt. Philosophische Bibliothek, vol. 387. Hamburg: Felix Meiner, 1988.
Dialektik, ed. Manfred Frank. Frankfurt am Main: Suhrkamp, 2001.
Dialektik, ed. Rudolf Odebrecht. Unveränd. reprograf. Nachdruck der Ausgabe Leipzig 1942. edn. Darmstadt: Wissenschaftliche Buchgesellschaft Abt. Verlag, 1976.
Dialektik, ed. Ludwig Jonas. Berlin: Reimer, 1839.
Ethik (1812–13), Mit späteren Fassungen der Einleitung, Güterlehre und Pflichtenlehre, ed. Hans-Joachim Birker. Philosophische Bibliothek, vol. 335. Hamburg: Felix Meiner, 1981.
Gelegentliche Gedanken über Universitäten in deutschem Sinn. Nebst einem Anhang über eine neu zu errichtende. Berlin: In der Realschulbuchhandlung, 1808.
Grundlinien einer Kritik der bisherigen Sittenlehre. Berlin: Realschulbuchhandlung, 1803.
Grundlinien einer Kritik der bisherigen Sittenlehre. 2. Ausg. edn. Berlin: Reimer, 1834.
Grundriss der philosophischen Ethik, ed. A. Twesten. Berlin: Reimer, 1841.
Handschriftliche Anmerkungen: Zum Ersten Theil Der Glaubenslehre, ed. C. Thönes. Berlin: Reimer, 1873.
Hermeneutik und Kritik, ed. Manfred Frank. 6th edn. Frankfurt am Main: Suhrkamp, 1995.
Kleine Schriften und Predigten, ed. Hayo Gerdes and Emanuel Hirsch. Berlin: Walter de Gruyter, 1969–70.
Kurze Darstellung des theologischen Studiums zum Behuf einleitender Vorlesungen, ed. Heinrich Scholtz. 1st edn. Darmstadt: Wissenschaftliche Buchgesellschaft, 1973 (orig. 1910).
Das Leben Jesu. Vorlesungen an der Universität zu Berlin im Jahr 1832, ed. Karl Rütenik. Berlin: Reimer, 1864.

Monologen. Kritische Ausgabe. Reprint of the 1914 ed., with introduction by Friedrich M. Schiele. Philosophische Bibliothek, vol. 84. Hamburg: Felix Meiner Verlag, 1978.

Pädagogische Schriften I (1826 Lectures), ed. Eric Weniger. Frankfurt: Klett-Cotta, 1983.

Pädagogische Schriften, ed. C. Platz. Neudruck der dritten Aufl. 1902 edn. Osnabrück: Biblio-Verlag, 1968.

Platon im kontext: Sämtliche Werke auf CD-Rom, in den Übersetzungen und mit den Einleitungen in die Dialoge von Friedrich Schleiermacher, Berlin: Karsten Worm, 1998.

Platons Werke (Translations of Plato's Dialogues). Berlin: Reimer, I.1, 1804; I.2 and II.1, 1805; II.2, 1807; II.3, 1809; III.1, 1828 (2nd edn. of pts. I and II, 1817).

Predigten, ed. Hans Urner. Göttingen: Vandenhoeck und Ruprech, 1969.

Schriften, ed. Andreas Arndt. Bibliothek Der Philosophie, vol. 134. Frankfurt am Main: Deutscher Klassiker Verlag, 1996.

Theologische Enzyklopädie (1831–2): Nachschrift David Friedrich Strauß, ed. Walter Sachs. Schleiermacher-Archiv, vol. 4. Berlin: Walter de Gruyter, 1987.

Über Die Philosophie Platons. Die Einleitungen zur Übersetzung des Platon (1804–1828); Geschichte der Philosophie; Vorlesungen über Sokrates und Platon (Zwischen 1819 Und 1823), ed. Peter M. Steiner, with contributions by Andreas Arndt, and Jörg Jantzen. Philosophische Bibliothek, vol. 486. Hamburg: Meiner, 2000.

English Translations of Schleiermacher's Work

Schleiermacher, Friedrich. "The Boat Ride (1786)," trans. Michael D. Ryan. *New Athenaeum/Neues Athenaeum* 2 (1991): 171–4.

Brief Outline of the Study of Theology. Translated by William Farrer. Edinburgh: T.&T. Clark, 1850.

Brief Outline of Theology as a Field of Study, trans. Terrence N. Tice. Schleiermacher Studies and Translations, 1. Lewiston, N.Y.: Edwin Mellen Press, 1990.

Brouillon Zur Ethik/Notes on Ethics (1805–1806), trans. and ed. John Wallhauser. Schleiermacher Studies and Translations, 22. Lewiston, N.Y.: Edwin Mellen Press, 2002.

Christian Caring: Selections from Practical Theology, trans. James O. Duke and ed. James O. Duke and Howard W. Stone. Fortress Texts in Modern Theology. Philadelphia: Fortress Press, 1988.

Christian Faith, trans. Catherine L. Kelsey, Terrence N. Tice, and Edwina Lawler. Louisville, K.Y.: Westminster John Knox, forthcoming.

The Christian Faith, trans. H. R. Mackintosh and James Stuart Stewart. Edinburgh: T.&T. Clark, 1928. Reprint, with a foreword by B. A. Gerrish, 1999.

The Christian Household: A Sermonic Treatise, trans. Dietrich Seidel. Schleiermacher Studies and Translations, 3. Lewiston, N.Y.: Edwin Mellen Press, 1991.

Christmas Eve, trans. Terrence N. Tice. Schleiermacher Studies and Translations, 4. Lewiston, N.Y.: Edwin Mellen Press, 1991.

"Comparison of the Political Philosophies of Plato and Aristotle (1794)," trans. Kostas Niafas. *New Athenaeum/Neues Athenaeum* 6 (2001): 33–50.

Dialectic or, the Art of Doing Philosophy: A Study Edition of the 1811 Notes, trans. and ed. Terrence N. Tice. Atlanta: Scholars Press, 1996.

Fifteen Sermons of Friedrich Schleiermacher Delivered to Celebrate the Beginning of a New Year, ed. and trans. Edwina Lawler. Lewiston, N.Y.: Edwin Mellen Press, 2003.

Hermeneutics and Criticism and Other Writings, ed. Andrew Bowie. Cambridge Texts in the History of Philosophy. Cambridge: Cambridge University Press, 1998.

Hermeneutics: The Handwritten Manuscripts, trans. Jack Forstman and James O. Duke and ed. Heinz Kimmerle. Missoula, Mont.: Scholars Press for the American Academy of Religion, 1977.

Lectures on Philosophical Ethics, trans. Louise Adey Huish and ed. Robert B. Louden. Cambridge Texts in the History of Philosophy. Cambridge: Cambridge University Press, 2002.

Letters on the Occasion of the Political Theological Task and the Sendschreiben (Open Letter) of Jewish Heads of Households, trans. Gilya Gerda Schmidt. Schleiermacher Studies and Translations, 21. Lewiston, N.Y.: Edwin Mellen Press, 2001.

The Life of Jesus, trans. S. Maclean Gilmour and ed. Jack C. Verheyden. Lives of Jesus Series. Philadelphia: Fortress Press, 1975. Reprint Mifflintown: Sigler, 1997.

The Life of Schleiermacher as Unfolded in His Autobiography and Letters, trans. and ed. Frederica Rowan. London: Smith Elder and Co., 1860.

Luke: A Critical Study, trans. Connop Thirlwall and ed. Terrence Tice. Lewiston, N.Y.: Edwin Mellen Press, 1993.

"Note on the Knowledge of Freedom (1790–1792)," "Notes on Kant's *Critique of Practical Reason* (probably from 1789)," and "Review of Immanuel Kant's *Anthropology from a Pragmatic Point of View* (1799)," trans. Jacqueline Mariña. *New Athenaeum/Neues Athenaeum* 5 (1998): 11–31.

Notes on the Theory of Virtue (1804–1806), trans. Terrence N. Tice. Schleiermacher Studies and Translations, 22. Lewiston, N.Y.: Edwin Mellen Press, 2002.

Occasional Thoughts on Universities in the German Sense with an Appendix Regarding a University Soon to Be Established (1808), trans. Terrence Tice with Edwina Lawler. Lewiston, N.Y.: Edwin Mellen Press, 1991.

On Colossians 1:15–20, trans. Esther D. Reed and Alan Braley. *New Athenaeum/ Neues Athenaeum* 5 (1998): 48–80.

On Creeds, Confessions, and Church Union, trans. and ed. Iain G. Nicol. Schleiermacher Studies and Translations, 24. Lewiston, N.Y.: Edwin Mellen Press, 2004.

On Freedom, trans. Albert L. Blackwell. Lewiston, N.Y.: Edwin Mellen Press, 1992.

On Religion: Addresses in Response to its Cultured Critics, trans. Terrence N. Tice. Richmond: John Knox Press, 1969.

On Religion: Speeches to its Cultured Despisers, trans. Richard Crouter (from the 1st German edn.). Cambridge Texts in the History of Philosophy. Cambridge: Cambridge University Press, 1988, 2nd edn. 1996.

On Religion: Speeches to its Cultured Despisers, trans. John Oman (from the 3rd German edn.), with a foreword by Jack Forstman. Louisville: Westminster/John Knox Press, 1994.

On Religion: Speeches to its Cultured Despisers, trans. John Oman (from the 3rd German edn.), with an introduction by Rudolf Otto. New York: Harper & Brothers, 1958.

"On the Discrepancy between the Sabellian and Athanasian Method of Representing the Doctrine of the Trinity (1822)," trans. Moses Stuart. *Biblical Repository and Quarterly Observer* 5–6 (1835): 31–5 (April); 1–116 (July).

On the Glaubenslehre: Two Letters to Dr. Lücke, trans. James O. Duke and Francis Fiorenza. American Academy of Religion Texts and Translations Series, vol. 3. Chico, C.A.: Scholars Press, 1981.

On the Highest Good, trans. H. Victor Froese. Schleiermacher Studies and Translations, 10. Lewiston, N.Y.: Edwin Mellen Press, 1992.

"On the Worth of Socrates as a Philosopher (1815)," trans. Connop Thirlwall. In *Life of Socrates*, ed. Gustav Freidrich Wiggers. London, 1840.

On What Gives Value to Life, trans. Edwina G. Lawler and Terrence N. Tice. Schleiermacher Studies and Translations, 14. Lewiston, N.Y.: Edwin Mellen Press, 1995.

Reformed but Ever Reforming: Sermons in Relation to the Celebration of the Handing over of the Augsburg Confession (1830), trans. and ed. Iain G. Nicol. Schleiermacher Studies and Translations, 8. Lewiston, N.Y.: Edwin Mellen Press, 1997.

Selected Sermons of Schleiermacher, trans. Mary F. Wilson. London: Hodder and Stoughton, 1890.

Selected Sermons of Schleiermacher, trans. Mary F. Wilson. Foreign Biblical Library. N.Y.: Funk and Wagnans. n.d.

Servant of the Word: Selected Sermons of Friedrich Schleiermacher, trans. Dawn DeVries. Fortress Texts in Modern Theology. Philadelphia: Fortress Press, 1987.

Soliloquies: An English Translation of the Monologen, trans. Horace Leland Friess. Chicago: Open Court Publishing Company, 1926.

"To Cecilie," trans. Edwina Lawler with Terrence N. Tice. *New Athenaeum/Neues Athenaeum* 6 (2001): 11–34.

"Toward a Theory of Sociable Conduct," trans. Jeffrey Hoover. *New Athenaeum/ Neues Athenaeum* 4 (1995): 20–39.

References

Adams, Robert Merrihew (1996). "Schleiermacher on Evil." *Faith and Philosophy* 13 4: 563–83.

Anderson, Benedict R. O'G. (1991). *Imagined Communities: Reflections on the Origin and Spread of Nationalism*. Rev. and extended edn. New York: Verso.

Aquinas, Thomas (1981). *Summa Theologica*, 5 vols., trans. Fathers of the English Dominican Province. Complete English edn. Westminster: Christian Classics.

Arndt, Andreas (2002). "Die Dialektik ... Will ein Organon des realen Wissens Sein." Eine neu zugangliche Nachschrift zu Schleiermachers Dialektik-Vorlesung 1818–19." *Zeitschrift für neuere Theologiegeschichte* 9: 1–23.

Arndt, Andreas, and Wolfgang Virmond (1992). *Schleiermachers Briefwechsel (Verzeichnis): nebst einer Liste seiner Vorlesungen*. Schleiermacher-Archiv, vol. 11. Berlin; New York: Walter de Gruyter.

Asad, Talal (2001). "Reading a Modern Classic: W. C. Smith's *The Meaning and End of Religion*." *History of Religions* 40/3: 205–22

Axt-Piscalar, Christine (1990). *Der Grund des Glaubens: Eine theologiegeschichtliche Untersuchung zum Verhältnis von Glaube und Trinität in der Theologie Isaak August Dorners*. Beiträge zur historischen Theologie 79. Tübingen: J. C. Mohr.

Barnes, Michel R. (2001). *The Power of God: Dunamis in Gregory of Nyssa's Trinitarian Theology*. Washington, D. C.: Catholic University of America Press.

Barnes, Michel R. and Daniel H. Williams, eds. (1993). *Arianism after Arius: Essays on the Development of the Fourth Century Trinitarian Conflicts*. Edinburgh: T.& T. Clark.

Barth, Karl (1957). *Church Dogmatics*, ed. and trans. G. Bromiley and T. F. Torranie. Edinburgh: T. & T. Clark.

(1973). *Protestant Theology in the Nineteenth Century*. Valley Forge: Judson Press.

(1982). *The Theology of Schleiermacher: Lectures at Göttingen, Winter Semester of 1923–24*, ed. Dietrich Ritschl. Grand Rapids: Eerdmans.

Barth, Ulrich (1983). *Christentum und Selbstbewusstsein: Versuch einer rationalen Rekonstruktion des systematischen Zusammenhanges von Schleiermachers subjektivitätstheoretischer Deutung der christlichen Religion*, Göttinger Theologische Arbeiten, vol. 27. Göttingen: Vandenhoeck & Ruprecht.

Baumgarten, Alexander Gottlieb (1757). *Metaphysica*. Halle: Hemmerde.

Bernecker, Karl (1915). *Kritische Darstellung der Geschichte des Affektbegriffes*. Berlin: Godemann.

Berner, Christian (1995). *La Philosophie de Schleiermacher*. Paris: Cerf.

Bierwaltes, Werner (1977). "Plotins Metaphysik des Lichtes," in *Die Philosophie des Neuplatonism*, ed. Clemens Zintzen, 75–111. Darmstadt: Wissenschaftliche Buchgesellschaft.

Birkner, Hans Joachim (1964). *Schleiermachers christliche Sittenlehre im Zusammenhang seines philosophisch-theologischen Systems*. Berlin: Walter de Gruyter.

(1996). *Schleiermacher-Studien*, ed Hermann Fischer. Berlin: Walter de Gruyter.

Birus, Hendrik, ed. (1982). *Hermeneutische Positionen. Schleiermacher, Dilthey, Heidegger, Gadamer*. Göttingen: Vandenhoek & Ruprecht.

Blackwell, Albert L. (1982). *Schleiermacher's Early Philosophy of Life: Determinism, Freedom, and Phantasy*. Chico, Calif.: Scholars Press.

(1985). "The Role of Music in Schleiermacher's Writings," in *Internationaler Schleiermacher Kongreβ Berlin 1984*, ed. Kurt-Victor Selge. Berlin: Walter de Gruyter.

Blackwell, Albert L., and Herbert H. Richardson (1991). *Friedrich Schleiermacher and the Founding of the University of Berlin: The Study of Religion as a Scientific Discipline*. Schleiermacher Studies and Translations 5. Lewiston N.Y.: Edwin Mellen Press.

Böckh, August (1808)."Rezension vom Platons Werke von F. Schleiermacher. Ersten Theiles erster Band Berhn 1804," in *Heidelbergische Jahrbücher der Literature* 1/5: 83.

Börsch, Ekkehard (1957). "Zur Entstehung Der 'Weihnachtsfeier'." *Theologische Zeitschrift* 13.

Bowie, Andrew (1990). *Aesthetics and Subjectivity from Kant to Nietzsche*. Manchester: Manchester University Press; Distributed exclusively in the U.S.A. and Canada by St. Martin's Press.

(1996). "The Meaning of the Hermeneutic Tradition in Contemporary Philosophy," in *"Verstehen" and Human Understanding*, ed. A. O'Hear. Cambridge: Cambridge University Press.

(1997). *From Romanticism to Critical Theory: The Philosophy of German Literary Theory*. New York: Routledge.

(2003). "Schleiermacher, Habermas, and Rorty," in *Schleiermachers Dialektik. Die Liebe Zum Wissen in Philosophie und Theologie*, ed. Christiane Kranich, Birgit Rehme-Iffert, and Christine Helmer. Berlin: Walter de Gruyter.

Brandom, Robert. (2000). *Rorty and His Critics*. Philosophers and Their Critics, 9. Oxford: Blackwell

Brandt, James M. (2001). *All Things New: Reform of Church and Society in Schleiermacher's Christian Ethics*. Louisville: Westminster John Knox Press.

Brandt, Richard B. (1941). *The Philosophy of Schleiermacher: The Development of His Theory of Scientific and Religious Knowledge*. New York: Harper.

Brandt, Wilfried (1968). *Der heilige Geist und die Kirche bei Schleiermacher*. Zürich: Zwingli Verlag.

Bretschneider, Karl Gottlieb (1914). *Handbuch der Dogmatik der evangelisch-lutherischen Kirsche*, vol. 1. Leipzig: J. A. Barth.

Brunner, Emil (1924). *Die Mystic und Das Wort. Der Gegensatz zwischen moderner Religionsauffassung und christlichen Glauben*. Tübingen: J. C. B. Mohr.

Buelow, George J. (1983). "Johann Mattheson and the Invention of the Affektenlehre," in *New Mattheson Studies*, ed. George J. Buelow and Hans Joachim Marx. Cambridge: Cambridge University Press.

Burdorf, Dieter, and Reinold Schmücker (1998). *Dialogische Wissenschaft: Perspektiven der Philosophie Schleiermachers*. Paderborn: F. Schöningh.

Calvin, Jean (1926–59). *Joannis Calvini Opera Selecta*, ed. Wilhelm Niesel, Peter Barth, and Doris Scheuner, 5 vols. Munich: Chr. Kaiser.

(1956). *Of the Eternal Predestination of God*. 1856, reprint, Grand Rapids: W. B. Eerdmans.

Capetz, Paul E. (1998). *Christian Faith as Religion: A Study in the Theologies of Calvin and Schleiermacher*. Lanham: University Press of America.

Clements, Keith W., ed. (1987). *Friedrich Schleiermacher: Pioneer of Modern Theology, Making of Modern Theology*. Augsburg: Fortress.

Clore, Gerald, and Andrew, Ortony (2000). "Cognition in Emotion: Always, Sometimes, Never?" in *Cognitive Neuroscience of Emotion*, ed. Richard D. Lane and Lynn Nadel. New York: Oxford University Press.

Cordes, Martin (1971). "Der Brief Schleiermachers an Jacobi: Ein Beitrag zu seiner Entstehung und Überlieferung." *Zeitschrift für Theologie und Kirche* 68: 195–211.

Crouter, Richard (1999). "Schleiermacher's *On Religion*: Hermeneutical Musings after Two Hundred Years." *Zeitschrift für neuere Theologiegeschichte/Journal for the History of Modern Theology* 6: 1–22.

Curran, Thomas H. (1994). *Doctrine and Speculation in Schleiermacher's Glaubenslehre*. Berlin: Walter de Gruyter.

Davidson, Donald (2001). *Subjective, Intersubjective, Objective*. Oxford: Clarendon Press.

Dawson, Jerry F. (1966). *Friedrich Schleiermacher: The Evolution of a Nationalist*. Austin: University of Texas Press.

DeVries, Dawn (1987). *Jesus Christ in the Preaching of Calvin and Schleiermacher*. Louisville: Westminster John Knox Press. [2nd edn. 1996]

Dilthey, Wilhelm (1960). *Zur Preussischen Geschichte*, 3rd edn. vol. 12, *Wilhelm Diltheys Gesammelte Schriften*. Stuttgart: B. G. Teubner.

(1972). *Leben Schleiermachers*, ed. Martin Redeker, vol. 13, *Wilhelm Dilthey, Gesammelte Schriften*. Gottingen: Vanderhoeck & Ruprecht.

Duke, James O., and Robert F. Streetman, eds. (1988). *Barth and Schleiermacher: Beyond the Impasse?* Philadelphia: Fortress Press.

Ebeling, Gerhard (1970). "Schleiermacher's Doctrine of the Divine Attributes," in *Schleiermacher as Contemporary*, ed. Robert W. Funk. New York: Herder and Herder.

Eberhard, Johann August, (1776). *Allgemeine Theorie des Denkens und Empfindens*. Eine Abhandlung welche den von der königl. Akademie der wissenschaften in Berlin auf das Jahr 1776 ausgesetzten Preis erhalten hat. Berlin: Friedrich Voss.

Ellis, Ieuan (1980). "Schleiermacher in Britain." *Scottish Journal of Theology* 33: 417–52.

Engel, Mary Potter, and Walter E. Wyman (1992). *Revisioning the Past: Prospects in Historical Theology*. Minneapolis: Fortress Press.

Fichte, Johann Gottlieb (1977). *Werke 1798–1799, Gesamtausgabe Werkeband 5*, ed. Reinhard Lauth and Hans Gliwtizky. Stuttgart: Fromman.

Fischer, Hermann (2001). *Friedrich Schleiermacher*, Beck'sche Reihe Denker, vol. 563. Munich: C. H. Beck.

Forstman, Jackson (1977). *A Romantic Triangle: Schleiermacher and Early German Romanticism*. AAR Studies in Religion, 13. Missoula: Scholars Press for the American Academy of Religion.

Frank, Manfred (1977). *Das individuelle Allgemeine: Textstrukturierung und Interpretation nach Schleiermacher*, vol. 1. Aufl. edn. Frankfurt am Main: Suhrkamp.

(1986). *Die Unhintergehbarkeit von Individualität. Reflexion über Subjekt, Person und Individuum aus Anlass ihrer Postmodernen Toterklärung*. Frankfurt am Main: Suhrkamp.

(1989). *Das Sagbare und das Unsagbare*. Frankfurt: Suhrkamp.

(1997). *"Unendliche Annäherung": Die Anfänge der philosophischen Frühromantik*, vol. 1. Aufl. edn. Frankfurt am Main: Suhrkamp.

(2002). *Selbstgefühl: Eine historisch-systematische Erkundung*, vol. 1. Aufl. edn. Frankfurt am Main: Suhrkamp.

(2004). *The Philosophical Foundations of Early German Romanticism*, trans. Elizabeth Millán-Zaibert. Albany: State University of New York Press.

Frank, Manfred, and Andrew Bowie (1997). *The Subject and the Text: Essays on Literary Theory and Philosophy*. Cambridge: Cambridge University Press.

Frege, Gottlob (1977). *Logical Investigations*. Oxford: Blackwell.

(1990). *Schriften zur Logik und Sprachphilosophie*. Hamburg: Felix Meiner.

Funk, Robert W., ed. (1970). *Schleiermacher as Contemporary*. New York: Herder and Herder.

Gadamer, Hans Georg (1975a). *Truth and Method*, trans. Garrett Barden and John Cumming. New York: Seabury Press.

(1975b). *Wahrheit und Methode: Grundzüge einer philosophischen Hermeneutik*. 4. Aufl., unveränderter Nachdruck der 3., erw. Aufl. ed. Tübingen: Mohr.

Gerrish, Brian A. (1978). *Tradition and the Modern World: Reformed Theology in the Nineteenth Century*. Chicago: University of Chicago Press.

(1982). *The Old Protestantism and the New: Essays on the Reformation Heritage*. Chicago: University of Chicago Press.

(1984). *A Prince of the Church: Schleiermacher and the Beginnings of Modern Theology*. Philadelphia: Fortress Press.

(1993). *Continuing the Reformation: Essays on Modern Religious Thought*. Chicago: University of Chicago Press.

Grillmeier, Alois (1975). *Christ in Christian Tradition: From the Apostolic Age to Chalcedon*, trans. John Bowden. 2nd edn. vol. 1. Atlanta: John Knox Press.

Grimm, Jacob (1999). *Deutsches Wörterbuch*, ed. Karl Euling, 33 vols, vol. 24. Munich: Deutscher Taschenbuch Verlag.

Grondin, Jean (1994). *Introduction to Philosophical Hermeneutics*. Yale Studies in Hermeneutics. New Haven: Yale University Press.

Guenther-Gleason, Patricia Ellen (1992). "Schleiermacher's Feminist Impulses in the Context of his Later Work," in *Schleiermacher and Feminism: Sources, Evaluations, and Responses*, ed. Iain G. Nicol, 95–127. Lewiston, N.Y.: Edwin Mellen Press.

(1997). *On Schleiermacher and Gender Politics*. Harrisburg: Trinity Press International.

Gunton, Colin E. (1997). *Yesterday and Today: A Study of Continuities in Christology.* Melksham: Cromwell Press.

Halleux, André (1986). "Personnalisme ou Essentialisme trinitaire chez les Pères Cappadociens?" *Revue théologique de Louvain* 17: 129–55 and 265–92.

Hamman, J. G. (1949–57). *Sämtliche Werke.* Vienna: Herder.

Hankey, W. J. (1987). *God in Himself: Aquinas' Doctrine of God as Expounded in the Summa Theologiae.* Oxford Theological Monographs. Oxford: Oxford University Press.

Hardtwig, Wolfgang (1998). "Die Verwissenschaftlichung der neueren Geschichtsschreibung," in *Geschichte: Ein Grundkurs*, ed. Hans-Jürgen Goertz. Reinbeck bei Hamburg: Rowohlt Taschenbuch Verlag.

Hegel, Georg Wilhelm Friedrich (1892). *The Logic of Hegel*, trans. William Wallace. 2nd edn. Oxford: Clarendon Press.

Helmer, Christine, ed. (2004). (in cooperation with Marjorie Suchoki, John Quiring, and Katie Goetz) *Schleiermacher and Whitehead: Open Systems in Dialogue.* Berlin: Walter de Gruyter.

Helmer, Christine, Christiane Kranich, and Birgit Rehme-Iffert, eds. (2003). *Schleiermachers Dialektik: Die Liebe Zum Wissen in Philosophie und Theologie.* Religion in Philosophy and Theology. 6. Tübingen: Mohr Siebeck.

Henrich, Dieter (1999). *Bewusstes Leben.* Stuttgart: Reclam.

Heppe, Heinrich (1978). *Reformed Dogmatics: Set Out and Illustrated from the Sources*, trans. G. T. Thompson. and ed. Ernst Bizer. London: George Allen & Unwin, 1950; reprint Grand Rapids: Baker House.

Herdt, Gilbert H. (1999). *Sambia Sexual Culture: Essays from the Field, Worlds of Desire.* Chicago: University of Chicago Press.

Herms, Eilert (1974). *Herkunft, Entfaltung und erste Gestalt des Systems der Wissenschaften Bei Schleiermacher.* Gütersloh: Gütersloher Verlagshaus Mohn.

(1992). "Platonismus und Aristotelismus in Schleiermachers Ethik," in *Schleiermacher's Philosophy and the Philosophical Tradition*, ed. Sergio Sorrentino, 3–26. Lewisten, N. Y.: Edwin Mellen Press.

(2003). *Menschsein im Werden: Studien zu Schleiermacher.* Tübingen: Mohr Siebeck.

Heydenreich, Karl Heinrich (1789). *Natur und Gott nach Spinoza*, vol. 1. Leipzig: Joh. Gottfr. Müllershen Buchhandlung.

Hick, John (1978). *Evil and the God of Love.* Revised edn. New York: Harper and Row.

Hübner, Ingolf (1997). *Wissenschaftsbegriff und Theologieverständnis: Eine Untersuchung zu Schleiermachers Dialektik.* Berlin: Walter de Gruyter.

Iamblichus (1973). *Iamblichi Chalcidensis in Platonis Dialogos Commentariorum Fragmenta*, ed. John M. Dillon. Philosophia Antiqua, Vol. 23. Leiden: Brill.

Iggers, Georg G. (1995). "Historicism: The History and Meaning of the Term." *Journal of the History of Ideas* 56: 129–52.

Jensen, Robert W. (1982). *The Triune Identity.* Philadelphia: Fortress.

Johnson, William A. (1964). *On Religion: A Study of Theological Method in Schleiermacher and Nygren.* Leiden: Brill.

Jørgensen, Poul Henning. (1959). *Die Ethik Schleiermachers*, ed. Ernst Wolf. Forschungen zur Geschichte und Lehre des Protestantismus, vol. 14. Munich: Kaiser Verlag.

Kant, Immanuel (1960). *Religion within the Limits of Reason Alone,* trans. Theodore M. Greene and Hoyt H. Hudson. New York: Harper and Row.

(1996). *Metaphysics of Morals.* Cambridge Texts in the History of Philosophy. New York: Cambridge University Press.

(1997). *Groundwork of the Metaphysics of Morals,* trans. Mary J. Gregor. Cambridge Texts in the History of Philosophy. Cambridge: Cambridge University Press.

(1998). *Critique of Pure Reason,* trans. Paul Guyer and Allen W. Wood. Cambridge: Cambridge University Press.

Kasper, Walter (1984). *The God of Jesus Christ.* New York: Crossroad.

Kelsey, Catherine L. (2003). *Thinking About Christ with Schleiermacher.* Louisville: Westminster John Knox Press.

Kloppenborg, John S. (2000). *Excavating Q: The History and Setting of the Sayings Gospel.* Minneapolis: Fortress Press.

Kraeling, Emil Gottlieb Heinrich (1955). *The Old Testament since the Reformation.* London: Lutterworth Press.

Kraus, Hans-Joachim (1988). *Geschichte der historisch-kritischen Erforschung des alten Testaments.* 4th edn. Neukirchen: Neukirchener Verlag.

Lamm, Julia A. (1994). "The Early Philosophical Roots of Schleiermacher's Notion of Gefühl, 1788–1794." *Harvard Theological Review* 87/1: 67–105.

(1996). *The Living God: Schleiermacher's Theological Appropriation of Spinoza.* University Park: Pennsylvania State University Press.

(2000). "Schleiermacher as Plato Scholar." *The Journal of Religion* 80/2: 206–39.

(2003). "Reading Plato's Dialectics: Schleiermacher's Insistence on Dialectics as Dialogical." *Zeitschrift für neuere Theologiegeschichte/Journal for the History of Modern Theology* 10/1: 1–25.

Landmesser, Christof (1999). *Wahrheit als Grundbegriff neutestamentlicher Wissenschaft,* vol. 113. *Wissenschaftliche Untersuchungen zum neuen Testament.* Tübingen: Mohr Siebeck.

Leibniz, Gottfried Wilhelm (1989). *Philosophical Essays,* trans. ed. Roger Ariew and Daniel Garber. Indianapolis: Hackett Pub. Co.

Lessing, Eckhard (1979). "Zu Schleiermachers Verstandnis der Trinitätslehre." *Zeitschrift für Theologie und Kirche* 76: 450–88.

(1985) *Fragments,* trans. Charles H. Talbert. Lives of Jesus. Philadelphia: Fortress Press.

Lücke, Friedrich (1834). "Erinnerungen an Dr. Fr. Schleiermacher." *Theologische Studien und Kritiken* 7: 771.

(1840). "Fragen und Bedenken über die Immanente Wesenstrinität, oder die Trinitarische Sebstunterscheidung Gottes." *Theologische Studien und Kritiken* 13: 63–112.

Luft, Eric von der, ed. (1984). *Hegel, Hinrichs, and Schleiermacher on Feeling and Reason in Religion: The Texts of Their 1821–22 Debate.* Studies in German Thought and History, 3. Lewiston, N.Y.: Edwin Mellen Press.

Mackintosh, H.R. (1952). *Types of Modern Theology: Schleiermacher to Barth.* London: Nisbet and Co. Ltd., distributed by Scribner.

Mariña, Jacqueline (1996). "Schleiermacher's Christology Revisited: A Reply to His Critics." *Scottish Journal of Theology* 49/2: 177–200.

(1998). "A Critical–Interpretive Analysis of Some Early Writings by Schleiermacher on Kant's Views on Human Nature and Freedom (1789–1799) with Translated Texts." *New Athenaeum/Neues Athenaeum* 5: 11–31.

(1999). "Schleiermacher on the Philosopher's Stone: The Shaping of Schleiermacher's Early Ethics by the Kantian Legacy." *Journal of Religion* 79/2: 193–215.

(2004a). "Schleiermacher between Kant and Leibniz: Predication and Ontology," in *Schleiermacher and Whitehead: Open Systems in Dialogue*, ed. Christiane Kranich, Birgit Rehme-Iffert, and Christine Helmer. Berlin: Walter de Gruyter.

(2004b). "Schleiermacher on the Outpourings of the Inner Fire: Experiential Expressivism and Religious Pluralism." *Religious Studies* 40: 125–43.

"Transcendental and Phenomenological Analyses of Religious Feeling: Friedrich Schleiermacher and Rudolf Otto," in *The Oxford Handbook of Religion and Emotion*, ed. John Corrigan. Oxford: Oxford University Press, forthcoming.

Massey, Marilyn Chapin (1985). *Feminine Soul: The Fate of an Ideal*. Boston: Beacon Press.

Mates, Benson (1986). *The Philosophy of Leibniz: Metaphysics and Language*. New York: Oxford University Press.

McGrath, Alister E. (2001). *The Christian Theology Reader*. Oxford: Blackwell.

Meckenstock, Günter (1988). *Deterministische Ethik und kritische Theologie: Die Auseinandersetzung des Frühen Schleiermacher mit Kant und Spinoza, 1789–1794*. Schleiermacher-Archiv, vol. 5. Berlin: Walter de Gruyter.

Meckenstock, Günter, and Joachim Ringleben (1991). *Schleiermacher und die wissenschaftliche Kultur des Christentums*. Berlin; New York: Walter de Gruyter.

Meding, Wichmann von (1992). *Bibliographie der Schriften Schleiermachers nebst einer Zusammenstellung und Datierung seiner gedrückten Predigten*. Schleiermacher-Archiv, vol. 9. Berlin: Walter de Gruyter.

Meeks, M. Douglas (1982). "Trinitarian Theology: A Review Article." *Theology Today* 38: 472–7.

Möhler, Johann Adam (1827). *Athanasius der Grosse und die Kirche seiner Zeit, besonders im Kampfe mit dem Arianismus*. Mainz: Florian Kupferberg.

(1996). *Unity in the Church or the Principle of Catholicism: Presented in the Spirit of the Church Fathers of the First Three Centuries*, trans. Peter Erb. Washington, D.C.: Catholic University of America Press.

Moltmann, Jürgen (1981). *The Trinity and the Kingdom: The Doctrine of God*. San Francisco: Harper and Row.

(1990). *The Way of Jesus Christ: Christology in Messianic Dimensions*. San Francisco: Harper and Row.

Murmann-Kahl, Michael (1997). *Mysterium Trinitatis*. Berlin: Walter de Gruyter.

Nicol, Iain G. (1992). *Schleiermacher and Feminism: Sources, Evaluations, and Responses*. Schleiermacher Studies and Translations, vol. 12. Lewiston, N.Y.: Edwin Mellen Press.

Niebuhr, Richard R. (1964). *Schleiermacher on Christ and Religion: A New Introduction*. New York: Charles Scribner's Sons.

(1970). "Schleiermacher and the Names of God: A Consideration of Schleiermacher in Relation to Our Theism," in *Schleiermacher as Contemporary*, ed. Robert W. Funk, 176–205. New York: Herder and Herder.

Nitzsch, Carl Immanuel (1829). *System der christlichen Lehre*. Bonn: A. Marcus.
(1841). "Uber Die Wesentlich Dreieinigkeiten Gottes." *Theologische Studien und Kritiken* 14: 295–345.

Nowak, Kurt (2001). *Schleiermacher: Leben, Werk und Wirkung*. Göttingen: Vandenhoeck & Ruprecht.

Ogden, Schubert M. (1982). *The Point of Christology*. San Francisco: Harper and Row.
(1986). *On Theology*. San Francisco: Harper and Row.

Palmer, Richard E. (1969). *Hermeneutics: Interpretation Theory in Schleiermacher, Dilthey, Heidegger, and Gadamer*. Northwestern University Studies in Phenomenology and Existential Philosophy. Evanston: Northwestern University Press.

Panksepp, Jaak (1998). *Affective Neuroscience: The Foundations of Human and Animal Emotions*. New York: Oxford University Press.

Pannenberg, Wolfhart (1991). *Systematic Theology*. Grand Rapids: Eerdmans.

Park, John Sungmin (2001). *Theological Ethics of Friedrich Schleiermacher*. Schleiermacher Studies and Translations, 20. Lewiston, N.Y.: Edwin Mellen Press.

Patsch, Hermann (1991). "Die Angst vor dem Deuteropaulinismus: Die Rezeption des 'Kritischen Sendschreibens' Friedrich Schleiermachers über den 1. Timotheusbrief im ersten Jahrfunft." *Zeitschrift für Theologie und Kirche* 88: 451–77.

Plantinga, Alvin, and Nicholas Wolterstorff (1983). *Faith and Rationality: Reason and Belief in God*. Notre Dame: University of Notre Dame Press.

Plato (1987). *The Republic*, trans. Desmond Lee. 2nd edn. London: Penguin Books.

Pleger, Wolfgang H. (1988). *Schleiermachers Philosophie*. Berlin: Walter de Gruyter.

Proclus (1963). *The Elements of Theology*, trans. E. R. Dodds. 2nd edn. Oxford: Clarendon Press.

Proudfoot, Wayne (1985). *Religious Experience*. Berkeley: University of California Press.

Raack, R. C. (1964). "A New Schleiermacher Letter on the Conspiracy of 1808." *Zeitschrift für Religions- und Geistesgeschichte* 16: 209–23.

Rahner, Karl (1970). *The Trinity*. New York: Herder and Herder.

Reble, Albert (1935). *Schleiermachers Kulturphilosophie: Eine Entwicklungs Geschichtlich-Systematische Würdigung*. Erfurt: K. Stenger.

Redeker, Martin (1973). *Schleiermacher: Life and Thought*. Philadelphia: Fortress Press.

Reimarus, Hermann Samuel (1985). *Reimarus, Fragments*, trans. Ralph S. Fraser and ed. Charles H. Talbert. Scholars Press Reprints and Translations Series. Chico: Scholars Press.

Reuter, Hans-Richard (1979). *Die Einheit der Dialektik Friedrich Schleiermachers: Eine systematische Interpretation*. Beiträge zur evangelischen Theologie, Theologische Abhandlungen, vol. 83. Munich: Kaiser.

Richardson, Ruth (1991a), ed. *Schleiermacher in Context*. Schleiermacher Studies and Translations, 6. Lewiston, N.Y.: Edwin Mellen Press.
(1991b). *The Role of Women in the Life and Thought of the Early Schleiermacher (1768–1806): An Historical Overview*. Lewiston, N.Y.: Edwin Mellen Press.
(1995). *Friedrich Schleiermacher's "Toward a Theory of Social Conduct" and Essays in Its Intellectual-Cultural Context*. Lewiston, N.Y.: Edwin Mellen Press.
(1998), ed. *Schleiermacher on Workings of the Knowing Mind: New Translations, Resources, and Understandings*. Lewiston, N.Y.: Edwin Mellen Press.

Rist, John M. (1967). *Plotinus: The Road to Reality*. Cambridge: Cambridge University Press.

Roessler, Beate (1990). *Die Theorie des Verstehens in Sprachanalyse und Hermeneutik*. Berlin: Dunker and Humblot.

Rosenkranz, Karl (1831). *Enzyklopädie der theologischen Wissenschaften*. Halle: C. A. Schwetschke & Sohn.

Rössler, Martin (1994). *Schleiermachers Programm der Philosophischen Theologie*. Schleiermacher-Archiv, 14. Berlin: Walter de Gruyter.

Rousseau, Jean-Jacques (1983). "The Creed of a Savoyard Priest," in *The Essential Rousseau*. New York: Meridian.

Ruether, Rosemary Radford (1983). *Sexism and God-Talk: Toward a Feminist Theology*. Boston: Beacon Press.

Sadie, Julie Anne (1990). "Johann Mattheson," in *Companion to Baroque Music*, 171–2. Berkeley: University of California Press.

Schelling, Friedrich Wilhelm Joseph (1856). *Friedrich Wilhelm Joseph von Schellings Sämmtliche Werke*, ed. Karl Friedrich August Schelling. Stuttgart, Augsburg: J. G. Cotta.

(1946). *Die Weltalter: Fragmente*, ed. by Manfred Schröter. Munich: Biederstein Verlag.

Schlegel, Friedrich von (1800). "Ankündigung," in *Intelligenzblatt der Allegemeinen Literatur-Zeitung* 43 [also in *Poetischen Journal* 1:2]

(1971). *Friedrich Schlegel's Lucinde and the Fragments*, trans. Peter Firchow. Minneapolis: University of Minnesota Press.

Schmid, Heinrich, ed. (1961). *The Doctrinal Theology of the Evangelical Lutheran Church*, trans. Charles A. Hay and Henry E. Jacobs. 3rd edn. Minneapolis: Augsburg.

Scholtz, Gunter (1981). *Schleiermachers Musikphilosophie*. Göttingen: Vandenhoeck & Ruprecht.

(1984). *Die Philosophie Schleiermachers*. Darmstadt: Wissenschaftliche Buchgesellshaft.

(1995). *Ethik Und Hermeneutik: Schleiermachers Grundlegung Der Geisteswissenschaften*. Frankfurt am Main: Suhrkamp.

Schröder, Markus (1996). *Die kritische Identität des Christentums: Schleiermachers Wesensbetimmung der christlichen Religion*. Tübingen: J. C. B. Mohr (Paul Siebbeck).

Schwarz, F. H. C. (1812). "Review of Schleiermacher's *Brief Outline*." *Heidelberger Jahrbücher der Litteratur* 5/33: 526–7.

Segundo, Juan Luis, and Alfred T. Hennelly (1993). *Signs of the Times: Theological Reflections*. Maryknoll: Orbis Books.

Selbie, W. B. (1913). *Schleiermacher: A Critical and Historical Study*. London: Chapman and Hall.

Sheehan, James J. (1989). *German History, 1770–1866*. Oxford History of Modern Europe. Oxford: Oxford University Press.

Smend, Rudolf (1991). "Schleiermacher's Kritik am alten Testament," in *Epochen der Bibelkritik: Gesammelte Studien*, ed. Rudolf Smend, 128–44. Munich: Chr. Kaiser.

Smith, Wilfred Cantwell (1991). *The Meaning and End of Religion*. 1st Fortress Press edn. Minneapolis: Fortress Press.

Sockness, Brent (2001). "Was Schleiermacher a Virtue Ethicist?: Tugend and Bildung in the Early Ethical Writings." *Zeitschrift für neuere Theologiegeschichte/Journal for the History of Modern Theology* 8: 1–33.

(2003). "The Forgotten Moralist: Friedrich Schleiermacher and the Science of Spirit." *Harvard Theological Review* 96/3: 317–48.

(2004). "Schleiermacher and the Ethics of Authenticity." *Journal of Religious Ethics* 32/3: 477–517.

Sorrentino, Sergio, ed. (1992). *Schleiermacher's Philosophy and the Philosophical Tradition, Schleiermacher Studies and Translations.* Lewiston, N.Y.: Edwin Mellen Press.

Steiger, Johann A. (1994). "Friedrich Daniel Ernst Schleiermacher, Das Alte Testament Und Das Alter: Zur Geschichte Einer Überraschenden Alterseinsicht." *Kerygma und Dogma* 40: 305–27.

Stein, Craig (2001). *Schleiermacher's Construction of the Subject in the Introduction to the Christian Faith in Light of M. Foucault's Critique of Modern Knowledge.* Schleiermacher Studies and Translations, 19. Lewiston, N.Y.: Edwin Mellen Press.

Stein, Karl (1931). *Briefwechsel, Denkschriften und Aufzeichnungen.* n.p.

Strauss, David Friedrich (1876–8). *Gesammelte Schriften*, ed. Eduard Zeller. Vol. 5. Bonn.

(1972). *The Life of Jesus Critically Examined,* trans. George Eliot and ed. Peter Hodgson. Philadelphia: Fortress Press.

(1977). *The Christ of Faith and the Jesus of History: A Critique of Schleiermacher's Life of Jesus,* trans. and ed. Leander E. Keck. Philadelphia: Fortress Press.

Suchocki, Marjorie (1994). *Fall Into Violence: Original Sin in Relational Theology.* New York: Continuum.

Takamori, Akira (1991). "Interpretation der Lehre von den gottlichen Eigenschaften in Schleiermachers Glaubenslehre," in *Schleiermacher und die Wissenschaftliche Kultur des Christentums,* ed. Günter Meckenstock and Joachim Ringleben. Berlin: Walter de Gruyter.

Tanner, Kathryn (1997). *Theories of Culture: A New Agenda for Theology.* Guides to Theological Inquiry. Minneapolis: Fortress Press.

Tennemann, W. G. (1792). *System Der Platonischen Philosophie,* 2 vols. Leipzig: Barth.

Thandeka (1995). *The Embodied Self: Friedrich Schleiermacher's Solution to Kant's Problem of the Empirical Self.* Suny Series in Philosophy. Albany: State University of New York Press.

Thiel, John E. (1991). *Imagination and Authority: Theological Authorship in the Modern Tradition.* Minneapolis: Fortress Press.

Tice, Terrence (1966). *Schleiermacher Bibliography.* Princeton Pamphlets, 12. Princeton: Princeton Theological Seminary.

(1991a). "Schleiermacher and the Founding of the University of Berlin," in *Schleiermacher and the Founding of the University of Berlin,* ed. Herbert Richardson, 45–82. Lewiston, N.Y.: Edwin Mellen Press.

(1991b). "Schleiermacher's Psychology: An Early, Modern Approach, a Challenge to Current Tendencies," in *Schleiermacher und die wissenshaftliche Kultur des Christentums,* ed. Gunter Meckenstock and Joachim Ringleben, 509–21. Berlin: Walter de Gruyter.

(1997). *Schleiermacher's Sermons: A Chronological Listing and Account.* Schleiermacher Studies and Translations, 15. Lewiston, N.Y.: Edwin Mellen Press.

(1998). "Translation as a Philosophical Art." *New Athanaeum/Neues Athenaeum* 5: 115–28.

(2002). "Speaking the Truth in Love: Schleiermacher's Perspectives on Church Governance and Service." *Toronto Journal of Theology* 18/1: 21–32.

(2003a). "Schleiermacher's Concept of Ministry: Proclamation in the Christian Life," in *Schleiermacher Festschrift for Michael Ryan.* Lewiston, N.Y.. Edwin Mellen Press.

(2003b). "Schleiermacher's Use of Philosophical Mindedness in Theology," in *Schleiermachers Dialektik: Die Liebe zum Wissen in Philosophie und Theologie,* ed. Christiane Kranich, Birgit Rehme-Iffert, and Christine Helmer. Tubingen: Mohr Siebeck.

Tigerstedt, E. N. (1974). *The Decline and Fall of the Neoplatonic Interpretation of Plato: An Outline and Some Observations.* Commentationes Humanarum Litterarum, 52. Helsinki-Helsingfors: Societas Scientiarum Fennica.

Tillich, Paul (1951). *The Protestant Era,* trans. and ed. James Luther Adams. London: Nisbet.

Trillhass, Wolfgang (1991). "Schleiermachers Predigten Uber Alttestamentliche Texte," in *Schleiermacher und die wissenschaftliche Kultur des Christentums,* ed. Gunter Meckenstock and Joachim Ringleben, 279–89. Berlin: Walter de Gruyter.

Twesten, A. (1837). *Vorlesungen über die Dogmatik der evangelisch-lutherischen Kirche,* ed. Wilhelm Leberecht de Wette. Hamburg: F. Perth.

Vance, Robert Lee (1994). *Sin and Self-Consciousness in the Thought of Friedrich Schleiermacher.* Lewiston, N.Y.: Edwin Mellen Press.

Virmond, Wolfgang (1985). "Neue Textgrundlagen zu Schleiermachers früher Hermeneutik." *Schleiermacher-Archiv,* vol. 1, 1271–310. Berlin: Walter de Gruyter.

Wagner, Falk (1974). *Schleiermachers Dialektik: Eine kritische Interpretation.* Gütersloh: Gütersloher Verlagshaus Mohn.

Wallmann, Johannes (1994). "Vom Katechismuschristentum zum Bibelchristentum: Zum Bibelverständnis im Pietismus," in *Die Zukunft des Schriftprinzips,* ed. Richard Ziegert, 30–56. Stuttgart: Deutsche Bibelgesellschaft.

Weisse, Christian (1841). "Zur Verteidigung des Begriffes der immanenten Wesenstrinität." *Theologische Studien und Kritiken* 14: 345–410.

Welch, Claude (1952). *In This Name: the Doctrine of the Trinity in Contemporary Theology.* New York: Charles Scribner's Sons.

de Wette, Wilhelm Martin Leberecht, and Friedrich Lücke (1818). *Synopsis Evangeliorum Matthaei, Marci et Lucae cum Parallelis Joannis Pericopis.* Berlin: Reimer.

Wiles, Maurice F. (1976). "Some Reflections on the Origins of the Doctrine of the Trinity," in *Working Papers in Doctrine,* ed. Maurice F. Wiles, 1–18. London: SMC.

Williams, Bernard Arthur Owen (2002). *Truth and Truthfulness: An Essay in Genealogy.* Princeton: Princeton University Press.

Williams, Robert R. (1978). *Schleiermacher the Theologian: The Construction of the Doctrine of God.* Philadelphia: Fortress Press.

Wolfes, Matthias (2002). "Öffentlichkeit und Nationalstaat. Friedrich Schleiermachers politische Wirksamkeit, insbesondere während des Jahrzehnts der preussisch-französischen Konfrontation von 1806 bis 1815." Ph.D. Dissertation, Christian-Albrechts-University Kiel (To be published by Walter de Gruyter in 2005 under the title: *Öffentlichkeit und Nationalstaat. Friedrich Schleiermachers politische Wirksamkeit*).

Wyman, Walter E. (1991). "The Historical Consciousness and the Study of Theology," in *Shifting Boundaries: Contextual Approaches to the Structure of Theological Education*, ed. Barbara G. Wheeler and Edward Farley. Westminster: John Knox Press.

(1994). "Rethinking the Christian Doctrine of Sin: Friedrich Schleiermacher and Hick's 'Irenaean Type'." *Journal of Religion* 74/2(April): 199–217.

(2001). "Testing Liberalism's Conceptuality: The Relation of Sin and Evil in Schleiermacher's Theology," in *Ethical Monotheism, Past and Present: Essays in Honor of Wendell S. Dietrich*, ed. Theodore M. Vial and Mark A. Hadley. Brown Judaic Studies, 329. Providence: Brown University.

Ziolkowski, Theodore (2004). *Clio the Romantic Muse: Historicizing the Faculties in Germany*. Ithaca and London: Cornell University Press.

Index

absolute 17, 19, 24–5, 31, 66–8, 79–80, 81, 263
absolute being 79
absolute blessedness 217
absolute communality of being 178
absolute dependence 30, 31, 156–9
absolute idealism 32, 79
absolute identity of being and knowledge 79
absolute identity of subjectivity and objectivity 260
absolute power 178
absolute Spirit 19
absolute subject 23, 24, 178
academic disciplines 113
act, intentional 30
action 54–8, 214–16
  morally indifferent 66, 69
  worth 56
aesthetic production 76
aesthetics 289
Aesthetics 88
affect 289–92
affection
  doctrine of 288–96
  moments of 289–92
affections 288–99
  pious 295
age of the apostles 117
agency, human 195, 196
alienation from God 129
all-one 193
analytic philosophy 88–9
analytic/synthetic distinction 81
An Cecilie 63
Anselm 171
anthropocentrism 35
anthropology 60, 152, 159, 214
anti-foundationalism 17
apologetics 115, 116, 120
Apology 95
Apostles' Creed 191
Aquinas, Thomas 44, 171, 174–5, 184
Aramaic *Urgospel* 234
Arianism 172
Arians 153–4
Aristotle 53, 61, 91
artist 292–4, 299, 302

art of disagreement (*Kunstlehre*) 80
arts 251, 265–7
Athanasius 172, 183
atheism 41
Athenaeumsfragmente 60, 63
atonement 140
Aufklärung 60, 63
Augustine 171, 186, 202
Augustinian tradition 130
author, relation to text 73–6
authorial intentions 73, 239–40

Barth, Karl 146, 159–60, 162, 171, 184, 186, 197–8, 202
Barthes 76
Baumgarten, Alexander Gottlieb 27
Baur, F. C. 159, 162
being 23, 25, 26–7, 28, 30, 31, 32–3, 77–8, 87
  as transcendent to consciousness 31–2
  common 34
  ground of 34
  highest 24
  of God in Christ 176, 181–2
  of God in the church 176
belief 259, 260, 265
benevolence 62–3
Bible 230, 233
biblical and credal teachings 112
biblical theology 111
Bildung 251–2
Birkner, Hans-Joachim 126
Bishop Berkeley 32
blessedness 138–43, 147, 166–8
Böckh, August 92
Boethius 185
Bolzano 75
Bretschneider, Karl Gottlieb 175, 202
Brief Outline 112–27, 214, 233, 263
Briefe über die Lehre von Spinoza 56
brotherly love 219, 227
Brouillon zur Ethik 53, 66–9, 301
Brunner, Emil 162

Calvin, John 111, 189, 200
Calvinism, divine decree 202

canon 230
  determination of 233–5
categorical imperatives 68
categories 76
Catholicism 144
causal relation
  experience of 40
  laws 54
  philosophical conception 176–8
causality 193–7
  epistemological significance 177
  general 193–7
  knowledge of 178
  ontological significance 177
  particular 193–7
  theological significance 177
causation, natural 193–7
causes
  free 195–7
  natural 195–7
chaos 23
character 56
Christ 138–43, 151–2, 180–2, 298
  activity of 198–202
  apprehension of 242
  as completion of human nature 160–2
  as expression of the divine 156–9
  as ideal 159–62
  as mere exemplar 159
  as second Adam 146
  as teacher and example 130
  atoning death of 130
  divine intellect 155
  divine nature 153–6, 157–9
  divine will 155
  human intellect 155, 157
  human nature 153–6, 157–9
  human will 155, 157
  incarnation of 195–6, 203
  influence 238
  moral development 157–9
  new life in 198–202
  original appearance 241
  Passion of 167–8
  person and work of 199
  person-forming activity 295–6
  person of 181–2
  priestly office 139
  prophetic office 139
  redemptive activity 129, 295–6
  redemptive work 219
  self-consciousness of 156–9
  sinless perfection 139–42
  Spirit of 219, 221–3, 227
  spiritual originality 48
  temptation of 158
  two natures 153

  unity of person 153–6, 157
  work of 162–3, 224–5
Christ–Scripture relation 230–3
Christian community 116–17, 165–6, 181–2,
    199, 211–12
  common spirit of 142–3
  role of 141
Christian consciousness 116–17, 120
  in history 117–18
  incentives of 217–20
  modern account of 112
  of God 176, 177
  of God as triune 180–2
  of redemption 179
Christian ethics 119, 124, 151, 209, 213–27
Christian Ethics 209, 214–27
Christian faith 209, 213–16
Christian Faith 26, 30, 35–50, 112, 125, 146–7, 159,
    172, 175–6, 190–205, 214–16, 235, 271
  Introduction 115, 130–2, 221–2
  reception 183–5
Christian history 114, 211–12
Christian household 223
Christian life 216–27
Christian mission 226
Christian pedagogy 226
Christian piety 129, 138
  as incentive 215
Christian theology, origin 116
Christianity 129, 236, 262–3
  as positive religion 263
  essence of 211–12, 213, 232–4, 241
  origin 232
Christmas Eve 288–9, 297–9, 301
Christological preference criterion 236
Christology 47–8, 151–68, 181–2, 273–5, 294–6,
    297–9
  Antiochene 154–5
  Apollinarian 168
  empirical view 273
  logos/sarx 156
  magical view 273
church 181–2, 199, 211–12, 225, 227
  actual life of 120
  community 115
  contemporary situation of 211
  discipline 222
  governance 123, 124, 125
    synodal meetings 125
    teaching and writing 125
  government 212, 281
  history 118–19, 212, 232–3
  improvement 223
  leadership 125
  life of 212
  organization 225
  origin 274–5

pastoral care 222
reform 281–2
service 124–5
  catechetics 124
  edification 124
  liturgics 124
  missions 124
  pedagogy 124
  preaching 124
  regulation 124
  statistics 120, 212, 233
church and state 280–2
Church Dogmatics 197
civil community 225–6
civil society 223–4, 226, 287
Colossians 1:15–20 229, 239
common Christian life 221–7
common human life 221–4
common life, new 199–200
communal life, forms of 225–6
communion with Christ
  (*Lebensgemeinschaft*) 200–02
community 274–5
  as originating in founder 273–5
  political 276
comparative procedure 86
comparison 86
compatibilism 56–8
concept 28, 178, 296
  a priori 33
  complete 22
  empirical 74
  extension of 22
  formation 240–2
  immediate 27
  individual 22
  innate 81
  Kant's understanding 22
  of God, metaphysical 178–80
  pure 74
  upper and lower limits of 23–4
  Wolffian school understanding 22
concepts and judgments, limits of 25
concupiscence 136
conditions of the identity of an object 16
confessional documents 135
confessions
  Evangelical 190
  Lutheran and Reformed 201
  sixteenth-century 129, 145
Consciousness
  common 142–3
  human 287, 289–90, 291–2
  immediate 255
  of guilt 200
  of sin 132–4, 162
  sensible 242

sensuous 218–19
theology of 133
transcendent unity 29
transformation of 143
consensus theory 80
constitutional monarchy 276
consummated church 46
contemporary dogmatics 117
content (sense-data) 76
conversion 144, 197–202
corporate life, as divinely effected 138–40,
  140–3, 166–8
correspondence theory of truth 32, 78–80, 242
cosmic dualism 195
counsels of prudence 68
creation 41, 190–1, 220, 224–5
  from nothing 26
creativity 293–4
Critias 106
critical discipline 113, 123
critical reflection 260
criticism 253–4
crucifixion 140
culture 251–67

Davidson, Donald 76, 79–83, 84, 87
deism 273
democratic equality 172
Derrida, Jacques 76
Descartes, René 75
desire 252
determinism 54–8, 67
developing creation, Irenaean picture 145
Dialectic 15–16, 17–33, 37, 43, 76–83, 84, 230, 237,
  240–2, 260–2, 263–4
Diatesseron 234
dicta probantia method 231, 244
Dilthey, Wilhelm 269
Dionysius 175
disposition, formation of 224–6
distinction between "is" and "ought" 68
divide
  spontaneous/receptive 83
  technical/grammatical 83
divided line 259–61, 265
divination 86–7, 238
divine activity 43–4, 174, 197
divine attributes 43–4, 44–5, 176–80, 187, 191
divine causality 44–5, 47–8, 137–8, 144, 160–2,
  173, 176–80, 182, 185–7, 190–7
  as absolute 194–7
divine essence 47, 175–87, impartation of 47
divine goodness 175–6
divine good-pleasure 204
divine governance 202–05
divine grace 182
divine knowledge 175–6

divine love 47, 159, 165–6, 179–80, 182, 191
divine omnipotence 194, 195
divine operations 175
divine persons 175
divine power 175–6
divine preservation 190–7, 203–04
divine punishment 201–02
divine wisdom 175, 179–80, 182, 191
divine world-governance 191–7
divine wrath 201–02
Docetic heresy 152–3
Docetism 168
doctrines/doctrine 38, 41–5, 151–2, 307–08
  Christian 111, 213–16
  development of 233
  of human affections 287
  of preservation 180
  of the soul 287
  practical 213–27
dogmatics 118, 119–23, 129
dogmatic theology 113–14, 115, 212, 230, 233,
  243–5, 263, 271
  relation to canon 122
  relation to history 120–3
doing 210, 214–16
Dülon, Friedrich Ludwig 288
duty 69, 217

earliest Christianity 118
Eberhard 17, 18–19, 27
ecclesiology 189
economy of salvation 178
education of children 223
egoism 62
election 189–90, 202–05
  universal 203–04
emerging blessedness 217–20, 224–5, 227
  as incentive 218–20
emotions, religious 132
empathy 86
empirical discipline 123
empirical world of nature 55
empiricism 40
encyclopedia 112–13, 125, 125–6
Encyclopedia of the Philosophical Sciences 112,
  115
Encyclopedia of Theological Sciences 113
ends of life 58–60
Enlightenment 129, 230, 253–4, 273
Enlightenment rationalism 129
ensoulment of nature through reason 210,
  214–15, 220, 221–2
Entwurf eines Systems der Sittenlehre 66
epistemological certainty 80
epistemology 23, 237
  of religion 35–50
Eros 99–100, 101

eschatology 46–7
essence of Christianity 116–17, 126, 130
eternal damnation 46
ethical life 221–7
ethics 15, 53–70, 113, 232–3, 237, 264–5
  as history 68
  its relation to physics 67
Ethics 88
Ethik 53, 58, 66–70
Eunomius 177
Eutyches 155
evil 137–8, 194–5
  as punishment for sin 137–8
  relation to sin 137
exclusivism 252, 254
exegesis, methodology 230–2
exegetical theology 118, 120, 212, 229–45, 233–6
expansive action (erweiterndes Handeln)
  218–20, 221, 224–6
experience 35
expressive action (darstellendes Handeln)
  219–20, 226–7
external order 223
extra-canonical literature 234

faith 35–45, 121, 144, 145, 200
  as assenting certainty 42
  as conceptually structured 41
  as grounded in religious consciousness
  35–50
  Catholic and Protestant understandings 145
  definition of 122
  expressions of 217
  in Christ 45–8
  in God 40–5, 49–50
Fall 130
  traditional doctrine of 134
Fall and restoration, Augustinian picture 145
false church 257–8, 261
family 223–4, 287–8
  devotions 223
fatalism 56
Father 180
feeling 28, 30, 36, 87–8, 131, 210, 255–6, 266–7,
  273–5, 287, 289–92
  as dependent on conceptual thought 39
  of absolute dependence 28, 37–44, 130–1, 152,
  191, 192–3
  of being 27
  religious 28, 42–3, 298
  sensuous world 217
fellowship
  of believers 140–3
  with God 129
feminism 63, 287, 300–04
feminist theory 303–04
fetishism 222

Fichte, Johann Gottlieb (1762–1814) 16, 30, 56, 65, 68, 80, 111, 184, 186, 232
fidelity to Christian tradition 129
filioque 186
final causes 68
finite 67
finite being 193–7
finite causality 160, 177–8
first philosophy 260
fixing or individuation of the object 16
Flacius 237
flesh 132, 133–4, 136, 138, 164, 165, 215, 216, 218, 220, 222, 224–5
refractoriness 220, 221–3
foreordination 192
forgiveness of sins 139, 144, 200–02
foundational power of the soul 20
foundationalism 87
four natural heresies 152–3
Frank, Manfred 76, 87, 240
freedom 31, 73, 178, 252, 253
absolute 131, 193
human 195
Kant's view of 55
relative 193
Frege 75, 78–9
Friedrich the Great 278
fundus animae 34
Fürwahrhalten, "Holding as true" 51
fusion of horizons 75, 83

Gabler, Johann Phillip 231
Gadamer, Hans Georg 75–6, 83, 122
Galen 177
Gass, Joachim Christian 198
Gefühl 28
gendered distinctions, reification 300–03
gender images and concepts 292–4, 297–9
gender superiority 301
general validity 84
of utterances 84
German idealism 17, 77, 80
Gespräche über die Freiheit 54–6
gesture 88, 291, 294, 295
given 88
God 24, 26, 35, 37–8, 131, 152, 215, 252, 253
activity of 161
as author of sin 146, 194–5
as love 44, 176
as omniscient 44
as One in All 193–7
as power 176, 178
as present in Christ 156–9
as triune 171–87
as unchangeable 197
as wisdom 176
doctrine of 151, 175–87, 189

external activity 175
idea of 264
nature 175–6
oneness 172
relation to world 160–1, 179, 190–7
God-consciousness 130–47, 152, 156–7, 242
as transcendental 163
God-feeling 217, 220, 222
God-forgetfulness 130, 133
Godlessness 130
good 69, 217, 259, 261
grace 132, 159, 189, 190, 224
as special divine impartation 48
consciousness of 138, 199–202
election of 202–05
phenomenology of 143–4
prevenient 198
grammatical analysis 238
Greek word for dialectic 15–17
Gregory of Nyssa 177
Griesbach, Johann Jakob 235
ground of the soul 27
groundfeeling 27
Grundlinien 16, 67
Grundlinien einer Kritik der bisherigen Sittenlehre 53, 64–6
Grunow, Eleanore 64, 288, 299
Gunton, Colin 168
Güterlehre 69

Habermas, Jürgen 80
Hamann 74
happiness 58–9, 62
hedonism 59
Hegel, Georg Wilhelm Friedrich (1770–1831) 16, 61, 79, 80, 111, 112, 115, 252
absolute knowledge 16
Hellenism 236
Henrich, Dieter 88
Herder, Johann Gottfried 231, 234
Herdt, Gilbert 301
hermeneutical art 124
hermeneutics 83–9, 95–8, 96–7, 230, 237, 272
as a "Kunstlehre" 80
circle 85
Hermeneutics and Criticism 83–8
Heydenreich, Karl Heinrich (1764–1801) 17, 18
higher criticism 114
higher ethical standpoint 63
highest good 58, 266
as a regulative ideal 58
Kant's concept of 58–9
hindrances 137–8
to life 194–5
historical–critical method 93
historical epistemology 114, 117
historical event 237

historical judgments 117
historical theology 117–23, 120, 126–7, 209,
  211–12, 213, 232–3, 243, 244
historicism, new 93
history 113, 126–7, 237
history of the church
  common life 118
  doctrine 119
Hobbes 61
Holy Spirit 142–3, 180–2, 221, 224–6
human activity
  modes of 210
  transcendental conditions 210
human affections, musical temperament 291–2
human condition 210–11
  Essential features 213, 216–17, 218–19, 220–2
human experience, male and female 300–03
human knowledge, theology's place in 209–12
human nature 152, 191–2
  as perfect 156–7
  doctrine of 151
humanism 60
humanity
  as divided into two groups 202–04
  as elected in Christ 203–04
  complete 210
  creation of 160–2
Humboldt, Wilhelm von 61, 269
Hume 40, 68
hypostases 186

Iamblichus 177
ideal and real, antithesis between 25
identity
  between knowing and willing 28–30
  great principle of 23
  indiscernables, of 18
  of thinking and being 264
  principle of indiscernables 23, 24
  real and ideal 25
  reason and sensation, of 20
  relation 19
  sameness 77
  theory of judgment 19–20
idolatry 263
illusion 259
imaginative improvisation (*fantasie*) 296–7
immanent Trinity 183–5
immediate self-consciousness 26, 27, 29, 30,
  30–1, 87–8, 131, 210, 231, 238, 241, 244, 295
  Christian determination 213–16, 217–20,
  226–7
impassibility of the divine 153–4
incentive 214–15
incompatibilism 56, 58
individual 85
  cultivation 251

in relation to community 218–23, 222–4,
  274–5
individual differences 60
individualism 116
individuality 62, 266–7, 273
  intrinsic worth of 60–1
individuals as *species infimae* 32
infinite 66–8, 256
innate ideas 20–1
Institutes 189, 200, 202
intellectual function 28
intelligence 260–2
intelligible world 55
intentionalism 73–6, 85
intentions 84–6
interest 214–15
interpretation
  divinatory method 91
  grammatical aspect 83, 85–6, 96–7
  individual aspect 83
  models of 73–6
  need for 82–3
  psychological aspect 83, 85–6, 96–7
  romantic paradigm 107
  structural aspect 83
  theory of 92
  technical aspect 83, 86, 96–7, 238
Interpretation of Plato
  artistic unity 99–100, 105
  authenticity of texts 102–03, 104
  dialectics 99–100, 101
  dialogue form 103–04
  elementary works 106
  esoteric tradition 101–02
  external method 94, 102, 105
  higher grammar 94–5, 97
  historical–critical method 93, 94–6
  internal method 94–5, 102
  middle dialogues 106
  modern 91, 93
  order of importance of dialogues 104
  organic unity 98–9, 102–03, 104
  Plato as artist 91, 97–8, 101–03, 104, 107
  Plato as pedagogue 104–06
  purpose of philosophy 100–01
  romantic 91, 93
  scientific works 106
  system 97
  unity of dialogues 97–100, 101–03,
  103–04
  trilogy of trilogies 106–07
intuition 28, 36–7, 76, 255–6, 266–7, 294
  empirical 74
  of the universe 259, 260, 261, 262–3
  pure 74
irony 94
Islam 236

Jacobi, Friedrich Heinrich 17, 26, 56, 184
Jensen, Robert W. 172
Jesus 274–5
John 239, 241, 244
Jonas, Ludwig 17, 24, 25
joy of the Lord 220
Judaism 181, 236
judgment 28, 87, 178, 240
  analytic 22, 81
  formation 18, 240–2
  responsibility, of 56–7
  synthetic 81
  true 22
  upper and lower limits of 24
justification 144, 145, 189–90, 197–205
  by faith 144, 197–202

Kant, Immanuel (1724–1804) 17, 18–19, 22, 27,
  32, 36, 40, 55, 62–3, 65, 68, 74, 76, 78, 80, 91,
  253
  Critique of Practical Reason 55
  Critique of Pure Reason 55, 78, 253
  Groundwork of the Metaphysics of Morals 55
  Metaphysics of Morals 55
  rational theology 116
  regulative idea 17
  Religion within the Bounds of Reason Alone
   55
  transcendental philosophy 209
Kantian view of Jesus 111
kingdom of God 140–3, 165–6, 167–8, 191–2,
  198–205, 216, 225–7
knowing 210, 214–16
knowledge 76, 78, 80–1, 214–16, 240–2,
  259–60
  absolute 79–80, 260
  as intersubjectively communicable 82
  conditions of possibility 209
  divinely revealed 252–3
  of Christianity (Wissen) 126
  positive 211
  speculative interest in 210
  transcendental 209–10
koinos logos 214, 216, 221, 224–5
Kultur 251–2
Kurze Darstellung des Spinozisteschen
  Systems 26, 28

language 73, 84–9, 272
  grammatical aspect 74
  logical side 302
  mechanization of rules 75
  musical side 302
  psychological aspect 75
  technical aspect 75
law 265
laws of nature 67

Leibniz, Gottfried Wilhelm (1646–1716) 16,
  18–19, 21, 22, 23, 24, 26, 31, 32, 80
Leibnizian–Wolffian theory of the soul 55
Lessing, Gotthold Ephraim 111, 234–5
liberation theory 303–04
Life of Jesus 157–8, 235, 243
life of the church 111
linguistic rule 87
liturgical reform 281–2
logia collection 235
logos 151
Lombard, Peter 174–5
Lord's supper 222
love 62–4
Lücke, Friedrich 183–4, 235, 243, 244
Luke 229, 235, Commentary on 229, 235
Luther 202
Lutheran and Reformed theological traditions
  198
lyric poetry 88

Magnus, Albertus 44
Maimonides 44
male and female, equality of functions 300,
  301–03
Malebranche 40
Manicheanism 152, 195
Mark 235
marriage 225
Massey, Marilyn 300–01
mathematical reasoning 260–1, 265
Matter 26
Matthew 235
maximum/minimum 18
meanings 73–4
metaphysics 15, 28, 33, 36, 66–8, 67–8, 255, 261
minimum/maximum continuum 241
miracles 190, 195–7
modalism 184
modern Christian thought 111
modernity 73, 74, 75, 146
Möhler, Johann Adam 172
Moltmann, Jürgen 171, 184–5
monads 18
monism, metaphysical 18
Monologen 60, 62, 210, 301
Monophysite
  Alexandrians 154
  Christology 168
monotheism 222
  political 171
monotheistic teleological types of religion 236
moral imperatives 58
moral law, as an object of pleasure 55
  responsibility 54–8
morality 36, 196, 255
morals 28, 261

motive of piety 214–15
music 88, 287, 288–94
myth 260

Napoleon 270–1, 276, 281
nationalism 277–8, 279
natural history 68
natural religion, essence of 259
natural science 264
   challenge to theology 231–2
naturalism 56, 143, 224–5
nature 67, 191
   relation to super-nature 161–2
   system 193–7
Nazarean heresy 152–3
necessity 178
Neo-Orthodox 171
Nestorians 154–5
new criticism 92–6, 105
New Testament 129, 141–2, 212, 229–45
   interpretation of 83
   oral sources 234
Nicomachean Ethics 53
Niebuhr, Richard R. 151, 172
Nietzsche 114
Nitzsch, Carl Immanuel 183–4
noumenal 56
   world 55
nous 224–5
Novalis 16–17, 60, 61

objective knowledge 84
objective representation (Darstellung) 84
objectivity 260
Old Testament 236
omnipotence 180
On Religion 28, 115, 251–67
On the Glaubenslehre, open letters 129
one and all 31
one gender 288, 302
Open Letter 121
opinion 259–60
organic affection 82–3
organic function 17, 20–1, 28, 241
organization 216
organizing activity 210
   capacity 265
original divine decree 146, 159–62, 168, 182, 189,
   190, 202–05
   as universally justifying men 144
   execution 204
original gender 292–4, 299

pain 158, 218–19, 220
paganism 181
Pannenberg 171, 184–5
pantheism 25, 41, 190

pantokrator 191
Papias-Fragment 235
Parmenides 106
partial dependence 131
partial freedom 131
particularity 252, 254–67
passibility of the human 153–4
pathological love 62–3
Paul 189, 229
pedagogy 100–01
Pelagian heresy 152
perceptions (Anschauungen) 131
perichoresis 179
person 186
person-forming presence of the Being of God
   181–2
personhood of God, anthromorphic notion
   184–7
Pflichtlehre 69
Phaedrus 98–101, 106
   introduction to 98–101, 105
phenomenal 56
   world 55
philology 93, 96–7
philosophical anthropology 130–2
philosophical ethics 209, 216–17, 264–5
philosophical theology 113, 115–17, 118, 120–1,
   123–4, 209, 211–12, 213, 232–3, 243, 254,
   259–67
   relation to historical theology 117
philosophy 115–16, 119, 121, 132, 159, 237
   relation to dogmatics 122–3
physics 67, 68, 113, 237
pietism 231
piety 37, 38, 42, 143, 147
   as determination of feeling 214–16
pious affections 297–9
pious emotions 40
pious reflections 297–9
Plato (427–347 BCE) 17, 61, 65, 111, 177, 259
   as a dialectician 97
   double philosophy 94
Plato's dialogues
   chronological sequence 93–4, 95, 102–03,
      105–06, 106–07
   General Introduction to 96–101
Plato's Works (Platons Werke) 92
Platonic philosophy
   esoteric tradition 94, 97, 100
   exoteric tradition 94
Platonic system 94
pleasure 55–6, 59, 158, 217–19, 220
pneuma hagion 221, 224–6
polemics 115, 116, 120
political reform, Christian roots 277–9
political sermons 276–9

political theory 60
politics 62
polytheism 222
power, as expression of essence 177
    highest living 25
    of God 182
powers as appearances 25
practical love 62–3
practical theology 113, 116, 120, 123–5, 211, 230, 233
    as crown of theology 123
    relation to historical theology 117
pragmatism 76, 80–3
prayer 133, 195
    power of 197
pre-Christian life 220–2
predestination 189, 192, 197, 203–04
    double 197
    to blessedness 203–04
preponderant synthesis 19–20, 22
primary divine triad 175
primitive Christianity 119
principium individuationis 61
procataric cause 177
procession of creatures 175
Proclean triad 175
Proclus 175
proposa 182
propositions
    about God 41–3
    compatible with piety 41–2
Protagoras 106
Protestant–Catholic controversies 144
Protestant confessions, unification 280–2
Protestant orthodoxy 190
proto-Mark 235
Proudfoot, Wayne 36, 38
providence 189–97
    as relating to individuals 190
    divine 201–05
    general 192–7
    most special 192–7
    special 192–7
Prussia 278
Prussian Correspondent 270, 279–80
psyche 225
    as organ of spirit 163
psychological androgyny 302
psychologism 75
psychology 159, 210, 214
punishments 166–7

Rahner, Karl 186
rationalism 146, 224–5
real and ideal series, upper and lower limits 18
realism 77–9
realist ontology 77–80
reality 77–9

reason
    having the power to create laws 55
    practical 264
    theoretical 264
    universal 253–4
rebirth 197
receptivity 20–1, 76–7, 82, 85, 131, 294
reconciliation 138–9, 262
    condition of possibility 139–40
    means of 140–3
redeemed
    community of 199–200
    individual 199–200
redeemer 138–43, 152, 181–2, 199, 299
redemption 45–6, 47–8, 129–30, 156,
    179, 181–2, 190, 203, 224–5, 236,
    263, 274, 295–6, 299
    as completion of creation 145–6
    concept of 152
    condition of possibility 139–40
    empirical 129
    experience of 152, 219
    magical view of 129, 166–7
    means of 140–3
    mystical view of 129
Reden 60, 61, 62
re-establishing action (*wiederherstellendes
    Handeln*) 218–20, 221–4
Reformation 144, 174
regeneration 143–4, 195, 197–202
    of the human race 203–04
regulative idea 78
    of complete interpretation 85
Reimarus, Hermann Samuel
    230, 234–5, 242
reinterpretation of traditional doctrines
    129–47
reinterpreting redemption 138–43
relation between religion and morality
    60, 63–4
religion 35–50
    absolute 263
    anatomy of 63–4
    as foundation for the recognition of
        individuality 64
    as historically conditioned 251
    comparative 251
    cultured despisers 256–7
    essence of 255–7, 259, 261, 262
    historical 252
    in its givenness 115–16
    natural 253, 254–5, 258–67
    positive 222, 252–3, 254–5, 256, 257–67
    relation to culture 251, 252–67
    revealed 252–3, 253–4
    social element 257–8
religious communities 116, 257, 287

religious consciousness 115
  as intentional 35
  preconceptual 36–9
religious experience 113, 151–2
religious pluralism 172, 262
repentance 144, 200–02
representation (*Vorstellen*) 214–16
representing action (*darstellendes Handeln*)
  219–20, 221, 226–7
Republic 106, 259
revelation 262–3
rhetoric as a false art 99
Richardson, Ruth 301–03
right 223–4, 226
ritual 260
Romans 9–11 189
Roman symbol 190–1
romantics 93
romantic circle, association with 60
romantic movement 256
Rorty, Richard 77–8
Rousseau 252–3
Ruether, Rosemary Radford 303
rules 80, 90

Sabellian modalism 186
Sabellius 172, 182
sacraments 222
salvation 165
sanctification 143–4, 145, 198
satisfaction, Anselmian theory 166–7
Schelling, Friedrich Wilhelm Joseph von
  (1775–1854) 16, 18–21, 22, 23, 25, 32, 232
schema 82–3
schematism 82–3
scheme 76
Schiller 61
Schlegel, Friedrich 60, 61, 92, 93, 94–5
Schleiermacher reception 309–13
Schleiermacher scholarship 313–17
Schmid 16–17
science 37, 89, 193
  as foundationalist 65
  positive 211
scientism 88
sciences, system of 113
Scripture
  as grounded in Christ 231–3
  doctrine of 230–2
  ecclesial interest 232–3
  historical research 231–2
  scientific study 232
sectarianism 258
Segundo, Juan Luis 303
self
  relation to God 216
  relation of world 216

self-consciousness 152, 163, 271, 296
  higher 130, 130–2, 134, 135, 136, 216
  lower 131, 136
  of the individual 201
  pious 212–27
  religious 191, 192–3, 215–16, 218–27
  sensible 130, 130–2, 134, 135, 136, 138,
    162, 289
  sensuous 145, 157–9, 165
  unity of 26
self-determination 73
self-realization 61
self–world relation 131
Sendschreiben 176
sense 20
sense experience 241
sensuous functions, independence
  of 163–4
Septuagint 236
sermon 222, 296–7
service of worship
  narrow sense 227
  wider sense 227
sexism 303
sexual equality 63
signifier, objective existence of 74
sin 40, 45–6, 129–47, 132–47, 156, 159, 162–5, 190,
    194, 201
  actual 134, 136–7
  as pain 133–4
  as unequal development of intellect and
    will 135
  developmental account 134–5
  forgiveness of 166–8
  origin of 158
  original 134–7, 164
  social account 135–6, 145, 164–5,
    199–200, 222
  universality of 134–7
skepticism 80
sociability (*Geselligkeit*) 61–2
social contract tradition, individualist
  anthropology of 61
social externalism 84, 85
social life 62
Socrates 99, 261
Socratic clues 98–101
Socratic method 100–01
sola scriptura 231
Son of God 173, 180
soteriological exclusivism 147
soteriology 146, 189
soul 253
  care of 123, 290
  doctrine of 288–96
  gendered 299–303
  original state 293–4

theological doctrine 294–7
unitive experience of 298, 300, 301–03
speculative rationalism 111
Speeches 36–7, 214, 236
Speeches on Religion 92
spheres of culture 264–5
Spinoza, Baruch (1632–1677) 18, 24, 26, 27, 28, 56, 61, 65, 91, 93, 184, 186, 193
Spinoza Studien 61
Spinozabüchlein 26
Spinozism 67
Spinozismus 26
Spirit 132, 133–4, 160, 165, 215, 216, 220
    reign over flesh 219, 221–3
    relation to flesh 224
Spirit and affect, relation 291–2
spiritual life, organic condition 290
spirituality 265–7
split consciousness 299–303
    female element 295
    male element 295
spontaneity 20–1, 55–6, 76–7, 85
state 223–4, 226, 265, 269–83
    as machine 272–3, 277
    as organic expression 277
    as organism 272
    freedom of individual 278
    origin 272–5
    relation to family 271–2
    relation to individual 271–5
    social contract 271
statements
    analytic 22
    synthetic 22
Stein, Karl Freiherr 270–1
Stoics 177
Stolp 64–6
Strauss, David Friedrich 115, 146, 229, 243
    lecture transcript 115, 125
structuralism 73–6
subject, highest 25
subject's relation to language
    receptive aspect 74–5
    spontaneous aspect 75
subjectivism 35, 84
subjectivity 260
subordinationism 184
suffering 138, 139
Summa Theologiae 175
supernatural 48
    becoming natural 195–6, 204
supernaturalism 111, 129, 137, 143, 146, 224–5, 231, 273
Symbol of Chalcedon 451 153–6
symbolic confessions 121
symbolization 216
symbolizing activity 210

symbolizing capacity 265
synectic 177
Synoptic dependence, problem of 235
Synoptic gospels 229, 235, 239, 241
System der christlichen Lehre 183
system of nature 137
system of powers and appearances 24
systematic theology 119, 120, 122–3

talent 224–6
Tatian 234
technē 123
technical discipline 113, 123
temptation 158
Tennemann, Wilhelm Gottlieb 93–4, 95
text 73–6
textual criticism 75
theological encyclopedia 112, 115
theological method 111–27, 307–08
theology 35–50, 289
    as intellectual discipline 111–27
    as positive science 114, 211, 232–3
    dogmatic's place in 209
    liberation 168
    of consciousness 130, 137
    practical orientation 232
    relation to political community 271–5
Tillich, Paul 198
Timaeus 106
Timothy 1 229, 239
Timothy 2 239
Titus 239
total depravity 136–7
transcendence 30
transcendent 31
    ground 15, 23, 87, 178
transcendental 15, 31
    freedom 55–6
transformation 144
    ethical 167
transition, theory of 20
triangulation 84
Trinity
    Athanasian interpretation 173–4
    distinction of persons 175
    doctrine of 171–87
    equality of persons 173
    eternal distinctions 173–4
    God as Father 173–4
    marginalization of 172, 175
    plurality of persons 184–5
    Sabellian interpretation 173–4, 180
    subordinationism 173
    traditional place of doctrine 174–5
    unity of essence 173, 173–87
    tripartite division of theology 112–25
    tritheism 173, 185

true church 258
truth 15–16, 77–83, 87
  criterion of 78
  definition of 16
  correspondence, as 16, 78–80
  correspondence theory of 23
  realistic theory of 16
Truth and Method 75
Tugendlehre 69
Twesten, August 41, 183
Über das höchste Gut 58–9, 63
Über den Wert des Lebens 58–60, 59
Über die Freiheit 54–8

ultimate reality 252
unconditioned, the 25
understanding 20, 28, 83, 179, 184
union of human and divine 157–9,
  180–2, 192
union with God 156–9
unitarianism 173, 184
unity between the ideal and the real 24
universal 85, 251
universal agreement 84
universal principles 260
universality 254–67
Urevangelium hypothesis 235
Use and Abuse of History for Life 114
utterances 84–6

value of life 59–60
vanishing contrast 204
Versuch einer Theorie des geselligen
  Betragens 62
Vertraute Briefe 60
vicarious atonement 139
virtue 58–9, 69, 217
voices, male and female 292

war, development of German state
  280
Welch, Claude 172
Wilhelm III, King Friedrich 270–1, 275, 279,
  280, 281–2
will 28, 179, 184
Wolfes, Matthias 279–80
Wolff, Christian 32
women, civil rights 287
women, liberation 287
women's suffrage 63
word 157
word of Christ 199–200
word of God 159
word of the Gospel 198
world
  as a living organism 67
  idea of 264
world-feeling 220, 222
worship service 227